# Poland

# THE MODERN WORLD
## *A SURVEY OF HISTORICAL FORCES*
### Edited by Rt. Hon. H. A. L. Fisher, F.R.S.

The aim of the volumes in this series is to provide a balanced survey, with such historical illustrations as are necessary, of the tendencies and forces, political, economic, intellectual, which are moulding the lives of contemporary states.

# POLAND

*By*

## ROMAN DYBOSKI 1883-

*Ph.D., Professor of English Literature
in the University of Cracow*

*With a Foreword by*

## H. A. L. FISHER

P.C., D.C.L.

NEW YORK
CHARLES SCRIBNER'S SONS
1933

PRINTED IN GREAT BRITAIN

# POLAND

## TABLE OF CONTENTS

Page

IV. Ten Years of the New Poland . . . 98

1. The difficulties of State-building : the crisis of Parliamentary
Democracy ; the large sphere of State activities.—2. Land
Reform in 1920 and agricultural reconstruction in 1921.—3. The
constitution of 1921 ; the first Capital Levy.—4. The early
Parliamentary Governments, and Grabski's financial reform,
1924.—5. The breakdown of the new currency, 1925.—6. The
foreign policy of Count Skrzyński, 1923–1926.—7. The *coup
d'état* of Marshal Piłsudski, 1926.—8. The new *régime* and the
Constitution.—9. Economic successes, 1926–1928.—10. Foreign
relations in the Piłsudski era, 1926–1930.—11. Domestic politics :
the election of 1928.—12. The economic crisis ; political
uncertainty ; the election of 1930.—

V. Geographical Aspects and Administrative
Structure . . . . . . . 125

1. Some common fallacies concerning Poland's geography : size,
structure, climate.—2. Types of the population.—3. Polish
towns : Bydgoszcz, Poznań, Katowice, Łódź.—4. Cracow and
Warsaw.—5. Lwów and Wilno.—6. West and East ; the beginnings of unification.—7. The administrative division into counties.
—8. Districts, cities, towns, villages.—9. The Catholic Church in
Poland.—10. The Codification of Polish Law.—11. Courts of
Law ; the prison system.—12. The Army and Navy.—13. The
Police Force and the Frontier Corps.—14. Foreign representation.
—15. The Parliament, the President, and the Cabinet.—

VI. Minority Problems . . . . . 153

1. National minorities in the new Europe.—2. National minorities in the old Poland and the new.—3. The Ukrainians : the
Uniat Church.—4. Austria's Ukrainian policy contrasted with
Russia's.—5. Essentials of the Ukrainian problem in the new
Poland.—6. The actual status of Poland's Ukrainian citizens.—
7. The Ukrainians in Poland's party politics.—8. The White Ruthenian problem ; the Lithuanians.—9. Russians in Poland : status
of the Greek Orthodox Church.—10. Armenians, Karaims, and
Tartars.—11. The Germans in Poland ; distribution and status.
—12. Protestantism in the new Polish Republic.—13. The
two nationalities in Silesia.—14. Danzig and the new Poland.—
15.—The Jews : their history in Polish lands.—16. The Jewish
problem in the new Poland's early years.—17. The Jewish problem since 1926 ; status of Jewish religious communities and
schools.—18. Polish minorities in other countries : the Poles
in France and in Russia.—19. The Poles in Germany.—20.
The Poles in Lithuania, Latvia, Rumania, Czechoslovakia, and
elsewhere.—

VII. Economic Life . . . . . . 191

The three main economic problems of the new Poland.—1. Land
Reform : legislation and its effects.—2. " Commassation."—
3. Drainage.—4. Co-operatives.—5. Agricultural education and
research.—6. Agricultural output : rye, wheat, oats, barley ;
mills, breweries.—7. The production of beet sugar.—8. The
production of spirit from potatoes.—9. General economic aspects
of agricultural production.—10. Gardening, seed culture, meadows
and pastures.—11. The forests of Poland.—12. Wood industries :
saw-mills, furniture factories, manufacture of matches, paper-
mills.—13. Poland's animal wealth : horses.—14. Horned cattle,

# FOREWORD

THE Treaty of Versailles has been termed a Carthaginian Peace. The epithet, which implies injustice, is misleading. Justice for justice, the political map of Europe, as it has been drawn in the Peace Treaties, compares favourably with the map which it replaced and is more closely in accord with the wishes of the populations concerned than any previous arrangements in European history. It would be truer to say of the Peace Treaties not that they are Carthaginian but that they are radical. As the revolutionary effervescence of the Napoleonic War was curbed by a Conservative Peace, so the Great War launched by the military Empires of Central Europe produced as a necessary consequence of their downfall a radical Peace. The Congress of Vienna suppressed, the Treaties of Versailles and Trianon released the minor nationalities from the thraldom under which they had long been fretting. The malady of Europe, diagnosed by the doctors of the Entente as repressed nationalism, was provided under these diplomatic instruments with an appropriate cure.

The real gravamen against the Treaties is not that they are unjust, but that they are speculative and uncertain. The Western Slav, the universal bondsman of the early Middle Ages, is delivered from the Teuton, the Muscovite and the Magyar whose predominance, rooted in energy, it has been the work of centuries to mature. Is it wise so suddenly to reverse the mighty engines of history? Will the Slav states which have been revived, created or re-fashioned by the Treaties establish themselves in the esteem and confidence of Europe and successfully resist the dangers which may proceed from the valiant unreconciled aristocracies of Prussia and Hungary? These questions the future alone can solve.

Of the new creations, Poland is the most important, the most interesting and the most controversial. All through history the Poles, like the Irish, have been in the centre of the storm, combative, adventurous, temperamental, irrepressible. Their annals have been marked by extreme vicissitudes of fortune. At one time they have been masters of a wide Empire, at another

9

time partitioned and obliterated. That the Polish stock is capable of bearing brilliant fruit, the names of Copernicus, of Joseph Conrad and of Leibnitz (for his pedigree too was Polish) are sufficient to testify. Yet there are few parts of Europe where by the evidence of travellers the peasantry were so long permitted to live in a state of abject and miserable abasement.

The future of the new Polish Republic being so speculative and controversial, it has been thought wise to invite a distinguished Polish historian who possesses a remarkable command of the English language, to contribute the volume on Poland to the series of *Nations of the Modern World*. Professor Roman Dyboski does not, of course, approach his subject with the glacial impartiality which might be expected of a commentator from Japan. He feels the call of the blood too strongly for that. It is, however, more valuable for English readers to have the full Polish case at first hand from an eminent scholar who passionately believes in it, than to be introduced to the estimate of an alien, which, even if it be more scrupulously balanced, will fail to do justice to the " stress and form " of Polish life. Here then is a volume written with great vigour and conviction as well as from an overflowing fund of knowledge which presents to the English public the case for the Polish Republic and such reasons as there may be for thinking that it deserves to have a place in the sun and may hope to retain it.

H. A. L. FISHER.

## AUTHOR'S PREFACE

HAVING lectured on Poland's history and literature, and on contemporary Polish problems, to numerous British and American audiences—academic and otherwise—and having published some of those courses of lectures in book form, it was with a relatively light heart that I accepted the proffered privilege of contributing a volume on my country to the Modern World Series.

The difficulties of attempting a comprehensive survey of all the essential domains of the collective life of a large modern State only became fully apparent when I had taken the task in hand. It was fortunate that the tenth anniversary of the existence of the new Poland happened to be celebrated while my work was in its early stages. The event called some valuable literary retrospects into being, and it is safe to say that the present book never could have been completed at all without the mass of information conveniently supplied by a brilliant band of first-rate experts within the covers of the sumptuous folio volume *Dziesięciolecie Polski Odrodzonej* (*Ten Years of Poland Reborn*), published by the *Ilustrowany Kurjer Codzienny* (*Illustrated Daily Courier*) Company at Cracow.

In spite of the valuable materials ready to my hand in this and similar Polish publications, it necessarily took me several years to finish the book while engaged on day-to-day academic duties in the widely remote field of English literature. In the meantime, political and other events were running their course in this post-war world, and the paradox of writing " contemporary history " became more glaring with the length of time which elapsed between the beginning and the end of the task. The reader will no doubt discern discrepancies between the presentation of the same problems in different chapters written at different times ; nor will he fail to note (with sympathetic forbearance, I hope) that those fluctuations between optimism and pessimism which agitate the mental atmosphere of our troubled time, have inevitably become reflected in the book.

The most serious of all discrepancies will no doubt be observed in the discussion of that domain with which the author himself is least immediately familiar, viz. of *economic life*. The book was begun when Poland seemed to have weathered the economic tempests of her early years, and to be entering on a steady course of progress towards prosperity. It is being finished when Poland is involved in a most ruinous world-wide crisis. Under the circumstances, nothing more than an outline of developments up to the coming of the crisis could be attempted, the effects of the crisis itself being hardly as yet even measurable, and certainly not mature for a critical survey.

Similarly, in the no less difficult field of *politics*, a feeling of comparative stability, which existed in 1928, has given way to greater anxiety and tension than ever. Here again, it was patently unsafe to attempt discussion, and sometimes even a detailed narrative account of the most recent events. As it is, the appreciations and forecasts, expressed particularly in the final chapter, may be belied by new facts before the book is in the hands of the reader.

These, however, are unavoidable contingencies, to be faced in dealing with a theme like the present. Whatever deficiencies the book may suffer from in the eyes of the student of politics, must yet additionally be accounted for by the fact—which I frankly admit—that my own principal interests do not lie in the field of politics, and that I feel constitutionally incapable of political controversy. I have, accordingly, devoted more space and labour to the constructive achievements of the new Poland in non-political fields than to the discussion of those political problems which are foremost in the mind of the average newspaper reader. The book might even, on that account, be accused of lack of proportion in its structure ; but it should be considered, in fairness, that the aspects of Poland which could seem unduly emphasised here are exactly those of which least has so far been heard in the outside world.

They are certainly most unfamiliar to readers in the English-speaking countries, and it is to them that the book is chiefly addressed. Having devoted my best energies, for many years past, to the task of making my countrymen better acquainted with the glories of the English heritage of literature, of states-manship, of thought, of manners, I may pardonably consider it a task of some importance also to bring what I consider the highest efforts and noblest achievements of my own nation, both in the past and the present, to the knowledge of the English-speaking communities. If, in doing so, I help them to realize that what may seem strange to them from afar, reveals itself at close quarters as merely the honest struggle against the common

world-wide difficulties and perplexities of our time—I may claim,
I trust to be doing a service to the cause of international
understanding and fellow-feeling.

*University of Cracow (Kraków), Poland.*
   *Easter,* 1933.

## CHAPTER I

# THE OLD POLAND

I

POLAND presents in many ways a unique, and therefore most fascinating, spectacle in European history. Developing out of a comparatively small Slavonic state, by dynastic union, into a large Empire on the confines of Central and Eastern Europe, which at one time bade fair to become the nucleus of an even larger federation of states on the vast territories between the Baltic and the Black Sea, Poland, after all this, is wiped out from the map of Europe by an unprecedented and hitherto unparalleled act of dismemberment—the partition of the Polish Kingdom between Russia, Prussia and Austria, in the latter eighteenth century.

And again—a spectacle even more wonderful—the divided and subject nation under three widely different systems of foreign rule, maintains firmly, through more than a century of captivity, its sense of unity and distinctness, it rises repeatedly in arms against its oppressors, it holds its own against the strongest pressure both administrative, economic, and even educational, and it keeps all the cabinets of Europe busy with " the Polish problem " as one of the unsolved international questions of Europe. What is more, the nation produces, under these abnormal conditions, its very highest achievements in learning, literature and art.

Finally—a third and certainly not a lesser historical marvel— a reborn Polish State, brought to life by the convulsion of the Great War in a thoroughly ruined and devastated country, a state considerably smaller than the historical Polish Empire, and placed in a most precarious international and a fairly desperate economic position, succeeds not only in repelling a massed attack of the huge forces of Bolshevik Russia, but gathers strength in ten short years to occupy a place of considerable importance both in the political and economic system of the new Europe.

Such extraordinary destinies could not but invite speculation on the secret mainsprings both of past disaster and of recent vitality. Faced by the unheard-of calamity of the destruction of a whole large state, Polish historians of the nineteenth century naturally were as unceasingly busy with discussion of the causes of old Poland's downfall as, in a wider field, historical scholars always are and will be with the vexed question of the reasons for the fall of the Roman Empire. For Poles, the problem of the fate of their country in the past, of course, had much more than a merely academic interest : it was inevitable that it should be envisaged from moral as well as intellectual points of view. Both " pessimistic " and " optimistic " interpretations of Polish history were bound to make their appearance, and historical pessimism necessarily grew in weight and authority after the reverses of struggles for liberty in the period of captivity. Even now, however, when the optimists' confidence in Poland's perennial vitality stands justified by post-war events, it still remains a fruitful subject for heart-searching and debate among philosophical students of national history in Poland whether the past fortunes of the country ought to yield more of encouragement or of warning to the Poles of to-day and to-morrow.

## 2

Certain solutions of the enigma of Poland's historical catastrophe, indeed, easily suggest themselves to the outside observer indifferently conversant with general European history. Thus, some bearings of Poland's *geographical position* on her fate are obvious enough. That position is a " key " position at the crossing of old-established and important trade routes between the northern and the southern seas, and the western and eastern lands, of Europe. As such, it was bound to make Poland a flourishing power in international trade in the Middle Ages ; but it inevitably lost its advantages with the blocking-up of the European south-east by the Turkish conquest, and the opening up of a new world across the western seas for European trade. Commercial wealth, and with it political power, was fated to ebb away from Poland in the modern era, quite as it was fated to ebb away from the Venetian Republic.

Viewed from yet another angle, Poland's fate may also seem to fall into line with certain wider developments in the European world. Those who hold it as an axiom of historical belief that, since the *Reformation*, Protestant powers in Europe generally advance in strength and importance while Catholic nations decay, may think of the old Poland as doomed together with

Spain and only affected more tragically than Spain itself because much less favourably situated on the map.   But even those who do not believe in Protestantism as an *elixir vitae* for nations, will be inclined to think that Poland perished, among other reasons, because she did not make the best of either of both worlds : neither turning resolutely Protestant (though at a time strongly permeated with Protestant doctrines), nor on the other hand, utilizing the Catholic Counter-Reformation for an active international policy of imperial aggrandisement, Poland, since her neutrality in the great religious war of the seventeenth century— the Thirty Years' War—lapsed into a passivity which made her a battle ground for foreign armies and an object of contention for foreign ambitions.   Her inactivity in the great wars of the eighteenth century and her consequent sufferings, are, from that point of view, but symptoms of vanishing prestige : irresolute religious tolerance is followed by the pacifism of paralysis.

### 3

But surely Poland's attitude—whatever it was—on the great religious issue of early modern times was not in itself a sufficient cause for the overthrow of what was then a vast monarchy of great international power, rich resources, and a high degree of culture.   Should we, then, perhaps find the seeds of the historical Poland's dissolution in the very process of her *territorial growth* ?

That growth, indeed, has certain peculiarities which have an evident bearing on Poland's extraordinary fate.   The very origin of a Polish state seems to have been due to a process for which the German historians have coined the apt phrase *Drang nach Osten*—the " Eastward pressure " of the expanding population of Germany.   Finding its way barred on the western side, since Charlemagne's successors, by a consolidating French kingdom, *Germany* begins to seek an outlet for its surplus force in the thinly-populated and politically unorganized regions on its eastern border, inhabited by a variety of Slavonic tribes.   The Slavonic peoples which spread in those early days over what are now the central German lands between Elbe and Oder, were gradually exterminated or merged in the advancing German element.   In the early tenth century, part of that prehistoric nebula of Slav races east of the Germans crystallizes—evidently under German pressure—into a *Polish monarchy*. We find that monarchy centring, in this its first period, considerably farther west than the Poland of later centuries : it occupies mainly the land between the rivers *Oder* and *Vistula*, and its earliest capital

B

Gniezno (still the traditional seat of the Primate of Poland's Church) it situated in the centre of what later became the western border province of Poland.   The first rulers of Poland attain the status of recognized sovereigns by entering, with their nation, into the fold of the *Roman Catholic Church*, that League of Nations of the medieval world.   While Christianity itself comes to Poland, through a dynastic marriage, from the neigh-bouring Slav kingdom of Bohemia, Church organization and personnel are provided mainly by Germany.   Skilfully playing upon the rivalry between the German monarchs as the temporal heads of Christianity and the Popes as its spiritual chiefs, some early Polish princes not only strengthen the independent position of their country, but actually extend its boundaries considerably ; the conquests of one of them, Boleslas the Brave, about the year 1000 of our era, range from the banks of the Elbe in the west to those of the Dnieper in the far south-east.

On the whole, however, in spite of the official relations between the new Poland and the political system of Central European Christianity, the aforesaid " Eastward pressure " of the German element, being an evolutionary necessity, continues to make itself felt.   It proves particularly effective with regard to certain smaller tribal units along the shore of the *Baltic*.   The Polish rulers, at the same time, with a proper sense for essentials, strive for permanent possession of the sea outlets of their territorial rivers—the Oder first and the Vistula later—and the clash between the two tendencies becomes an age-long struggle for the foothold on the Baltic shore between Poland and Germany. Poland, in the later part of the twelth century, is ultimately pushed away from the lower and middle reaches of the *Oder*, and, as a necessary consequence, the region of the upper course of the Oder, the ancient Polish Province of *Silesia*, is drawn into the orbit of German influence, and a large portion of it, in the early fourteenth century, lost for ever.   Those losses are facilitated by the disastrous fact that Poland, like some other neighbouring Slav States, becomes for two centuries—the twelfth and the thirteenth—divided between several branches of the ruling Piast dynasty, and the minor territorial princes naturally cannot hold their own so well against the German onrush as a united kingdom could.   In the course of their quarrels, in fact, a strong German military organization of monks, which had originated in the crusades and found itself temporarily homeless, is called in to help, and allowed to settle near the mouth of the Vistula, thereby intensifying the Polish-German problem in that region, and creating the embryo of the *East Prussia* of to-day.   To these factors of destruction is added, in 1241, the first great *Tartar invasion* of Europe, which ravages Poland and sweeps away much of its population : it entails the necessity of calling in German settlers to re-people the devasted country, and of thereby strengthening the growing German influence in Poland.

4

In the midst of such calamities, the mysterious national vitality of Poland which was to be manifested again so often until our own day, asserts itself by *re-union*, conquest, and vast constructive effort in the fourteenth century. The Poland which re-emerges from disruption, already centres mainly round the Vistula and its tributaries ; of the tributaries of the Oder, only one, the Warta, whose course is enclosed on three sides by opposite courses of the tributaries of the Vistula, remains firmly in the grip of Poland. The loss of the Oder itself, and of best part of Silesia with it, has to be admitted, while access to the mouth of the Vistula is not yet permanently gained. At this juncture—the most important turning point of Poland's territorial history—the diplomatic genius of Poland's " Prince of Peace " in the fourteenth century, *King Casimir the Great*, devises the means of compensating for the losses in land on the western side by opening up expansion on a large scale in the direction of the *East*. It was not Poland only but her south-eastern neighbour, the original Russian Empire round Kiev, which had been disastrously affected by dynastic divisions ; and by skilful intervention in these disputes, Casimir ultimately secures for Poland the territory now best known by its Austrian name *Eastern Galicia,*—a large and fertile tract of land which had been an object of contention between Poland and Southern Russia since the dawn of their historical existence. While Poland's area is thus definitely extended on the southern side, along the bordering Carpathian ridge, the idea of strengthening and correspondingly extending Poland's hold on the *Baltic shore* in the north suggest itself in the shape of dynastic alliance with Poland's north-eastern neighbour *Lithuania*. That thorn in the flesh of Poland—the militant German monks settled on the Baltic since the early thirteenth century—had a moral justification in European opinion for the existence of their settlement, in their crusading activities against the heathen tribes of the neighbourhood : first the original Prussians (whom they gradually exterminated and supplanted), and then the Lithuanians. The peaceful conversion of Lithuania to Christianity from some other neighbouring state, and union with that state, would take away the justification for the raids of the German Knights and at the same time crush their growing power. Such a union appeared particularly tempting when Lithuania, under one of her greatest rulers, in the fourteenth century, expanded considerably into the south-east and became a large state, extending along the eastern border of Poland. Christian influences came into the pagan country first in the shape of Greek Orthodox Christianity from its eastern neighbour, the North Russian principality of White Ruthenia ; then in the shape of Roman Christianity from Poland. Ultimately Poland, being the larger and more civilized power, got the upper hand. What had been initiated by the far-sighted Casimir the Great through his marriage with a Lithuanian princess, was finally perfected by the union of his grand-niece Queen *Jadwiga* with the Lithuanian ruler Jagello in 1386.[1] The Polish-Lithuanian federation, after nearly two centuries of territorial and constitutional disputes and re-adjustments, received its definite legal form only by the pact of Lublin in 1569 ; and shortly afterwards, the definitely united monarchy, in place of its two old capital cities,—*Cracow* for Poland in the south-western corner, and *Wilno* for Lithuania in the extreme north-east,—received one capital in the city of *Warsaw*, situated in the very centre of the new system, on the middle course of the Vistula. But long before these measures of unification were agreed upon, the *Polish-Lithuanian Monarchy* had advanced by strides towards the height of its imperial importance. While in the fourteenth century first a Bohemian, and later a Hungarian king had occupied the throne of freshly re-united Poland, now princes of the Jagellonian dynasty wear, for a time, both the Bohemian and the Hungarian crown, and at certain moments in the fifteenth century, the formation of a great block of states between the Baltic and the Black Sea—comprising Poland, Lithuania, Bohemia, Hungary, East Prussia and Rumania—seems to be fairly within sight.

The original aim of the Polish-Lithuanian union—the suppression of the power of the *German Knights* on the Baltic—was attained, after prolonged struggles, in the course of the fifteenth century, and Poland now gained for good her natural outlet on the sea at the mouth of the Vistula—the port of *Danzig*—which, with great benefit to her export trade in corn, she held more or less securely for over three centuries.

---

[1] See Charlotte Kellogg : *Jadwiga, Queen of Poland* (New York, Macmillan, 1931), third Ed., 1933.

## 5

But more was involved in the new territorial extensions. The possession of Eastern Galicia, with its main waterway, the *Dniester* flowing into the *Black Sea*, pointed towards that sea ; so did the possession of the upper reaches of the great river Dnieper, farther east, after the union with Lithuania. Access to the Black Sea henceforth becomes one of the objectives of Poland's policy ; that aim is part of the persistent, age-long struggles of Poland against the Turk and Tartar invasions ; it is with that aim in view, also, that Poland avails herself of the services of the military community called " *Ukrainian Cossacks* " which grows up, out of waifs and strays of fugitive peasant population, on the vast south-eastern plains. But the Cossacks are a refractory element, and out of a tool of Polish policy become a distinct and constant source of troubles ; the trouble is increased by the high-handed policy of Polish border magnates, owning large tracts of land in that region. Besides, the principalities composing the present-day *Rumania*, placed between Pole and Turk as between hammer and anvil, are driven by their precarious position into a policy of veering and tacking between the two powers, and never constitute the reliable outpost which Poland needed in that quarter for the purposes of her Black Sea policy. Finally, Poland's many and brilliant victories checking the advance of the Islam upon Christian Europe, and culminating in King *John Sobieski's* gallant rescue of Vienna from the Turk in 1683, are fructified by her growing rival neighbours, first *Austria* and ultimately *Russia*. If Poland, hesitating in the seventeenth century between an Austrian and a French alliance, had resolutely sided with *France* throughout, this would have meant the avoidance of many a Turkish war and would have enabled Poland better to arrest the advance of the growing power of Russia.

In the sphere of the Black Sea, then, the later centuries of Polish history present a spectacle of only partial and fitful success in Empire-building. Nor was achievement in the *Baltic sphere*, although more definite at first, ever to be complete. Here again, the extension of Poland's possessions along the curving sea-coast line to the north-east was as vital to Poland's Imperial safety as her south-eastward expansion along the curve of the Carpathian ridge towards the Black Sea. Ever since the union with Lithuania, the monarchy, with a narrowed western and a long and open eastern frontier, was spreading out like a fan in the direction of the European east ; and the extreme points of the fan north and south—had to be well secured if the fan was not to be rolled up by force instead of broadening farther. In the north, a good beginning had been made by the acquisition of Danzig ; but the stumbling-block of East Prussia remained unremoved on the way farther east. Like Rumania, East Prussia was an untrustworthy and tricky vassal, and when, in Poland's days of enfeeblement, a strong *Prussian kingdom* was built up by the dynastic union of East Prussia with the Marchy of Brandenburg, Poland was outflanked along her northern shore, and her vital artery of access to the Baltic was doomed. Long before that artery (the so-called " Corridor " of to-day) was finally cut, the Polish-Lithuanian monarchy had still achieved apparent further success in the Baltic region by obtaining control over parts of the *Latvia* and *Estonia* of to-day, and even reaching out into *Finland* by dynastic marriage. In these recesses of the Baltic, Poland's interests clashed with the ambitions of *Sweden* for command of both Baltic shores ; and when a Polish king from the Swedish Vasa dynasty in the seventeenth century—Sigismund III—was possessed with an imprudent desire for the Swedish crown and for the re-establishment of Catholicism in Protestant Sweden, Poland became embroiled in long ruinous wars with Sweden, which were repeatedly renewed throughout the whole heroic age of Swedish history—the seventeenth and early eighteenth centuries. Although Sweden had ultimately to resign her territorial ambitions on the southern side of the Baltic, it was not Poland but *Russia* which gained the disputed sea-coast lands in the end. Russia's Baltic aims, in fact, had collided with Poland's as far back as the middle of the sixteenth century, and more danger-ously than Sweden's, because the southern Baltic shore was more vital for Russia than for Sweden.

And when Russia, in *Peter the Great*, received a ruler gifted with particularly keen vision for the Imperial importance of the sea, the Baltic plans were sure to be relentlessly pushed to a con-clusion, while Poland by that time was too weak to resist them effectively.

## 6

In thus surveying in broadest outline both Poland's Black Sea and her Baltic policy, we have seen both lines of develop-ment converging on the danger to the Polish-Lithuanian Monarchy from the growing power of Russia. Ever since Ivan the Great, in the fifteenth century, had constituted himself, by marriage, the inheritor of the *Byzantine Empire* destroyed by

the Turks, and begun to build up, in its place, the Tsardom of
Moscow in the north, this new power was obviously the most
formidable check in the way of the predominance of the Polish-
Lithuanian Monarchy in eastern Europe. At the same time,
one obstacle after another prevented Poland from dealing with
the Russian issue effectively. In the sixteenth century, the
cultured humanist King Sigismund Augustus, who achieved
successes against Russia mainly by his brilliant diplomacy, was
followed by the Transylvanian Stephen Bathory, one of Poland's
greatest rulers both in peace and war, who came near to breaking
Russia's power definitely by triumphant military effort ; but the
later king's hand was held by Rome, because Moscow held out
hopes of Church reunion. On the occasion of a royal election
in Poland in the later sixteenth century, and again, through
Poland's intervention in Russian domestic wars in the early
seventeenth, prospects were temporarily opened up for a
dynastic union, which would have created a vast Eastern European empire out of Poland, Lithuania, and Russia together ; but
every time those prospects came to nothing, through short-
sightedness or narrow-mindedness in decisive quarters. Perhaps,
in fact, the combination was too vast to be realizable ; too deep a
gulf was by that time fixed between Poland, Roman Catholic in
faith, Parliamentary in her political constitution, and Western
European in her intellectual life,—and Russia, Greek Orthodox
in religion, autocratic in government, and largely Eastern in
mentality after centuries of Tartar domination. Polish culture
and manners still spread their influence far and wide through
Russia in the early seventeenth century, but Poland as a political
power, undermined by the successful Imperial competition of
the Hapsburgs, absorbed by Turkish wars, devastated by Swedish
invasions, never in full command of the Baltic, was too weak even
in that century to withstand Russia's westward movement firmly,
and had to abandon such strongholds of her long eastern front
as Smolensk in the north and Kiev in the south as early as 1667.

In the eighteenth century, Russia, violently invigorated by
Peter the Great, exercises more and more influence in Poland's
domestic politics. That influence is occasionally exercised even
on behalf of political reform and for protection against *plans of a
partition of Poland*, which begin to make their appearence in
international negotiations in the early years of the eighteenth
century. It is perfectly true to say that Russia herself did not
really contemplate a partition of Poland : things seemed to be
tending towards the incorporation of the complete Polish-
Lithuanian monarchy in Russia alone. It was the superlative

diplomatic astuteness of *Frederick the Second* in playing upon the
jealousy between Russia and Austria which finally brought
*Catherine the Great* to consent to the compromise of a partition
of the Polish spoils with the two other neighbours.  In the two
further partitions which followed the first within a quarter of a
century and completed the work of Poland's extinction shortly
before 1800, great events in other sections of Europe played their
part : revolutionary *France* sacrificed the remainder of Poland to
the appetites of her three enemies in order to divert their energies
temporarily, at least, from the cause of the European Coalition
against the French Revolution.

## 7

The above rapid examination of the old Poland's territorial
growth and decay shows that the impediments surrounding the
construction of the Polish-Lithuanian empire on all sides were
indeed too great to allow of its complete realization and continued
safe existence.  The rival power of the Hapsburg dynasty, the
unending preoccupation with the Islam, the huge growth of
Russia, and finally, the German barrier on the Baltic fixed since
the early Middle Ages, all this, combining, would have baffled the
strength of a state even much larger, richer, and more firmly
settled in its internal conditions than the Polish-Lithuanian
monarchy ever became through the four centuries of its united
existence.

This brings us to the question how far Poland's *internal
conditions* contributed to the decay of her political power and to
her final undoing.  It is on this great problem that the opinions
of historians are most sharply divided, and optimism and pessimism stand out most glaringly against each other.  Poland had a
fully developed *Parliamentary system*, while the monarchies
which dismembered her were more or less absolute.  Hence the
opinion of the modern " *optimists* " in Polish historical thought,
in whose view Poland's parliamentary institutions were too far
advanced for the age, and Poland perished as a martyr for
progressive ideas to be realized generally only in a later period.
This interpretation is opposed to the older doctrine of the so-
called " *Cracow school* " of historians, a doctrine dominant in
Polish scholarship for a long time, and largely consonant with
the views of foreign—especially German—students of Polish
history.  According to this doctrine—which had its origin in the
depressed mood of the nation after the downfall of the insurrection of 1863—the old Poland brought her catastrophe upon
herself through ill use made of Parliamentary liberties : freedom

degenerating into licence, the rights of the individual being unduly extolled and his duty to the State neglected, all attempts at administrative or social reform baffled by this anarchic individualism and by the class egoism of the nobility and gentry, Poland perished through lack of a strong central Government authority and ensuing lack of enforcement in all matters vital to the life of the State—justice, finance, military organization and consistency in foreign policy.

This gloomy view, which certainly had a large body of fact in Polish history to support it, suffered from the limitations proper to all such general theories ; it often overlooked positive achievements, or minimized their relative importance, which in some cases only became apparent in our own days. Accordingly, the doctrine of the Cracow school, while admitted to contain a measure of wholesome, if bitter moral truth, has undergone, and is still undergoing, considerable modification. And this not only, because the re-birth of a Polish State before our own astonished eyes would have been impossible without roots of this new life stretching far back into old Polish history, but also because the old Poland's domestic difficulties are bound to be viewed more sympathetically and indulgently by the Parliamentary democracies of post-War Europe, all without exception proving singularly incapable to form strong and permanent governments, and struggling desperately against the same fundamental dilemma. To combine a full measure of popular liberty with the necessary strength of central state authority seems to-day more than ever like squaring the circle.

Yet this was the task which Poland had to face just at the time when her territorial growth and international prestige were at their height, and her political and moral responsibilities accordingly the gravest.

## 8

The *constitutional history of Poland*, viewed in retrospect, falls into evolutionary stages closely corresponding to those passed by other political organisms in Europe.

The first of them has been aptly called the *patriarchal* stage. The State is built up by a succession of strong rulers, who govern it as they would a private domain, and whose authority, gladly recognized by subjects in need of protection from foreign violence, is very much like that of the *paterfamilias* in a family grown into a tribe. In this state of things, prevailing in the earlier Middle Ages, the obvious dangers to state unity are, firstly, competition for moral authority over the people between the two supreme powers—the King and the Church ; secondly, revolts of individual great nobles from among the King's Council, or the joint pressure of that Council upon a weak monarch ; thirdly, rebellions of strong-minded younger royal princes against a ruling elder brother ; and fourthly—a remedy worse than the disease—disruption of the kingdom between the several sons of the King. The Polish Kingdom of the first medieval centuries, having repeatedly overcome the first three dangers, finally succumbed to the fourth.

The second stage of constitutional evolution was hurried on by peculiarly disastrous Polish developments. The division of the country, the civil wars consequent upon it, and finally wholesale ruin through the great Tartar invasion of 1241, made it impossible for the rulers, even after reunion, to shoulder the huge reponsibility for reconstruction ; it had to be delegated to, and distributed among, the main social forces of the medieval community : the clergy, the landowning gentry, and the burghers of the towns (who were enjoying self-government on the German model). The autonomy of the *three estates* within their spheres of activity is guaranteed by pacts with the monarch, which take the form of *charters of privilege*. These charters also determine the material duties of the three estates towards the commonwealth. The King's functions are limited to foreign policy and, in domestic affairs, mainly to holding the balance between the dominant social forces ; the expenses of Royal administration are defrayed out of the income from crown lands.

Within the framework of that system—which might be called something like " Syndicalist Government " in modern parlance —splendid constructive work is done, in fourteenth and fifteenth-century Poland ; the learning of the clergy, the chivalry of the gentry, and the industry of the townsmen, all contribute their share to the common stock of organized achievement.

The transition to the third stage of constitutional development is hastened by Poland's growth into a large empire through the *Polish-Lithuanian union*. The tasks of political existence on such a large scale—tasks military, administrative, economic and cultural—can no longer be adequately carried out by the medieval three estates of the realm. All Europe, on the threshold of the modern era, reshapes itself into more centralized political systems, which develop organs for the manifold new functions of the State. In most cases that reorganization takes the form of strong *absolute monarchy* ; under the Tudors in England, under Louis XI and his successors in France, under the Renascence tyrants in the Italian cities. Poland, like her neighbour

Hungary, evolves one of the few representative *Parliamentary constitutions* of Continental Europe in the early modern era, the old precedent of thirteenth-century England and her unbreakable Parliamentary tradition remaining something quite apart from the main stream of Central European political life. Poland and Hungary (somewhat like Spain), being, of necessity, perennially militant nations, possessed in their gentry a class which was the mainstay of the State's very existence, and the honourable duty of defending the country naturally went together with certain civic privileges, symbolized by the coat of arms. It was that class, then, which became the social centre of the new political system. The custom had developed for the gentry to send delegates of their local conventicles or "dietines" to submit their wishes to the king and council. From a practice this developed into a right, and out of the occasional meetings of the "Diet" or general assembly of local delegates, there developed a *Parliament* meeting periodically and at fixed places ; the existence and constitutional prerogatives of that Parliament were ultimately legalized in the year 1505. In that year, then, a *Parliamentary democracy of the Polish gentry* may be said to have definitely come into being. The new parliamentary system certainly has its organic faults : the members of Parliament were delegates from local bodies and not national representatives ; hence, breadth of view was often lacking, and local prejudice was apt to paralyse national action. Again, the Upper Chamber or *Senate*, having evolved out of the king's council, remained in the anomalous position of being a parliamentary assembly composed of the highest office-holders in the State ; and the irremovable tenure of those supreme offices gave ample scope for abuses.

### 9

But the Polish parliamentary system had also its essential qualities of soundness and its inherent possibilities of prosperous development. Parliament, after all, was broadly based on a large body of voters—the whole mass of country gentlemen ; and that democratic foundation might gradually have been extended by granting the civic rights of the gentry to increasing numbers of *townsmen*, and, in course of time, also to the *peasants*. A beginning in that direction was only made in the last years of independent Poland by the memorable reform of the Polish Constitution on May 3, 1791 ; throughout the preceding three centuries of Poland's parliamentary life the class selfishness of the gentry not only left the towns unrepresented and the peasant masses in serfdom, but, by economic legislation in a purely agrarian spirit, brought the ancient commercial wealth of Poland's cities to decay.

Bad as the neglect of the cities and the ill-treatment of the peasantry was from the point of view of social welfare and economic interests, it was at least equally harmful politically. A strong and well-to-do middle class in the towns, had it been allowed to grow, might have given support to the *Crown* against the lawless privileged elements in the State, as it did for instance, in early modern France. As it was, the process of struggle for government authority found the kings and reforming statesmen in face of two elements, both possessed with the doctrine of " golden liberty " in its extreme and anarchic application, viz., the large mass of the *country gentry*, poor and unenlightened, hence politically short-sighted, and the *great nobles*, fabulously rich and inspired mostly by family pride and personal ambition. Even in that situation, a skilful and statesmanlike policy might have rallied the minor gentry round the king and the banner of administrative reform, and might have turned that gentry into a powerful instrument to curb the lawlessness of the noble families and make law and order prevail. Such a policy was resolutely conducted by the great king *Stephen Bathory* (1575—1586) with the able assistance of his chancellor *Jan Zamoyski*, who has justly been called, by a modern historian, the *tribunus populi* of Poland's gentry. But Bathory's reign came too late in the day and was too brief to make his salutary firmness and his epoch-making reforms permanently effective. The gentry in the seventeenth century, instead of strengthening the Crown, fatefully lapses into increasing dependence on the noble families and serves them in factious warfare.

On the unhealthy soil of such a social foundation excrescences develop, which indeed make Poland's advanced parliamentary constitution ruinous in the working. The principle of *electing kings* by popular vote convulsed the country with excitement at the end or every reign, resulted often in civil war, and weakened the royal power through a traditional pact which had to be entered into with the electors, and which even guaranteed to subjects the right of rising in arms against the king. Legislation became cramped by the recognition of the individual member's right to nullify a majority vote by personal protest—the disastrous *liberum veto*, which thwarted many useful reforms. It came to pass that the only way to carry out a reforming programme was to conclude an armed covenant of its supporters, alled a *Confederation*, and enforce it. Polish history of the seventeenth and eighteenth century is rife with such " Confederations," some of them formed for good ends and some for bad. It was a confederation which made the first stand against Russian intervention in Poland at the time of the first partition ; but it was a confederation also, which, by invoking Russian assistance against the political reform of May 3, 1791, paved the way for the second and the third partition.

10

The history of the Polish constitution, then, certainly presents in its later stages a desolating spectacle of growing disorganization. And yet, proofs of national vitality and elements of hope are not lacking even in that picture. From the beginning of the sixteenth to the end of the eighteenth century, throughout the nearly three hundred years of the old Poland's Parliamentary annals, honest efforts never cease to be made to *reform* the system. Partial successes are achieved by enlightened kings, far-sighted statesmen, inspired writers and noble-minded military leaders ; thanks to their endeavours, Poland still occupies a truly commanding position in the Eastern European system throughout the sixteenth century, she shakes off an overwhelming flood of foreign invasions in the seventeenth and, what is more, she makes great progress towards thorough reform in the eighteenth, when her international position is already too weak to be tenable.

That Poland, on the eve of her dismemberment, gave herself a really modern administrative system, that she retrieved, by legislative act, old social wrongs toward the burgher and the peasant, that she reorganized her currency and her army, that she did away with such rooted old abuses as the election of kings and the " free veto,"—all this means not merely " death-bed repentance," as it has been called, but it gives earnest of vigorous constructive effort and unceasing advance throughout the coming century of captivity, and of that unbroken will to regain freedom which animates Poland until she rises again. The uninterrupted record of endeavours at reform must not be forgotten over the record of political decay ; and the ray of light shed over the last years of the old Poland by the glorious new *Constitution of May* 3, 1791, must be rightly interpreted not as the last glow of sunset, but as the dawn of national revival. Not in vain was an allusion to that constitution included in the preamble to the first Constitutional Charter which the reborn Republic of Poland gave itself in 1919.

## II

From the much discussed subject of the old Poland's political constitution let us now turn to a more general and equally important aspect of pre-partition Polish history, viz., to the old Poland's record in *culture and civilization*.

Poland, in the earliest phases of her cultural development, is tutored by Germany through the common medieval medium of *ecclesiastical education*. Polish lands had their due share in the great intellectual revivals of the Middle Ages originating in reforms within the Church : the *Benedictine reform* of the tenth century led to the foundation of many abbeys, schools and churches on Polish soil, and the *coming of the Friars*, in the early thirteenth century, gives a great impulse, in Poland as elsewhere, both to piety and to learning : that century of grave domestic disasters—civil wars and Tartar invasions—is also marked by the appearance of a number of *Polish saints*, several of them being ladies of royal birth. When after the calamities of that century, the towns begin to fill with *German colonists*, and are practically rebuilt on a more regular plan, as well as reorganized according to Magdeburg municipal law, those reborn cities become the centres of German cultural influence of Poland, and of flourishing architecture as well as other arts, both ecclesiastical and civic. But a breath of inspiration from an even wider field and from higher regions of culture came into Polish life with the last king of the Piast dynasty, *Casimir the Great* (1333—1370), mentioned above as a " Prince of Peace " after a stormy period of dynastic wars and foreign invasions. Casimir had been educated at the royal court of *Hungary*, then connected through the *Angevin dynasty* with *Naples* and its magnificent blend of *Arab and Norman civilization*. Through the person of this great king, in fact, Poland was placed in touch with that earliest phase of the *Renascence* movement of which " *greater Greece* " was the proper home. Under Casimir, Poland advanced by leaps and bounds in all domains of civilization. His capital, *Cracow*, became the seat not only of commercial wealth hardly ever equalled in the modern history of the city, but also of a new refinement in intellect and art. Inspired by the example of the neighbouring kingdom of *Bohemia*, which had received, in 1348, in the *Univerity of Prague*, one of the earliest seats of academic learning in that part of the world, Casimir the Great founded, in 1364, Poland's oldest *University* at Cracow. Primarily constituted as a training college for Poland's clergy and administrative officials, the University was destined soon to see

greater days.  For the best traditions of Casimir's educational
and constructive efforts were inherited by his grand-niece,
Jadwiga, herself a fine flower of the cultured Anjou stock.
Ascending the throne of Poland while still half a child (1384), and
soon afterwards laying the foundation of the great Polish-
Lithuanian Monarchy through the sacrifice of her personal
happiness to the union with the Lithuanian Prince Jagello,
Jadwiga not only opened a new chapter in Poland's political
history, but made herself memorable as a great promoter of the
cultural development of the country.   It was largely due to her
enlightened initiative and personal generosity that the University, originally modelled on the old law school of Bologna, is
re-established on a more comprehensive plan in 1400, now taking
the flourishing University of Paris for its model.   The fifteenth
century becomes a true golden age for the *Alma Mater* of Poland's
academic learning.   At the very beginning of the century, the
Polish school wins laurels at an illustrious international gathering
—the *Council of Constance*, at which the Rector of Cracow
University, Paulus Vladimiri, side by side with Jacques Gerson,
the famous Rector of Paris, attracts universal attention by the
skilful defence of his own thesis (directed against the German
Knights on the Baltic) " that it is not permissible to convert
pagans to Christianity by force of arms."   And towards the
end of the century, the Cracow undergraduate gown is worn by
the greatest man of science of the early modern era—the immortal
astronomer *Nicholas Copernicus*.

### 12

The lustre of the Cracow schools grew somewhat dimmed in
the sixteenth century, while noble Polish youth began to flock in
increasing numbers to celebrated foreign universities, especially
to Padua and Paris.   The spirit of *Italian Humanism* found
entrance into Poland's intellectual life, and the last two kings of
the Jagellonian dynasty, *Sigismund I* and his son *Sigismund
Augustus* (1506-1548, 1548-1572), represented it at its best on
the heights of the throne.   Sigismund the father married an
Italian princess, *Bona Sforza* of Milan, and with her, a crowd of
Italian artists of every kind came to the Polish Court.  Italian
monks had been among the teachers of Poland in her earliest
centuries, Italian bankers and merchants had made their mark
in her economic life in the later Middle Ages, and the Italian
Renascence art of diplomacy had been represented by an astute
diplomatic adviser at the Polish Court of the fifteenth century.
But now only, in the heyday of humanism, the Italian influence

reached its height. Italian came to be spoken as familiarly in the streets of Cracow as German had in the preceding centuries been spoken there. As the towering Gothic cathedral of St. Mary in the market-place stands there to commemorate that earlier age of culture, so now the Renascence splendours of a new royal castle arose on the hill overlooking the town as a monument to the new era.

Humanism stood for broadest religious tolerance, and in its favourable atmosphere the doctrines of the *Reformation*— heralded a century before by the popularity of Bohemian Hussitism in Poland—now spread rapidly among the most cultured classes of the nation. The *University of Königsberg*, founded on the confines of Poland in 1544 by Poland's Prussian vassal as a centre of Protestant thought, for a time exercised even a greater attraction on the best young minds of the country than did the ancient *Alma Mater* of Cracow. As elsewhere in Europe, the Reformation became a powerful stimulus to *literary production in the vernacular*: after her distinguished Latin writers on philosophy, history and science in the later medieval ages, Poland in the sixteenth century began to produce literary classics of her own language both in verse and prose, like *Jan Kochanowski*, in whom the nation, in 1930, on the 400th anniversary of his birth, enthusiastically honoured one of its foremost poets. What is perhaps even more significant, the Reformation inspired one of the soundest programmes of political reform which stand in Poland's annals to her credit, and it helped to consolidate the best-organized reform party in early Polish history. The political philosophy of a distinguished Polish writer of the period, *Andreas Fricius*, expounded in his Latin work *De emendanda republica*, acquired a wide vogue throughout Europe. And in the strictly religious field, an ardent Polish Protestant, *John Łaski*, played an important part in the history of the Reformation in western European countries.

Great as was the hold of the Reformation on the intellectual *élite* of the country, the new doctrines never took root among the masses : to them, they remained " a German religion," quite as the eastern type of Christianity, to the plain man in Poland, will always wear the colours of Russia. It is perhaps to the nation's obscure self-preserving instinct between the Scylla of Protestant Germany and the Charybdis of Greek Orthodox Russia, that the ultimate victory and lasting vitality of *Roman Catholicism* in Poland is chiefly due. But other causes were not lacking. The establishment of a *Polish National Church* of the reformed type failed to be achieved, largely through the subtle irresolution of

King Sigismund Augustus' humanist mind in the matter. And the incurable dissensions between extreme and moderate forms of Protestantism weakened the united Protestant front, although a show of it existed for a time. The Catholic side, on the other hand, scored through the authority of Poland's great representative at the *Council of Trent,* her learned Cardinal Hosius, and soon after through the brilliant part at first played by the *Jesuits* in Polish education. What were to become the flourishing eastern Polish Universities of *Wilno* and *Lwów* (Lemberg), arose as Jesuit colleges in the first period of the Counter-Reformation. And even in the seventeenth century, at a time of great political distress and calamity, Catholic learning in Poland's eastern borderlands is the motive force of a truly amazing predominance of Polish culture and even of the Polish language among the eastern Christians of Russia and of the Ukrainian lands.

Protestantism, however, although receding towards the end of the sixteenth century and even actively repressed in the early seventeenth, still continues for a long time to exercise a vivid influence on Poland's intellectual life. Among the liberal religious doctrines which owe their origin to the Reformation, one principally—the noble teaching of *Unitarianism,* propagated in early seventeenth century Poland by its founder, *Faustus Socinus,* and known then by the old-world name of " Arianism " —leaves a distinct mark in Poland's cultural history[1]. That the greatest Polish poet of the seventeenth century, *Venceslas Potocki,* was an " Arian " seems like a last after-glow of the irradiation of Poland's early literature by the Reformation.

### 13

Of the seventeenth century, for a long time, little but evil used to be thought and said by the Polish historians both of politics and of civilization. Politically, the century, marked by ruinous foreign invasions and growing constitutional decay, seemed to be one of the most decisive stages on the road of the old Poland towards catastrophe. In the sphere of culture, the restlessness of the stormy epoch, the stiffening formalism and obstinate conservatism of education now held in monopoly by the Jesuits, the fanaticism of the Counter-Reformation campaign and the rigour of Ecclesiastical censorship, and over and above all this, the mannerism and wild exaggerations of the Baroque style in literature as well as in the plastic arts—these certainly

[1] See Earl Morse Wilbur : *Our Unitarian Heritage* (Boston, Mass., U.S.A., The Beacon Press, 1925).

C

appeared to be factors conspiring to mark out the age as one of decadence in art, stagnation in intellectual life and increasing provincialism in outlook.

Recent research had rendered this picture considerably brighter and more hopeful. To begin with, the period of disastrous *invasions* of Poland by all her neighbours now stands revealed as a period of unparalleled Polish *heroism* : products of historical scholarship furnished a secure foundation for the apotheosis of seventeenth-century Polish bravery in the great " Trilogy " of his historical novels by Sienkiewicz, and these novels, amidst the seemingly utter helplessness and hopelessness of a subject and divided Poland in the later part of the nineteenth century, inspired the nation with a new conception of its own vitality and of its great historical tradition. The new presentation of the seventeenth century helped to live down the nineteenth and to reach out for renewed independence in the twentieth.

Even more strange is the transformation which the accepted view of Poland's cultural history in the seventeenth century has undergone within a few decades. We are all familiar throughout Europe with the complete revaluation of *Baroque art and literature* which is taking place in our days. In Poland, it received strong support by the discovery of a large body of literature which lay hidden away in *manuscript* on account of the ecclesiastical censorship. In the light of such discoveries (particularly numerous in our own century) *Polish literature of the seventeenth century* now presents itself as highly important and interesting in achievement, notable personalities of great authors have come to stand out clearly, and the very quantity of the output appears quite amazing, when we consider the tempestuous destinies of the nation at the time. What is even more creditable is the fact that in spite of the undeniable narrowing-down of the educated Pole's intellectual outlook in the seventeenth century through degenerating Jesuit education, literature on its heights maintains contact with the west and keeps Poland open to progressive inspiration from abroad. In addition to the old-established Italian influence—now manifested, e.g., by the efflorescence of Italian opera at Court—the new factor of *French leadership* in post-Renascence Europe's culture comes into fuller play in Poland now. In the sixteenth century a French prince of the Valois dynasty—later to become King Henry III of France—had occupied the Polish throne for a few short months, and, through his following, introduced that French factor bodily into Poland's life. Now, two French queens appearing in Poland's annals of the seventeenth century, and the sojourn of many young Polish nobles in Paris for the completion of their education, constitute other such links. A Polish poet of the noble family of *Morstin* ably translates Corneille's *Cid* and himself composes graceful sonnets and madrigals ; and the long-winded sentimental novels of seventeenth century French authors, such as d'Urfé and Mlle. Scudéry, find a grateful reader even in the hero-king John Sobieski.

### 14

But the new *French influence* was to be productive of much greater things in the very last century of the old Poland's existence. The emancipating spirit of rationalist philosophy, sweeping Europe from France in the *Era of Enlightenment*, shakes Poland out of the torpor into which the routine of Jesuit education had plunged her. Even in the intellectually stagnant and politically disastrous reigns of two *Saxon kings* on the Polish throne (1697–1763) an exiled Polish rival of theirs, *Leszczyński*, who becomes father-in-law to the King of France and resides at Nancy, himself writes wisely on the reform of the Polish commonwealth and trains young Polish patriots to promote it. Through his influence reformers of education, research and government begin to raise their voice in Poland—foremost among them the Piarist priest *Stanislas Konarski*, who, by a monumental work on Poland's political abuses and by his memorable activities as a reorganizer of education, earned the title of *præceptor Poloniae* and the honourable epithet *sapere ausus* (" he who dared to be wise.")[1]

It was, however, only the reign of the very last king of Poland which was to produce the unique spectacle of magnificent cultural advance and national regeneration coupled with political downfall. Stanislas Augustus Poniatowski, king from 1764 to 1795[2], did not possess the qualities of moral fibre which the epoch of imminent political catastrophe required, and his vacillating and diffident policy only plunged Poland into deeper and deeper dependence on Russia. At the same time, however, his enlightened patronage of all intellectual and artistic endeavour turned his capital, Warsaw, into a centre of high refinement and truly creative effort. He adorned the city with some of the most charming specimens of *Rococo architecture*—such as his own summer palace called *Łazienki* (" the bath-house ") ; under his protection, the *theatre* and the *Press* enter into their important

[1] See William J. Rose : *Stanislas Konarski* (London : J. Cape, 1930).
[2] See R. Nisbet Bain : *The Last King of Poland and Some of his Contemporaries* (London : Methuen, 1909).

modern functions among Polish society ; *research*, both historical and scientific, begins to flourish and produces great works ; a
beginning is made with *industrial organization* and with the
building of *water-ways* ; *education* is reorganized on a secular
basis and in a thoroughly modern spirit by a *State Department of
Education* (the first of its kind in Europe ) ; a school of Polish
*painters* grows up under Italian and French tutorship ; and
*literature* with the marvellously prolific and many-sided poet and
prose writer, Bishop *I. Krasicki,* as its chief representative,
has a second golden age after the glorious outburst of the
Renascence era.  Some of the best literary talent runs, as
everywhere in Europe in the eighteenth-century, into didactic
channels, and Poland's needs dictate one particulary didactic
application—that of political and social reform.  Accordingly,
many of the greatest minds of the age—such as that of the
great scientist, scholar and national teacher *Stanislas Staszic*—
devote their best energies to strong appeals and elaborate
proposals of a political nature.  It is to a large extent the merit
of those *political classics* of eighteenth-century Polish literature
that the old Poland goes down to her grave redeemed from the
reproach of having failed to shake herself free from ancient abuses
and wrongs. The achievements of eighteenth-century Polish intellectual effort and literary genius, perhaps to a higher degree even
than the partial accomplishment of political reform, proved the
nation to be spiritually fit and morally worthy to live, in spite of
the violence committed upon its people and territory.  Those
achievements gave the initiative and supplied the foundation for
the unceasing creative activity in thought and art which enslaved
and divided Poland continued to display throughout the
nineteenth century in constant harmony with the march of the
European mind in that mighty age.  A nation thus remaining
alive spiritually, was, by virtue of that very fact, bound to be
recognized as politically alive also, as soon as events made an
outward change of the political face of Europe feasible and
imperative.

Having, then, examined in brief survey the possible inner and
outer causes of the old Poland's fall, and the possible explan-
ations of her mysterious survival after political death, we arrive,
as so often in human affairs, at the deep truth that the *forces of
the spirit are the true mainspring of life.*  Never extinguished in
the social organism of Poland, and more active than ever in the
last stages of its material decay, they were to tide that organism
across the dark abyss of captivity into renewed fullness of
existence.

## CHAPTER II

# POLAND UNDER FOREIGN RULE

I

THE century and more of Poland's division between the three neighbouring empires, and of the government of the nation by foreign rulers, might at present, with a reunited and free Poland once more on the map, appear to be but a dark interval which it will be best resolutely to overlook now in surveying the past with regard to its bearings on the present.

Indeed, the foreign policy of the new Poland constantly finds itself faced by the same problems which the old Poland had to grapple with, not merely in the eighteenth but as far back as fifteenth and even the fourteenth century. The more remote past seems to contain the more vital lessons for to-day, and the period of captivity seems as devoid of them, except by way of warning, as the comparatively negligible and uninteresting two centuries of early medieval Poland's break-up into territorial principalities.

Yet the century during which modern Poland was deprived of unity and freedom, was no other than the great nineteenth century, the era of the new growth of democracy, of gigantic achievements in science and technical progress, of the awakening of nations long submerged or so far unconsolidated, and of developments in empire-building and in international economics which lead up to the greatest convulsion in universal history. If, then, we are bound, in the presence of a reborn Polish State, to admit the marvellous fact that a subject and divided Poland never ceased to live its own individual life as a national unit, we find ourselves obliged also to consider how this unbroken national existence was affected by the great social and intellectual movements of the century, and how far altered the Polish nation was when it came forth at last into renewed independence. Without this, we certainly could not understand many of the most essential issues in the new Polish life of to-day.

To begin with, the record of nineteenth-century Poland was one of untiring *active resistance* to foreign domination by every possible means and on every occasion which the course of international affairs seemed to offer. Hence the reputation which the Poles in that century acquired all over Europe, of being the most persistent revolutionaries and the most romantic military adventurers in the world. Not only did they for twenty years follow Napoleon's eagles and shed their blood on all his battle-fields in the unflagging hope that out of his drastic rearrangements of the map of Europe a complete and redelivered Poland would ultimately arise ; but the spirit of those years bore further fruit again and again.

Wherever a nation struggled for liberty, Polish knights-errant were sure to be found in its front ranks. In the eighteenth century, two gallant Polish leaders—Pułaski and Kościuszko—had carried their swords across the sea into the service of the rising North American Republic. In the nineteenth, Polish officers of Napoleon's army played their part in the Greek war of independence ; Polish generals organized the young armies of Belgium and of Egypt ; Poland gave a great leader (General Bem) to the Hungarian rising of 1849 against Austria ; the greatest of Polish poets—Mickiewicz—in his days of exile formed volunteer bodies of Polish troops to assist Italy in her struggle against her Austrian oppressors in 1848, and again, Turkey in the Crimean War against Russia, and he laid down his life on the threshold of the later enterprise ; there were Poles among the soldiers of Garibaldi, and numerous Poles fought with distinction as volunteers under the French banner against Prussia in 1870-71.

In Poland itself, the flame of this militant spirit was never dormant for long. In the eighteenth century, the two gallant leaders mentioned above as Polish-American heroes—Pułaski and Kościuszko—had given an example to all succeeding generations by raising the standard of revolt against Russian intervention—the first one on the eve of the first partition, the second one after the second.

In the nineteenth century, the partial and fitful concessions by which the partitioning powers at various times met the irrepressible desire of the Poles for complete political freedom did not prevent the nation, through two-thirds of the century, from rising in arms again and again. Two insurrectionary wars against Russia—in 1830-31 and 1863-64—each taxed her huge military strength to the utmost ; and the " springtime of nations " in 1848, sweeping the whole of Europe with gusts of revolutionary movements, had its stormy reverberations both in the Austrian and the German sector of Poland.

2

The two outstanding events in this military history of enslaved Poland—the national risings of 1830 and 1863—deserve particular attention, because they have far-reaching consequences of other than merely political importance.

Their political bearing, to begin with that, is obvious enough to-day, although it was not so comfortingly clear at the time to their own heroes and victims. There was this difference between the two insurrections that the first one, in 1830, on its outbreak, had the well-equipped army, well-filled treasury and well-organized administrative machinery of the " Congress Kingdom " of Russian Poland at its disposal, while the second rising was a frantic and desperately unprepared revolt of ardent youth not only against the exasperating measures of repression, but against the very dictates of reason and experience. The first rising continued for a year as a regular war, the second one dragged on for two in the way of guerilla warfare ; but both were doomed at the outset in view of the immense preponderance of Russian forces on the one hand, and of the apathetic attitude of the western powers on the other. These, while generally friendly towards Polish aspirations, never would run the risk of a European war over the Polish issue. France, in the throes of revolution again in 1830 as in 1794, once more was saved, by the tragic struggles of Poland, from Russian intervention and invasion. But neither in 1830 nor in 1863 did she find it possible to act decisively on Poland's behalf, although at the later date Napoleon III was at the height of his international authority as the professed protector of all oppressed nationalities in Europe. Britain, again, the chief opponent of Russian imperialism in the arena of world politics, was not sufficiently interested in a remote inland country of Continental Europe to take determined action in its defence.

If, however, the cause of Poland failed to receive active support from Western Europe at critical moments, the risings, nevertheless, achieved one end : they kept the Polish issue alive in Europe's international politics, and did not allow it to sink to the insignificance of a merely local and provincial matter.

Even more important were some indirect consequences of the two insurrections. After the first one, in 1831, France offered hospitality on its soil to the remnants of the Polish army, and soldiers as well as other servants of the insurrectionary cause gathered in great numbers in Paris and elsewhere in the west. The " Great Emigration," as Polish historians call it, was politically as passionately divided and, on the whole, as in effective as is the Russian emigration in western Europe to-day. But the abnormal and feverish conditions of exiled existence became a true hot-bed of intellectual production. The poetry of the Polish Romantic Movement, which had begun at home under various foreign influences before the rising, developed in exile into a true national gospel, framed in works of immortal beauty by Mickiewicz, Słowacki, Krasiński and other poets ; to the fruits of their genius there were added the musical master-pieces of Chopin, which also drew very largely on national suffering and past national greatness for their inspiration. The recent national tragedy, as interpreted by creative Polish thinkers, who applied to it the ideas of Hegel's new philosophy of history, became a source of metaphysical comfort, being idealized into vicarious suffering for the promotion of a higher international morality. The nation, deprived of political organs of self-expression, lived on the spiritual food supplied by the poetry, the philosophy, and the art of the great emigrant masters ; and however insufficient sustenance this might have been under normal conditions of existence, it certainly served in those days to keep national consciousness awake, and to produce a sense of national dignity in the degradation of slavery. The Polish poets did for their nation what the Hebrew prophets of old had done for theirs. And they also made the name of Poland more famous among western European nations than it had ever been before. The lectures delived by Mickiewicz, in the early ' forties, from the newly created chair of Slavonic literatures in the University of Paris, were the first great revelation of the achievements of Slav genius, and of the importance of the Slav nations, to the mind of the European West.

### 3

Very different, but equally important in their way, were the consequences of the second national rising—that of 1863. The attempt was much more desperate, and the catastrophe accord-ingly more crushing than in 1830. Hence the fact that the spirit of armed resistance to foreign rule was quelled much more thoroughly this time ; not till a few years before the World War was the idea of national military organization in Poland taken up again. To this change in mood there was also a contributory cause. The romantic nationalism prevalent in Europe in the earlier part of the century, and leading up to the revolutionary events of 1848, had, by the time of the Polish defeat of 1863, given way to other preoccupations in the public mind. In the industrialized communities of Western Europe the *social problem* constituted by the growth of modern industrial labour was becoming one of the dominant issues of national life. In the countries industrially still undeveloped, the problem of the *peasantry* and of *rural labour* was rapidly advancing to a corresponding place in general attention ; thus, in Russia, the aboliton of peasant serfdom by Tsar Alexander II in 1861 produced, for the newly emancipated class itself, difficulties analogous to those which the abolition of Negro slavery at the same time was creating in the United States, and the grave problem of economic readjustment to a reformed social order necessarily became one of prime importance and universal interest.

In addition to these new phases of the democratic movement, the great achievements of *natural science* were beginning, in the 'sixties, to affect the general mentality of European nations ; scientific materialism was about to clash with many old beliefs, and the ideals of the romantic era were retreating before its advance.

In Poland, as elsewhere, the transition from romanticism to realism, and from national to social interests, became a marked feature of intellectual evolution and of public life after the catastrophe of 1863. " Positivism " (the word framed by Auguste Comte to denote his philosophical system) became a fashionable intellectual slogan in post-insurrectionary Warsaw, and " organic work "—meaning day-to-day efforts at social, economic and educational improvement—was made the programme of national effort, in place of political conspiracy. The necessity of such patient spade work amidst the grey social realities of modern life was indefatigably preached for decades, through the medium of great novels and of newspaper articles by one of the most gifted, and at the same time, the most typical writers of the period : B. Prus.

The insurrections of 1831 and 1863 had been mainly the work of the land-owning gentry, and the consequent losses of this class through death, exile or confiscation of estates, undermined its importance for the social structure. The middle class, weakened in the old Poland through centuries of agrarian rule, and replaced to a large extent by an unassimilated body of Jewish tradesmen in the towns, now received reinforcements from the ranks of the dispossessed gentry, and the professional classes—that *intelligentsia* which plays such an important part in the modern life of Central European communities—in Poland came to be recruited largely from among the country gentry.

The peasantry of Poland—over two-thirds of the population—

whose neglected lot the political reformers of old Poland's last days had earnestly attempted to improve, became, after 1863, an object of greater national concern than ever. Even in the emigrant period, after 1831, numerous secret political emissaries from radical emigrant organizations in France had carried on in Poland an ardent propaganda of advanced democratic ideas ; but in the country itself, the land-owning gentry, when it had a voice at all in the matter, tackled the problem but half-heartedly. The credit for peasant emancipation was taken out of the hands of Poland's landlords by the partitioning governments, and those governments, posing as the protectors of the Polish peasant, sowed ruinous disunion between the peasantry and the gentry. In 1846, the peasants of Austrian Poland, at the instigation of Government officials, massacred thousands of the country gentlemen who were then preparing a new armed rising. In 1863, while the middle class of the towns of Russian Poland had a creditable share in the insurrection, the peasantry was largely indifferent and partly even hostile. All the more imperative, then, did it appear to be henceforth to devote energy to the civic education of the peasant and to the improvement of his material condition, if the struggle for the peasant's soul with Poland's foreign rulers was to be won and Polish national life to assert itself successfully in a democratic world by receiving a broad foundation in the masses of the people.

### 4

Here, indeed, was a new spirit of realism, and a new programme of democratic national endeavour. The romantic and aristocratic type of Pole, which, through the emigration after 1831, had become imprinted on the European imagination (and still largely remains there), could no longer be taken as representative of the new age. Even among the new—and much less numerous—wave of Polish emigrants going forth into foreign countries after 1863, the difference is marked ; we hear of Poles achieving distinction abroad in engineering, medicine or scientific research, rather than in literature or art. Joseph Conrad, the greatest Polish emigrant of modern times, by becoming a captain in the British Merchant Service first and a great English writer afterwards, marvellously combines the two phases of Polish emigration in his life and achievement, as indeed he combined the older vein of romance with the new realism in the nature of his genius. In place of the large and representative emigrant community of Poles in France, which had come into existence after 1831 and exercised a powerful

influence both on foreign opinion and on the destinies of the
nation at home, we now witness an enforced, mute dispersion of
exiled insurgents of 1863 over the huge spaces of Russia's
Asiatic domains in Siberia. Many of these, having survived their
long terms of imprisonment, forced labour, or residence in penal
settlements, become prosperous citizens of that vast country and
contribute to the exploration of Siberia, to the development of
its enormous natural resources, and to the introduction of
European civilization among its manifold native races. The
ranks of these pioneers are swelled by later generations of new
political exiles, and partly also of voluntary emigrants. The
repressive Russian *régime* closing all official careers to Poles in
Russian Poland itself, enterprising young Poles with a higher
education betake themselves to all parts of the Russian Empire,
and make their mark in scholarship, science and art, in the
legal profession and in administrative service, in architecture and
engineering, in trade and industry. This permeation of later
nineteenth-century Russia by the cultured and active Polish
element at a time when the hand of Russian autocracy lay most
heavily on Russia's Polish provinces, is another interesting and
surely not inglorious addition to the remarkable story of Polish
emigrant activities in many lands during the century of Poland's
captivity.

On the whole, however, the activities of emigrants after 1863
are of much lesser national importance than were those after
1831, and this fact is an outstanding characteristic of the new
period. It is in accordance with the dominant spirit of realism
that the main efforts of Poles to serve the Polish cause should
now be made at home, on Polish soil, under however adverse
circumstances.

This change, viewed in historical perspective to-day, may
seem favourable ; yet it had one consequence to begin with,
which told against the very substance of Poland's national
aspirations. While the emigrants of former decades, from
their vantage-ground abroad, could envisage the cause of Poland
as a whole and keep up an attitude of protest against the division
of the country, the Poles active in their homelands now are
perforce obliged to reckon with the realities of the situation and
to adapt their doings, and even their programme, to the framework of the several empires whose subjects they are. It is
indeed after the extinction of the spiritual Polish commonwealth,
maintained by the emigrant thinkers and poets in Paris, that
Poland becomes thoroughly divided in her inner life as well as in
hard political and geographical fact. During the decades between

the last rising in 1863 and the eve of the World War, the stream of Poland's national existence flows in three completely separate channels as widely distinct from each other as are the social and intellectual conditions of Russia, Germany and Austria respectively ; and three different types of Polish mentality, fashioned under the influence of the three foreign systems, definitely begin to crystallize. In spite of all the enthusiasm always alive for a great common tradition, and of many common racial traits of character, the three national temperaments which now take the place of one, are bound to form a considerable obstacle in the way of real reunion after the political deliverance of the nation in our own days.

Yet, as there is no evil out of which some good does not in-directly arise, it must be stated at once that the necessity of adaptation to three different political and economic systems had the advantage of enriching and diversifying national experience, and so preparing the nation better to encounter the manifold problems which the reunited and free Poland of to-day has to face. As a result of its different fortunes, each of the three parts of Poland brought different positive contributions with it into the re-established common household of the people. For this very reason, it will be necessary now briefly to survey the record of each of the three sectors of Poland after 1863 separately, with a view not so much to repeating the old tale of different forms of political persecution as to ascertaining what qualities were developed in the Poles under Russia, Germany and Austria respectively by the struggle against their different handicaps, and what moral and material capital, as a fruit of these struggles, they have now introduced into the common national stock.

## 5

We will begin our survey with the section which was under the rule of *Russia*. Being the largest of all three, it naturally was most prominent in the world's eye, and the phases of the Polish problem on the stage of international affairs were largely determined by its fortunes.

Twice in the nineteenth century had Russian Poland been temporarily in possession of a fairly lage measure of self-govern-ment : once during the first fifteen years after the Congress of Vienna, when the province was constitutionally a separate kingdom, with an army, a parliament, and an administration of its own, and the Tsar for its king,—and again in the early 'sixties, when the distinguished but too dictatorially-minded politician,

Count Wielopolski, had wrested from the St. Petersburg authorities a series of concessions amounting almost to a scheme of full provincial autonomy. Both these spells of comparative freedom had been productive of memorable progress, expecially in the economic and the educational field ; both were politically disturbed by glaring contrasts between constitutional theory and administrative practice ; in consequence both had come to an end through outbursts of national impatience, taking the form of armed insurrections. In both cases, the defeat of the insurgents was followed by a wave of measures of repression ; but, while in 1831 it had still been necessary to reckon with a remnant of international respect for the settlement effected by the Congress of Vienna, in 1863 that settlement had lost its vital force in European consciousness through intervening revolutions, and accordingly Russia had much more of a free hand than after the first rising.

Throughout all the changes in the treatment of her Polish spoils, Russia had persisted in making a distinction between the purely Polish province of Central Poland around Warsaw, and the eastern borderlands, which had also belonged to the old Polish Monarchy, but in which only the governing class—the landed gentry—was Polish, while the inarticulate peasant masses were largely Ruthenian and Lithuanian in speech, and partly Greek and not Roman Catholic in their religion. These border provinces had never had a share in whatever of self-government was at times granted to Russian Poland, and the most determined efforts were made by Russia throughout to uproot the two factors which had been the mainstay of Polish supremacy there, viz., the Roman Catholic Church and the Polish landed gentry. The Polish land-owning class in those districts—as is apt to be the case with such border outposts of a national civilization—had been, if possible, more ardent and self-sacrificing in its patriotism than the Poles of the centre ; the share of Lithuania, in particular, in the insurrectionary struggles was more heroic, and accordingly her martyrdom more intense, especially in 1863, than even that of the former Congress Kingdom.

The " Kingdom " itself, however,—as Poles always continued to call it—was by no means spared after the suppression of the second rising. A wholesale system of administrative and educational Russianization of the country was instituted and consistently developed through many years. In the country, it resulted in maintaining a state of dull indifference to national aspirations among the neglected peasant masses. In the towns, it could have no such effect ; yet its moral consequences were no less disastrous in their way. The utter corruption of the old Russia's administrative officials had long been a byword among nations ; it was well known throughout the world how the discretionary power of the bureaucracy made the free administration of justice impossible ; how the omnipresent control of the secret police and the stupid brutality of the official censorship interfered not only with all expressions of political opinion, with all endeavours at social improvement, but also with all creative effort in research, literature and art. Now it was one of the worsts faults of the Tsarist *régime* that, rotten as the whole machinery of administration was, its very worst elements were thought good enough to act as tools of the Russification of Poland. An attempt which would have been hopeless even when undertaken by picked men, was thus turned into assured failure. But it was also a fact that all idea of moral authority of the State and all respect for a legal order of things was even more thoroughly obliterated in the minds of Russia's Polish subjects than in those of the Russians themselves. The notion of bribery as the normal form of approach on the part of the citizen towards public authorities, of opposition and passive resistance as his permanent and only meritorious attitude towards all state action, of conspiracy as the habitual mode of all social activities, became implanted in the minds of a large part of the Polish nation ; and it will take the lifetime of a generation in the new free Poland to produce a general sense of legality, a spirit of confidence in the administrative apparatus of the State, and a consciousness of active loyalty being the individual's natural duty towards the Commonwealth.

### 6

Yet the picture was not all dark. In some domains of life the evils of Russian rule were inextricably combined with certain advantages of it. There were, to begin with, certain obvious *economic gains* reaped from the definite inclusion of Russian Poland in the Russian Empire. The foundations for modern *industrial development* had been laid in the semi-independent " Congress Kingdom " by the initiative of the far-sighted Polish scientist and statesman, Stanislas Staszic, by the financial assistance of the Bank of Poland (founded in 1825 by the great Finance Minister Prince Lubecki), and—last not least—by the thrift and sheer hard work of immigrant German families, which created large business undertakings. When these budding industries of Poland found themselves sheltered behind one common wall of high protective tariffs with the whole of the immense Russian Empire in Europe and Asia, and had its vast markets thrown open to them, they burst into rapid and powerful growth. Russian Poland became the chief industrial reservoir of the Russian Empire, and remained so, with great profit to the general prosperity of the province, till about the turn of the century. It was only then that the Russian Government began to favour the development of certain industrial centres in Southern and Central Russia by exercising a policy of discrimination in the matter of railway transport charges against the Polish industries. But by that time, the position of the Polish industrial products in the Russian market had become well-established and difficult to attack. Especially the great textile centre of Łódź in the western part of Russian Poland, growing up out of a village into a large industrial city in the course of a few decades, flourished chiefly through providing large masses of the village population all over Russia with cheap fabrics for daily use.

Besides these favourable industrial developments, *agricultural prosperity* in the country-side maintained a high level. Although the anti-Polish policy of the Government was directed mainly against the land-owning nobility and gentry, yet neither all the punitive measures of confiscation after the insurrections, nor the hostile legislation of later decades, nor even—be it said— the light-hearted and spendthrift habits of the landowners themselves could do away with the strong natural foundations of the wealth of that class. The abundance of extraordinarily cheap rural labour, constantly provided by the rapidly growing peasant population, made lucrative farming possible even under primitive conditions, and nullified the effects of the abolition of serfdom for the landowner. Especially in the Lithuanian and Ukrainian borderlands, with their fabulously large and old-established estates of Polish aristocratic families, the former luxury of these owners of vast tracts of land largely continued under modern conditions, and their palaces were often perfect treasure-houses of exquisite objects of art. It was only in our own days that the calamities of the World War were to deal a shattering blow to these old homes of high cultural refinement, and Bolshevism was to wipe them out ultimately.

This strange picture of economic prosperity in the midst of political persecution combines lights and shadows very curiously indeed. They are also combined, even more glaringly, in the field of *education*, although here we are more inclined, from the point of view of to-day, to observe a predominance of shadows.

The Russian school system, established from top to bottom in place of the Polish one, was not only calculated for the brutish destruction of all Polish national traditions, beginning with those of language, literature and history, but it was also in itself a thoroughly bad system, consisting of mechanical drill of the minds and anxious official supervison of all their movements. The Russian sector of Poland, during its brief periods of comparative liberty in the earlier nineteenth century, had achieved great things in the organization of education : the University of Wilno (closed after 1831) and that of Warsaw (turned shortly after 1863 into a second-rate Russian one) had been the shining summits of excellently built and broad-based structures. The succeeding period of purely Russian schools lowered the general standard of culture. This effect was particularly marked in the countryside ; the Russian practice of maintaining darkness in the village as a guarantee of passive obedience was extended to the Polish province, and peasant illiteracy became much more rampant under purely Russian rule than it had been under Polish provincial self-government.

In this domain, it was unmitigated evil itself which called forth good by way of reaction. It was certainly deplorable that gifted Polish scholars and scientists in Warsaw, being deprived of a university as a centre for their efforts, were compelled to waste their energies on ill-paid private lessons in secondary schools, and could only give a margin of their time to research work, conducted under most unfavourable conditions. Yet at the same time the suppression of all official Polish institutions of learning gave a powerful stimulus to private initiative among the Polish communtiy in educational matters. At a time when happier countries in the West, such as Denmark, became known throughout the world as examples of organized adult education, Russian Poland under conditions of necessary secrecy and constant personal danger to the organizers, was building up a variety of substitutes for the abolished national schools in the form of institutions for adult and extra-mural education, as well as private schools of all grades. When, in the growing excitement of the early years of the twentieth century, the youth of Russian Poland was emboldened to proclaim a boycott of all Government schools, and when, for a short time after the first Russian Constitution of 1905, all private educational activities were allowed to be conducted openly, the extent of the nation's effort in organized educational self-help was fully revealed. It certainly constitutes one of the proudest chapters in the history of Russian Poland.

No less proud a spectacle is presented by the development of *literature* and *art* in the Russian sector of Poland. In spite of the cramping fetters of the censorship, H. Sienkiewicz (himself a student of the Polish University of Warsaw in its palmy days) roused his fellow-citizens, in the period of deepest political degradation, to a revived sense of historic national dignity by his famous *Trilogy* of novels on the subject of Poland's heroic wars in the seventeenth century; and he was to win even wider fame all the world over by his *Quo Vadis*.[1] Both he and the only other Polish laureate of the Nobel prize, W. Reymont, the author of the grandiose prose epic *The Peasants*, wrote and published their masterpieces under the difficult conditions of their native Russian Poland. These conditions did not prevent a galaxy of other literary talents from arising in the grey and depressed period after 1863—including Poland's greatest poetess M. Konopnicka. It was under Russian rule also that the musical genius of St. Moniuszko—next to Chopin in greatness among Polish composers—flourished in spite of hard material struggles; it was there that Paderewski's wondeful talent first was made manifest to the world. Downtrodden and gagged, Warsaw never ceased to be a centre of refined culture and to produce works of art of the very highest quality.

Yet the abnormal position of Russian Poland in point of education could not fail to tell in the long run. Highly laudable as the works of the community's self-help in educational matters were, they could at best constitute only a makeshift for a normal system of public educational institutions. And this substitution of privately-organized instruction for a complete and regular school training became an all too frequent type of education among the people of Russian Poland. In consequence, when a new Polish State at last once more came into being, that large portion of Poland found itself suffering from a scarcity of people with a rounded and finished educational curriculum, especially as far as the academic professions are concerned; many important posts in the service of the State, requiring a university education, had temporarily to be filled by men without full qualifications, and many deficiencies in the working of the new administrative machinery in its first years are due to that state of things. What is worse, a virtue was often made of necessity: quite as in the field of politics the methods of the conspirator had come to be extolled exclusively, and the sense for legal order and normally organized public life had been obliterated, so in

[1] See *The Patriot Novelist of Poland, Henryk Sienkiewicz*, by Monica M. Gardner (London : J. M. Dent, 1926).

D

education, the ways of the free-lance adult educator and of the purely self-taught man were apt to be raised in estimation above the ordered, traditional teaching of schools and universities.

Remnants of this mood subsisted in the new free Poland : those who came into its public service with the regular university degrees and the normal administrative experience for which Austrian Poland gave opportunity, were apt to be looked at askance in Warsaw as pedants and bureaucrats.　Time, and the new unified education in Polish Government schools, are gradually doing away with this mental heritage of Russian rule.

## 7

Turning now from the Russian to the *Prussian* section of Poland, we find that here also certain useful moral qualities were developed in the community under political pressure.　But the circumstances were widely different, and the result bears the imprint of that difference.

Frederick the Great, who was, as we have seen, the real originator of the partitions of Poland, was also the initiator of the policy (suggested by the history of medieval German colonization in Poland) of establishing, with goverment aid, a growing number of German settlers among the population of Prussia's newly gained Polish province, and so gradually giving it a German character.　But this programme of Frederick's was to be realized resolutely only about a century after his death, when Prussia had gained enough political and economic strength to carry it out.　In the meantime, during the period of European troubles after the great shock of the Napoleonic wars, the aim of Germanizing Prussia's Polish spoils was pursued, for various reasons, on the whole but fitfully and irresolutely.　In one respect, however, Prussia even then firmly established a practice from which she never departed,—a practice which distinguished her favourably from Russia, but made her, in a way, more formidable to Polish nationality.　While Russia, as we have seen, to the great detriment of her *prestige* sent the very scum and offal of her corrupt bureaucracy to Poland, Prussia, developing in modern times a most efficient and incorruptible body of officials in her service, always thought the very best of these excellent public servants barely good enough for the exposed positions on the border.　The easy way of bribery, always open under Russia, was precluded by the Prussian system, and Poles under Prussia, contrary to their compatriots under Russia, acquired a strong sense of the authority of the State, the rigour of the law, and the accurate and correct, if occasionally ruthless, working of a well-ordered administrative machinery. Something of the German's discipline and thoroughness entered into their own mental composition. Armed by such partial assimilation to their oppressors, the Poles of Prussian Poland also thereby became qualified to reap the full benefits of such material and organizatory improvements as went with Prussian rule. The neat and orderly condition of the former Prussian Poland, as contrasted with the sad inheritance of slovenliness and neglect in the former Russian section, still bears evidence to-day of the gulf which separated German conditions from Russian. It is as if on the soil of the reunited Poland a European and an Asiatic sphere of influence met. And while the traces of Russian mis-rule are being gradually and painfully removed from the face of town and country in former Russian Poland, it is to the credit of former Prussian Poland to state that she has not allowed any of the commendable outward features of the German order of things to deteriorate within her borders, in spite of all the economic hardships of post-war time.

The anti-Polish Policy of Prussia, although really as old as the annexation of Prussian Poland itself, only became entirely determined and sustained when Bismarck made it part of his scheme for the national consolidation of the new German Empire of 1871 under Prussian leadership. In carrying out (with very imperfect success) another part of that scheme, viz., the struggle against the Catholic element in Germany (called by himself the "struggle for culture"), he had already come up against solid resistance on the part of the Poles, who represented a large united *bloc* of Catholic population dangerously near Berlin.

The *Kulturkampf*, as far as Prussian Poland was concerned, had only the effect of establishing a closer union between religion and patriotism in this part of Poland than in any other, and of turning the clergy into capable and popular national leaders when the struggle was no longer concerned with religion.

For purposes of the immediate attack on the Polish element by itself—an attack which Bismarck thought vital to the political welfare of the new Germany—the ground was shifted from religious to economic issues. The Poles—particularly the peasantry were (and are) a race of large families, and by sheer force of numbers they would always overcome every attempt to dissolve them in the large national unit of the new Germany : it was a successor of Bismarck's who spoke of their "rabbit policy " (*Kaninchen-Politik*) as the secret of their indomitableness. The vast majority to them being tillers of soil, the only effective way of dealing with them appeared to be a return to the plan of Frederick the Great, viz., organized purchase of Polish soil and the systematic establishment of German settlers on it with a view of gradually supplanting the entire Polish land-owning population both great and small. This accordingly was what Bismarckian and post-Bismarckian Prussia, more or less backed by the whole of German opinion, strenuously endeavoured to accomplish. A " Colonizing Commission " amply subsidized by the government, took the matter in hand, and its work was facilitated by various legislative measures, culminating, a few years before the World War, in an act which authorized the forcible expropriation of such Polish owners as refused to sell.

## 8

In spite of all the powerful financial, legislative, and administrative support which it enjoyed, the colonizing campaign achieved very little success. It was opposed by the Poles through excellent economic organization, in which priests (headed by Father Wawrzyniak) played a leading part. While in the other sections of Poland the partitioning governments had succeeded to some extent in sowing discord between the country gentleman and the peasant farmer, Prussia, a largely agrarian state, had not only abolished peasant serfdom much sooner than the other two (as early as 1823), but had taken well-devised measures to prevent all economic friction which could arise between peasant and landlord in consequence of emancipation. As a result of this fact, the colonizing campaign found the Polish landlords and the peasantry united in a common national front for the organized economic defence of their soil. As the struggle gained in intensity, the Poles were able to pass from the defensive to the offensive, and more land began actually to go out of German hands into Polish, than the opposite way. Incidentally, the sharp competition between the two nations for the possession of land pushed the price of land upward, and a considerable all-round increase of prosperity in the countryside became the desirable by-product of the struggle for the land. Wealth and enlightenment led to the adoption of mechanical improvements and scientific methods in farming : the soil of Prussian Poland—being by nature rather mediocre—became the best-tilled throughout the Polish lands, and produces the highest average yield to this day.

Another incidental result of the colonizing campaign proved also highly beneficial to the Polish cause. Those Polish landowners and farmers who could not, after all, hold their own and were obliged to relinquish the land, wandered largely into the towns, and were for the most part sufficiently equipped with capital through the sale of their land to go into trade on their own account. Thus the Polish middle class in the towns, weakened since the days of the old Poland, began to gain in strength. The towns, to which a German physiognomy had artificially been imparted through German officialdom, reassumed more and more of their native Polish complexion. Aware of this indirect result of the struggle for the land, the Prussian Government started another financial campaign, analogous to that of the Colonizing Commission, and began systematically to subsidize the middle-class German element in the towns. But this policy never reached the dimensions of the other and produced no appreciable result.

Apart from these huge economic efforts of the government in town and country, all means of administrative pressure and educational influence were used for the extinction of Polish nationality under Prussia. The use of the Polish language in all domains of public life was gradually done away with as completely as in Russia ; all branches of the administration were staffed with Germans, who received additions to their salary for service in the border provinces ; the schools were turned into engines of Germanization with a ruthless efficiency which even called forth, in 1906, the unheard-of phenomenon of a strike of school children.

The effects of German education were encountered, in the same way as Government education in Russian Poland, by voluntary private organization of Polish educational activities on a large scale. German efficiency producing a similar quality in Polish counter-efforts, Prussian Poland was soon able to boast of the highest standard of education among its masses that any part of Poland in the nineteenth century achieved. Illiteracy became unknown among the Poles under Prussia, and the peasantry, in particular, surpassed that of other parts of Poland in general culture and civic consciousness. The ends of higher education and of research were served by private organizations at Poznań (called by the Germans Posen), the ancient capital of the province ; the organizing efforts of an enlightened citizen of Poznań, Dr. K. Marcinkowski, as well as the munificence of a noble family—the Raczyńskis—played a memorable historical part in providing the city and province (which possessed

no university) with a fine framework for all Polish cultural
endeavour.

9

With all these memorable successes in upholding the national
tradition of culture, it was inevitable that Prussian Poland's
constant and severe struggle against aggression by sheer material
power should have a somewhat detrimental effect on the breadth
of intellectual outlook, and even on moral refinement, among
that section of the divided nation.

The Poles under Prussian rule, in their very struggle against it,
necessarily became somewhat tainted with the crude materialism
which characterized the new industrial and imperialist Germany
after 1871. Being driven by necessity almost exclusively into
economic fields of activity, the Poles of Prussian Poland came to
rate professional efficiency more highly than abstract knowledge
and intellectual speculation. The Prussian section of Poland
became somewhat deficient in that subtle and versatile type of
Polish intellect which, in other parts of the country and among
the emigrants abroad, often so attractively represented the old
cultural tradition of Poland's country gentry in the ranks of the
modern professional *intelligentsia*. The Poznań province remained characterized rather by a highly satisfactory average of
popular education than by such individual fine flowers of high
and wide culture. In that sense, we may call its intellectual life
more democratic than that of the rest of Poland. But it must be
added that at the same time the province, by the conditions of its
existence under Prussian rule, was unfitted for some of the most
essential functions of democratic self-government ; all official
careers, particularly at home, being closed to the Prussian Pole
as much as to the Pole under Russia, Prussian Poland, although
ably if scantily represented in the Prussian Parliament and in the
Reichstag, did not produce a body of trained public servants,
and found herself almost quite as resourceless in that respect as
Russian Poland, when the hour of deliverance came.

With all these inevitable deficiencies, the achievement of
Prussian Poland in economic organization and national character-
training was imposing indeed, and her fine record of successful
resistance to the most powerful instruments of oppression
naturally called forth admiring sympathy in all other parts of
Poland. Great artists, like Sienkiwicz the novelist and Paderewski the pianist, took occasion to do public homage to the
heroism of that province. Prussian Poland came to be looked
upon as another Alsace-Lorraine in Europe, and the struggle
it conducted so bravely aroused international interest.

But even within Germany, the Polish problem, instead of gradually disappearing, widened under repression. The traditional connection between Roman Catholicism and Polish nationalism had been strengthened by Bismarck's policy ; this connection quickened the new growth of Polish national feeling in the province adjoing Poznania on the southern side, viz., Silesia, which had been separated from the body of Poland since the early fourteenth century, but had remained Roman Catholic and largely Polish-speaking. On the other hand, the sympathies of all Poland fomented a similar development in Poznania's north-eastern neighbour province, Pomerania, which had once formed Poland's pathway to the sea, and also retained an overwhelming majority of Polish-speaking country people along the banks of the lower Vistula (in the present " Polish Corridor "). The Kassubians, dwelling along the Baltic coast in the neighbourhood of Danzig and speaking a dialect most closely akin to Polish, were also drawn into the orbit of the Polish national movement.

Thus Germany, in consequence of adopting too drastically simple methods of dealing with a national minority, found herself confronted by a problem of increasing magnitude, involving a province which was the principal granary of her industrial regions, another which was one of her main reservoirs of coal, and part of a third, which was vital for her maritime interests in the Baltic. The Polish nation, on the other hand, had the comforting consciousness of having shown superlative vitality by effectively withstanding the presssure of the most formidable modern imperial organism, whose rapid growth and unbounded ambition were beginning to make the greatest powers in Europe anxious.

### 10

As we have seen, both the Prussian and the Russian sector produced a considerable amount of wealth from different sources ; both in their several ways gave scope to voluntary social organization for national ends ; but both also were handicapped with regard to the attainment of highest culture, and both were deprived of opportunities for administrative training and practice.

The destinies of *Austrian Poland* were exactly the reverse. That sector was fated to combine comparative poverty with full opportunities for higher learning and achievements in research and art, as well as for the schooling of public servants in all domains of modern state administration.

At first, indeed, for a long series of years, the record of Austrian Poland was particularly dreary, and it was then that its permanent state of poverty originated. The first half-century and more of Austrian rule was marked by uncompromising centralism and unmitigated exploitation. The province was administered by imported government commissioners without any regard for local traditions ; the German language was introduced into government offices and schools ; Joseph II followed the Prussian example of Frederick in planting groups of German colonists on the land ; and fiscal and economic policy was purely predatory throughout, as if the Vienna Government never felt assured that it would keep the Polish spoils, and wished to " make hay while the sun was shining." It was during that period that the Austrian official mind adopted a principle which was persistently acted upon, even in the later days of self-government, viz., that the Polish province must be kept in the condition of a purely agricultural country, so as to serve as a granary for the rest of Austria and as a never-failing market for its industrial articles. It was then also that Austria began to apply to her Polish province, as well as to her other composite domains, the Roman rule of government, *Divide at impera*. The peasantry, as has already been mentioned, were taken under special government protection, and their class antagonism against the country gentry was fostered in order to keep the patriotism of the latter from active outbreaks. What became even more important as a fully-developed policy, was the early habit of the Austrian authorities of favouring a growth of separatism among the Ruthenians (or, as they later came to call themselves, the Ukrainians) of the eastern part of the province. It was after the early medieval Ruthenian duchy of Halicz (incorporated in the fourteenth century into Poland) that Austria called the whole province *Galicia*, it was out of regard to the Ruthenian element that the administrative centre of the province was fixed in the eastern city of Lwów (Lemberg) and not in Poland's ancient capital, Cracow, this being situated in the western and purely Polish part of the country.[1]

For a time, in the course of the ealier half of the nineteenth century, the province was even actually divided into two administrative units, a western, or Polish, and an eastern, or Ruthenian,

[1] Cracow with a small patch of territory around it was erected, by the Congress of Vienna, into a free City Republic, and enjoyed a brief thirty years' period of great prosperity under that arrangement ; but during the revolutionary troubles heralding the European storm of 1848, Austria unceremoniously annexed it. There was no question, then or after, of making the old royal city the capital of Austrian Poland.

one. And although this division, in view of the strength of the Polish element in the east, proved untenable, yet enough of ferment was created by Austrian policy to make Eastern Galicia the centre of one of the new Poland's gravest minority problems.

The old Austria was an absolute monarchy, supported by an elaborate bureaucratic machinery, and its Chancellor Metternich was for many years the mainstay of tottering absolutism in Continental Europe against the onrush of new democratic ideas. The Austrian absolute *régime* was doomed to fall first of the three autocratic powers of the Holy Alliance, because the Monarchy, built up during centuries out of the most heterogeneous racial elements, lacked inner cohesion, which dynastic unity alone could not give. Yet Austrian absolutism died extremely hard. Even after 1848, when the nations of Austria had risen in revolution to claim representative government, and a Pole (F. Smolka) had presided over their first Parliament, a long relapse into autocratic methods followed. Russian aid was called in to subdue Hungary's gallant effort to gain independence ; and it was not till defeats in war had seriously shaken the international prestige of the Empire that Austria definitely entered on the path of parliamentary government and provincial home rule. It needed the loss of Austria's Italian possessions, and, what was more, her deposition, by Prussia, from her former dominant place among German States, to induce her to grant a status of constitutional parity to the Hungarian half of the monarchy, in 1867. The same was not granted to the Poles and the Czechs under Austria, or to the Croats and Serbs under Hungary : the dual monarchy never became a triple or quadruple one, or a multiple federation, which might still have prolonged its existence and even possibly enlarged its boundaries. Yet Galicia, like other provinces of Austria, received in 1867 a complete system of self-government, which thoroughly changed the political state of affairs in the country and lifted it in constitutional privileges far above the Prussian and Russian sectors of the divided Poland.

## II

Self-governing Austrian Poland after 1867 had a provincial Parliamentary Assembly of its own, as well as representation in the Imperial Parliament at Vienna. A special post of Minister for Galician Affairs was soon created in the Austrian Cabinet. The administration of the country was divided between two categories of officials—imperial and provincial ones ; but both bodies were henceforward recruited exclusively in the country itself. The Army alone was not reorganized on territorial principles and retained German as its official language. In all other departments of public service, the Polish language became dominant throughout Galicia ; it reigned once more in the courts of law and in the schools. The two universities of Cracow and Lwów (Lemberg), which had been compelled to use German for a number of years, once more became Polish seats of learning, and an " Academy " founded on the ground-work of an older society at Cracow in 1871, became the central and supreme organization of research workers in all Polish lands.

The Austrian Poles, having obtained such far-reaching concessions, naturally came to see their interest in supporting the Empire within whose structure they had secured this comfortable political position. The strong Polish group in the Vienna Parliament became a mainstay of every Austrian Govern-ment, and had seriously to be reckoned with by each. Poles occupied important positions in all government departments at Vienna ; there never was an Austrian Cabinet again without two or even more seats in it being occupied by Poles ; the Polish element gave to Austria a number of distinguished Finance Ministers in particular ; Poles rose repeatedly to the rank of Prime Minister in the next few decades, and more than once the most vital issues of the Monarchy's domestic and foreign policy were decided upon by a Polish statesman.

Both in this sphere of activity and in the autonomous govern-ment of the Polish province it was in the first place the landed gentry which supplied the higher personnel.

Parliamentary representation, both provincial and imperial, was also constructed in such a manner as to secure predominance for that class. The fate of Galicia, it may be broadly said, was for several decades in the hands of the landed gentry—essentially a conservative class. Hence it came that although considerable improvements were indeed effected to retrieve the consequences of a half-century of Austrian bureaucrats' misrule, yet on the whole the progress of the province did not keep time with what was simultaneously going on so feverishly in the world outside. The governing class of country gentlemen had no proper sense of the importance of industrial development, in the direc-tion of which things were rapidly tending everywhere else ; they acquiesced in that purely agricultural destination which Austria's economic policy assigned to Galicia, and which coincided with their own class interests. They showed no eagerness to lift up the decayed welfare of the towns, and to foster the growth of a

really strong Polish middle class. Neither did they take the
corporate interests of the peasantry—the bulk of the population
—overmuch to heart, until that rapidly rising social power began
to take care of itself.

It was through changes in the social composition of the administrative staff and of the parliamentary representation that the
public life of Galicia began, towards the end of the nineteenth
century, to assume a different complexion. Members of that
newly consolidated class, the *intelligentsia*, in greater and
greater numbers began to reach high positions not only in the
professions, but also in the administration and in politics.
And the ranks of the *intelligentsia* began to be swelled by growing
influxes of men born in peasant cottages in the country. The
structure of the governing class thus becoming more democratic,
two things came to be better understood. One was that " Galician misery " (which had become proverbial) could only be
turned into competence by the development of industries on the
Western European model. Another was that a profound
change in the conditions of land ownership in the countryside
would be the enevitable consequence of the abolition of peasant
serfdom ; that the hitherto ruling class of country gentlemen
would gradually dwindle down, and a body of peasant farmers
grow up in its place, and that it was a primary duty of truly
far-sighted statesmanship to provide betimes for the highest
possible education and the best possible economic organization
of this rising social class of peasant proprietors.

12

In spite of considerable difficulties, some progress was made in
both directions. As regards industrialism, one calamity indeed
marked its course : the attempt to use the savings of the
population, accumulated in the central savings-bank of the
province, for the development of the oilfields on the northern
slope of the Carpathians, broke down through lack of vision in
decisive quarters ; an " oil boom " among private investors
ended mostly in losses, and foreign capital ultimately came into
control of the oil wells. But industrial developments in other
domains, thanks to a " League of Assistance to Industry," were
taking a fairly promising course in the early years of the
twentieth century.

With regard to the rise of the peasantry, certain definite and
most successful achievements in organization stand to Galicia's
credit. On the model of the German Raiffeisen banks, a network of small credit institutions for peasant farmers was created ;

another network of organizations, the " Farmers' Circles," served the ends of co-operation, and also of agricultural instruction, very usefully.

With growing prosperity and enlightenment, the peasantry began to show an active interest in politics ; peasant deputies made their appearance in Parliament, a " Peasant Party " arose, and one of the peasant leaders trained in the school of these political activities under Austria—Wincenty Witos—was to become not only leader of the Parliamentary Peasant Party, but also Prime Minister in the new Poland.

Side by side with the peasant movement, *Socialism* began, towards the end of the nineteenth century, to become a feature of Austrian Poland's political life.

It grew in strength particularly when Austria, shaken more and more violently by quarrels between her nationalities, resolved to divert attention to other issues by imitating Disraeli's "leap in the dark " thirty years later and introducing, in 1897, universal (male) suffrage as the basis of elections for the Imperial Parliament. A number of Socialist leaders trained in the Austrian Parliamentary school were to make their mark in the early history of the new Poland—foremost among them, Ignacy Daszyński, who was to become Speaker of the Lower House of Poland's Parliament in 1928.

Both personalities and problems, then, as we have seen, were to be bequeathed by Galicia's political life to that of reborn Poland. In historical retrospect, indeed, the politics of pre-war Galicia may now be viewed as a microcosm of political conditions on the larger stage of the new Republic. This is particularly and painfully true of two issues which Austro-Polish politicians grappled with in vain. The Ukrainian question has already been mentioned : carefully cultivated by Austria for purposes of its own, and fanned into flame by the ambitions of a growing class of Ukrainian *intelligentsia*, it threatened, in the last years before the World War, to disorganize the entire working of Galician self-government. The assassination of a Polish Governor-General of Galicia, Count Potocki, by a fanatical Ukrainian student in 1908 was a violent manifestation of the acuteness of the problem. At the same time certain sensational revelations concerning the support given to Ukrainian activities in Galicia by the chief anti-Polish organization in Prussia, and, on the other hand, the Austrian dynasty's demonstrative sympathies for Ukrainian nationalism—expressive of ambitions in the direction of Russia's Ukrainian domains—indicated the wide and serious international bearings of what might have seemed a purely provincial issue.

If, accordingly, Galicia was destined to introduce into the political organism of the new Poland some of the most momentous problems which agitate it to-day, she was also preparing a highly useful positive contribution of her own. Half a century of full provincial self-government and of active share in the Imperial politics of Austria made Galicia a well-stocked reservoir of experienced public servants—legislators, administrators, economists, judges, educators—and in view of conditions under Prussia and under Russia, she was the only reservoir of the sort which the new Poland found ready to draw upon. Administrative positions of all sorts in the new Republic had to be filled by Austro-Polish officials, and the resources which Galicia provided in this manner for the beginnings of organized life in the new State, certainly may be considered as an equivalent for the wealth which she lacked, and of which other portions of Poland brought a fuller measure into the common stock.

## 13

One other important contribution of Austrian Poland must be singled out. It is her share in the history of Polish *intellect* and *art* during the later nineteenth century. While, in the Russian and the Prussian sectors, the Polish language was being rapidly ousted from all stages of education, the Austrian province, on the contrary, after 1867 came once more into possession of a complete Polish school system, with an autonomous provincial school board as practically its supreme administrative authority. Under the circumstances, Galicia became the only part of Poland in which the entire body of the nation's youth was brought up not only with methodical school training in the national language and its literature, but with a systematic knowledge of Poland's place in European history and civilization. And international effects were quite as important as national ones. As the writings of Poland's great romantic poets in their Parisian exile after 1831 had kept the national flag flying in literature when torn down and trampled upon in political life, so now, after 1863, the same flag again flew proudly in the spiritual air of art as well as of learning through the revival of free institutions devoted to them in Austrian Poland. The Cracow Art School rose into a commanding position mainly through the genius of Poland's greatest painter, J. Matejko, who, in a series of huge historical canvases, presented to the eyes of the nation all the splendour of its past glories. The theatre of Cracow became the central home of Polish theatrical art and dramatic literature. Above all, however, it was the ancient University of Cracow which now once more, as in the fifteenth century, became the true *Alma Mater* of the best intellect throughout the Polish lands. Its chairs were filled with the most eminent Polish research workers and teachers from all parts of Poland and, indeed, from all over the world ; its lecture-rooms attracted not only the youth of Austrian Poland, but, in increasing proportion, that of the Russian and Prussian sectors as well. The Polish Academy at Cracow, year after year published scores of volumes of important Polish research work in all fields. The investigations of Cracow physicists and chemists like Wróblewski and Olszewski, which led up to the liquefaction of air, attained world-wide celebrity. But it was principally as a centre of studies in Polish history and literature that Cracow became a dominant force in national life. Eminent historians, such as J. Szujski and M. Bobrzyński, created a school of historical research which moulded its results into a philosophy of national history ; and workers in other fields, like the brilliant historian of Polish literature, Count Stanislas Tarnowski (for many years President of the Polish Academy) and, more recently, a great Professor of Law, W. L. Jaworski, were instrumental in building up, on the basis of that philosophy of history, an actual political programme. The philosophy was essentially critical, and the programme essentially conservative. Dwelling, by way of warning, on the faults of the old Polish commonwealth which had contributed to its undoing, and on the disastrous rashness of the armed risings in the earlier nineteenth century, the Cracow political doctrine recommended peaceful effort at educational, economic and legal improvement under the given political and social conditions. It gave moral support to the country gentry as the ruling force in Galician affairs, to the Roman Catholic Church as a spiritual mainstay of Polish national tradition, and to the Hapsburg monarchy as the only safe shelter left for free manifestations of Polish national life.

## 14

The Cracow programme, inspired by the sober wisdom of political realism, certainly lent itself to positive achievements at the hand of eminent personalities : administrative careers like that of J. Dunajewski as Finance Minister of Austria, or M. Bobrzyński as Governor of Galicia—both of them originally Professors of Cracow University—bear eloquent witness to the soundness of the Cracow doctrine.

Yet it is not to be wondered at that the doctrine failed to satisfy ardent youthful minds and even intellects of wider outlook.

In art, it was not only the paintings of Matejko but, even before them, the great historical novels of H. Sienkiewicz which had, in a way, countered the Cracow view of older Polish history by displaying the magnificence of the old Poland's heroism and power. In scholarship, historians like L. Kubala and O. Balzer at Lwów, T. Korzon and Smoleński in Warsaw, more or less deliberately in opposition to the Cracow school, dwelt on successful constructive efforts in Poland's political, economic, social and intellectual past. In politics, finally, men of vision chafed at the limitations of a view which confined national activities to the conditions given in each of the three different sectors, and seemed to exclude every prospect of reunion and deliverance. In the midst of what appeared to be a general mood of resignation in this matter, Stanislas Szczepanowski, whose writings now count among Poland's political classics, bodly began to speak again of the spiritual essentials of national unity, and of the value of a national tradition in a world of international currents of ideas. Educated in England for the engineering profession, he became the ardent advocate of industrialization as a means to raise the well-being of poverty-stricken Galicia.

Surrounded by a growing disposition, in Austrian Poland, to rely upon the action of public authorities in all social matters, he, with the fine examples of British self-help before his eyes, endeavoured to rouse the decaying spirit of private initiative in his fellow citizens. Brought up on the conventionalized " facts" of the positivist era, he went back for ideas to the work of the great educational reformers of the Poland of an earlier day. Suffering from a hunger and thirst for transcendental beliefs in the midst of his agnostic generation, he drew mystical religious inspiration from the great Polish romantic poets.

Szczepanowski, the herald of renewed and richer Polish national life, did not become a prophet in his own country. Yet, as the turn of the century drew near, other symptoms of change quickly followed one another. The official Polish school system of Galicia, found insufficient by the growing new democracy, was supplemented by the wide educational activities of a " People's School Society " (*T.S.L.*) founded by the poet A. Asnyk in 1891, and working particularly in the eastern and western border districts. A network of " Falcon Societies " (Sokols), on the model of Czech and other Slavonic organizations of the same type, served to popularize not only new ideals of physical culture, but also the notion of a trained and disciplined national force, to be kept ready for emergency. Animated by

new ideas of a more active national policy, Galicia began to look
beyond her provincial boundaries ; quite as, in Prussian Poland,
the national movement had extended to Pomerania and Silesia,
so now under Austria, assistance from Galicia and other parts of
Poland promoted the revival of Polish national consciousness
among the Polish-speaking country population in that southern
part of Silesia which had remained under Austria—the Duchy of
Cieszyn (Teschen), Galicia's neighbour province on the western
side.

It was the prophetic voice of literature which announced that
greater and more powerful changes were to follow.   All Europe,
growing weary of the narrowness and dullness of extreme
literary realism, was pervaded, towards the end of the century,
by new waves of individualism and romance.

Among those who expressed the new mood in Poland, there
arose, about 1900, at Cracow, the wonderful genius of Stanislas
Wyspiański, a painter and poet steeped in the historical glories of
Poland's ancient capital.   In his verse play *The Wedding* and a
succession of other dramatic visions of great poetic force,
Wyspiański shook the nation out of the torpor of acquiescence by
remorseless criticism of it's self-deluding indolence, as well as
by thunderous premonitions of another great sacrificial effort to
come, with the dawn of freedom in its wake.   At the same time,
an almost feverish note of patriotic exaltation, and of tragic
glorification of suffering, was struck in the novels of St. Żeromski
in Warsaw, who became the idol of youth and was to end his
career in a restored free Poland.

Whilst literature was dreaming its dreams of struggle for a
new existence, in the reality of political life Socialism was acting
as a powerful ferment, portending thorough and possibly violent
changes.   Polish Socialism soon after its birth both in Russian
and Austrian Poland (for it played hardly any part under
Prussia) assumed a deeper national colouring than in other
countries.   Under Russia in particular, the Socialist hopes for an
overthrow of the Tsarist *régime* by revolution became closely
associated with a Polish programme of emancipation by active
struggle, and of democratic reconstruction.   The revolutionary
activities conducted in this spirit by the Polish Socialists of
Russian Poland found a sympathetic echo among the Socialists of
Austrian Poland, and active co-operation was not slow in coming.
It was then that Galicia chiefly justified its description by foreign
onlookers as a " Polish Piedmont."   The hitherto peaceful and
law-abiding Austrian province became a basis of operations for
revolutionary action across the Russian border, and a seething

cauldron of conspiracy. Sympathies with the active spirit of revolutionaries in Russian Poland soon ceased to be limited to the Socialists under Austria : all democratic parties were drawn into their orbit, and ultimately—greatest surprise of all—a strange approximation was to be effected between the Russo-Polish revolutionary spirit and the political realism of the Cracow conservatives, and was to manifest itself by joint action at the beginning of the World War.

### 15

It used often to be said before the War, that while Poland remained divided into three parts, a fourth and most important sector of Poland was consolidating across the seas, in the *United States of America*. Emigration to America had become a feature of Western European life early in the nineteenth century, partly as a consequence of political convulsions in various countries, partly under the constant pressure of a rapid increase of population, far surpassing (as we see now) the record of earlier centuries. From Poland, groups of exiled fighters for liberty had occasionally gone to America, especially after the suppression of the rising of 1831, and some of them had made their mark among the pioneers of cultural development in the States. But a mass exodus of mere manual workers from Poland, as from other countries in eastern and south-eastern Europe, only set in during the second half of the century, and its reason may be sought, as far as Poland is concerned, mainly in the conditions of rural pauperism consequent upon the abolition of serfdom : the lack of land to support the crowded village population became painfully felt when that population was turned adrift by emancipation. The remedy of " land reform " was to be applied on a large scale only in our own days ; the purchase of land by the peasants, although in due time assisted by credit organizations, was necessarily a slow process ; meanwhile, crowds of peasants left the country either in search of temporary employment, especially during the harvest season, in the rural districts of neighbouring lands (a practice equally common to-day) or in search of a new existence altogether in the Promised Land across the ocean. America's rapidly developing industries demanded an abundant supply of cheap labour ; accordingly the new type of immigration was welcomed, and no obstacles were at first placed in its way. The crowds of landless peasants were soon swelled by other crowds of proletarian Jews, especially from the congested towns of eastern Russian Poland, where Russia kept them huddled together and exposed to waves of cruel

E

administrative persecution, and where their traditional occupation could not provide sustenance for all.   This new immigration from eastern Europe did not spread westward over the
American Continent, but peopled the growing suburbs of the new
colossal industrial cities, along the Great Lakes, in the Pennsyl-
vanian mining districts, and on the north-eastern coast of the
States.   The Polish peasant farmer mostly went to work in
factories and mines ; the Jewish element largely was absorbed by
the sweated home industries, especially the tailoring trade in
New York.   In a few decades, the accumulations of this emigrant
element from Poland became prodigious in numbers : the total
of Polish emigrants in America, and of descendants of emigrants
in the first generation, is estimated to-day at four millions and a
half, and Chicago alone has a Polish population of nearly half a
million.   Of the nearly four million Jews in America, over two
millions inhabit New York, and the majority of them are of
eastern European origin.

With the growth of the emigration movement, its commercial
exploitation set in : the masses of emigrants were herded off to
America by shipping agencies which flourished on a traffic in
emigrant labour comparable, in its conditions of transport, to
the extinct slave trade.

It was, however, not only in the crowded steerage quarters of
Transatlantic liners that pictures of human misery almost like
those of Dante's *Inferno* could be seen now.   In America itself,
both Polish and Jewish emigrants, being included in the lowest
ranks of American labour, lived for a long time under conditions
of unspeakable squalor and privation.   Dwelling together in
their own districts of the cities, they did not profit by contact
with the native American element even to the extent of acquiring
a tolerable knowledge of the language.   They seemed debarred
from all share in the rising prosperity of America.

### 16

And yet they began to thrive.   Of the Jews, many became—
or brought up their children to become—commercial magnates,
and some of their descendants now rank socially with the off-
spring of the earlier and more cultured type of Jewish immigrant
from western Europe.   The Polish peasant element rose more
slowly in the social scale.   With their inherited small-farmer
mentality, they were much less adaptable than the Jews, and
more hopelessly lost in the wilderness of American city life.
Having been used, in their old homes, to a much lower standard
of life than the average American worker, they managed,

amazingly, to save money on the low wages paid to them as unskilled labour ; but their ambition at first uniformly was to invest these savings in land purchase in the old country. Many returned to live on farms increased out of American savings ; some repeated the process of emigration and return home even several times in their lives. Others, having got into agricultural employment in America, by sheer industry and thrift worked their way up out of the position of farm hands into that of farm owners : of such are the prosperous Polish onion and tobacco growers in the Connecticut valley to-day. Some, finally, succeeded in business on their own account in the cities, especially in the districts inhabited by their countrymen ; a very few became the founders of larger industrial concerns, of banks, or of real estate agencies.

The general level of education among the emigrants remained, for a long time, low. America being full of self-made rich men without a higher education, there was no inducement for the emigrant even to let his children pursue any studies beyond the earliest age at which they could begin to earn money themselves. Gradually, professional groups of men seeking their *clientèle* among their own native emigrant community—first priests, then doctors, lawyers, architects—began to rise from among the mass ; it was these groups also which began to furnish lay political leaders, all leadership in organizations having at first been (as in the case of the Irish) entirely in the hands of priests.

But it is only with the recent rush towards institutions of higher learning in America that something like a mass movement in favour of higher education has begun to manifest itself among the Polish-American community. The type—now more and more frequent—of the " American of Polish origin " with a university education, entering actively into all the interests of cultured American society, contributes greatly to the increase of the prestige of his race, which until now has been deplorably low. In fact, the widely accepted theory of the superiority of the Nordic races ranked the Poles generally among the undesirable foreign elements in the United States. The quickly multiplying new type of cultured Polish-American citizen may become instrumental in removing that racial prejudice. He may do an even higher and more vital service to American civilization by acting as one more of its links with its " ancient mother," Europe. The Polish-American of really fine and intellectual fibre feels the desire of the man of true culture for some spiritual roots in the European past of the race, and he shows the same kind of affectionate interest in Poland's historical civilization

and renewed free life as the best type of American of old New
England stock is apt to show in England. It is needless to dwell
on the great value of such ways of thinking for the cause of
cultural co-operation among civilized nations.

In this manner, the descendants of emigrants, though
thoroughly Americanized in speech and manners, may in some
cases become more useful as exponents of Poland's historical and
cultural achievements in the American world than their fathers
ever could have been. At the same time, it is safe to predict of
the rank and file that they will, with higher education and the
concomitant change in social surroundings, become entirely
merged in the American nation. As, on the other hand, the
post-war anti-immigration laws of the United States have
brought emigration from Poland to the States to an almost
complete standstill, the history of the movement may be considered as, in a way, closed, and mature for a conclusive survey.
Such a survey from the point of view of Polish national interests
reveals, above all, one amazing fact : low as was the standard of
civic or any other education which the original emigrants
carried with them out of the old country—miserable as were the
conditions which drove them forth—yet such was the vitality of
racial tradition, that out of the hard-earned and much-needed
American savings, money, after a time, began to flow into
national institutions at home. It is well known how much such
national movements in Europe as the Irish or the Ukrainian
movement, owe to financial support from overseas. The
Polish cause was not, perhaps, materially quite so fortunate, yet
the American Poles, besides investing in their own insurance
societies, building co-operatives and other communal institutions,
certainly did find a considerable amount of money to spare for
the support of national organizations in the old country.

In yet another way, Poland long before the war profited by
the emigration movement, viz. through the fact that emigrants
who returned to Poland for good, not only brought capital with
them, but used it to build dwellings and develop farms which
served as models to the countryside and raised the standards
of domestic comfort, agricultural efficiency, cleanliness and
hygiene.

Apart from the United States, it was chiefly South America,
and especially Brazil which, even before the War, began to
serve as an outlet for Poland's landless rural labour. Here,
again, great hardships were endured ; they were enhanced by
the climate ; the records of much real suffering went into the
making of Mary Konopnicka's high-coloured emigrant epic *Mr.*

*Balcer in Brazil.* Here, also, as in the United States, emigrant communities leading a somewhat more normal life began gradually to grow up. But in the case of the South American States, contrary to North America, the movement is in full progress and has assumed considerably increased dimensions since the War.

## CHAPTER III

# THE WORLD WAR AND THE RE-BIRTH OF THE POLISH STATE

## I

POLAND'S greatest poet, Adam Mickiewicz, writing for the comfort of his fellow-exiles in Paris a book of parables, admonitions and prophecies in Biblical prose, called *The Books of the Polish Nation and of the Polish Pilgrimage* (1833), had ended it with a *Pilgrims' Litany*, containing a prayer to God " for a great war which would bring deliverance to oppressed nations." And, indeed, as the nineteenth century was drawing towards its close, it seemed that little short of the terrible fulfilment of Mickiewicz' inspired prayer could bring the Polish cause back to life. Forty years after Poland's last armed rising, the Polish problem, as an issue of international politics, seemed thoroughly dead and buried. France, which had repeatedly manifested a sympathetic and protective interest in Polish national aspirations, now, after her defeat in 1870-71, had sought security in an alliance with Tsarist Russia, which implied the tacit abandonment of the largest section of Poland to Russian oppresson. Austria, which, for cogent reasons, had allowed self-government to its Poles, was drifting into greater and greater dependence on her powerful German ally. Germany herself was as determined as ever to suppress Polish nationality within her borders ; her endeavours in that respect went exactly parallel to Russia's, and it seemed that, whatever other differences might arise between them, Berlin and St. Petersburg would always see eye to eye on the question of Poland.

In Poland itself, not only had the interests of the three sections of the country come to diverge widely from each other, but the generations growing up since the last armed struggle of 1863, had become too absorbed in the pursuit of the material ends of modern economic effort to retain a vivid sense of the reality of national aims. The land-owning gentry, which had been the backbone of resistance to foreign rule in the past, now professed acquiescence, and actually evolved a political programme

of " reconciliation " and " threefold loyalty " ; even under
Prussia, where it was engaged in a struggle for the land, that
class never thought of any but legal weapons in the contest.
The manufacturing and commercial communities in all three
sections, but particularly under Russia, had excellent reasons to
cling to the connection with large imperial organisms. The
peasantry, for the most part nationally unawakened, always
essentially conservative, and now bent with might and main
upon the acquisition of more and more land, naturally could not
be expected to pursue what seemed the chimera of national
reunion and freedom.

Under the circumstances, it was only the professional *intelligentsia* of the towns—that class of determining importance for all
spiritual movements in latter-day continental Europe—which
kept the torch of national aspirations burning. The intellectual
class, in Poland as elsewhere, at this time came to be pervaded
by those two currents which remain to this day the most powerful two opposite forces in the political life of European
communities, viz. Socialism and Nationalism. Socialism has
already been mentioned as a factor of revolutionary unrest in
later nineteenth century Russian Poland ; since 1885, the dark
recesses of the Russian Citadel in Warsaw had become once more
the scene of executions of political prisoners, as in the insurrectionary days of 1863. Nationalism as a modern political party
in Russian Poland also began its course necessarily in the guise of
conspiracy : many if its early leaders, while still university
students, suffered imprisonment and deportation to Siberia.

2

The attitude of the two movements only became differentiated
from each other when events in Russia, at the beginning of our
own century, seemed to move in the direction of great changes.
The disastrous defeat in the war with Japan hastened the
outbreak of a revolutionary storm which had long been brewing :
this was met by concessions to popular demands ; Russia
received a Parliament and seemed to be entering on an era of
constitutional life.

The *P.P.S.* (Polish Party of Socialists) with the patriotic
fervour alluded to before as its distinctive feature from the very
outset, had thrown itself into the vortex of revolutionary happenings under Russia : it kept up a running fire of acts of organized
violence against the Government, and became now definitely
inspired with the hope that complete national independence for
Poland would emerge out of the collapse of old Russia's imperial

fabric. It was in the stormy year 1905 that a man who was afterwards to play an historical part of supreme importance for Poland—Joseph Piłsudski—rose into prominence among the revolutionary Socialists. Editor, for years, of the secretly-circulated Socialist paper *Robotnik* ("The Workingman"), he had been the very heart and soul of the movement which tended to make Socialism in Russian Poland an instrument, above all, of national deliverance. It was after 1905 that he gave organized shape to this tendency by creating an " Association of Active Struggle," soon to be transformed into the " Riflemen's Associations," which were to be the nucleus of a reborn Polish Army.

It was at this decisive point of his activities that Piłsudski found himself confronted by the figure of an opponent who, on his part, gained equal prominence in the ranks of the Nationalists— Roman Dmowski. The Nationalists (" National Democrats," as they called themselves), in view of the new promise of con-stitutional liberties under Russia, resolutely abandoned their early tactics of conspiracy and embarked on a policy of legal endeavours to obtain a maximum of provincial self-government. This was to be attained by co-operation with those parties in the new Russian Parliament which stood for gradual extension of the constitutional privileges and for autonomy to the non-Russian provinces of the Russian Empire. At the same time, wider inter-national prospects were opened up by Dmowski's programme ; the growth of German imperialism and the relentless course of Prussia's anti-Polish policy promoted sympathies, among the Polish Nationalists, for the Pan-Slavic idea, which seemed to be reviving. Russia was to become the powerful centre of a group of Slavonic nations, seeking security, in their union, against German oppression and expansion.

Viewed in historical perspective, Piłsudski appeared upon the scene as the direct continuator of the early nineteenth-century tradition of armed struggle for independence, and of the doctrines of the radical wing of Polish emigration in Paris, according to which, hope for Poland lay only in revolutionary upheavals of international magnitude. Dmowski, on the other hand, was resuming the thread of ideas of those Polish statesmen of the earlier period, who had believed in the possibility of freedom for Poland in union with Russia, and had trusted in the efficacy rather of diplomatic than of militant methods of activity.

In the years immediately following 1905, it seemed that both Piłsudski's and Dmowski's hopes were doomed to utter disap-pointment. On the one hand, the revolutionary movement in Russian Poland did not widen into a national insurrection ; on the other, the beginnings of Parliamentary life in Russia were soon quenched almost entirely by reaction. Yet both political doctrines found powerful support in interested quarters. Austria, having constituted herself the vanguard of German expansion into the Balkans and the Near East, had to reckon with a clash between German and Russian ambitions in that sphere, and accordingly began to foment all anti-Russian movements among the Poles. Piłsudski having transferred the headquarters of his activities to Cracow, his " Associations of Riflemen " were tolerated and assisted by the Austrian Government as auxiliary organizations of military training. On the other hand, Russia, investing her Mediterranean ambitions with the traditional garb of "protection to the Balkan Slavs," and aiming, besides, at the disintegration of Austria, encouraged Pan-Slavic demonstrations (such as the Pan-Slav Congress at Prague in 1908) and observed with satisfaction how Prussian policy was naturally producing a wide-spread feeling among the Poles that Germany, after all, was the most dangerous enemy of the Polish nation.

3

In spite of all preparatory activities, the World War, when it broke out, placed the body of Polish opinion before a dilemma which it was extremely difficult to solve. It was clear that while the main underlying issues had nothing to do with the Polish cause, Poland would suffer as being necessarily one of the theatres of warfare, but she could also ultimately gain in consequence of drastic rearrangements of the map of Europe at the conclusion of the peace. The Powers concerned had shown a renewed inclination to reckon with the Polish factor, and it was evident that even more attention to it could be enforced by the Poles themselves, if they played an active, and not merely a passive part in the great struggle. Yet to play an active part meant taking sides, and here were Poland's two principal enemies and oppressors—Germany and Russia— arrayed against each other. True, on the same side as Germany was Austria, the only Power which had done something definite in satisfaction of the Poles' desire for political freedom : but Austria was by that time practically a vassal of Germany. True again, on the other side there were France and Britian—two Powers which had repeatedly shown sympathy for Polish aspirations in the nineteenth century ; but now they were deprived of liberty of action in this matter by consideration for their Russian ally, who persisted in treating the Polish problem as Russia's own domestic concern.

⌊Under the circumstances, it was natural that the active elements of the nation were divided into two opposing camps—a division which was to leave its traces in the political life of united and free Poland after the war.⌉ That Austro-Polish Parliamentary politicians emphatically declared themselves loyal supporters of Austria, and that the Polish representation in the Duma equally emphatically declared its sympathies for Russia was natural enough in the light of what had gone before ; only the Prussian Poles found it impossible to muster up any show of loyalty. It was also necessary, if highly tragic, that Poles called up as soldiers of the conscript armies of the three partitioning Powers now had to fight each other. But it was superlatively pathetic, while psychologically inevitable under the circumstances, that Polish volunteer troops took the field under opposed colours. A Polish formation in France, organized at Bayonne, perished heroically almost in a body in the early stages of the war ; a " Polish Legion " under Russia never developed into anything of importance. But highly important consequences were to follow from the action of the small body of Piłsudski's Riflemen who, in the very first days of the war, marched from Cracow into Russian Poland as the nucleus of a Polish army taking the field against Russia. The Austro-Polish politicians took care at once to obtain legal recognition of the movement from the Central Powers ; and Piłsudski's " Legions " (growing to the size of two brigades in time) co-operated with the Austrian and German armies as a Polish Auxiliary Force placed under the political protection of an Austro-Polish " Supreme National Committee."

⌈In spite of Piłsudski's resolute action⌉ and the distinction with which his soldiers fought against Russia,⌈silence lay over the Polish problem for a considerable time in the early years of the war. In its first days, indeed, manifestoes had been addressed to the Polish nation both by the Russian and Austro-German Supreme Command. Carefully circumscribed in their wording, and issued not by the Governments, but by military General Headquarters merely, the documents could not possibly be interpreted as having any political importance ; yet one of them at least—the Russian one—aroused a certain amount of enthusiasm, because it held out the mirage of reunion of all Polish lands by a victorious Russia. Russia's Western Allies observed diplomatic silence on the Polish issue, and censored all unofficial allusions to it ; only the Parliament of a new ally— Italy—spoke up boldly on behalf of complete independence of Poland in a resolution passed in 1916, and always gratefully remembered in Poland. But it was only when the course of strategic events made it quite imperative that a decision was taken on the subject of Poland by the Powers immediately concerned.

### 4

Instead of the reunion promised by Russia, reunion of all Polish lands under Austro-German military occupation had, after the victories of the Central Powers over Russia, become an accomplished fact since 1915. The status of the occupied area required some definition, because it would not do to keep a province in a doubtful position and accordingly in a distrustful mood, in the rear of the armies ; besides, the moment seemed to be drawing near when the exhaustion of Austria's and Germany's man-power would raise the question of drawing upon the occupied Russian Poland for recruits. After much discussion between Berlin and Vienna, a solution was adopted which had Napoleon's creation of the " Duchy of Warsaw " (in 1807) for its precedent. By a joint proclamation of the Austrian and German Emperors, the occupied territory of Russian Poland was declared " an independent State." Practically every question relating to the definite shape of that State—except that it was to be a Constitutional Monarchy—was left open, including the question of its ruler and that of its frontiers. No allusion was made, on the one hand, to any prospect of reunion with Austrian and German Poland ; reunion with the historical eastern border provinces of Poland, on the other hand, was barred in advance : it was evident then that the creation of other vassal states of the Central Powers in those regions, particularly of a Lithuanian and a Ukrainian unit, was contemplated. Thus, the new State seemed destined to remain confined to narrow limits, which would make real independence impossible. Even within those limits, the division into a German and an Austrian sphere of military occupation was maintained, and the prerogatives of the military authorities overshadowed all government machinery which was set up in the new State. Such institutions as were gradually created and endowed with a show of power—a " Regency Council " of three distinguished citizens, a semi-Parliamentary " Council of State," and a Cabinet—remained more or less mere *simulacra*. Only in such non-political spheres of state action as the administration of justice and the organization of education, some real progress was made, and part of the ground-work for the fabric of a new Poland was prepared.

In spite of its very limited range and the unpromising conditions of its issue, the proclamation of the Central Powers was

looked upon by Polish opinion as a definite step forward towards
the recognition of the problem of Poland as an international one.
If no other effect, it was hoped it would have that of forcing the
hands of the western Allies in the matter of Poland. Some of
the best men whom Poland could muster, were by that time
active in trying to engage the interests of the western nations in
the fortunes of Poland. Purely charitable appeals for relief to
the population of the devastated regions of the war-stricken
country were successfully launched from Switzerland by the
great Polish novelist, Sienkiewicz (who died while working in
this field) with the co-operation of the famous pianist, Paderewski
(whose world-wide renown and personal charm were soon to work
other wonders for Poland yet) and of the Warsaw lawyer A.
Osuchowski, an experienced organizer of charities and private
educational activities. It was more difficult to rouse those in
power to political action on behalf of Poland. Dmowski,
disappointed with Russia's utter inactivity while she still held
Poland, had, since the German advance, transferred his indefatigable propagandist activities to the west of Europe. A
Polish National Committee, formed in Switzerland of pro-Ally
Polish politicians and transferred to Paris later, conducted a
zealous campaign of lectures and publications as well as conferences with statesmen and diplomatic memoranda addressed to
the Cabinets. But all this bore hardly any visible fruit as long
as Russia's position in the allied camp remained what it had been.

It was only the Russian Revolution which was to exercise a
decisive influence on the counsels of the Allies and on the destinies of Poland. It did so even in its first stage, while it still
seemed that changes would be moderate and Russia would
hold out in the ranks of the Allies. The Provisional Government
of the first revolutionary period issued on March 30, 1917, a
manifesto to the Polish nation, recognizing its right to political
independence. Although this contained an allusion to some
sort of union between the new Poland and Russia, it was justly
hailed by Polish opinion as a highly important further step in the
direction of deliverance. A beginning had been made by Russia
herself with a thorough readjustment of age-old relations
established by conquest : a special " Commission for the Settlement of Russo-Polish Affairs " was set up with the powers of a
Ministerial Department, and with a distinguished Polish lawyer
of Moscow, Alexander Lednicki, at its head. Lednicki, a
former member of the first Duma, had been the President of a
" Polish Committee " in Moscow, whose charitable and educational activities since 1915 had earned the gratitude of many

Polish exiles driven into the interior of Russia by the war. Lednicki's appointment to the position of High Commissioner for Polish Affairs in Russia seemed to indicate unmistakably that the new Russia meant business with regard to the Polish problem. At any rate, the fact was there that after Germany and Austria, the other factor most immediately concerned, viz., Russia, had officially admitted Poland's claim to restored independence. Poles could now confidently expect the Powers not directly interested to draw their conclusions from the situation so created; they could also formulate their own demands more expressly and resolutely, which they soon proceeded to do on both sides of the front.

### 5

Even before the manifesto of revolutionary Russia, the voice of America—a Power still neutral at the time, but soon to be a determining factor in the European struggle—had rung out clearly on the subject of Poland. President Wilson, in a message to Congress foreshadowing America's possible share in the conclusion of the peace, had declared that a reunited and free Poland was one of the war aims admitted on all sides. A similarly emphatic statement with regard to the reconstruction of Poland was afterwards made part of President Wilson's famous Fourteen Points, and it is important to remember that free and secure access to the sea is considered by Wilson from the very outset as a vital necessity for Poland. No wonder that the name of the man who, after all, did not become a prophet in his own country, has never ceased to be held in high honour in Poland ; and that of his inspirer in Polish matters, Colonel House, is also widely known.

It was also still before the Russian manifesto that Dmowski had submitted to Balfour a memoir embodying his own and his fellow-workers' ideas on the territorial composition of a reconstructed Polish State—ideas which essentially remained his programme still when he afterwards represented Poland at the Peace Conference.

It was, on the other hand, under the encouraging impression produced by President Wilson's utterance and by revolutionary Russia's recognition of Polish claims that the Austrian Poles, on their part, now ventured to state national aims more frankly than had ever been done before in the Central Empires. A resolution passed by the Austro-Polish Parliamentary Deputies assembled at Cracow in May 1917, expressely defined a complete and independent Poland as the goal of national aspirations. It was also in this resolution that Austria was for the first time treated by her Polish subjects not as a Protecting Power, but as an Ally, whose services were only welcome if helpful for the attainment of the clearly defined national aims.

That such an unprecedented note should have been struck, was rendered possible not only by the turn which affairs had taken in Russia, but also by a recent happening under the Austro-German occupation. The question of drawing upon the occupied territory of former Russian Poland for recruits was becoming an actual one for the Central Powers. It was cautiously proposed to widen the framework of Piłsudski's Legions so as to create a larger Polish armed force, which, however, would at the same time be more unreservedly at the disposal of the Central Powers for their war aims. While some of Piłsudski's officers, such as General Sikorski, were willing to pay this price for the opportunity to call a large Polish army into being, Piłsudski himself, at this critical point, parted company with the Central Powers, to whom he had always professed only conditional allegiance. He forbade his loyal followers to take the new military oath required of them, and refused it himself. He resigned his seat in the Council of State, and returned to his old-accustomed *rôle* of conspirator, beginning to form a " Polish Military Organization " (P.O.W.) as the groundwork for a new Polish army. In return, his faithful legionaries were disbanded and interned, and he himself imprisoned in the fortress of Magdeburg. This imprisonment added considerably to his prestige in the eyes of the nation : it raised him to the dignity of a symbol of national resistance to foreign rule. That part of his forces which was not disbanded remained in separate existence as a " Polish Armed Force " (*Polnische Wehrmacht*) under close control of the German Powers, and was to act as one of the several partial foundations of the new Polish army afterwards. But very little headway was made with recruiting activites on behalf of the Central Powers in occupied Russian Poland ; nor was the attempt pushed to any great lengths, in view of the determined passive resistance of the population, and also of the new preoccupations created for Germany through America's entry into the War, and of the hopes that were placed in relentless submarine warfare as a short cut to victory. Also, the situation on the eastern front now became thoroughly changed by the Bolshevik landslide in Russia.

6

The coming of Bolshevism—soon to develop into a formidable menace to Poland—was at the first moment a factor of prime positive importance for the Polish problem. The attitude of the new Bolshevik Government towards the War created a new conception of Poland's possible function in the minds of the allied statesmen. Poland could become a useful safeguard against German-Bolshevik co-operation, and against the danger of Bolshevism itself to western Europe. France now at last saw her way to authorize and assist the formation of a Polish army on the Allied side, and shortly before the close of the War, on July 3, 1918, Poland was raised, by a decision of the allied statesmen at Versailles, to the rank of a belligerent allied nation. The Polish National Committee in Paris was thereby recognized in the allied camp as an official representation of the Polish people.

All this was the fruit of the new relations between Germany and Russia, as sealed and made manifest to the world by the German-Soviet Peace Treaty of Brześć (Brest) in 1918. That Treaty had also its important reverberations in Poland itself. By that Treaty—concluded without the admission of a Polish representative—a definite attempt was made to realize Germany's plan of carving out of Russia's western provinces a series of pseudo-independent small buffer states, which were in practice to become Austro-German protectorates. In favour of Austria's long-cherished Ukrainian conceptions of this kind, a portion of south-eastern Russian Poland—the district of Chełm —was to be detached from the body of Poland. This very district (inhabited partly by a Ukrainian-speaking peasantry) had already been administratively separated from Russian Poland proper by the old Tsarist Russia in 1912, and at that time loud protests against this "fourth partition of Poland" had resounded throughout all Polish lands. Now that the process was repeated under different auspices and in a changed historical situation, Polish protests were naturally even more emphatic and universal. The most important manifestation of all was that of General Joseph Haller, one of Piłsudski's fellow-workers, who was in command of a portion of Piłsudski's legions left intact and operating in the south-eastern region of the Russian front—the "Carpathian brigade." That brigade now revolted against the Austro-German command, and, after a pitched battle against German forces, partly succeeded in making its way into the Ukrainian part of Russia. Haller himself, by way of North Russia and the sea, ultimately arrived in France, to be placed at the head of the Polish army, which was organizing there under allied protection. Some of Haller's soldiers, scattered all over Russia, swelled the ranks of the manifold volunteer military formations which were spontaneously springing up everywhere, and which included both former Russian soldiers of Polish nationality as well as Poles who had served in the Austrian and German armies and found themselves in the interior of Russia as prisoners of war. The fate of these various formations, which inevitably were drawn into the welter of the Russian Civil War, was largely tragic ; but most of them succeeded in reaching Poland—if sometimes by fantastic roundabout ways and after unspeakable sufferings—and some were even included in the Polish army in time to take part in the struggle against the Bolshevik invasion of 1920.

While thus, all soldiers of Polish nationality who had served in the Great War on its eastern theatre, were instinctively drawing together under a common flag regardless of antecedents— on the western front Haller's army was growing into an allied fighting unit of respectable size—ultimately five divisions. This increase was largely promoted by the influx of volunteers from America, whom Paderewski's eloquence had roused, and who had begun to organize on Canadian soil. Nor was the contribution of the emigrant Polish element to the American army itself at all insignificant : it stands on record that the first American soldier to be killed in France was a Pole.

Another source of additions to Haller's ranks was Italy : former Austrian and German soldiers who were Italy's prisoners of war, were released to form Polish Legions, and they increased Haller's army, in the last resort, by nearly 40,000 men.

Thus in the later stages of the War, Polish combatants, whatever their former allegiance, were anticipating events and manifesting their determination to create and serve a new Poland.

## 7

The same desire to call a free Poland spontaneously into being before it emerged from the War and the Peace Treaties, was strongly manifested in the country itself, as the War was drawing to its close. The unexpected and seemingly impossible had happened : the three empires which had divided Poland between them, all collapsed in quick succession, although at the beginning of the War, when they were placed in opposite camps, it had appeared unthinkable that they should fall together. Now that the proud fabric of Imperial Germany seemed to be going the way of Tsarist Russia, the Poles in Poland hastened to take matters into their own hands. The Armistice having left the occupied area of Russian Poland temporarily still under occupation, and Prussian and Austrian Poland still in German and Austrian possession, the people began, after October 31, 1918, in Warsaw and elsewhere in the occupied area, themselves to disarm the bewildered and war-weary German soldiers. The same was easily done with the Austrian forces in the Austrian sector of the occupied territory and in Austrian Poland proper, where a Commission for the severance of the ties between Galicia and Austria was organized. Prussian Poland was the last to follow suit ; it was not without a sanguinary struggle that German power was shaken off there, but in the last days of 1918, that province was also *via facti* freed from German domination. Piłsudski's " Polish Military Organization " had emerged from underground and joined hands with the " Polish Armed Force " maintained by the Germans, so that immediately after the expulsion of the military occupants the nucleus of a Polish army was in being in their place.

While the removal of foreign military rule had thus been accomplished with comparative facility, it was much less easy, in the midst of ruin, starvation, turmoil, and revolutionary excitement, to create a unified Polish Government. The Regency Council in Warsaw had, in fact, immediately after the Central Powers' appeal to President Wilson for mediation, issued a manifesto declaring Poland free, and announcing that its form of government would be determined by a Constituent Assembly. But a month later, a self-appointed Government sprang into power at Lublin, the former centre of the Austrian occupation : that Government was a Socialist one, and its purpose was to outbid, by radicalism, the tempting offers of Bolshevik propaganda which were spreading among the famished masses. The Regency Council, wielding no real power itself and faced by the danger of anarchy, voiced the universal demand for a strong hand by asking the German Government to set Piłsudski free. The semi-Bolshevik conditions of revolutionized Germany made his release from Magdeburg possible. He arrived in Warsaw on the very day of the conclusion of the Armistice, took power into his hands, and, a few days later, officially notified all the Powers that a Polish State had come into existence. First the Lublin Government, and then the Regency Council, submitted to his authority, and he entrusted an old fellow-worker of his, a Radical, with the formation of a Cabinet.

The arrival of Piłsudski on the scene, while averting the danger of chaos in Poland itself, still left a major problem in Polish Government formation and Poland's international

F

representation open. The Polish National Committee in Paris retained its status as recognized by the Allies, and as it was composed of politicians diametrically opposed to Piłsudski in opinions and programme, the co-ordination of the two political forces seemed difficult. It was facilitated by the patriotism and personal charm of Paderewski : his arrival in Poland at the end of 1918 became an event only second in importance to Piłsudski's own return. Piłsudski by that time had shown plainly enough that national considerations outweighed his early Socialist convictions; the Socialists refused support to the Government appointed by him, as not being radical enough for their purposes, and it made room for one formed by Paderewski. The co-operation between Piłsudski as Chief of State and Paderewski as Prime Minister practically saved the situation. It now became possible that Piłsudski's lifelong antagonist Dmowski, together with Paderewski, represented Poland at the Versailles peace negotiations with the full authority of the nation behind them ; also that, in Poland itself, a Constituent Assembly met in February, 1919, and voted a Provisional Constitution. Piłsudski laid down his powers, but was re-entrusted with them by the Assembly and continued to act as Chief of State until the meeting of the first regularly-elected Parliament in 1922. At the same time, the conflicting political opinions among which the new Polish State had come into being, left their trace in the Provisional Constitution ; the prerogatives of the Head of the State were drastically circumscribed at once, and fullness of authority vested in the Assembly, on the model of the French Republican Constitution. This made much hasty legislation, and much parliamentary interference with the working of administrative institutions possible in the early years of the new Poland, and was finally to lead her to a crisis of parliamentary government. Poland was not fated to be happier in this respect than most other democratic states of post-war Europe.

## 8

It is well known that the representatives of the so-called " smaller " nations at the Peace Conference, although themselves men of authority and surrounded by imposing staffs of experts on all questions, had very little influence on the rearrangement of the map of Europe, which, in the last resort, was accomplished by a closed council of four men, afterwards reduced even to three.

With regard to the settlement of the Polish problem, however, it must be admitted that out of the clash of conflicting opinions within the small inner ring of peace-makers there resulted a certain measure of satisfaction to Polish aspirations as represented by Dmowski and his associate Paderewski.

Dmowski's conception of the reconstruction of Poland was known to the Allies from his memorandum addressed to Balfour in 1917.

True to his pre-war view that Germany was the most dangerous enemy of Poland, Dmowski laid stress on a maximum of territorial acquisitions on the western side, which would ensure Poland's complete economic and strategical independence as against Germany. Not content, accordingly, with the recovery of the province of Poznania, lost through the partitions, he desired to see Poland's historical access to the sea by way of Danzig safeguarded through the possession of a wide stretch of territory on both banks of the lower Vistula, including, if possible, Poland's sometime vassal, the province of East Prussia. He wished to see Poland's economic development in the direction of industrialization placed on a firm basis by the incorporation of Silesia, which had been separated from Poland since the fourteenth and included in Prussia since the middle of the eighteenth century. On the eastern side, on the other hand, he was prepared to sacrifice a large portion of the borderland possessions included in Poland before the partitions—partly because they were largely inhabited by non-Polish populations which had since reached a troublesome degree of national consciousness of their own, and partly also because he wished to leave the door open for a future understanding with Russia.

Dmowski's views on this, as on most other points, were fundamentally different from those of Piłsudski and his political friends, who continued to see in Russia the principal danger to Poland's existence. Piłsudski inherited with the blood of the eastern borderland gentry from which he had sprung, a vivid sense of the great historical tradition of Poland's imperial union with her eastern neighbour Lithuania, and of Poland's civilizing mission in the Lithuanian and Ruthenian border countries. His programme was, accordingly, more extensive and ambitious on the eastern than on the western side. Reckoning with the development which Ukrainian, White Ruthenian and Lithuanian national separatism had (not without fomentation by Poland's foreign rulers) attained, Piłsudski imagined the eastern borderlands constituted as a series of small buffer states between Poland and Russia, which would by the superior civilization of Poland gradually be drawn into some sort of federative union with her. On the western side, he would have remained satisfied with the restitution of the Polish-German frontier as it existed before the first partition in 1772.

9

If, now, we compare the settlement actually effected by the
Peace Treaties with these two different Polish conceptions of it,
we observe first of all that the solution given to the Polish
problem by the peacemakers of Versailles was, like their solutions
of most European questions, necessarily somewhat hasty and
accordingly sketchy. It was bound to be particularly sketchy
because one great factor of the problem—viz., Russia—was
absent from the Conference table, and from the signing of the
treaties. The Polish-Russian frontier was therefore left undefined, and this, the largest territorial question affecting the
new Poland, had accordingly to be determined between the new
State and its powerful eastern neighbour. This attitude towards
the major Polish-Russian issue implied also that the problem of
Poland's relations with the minor nationalities along her Russian
border, which were struggling for self-determination and independence—chiefly with the Lithuanians in the north and the
Ukrainians in the south—was largely left to the parties concerned
to settle between themselves. Only with regard to that troublesome heritage of Austrian rule, the Ukrainian question in Eastern
Galicia, did the Conference come to a definite desision, giving
Poland a mandate over that province for twenty-five years, to
be followed by a plebiscite : but that decision, like some others,
was modified by later events.

While unavoidably irresolute over Poland's eastern frontiers
in view of the Russian enigma, the Conference was naturally
more definite in its decisions with regard to the western side.
The Polish-German settlement, as laid down by it, followed
to some extent the lines of Dmowski's conception. But the
friction, within the governing body of the Conference, over the
question of the treatment of defeated Germany resulted in the
fact that Dmowski's territorial projects came out of the furnace
of the Conference like a highly controversial bill out of Parliament :
amended, that is, if not beyond recognition, yet so as to lose a
good deal in efficacy. The central part of Prussia's Polish-
speaking border domains, the province of Poznań (Posen), was
restored to Poland in the bulk, though not without some
curtailment of its western fringe. The two other vital items of
Dmowski's plan fared less favourably. As regards the vexed
question of Poland's access to the sea, the fact was there that the
province of East Prussia, built up out of the domains of the
medieval German Order of Knights, though for a long time a
vassal state of Poland, had remained a patch of German land

east of the essentially Polish province which connected the body of Poland with the sea ; also, that Danzig, Poland's natural outlet on the sea, though definitely under Polish domination for over three centuries, had remained a German city and often revolted against the kings of Poland. In view of this, the Conference determined on a compromise foreshadowed by Napoleon's solution of the Danzig problem : Danzig was made a free city under international control, but to be represented abroad by Poland's diplomats, to be included in the Polish customs frontier, and to be used by Poland as her harbour with special military and commercial privileges. The historical seaside province of Poland was considerably narrowed down—hence the misleading, widespread term " the Polish Corridor ";—in this shape it includes a stretch of seacoast, on which Poland has since built up her own harbour of Gdynia. East Prussia thereby found herself once more " a German island," separated from the main body of Germany, as she had always been before the partitions of Poland. The fate of two million " Mazurian " peasants, Protestants speaking a Polish dialect and inhabiting the southern fringe of East Prussia, was to be determined by plebiscite.

In this somewhat complicated condition, obviously bristling with possibilities of conflict, the problem of Poland's access to the sea left the hands of the Conference. No less difficult and complex was the third item which the Conference had to deal with in settling German-Polish relations. The province of Silesia, justly considered by Dmowski as vital to Poland in the capacity of a coal reservoir to feed her economic life, had, in spite of long centuries of separation, remained largely Polish-speaking as far as its country people were concerned ; but the towns had become more or less German. Here, as at so many other points of eastern Europe, a hard and fast frontier line between the two languages was impossible to draw. In this instance again, the plebiscite—that favourite device of the Conference, which seemed such an obvious realization of the principle of the " self-determination of nations "—was to be resorted to for a decision.

Plebiscites also were to decide on the fate of some frontier districts which became objects of dispute in consequence of the break-up of the Austro-Hungarian empire. Poland, in arising, found herself at odds with her new Slav neighbour, the Czecho-Slovak Republic, over the eastern section of the former Austrian Silesia—the Duchy of Cieszyn (Teschen), largely Polish-speaking, but historically a province of the Bohemian Crown since the later Middle Ages. And, in addition to this, some mountain districts on the Polish-Slovak border were claimed by both Republics : there had been a historical Polish province of Spisz on the southern side of the border mountains, and Polish is still generally spoken in large parts of this and the neighbour district of Orawa.

It was more than at one point, then, that the Conference found itself unable to define the frontiers of the new Poland, even on the western side. The new Polish Republic emerged from the Peace Treaties only half-ready. It is not to be wondered at that the long-accumulating impatience of an oppressed nation, quite as it had anticipated the formation of the new State itself, should also have been tempted now to take the disputed frontier problems out of the hands of the hesitating diplomats. It is not to be wondered at, either, in view of the pitch of excitement which all national aspirations in Europe had reached by that time, that the settlement of the outstanding questions between neighbours became in most cases a matter of armed conflict. Local wars between the Poles and the Ukrainians on the one hand and between the Poles and the Czecho-Slovaks on the other, were actually being waged while the Conference was sitting ; and the peace-makers had still to learn by experience that a plebiscite was less easy to conduct than it seemed, and did not at all exclude sanguinary conflicts.

The aftermath of little wars over the disputed frontier regions, however, was not to be the only thing which increased the natural difficulties of constructing the fabric of a new State in a thoroughly devastated country. Poland alone, of all the new States created at Versailles, was fated, by her geographical situation, to begin her renewed existence by a struggle on a much larger scale—a struggle in which not only this or that border province was the object, but in which the whole of national existence was at stake. What is even more, at this most difficult moment of political re-birth, she had at once to assume the historical part which she had once played as a powerful empire : she was compelled, single-handed, to shield the entire political and social system of Europe, the entire structure of European civilization, from the onslaught of a Power as dangerous to its very foundations as Islam had been. She had to save herself and Europe from the invasion of Bolshevism.

10

The plan of forming out of the large and extremely fertile Ukrainian lands a separate state under Austro-German protection had long before the War been a cherished aim of Austrian dynastic policy, and was adopted in war time into the larger programme of German Imperialism. It was not abandoned even at the moment of defeat. While unable to retain any hold on the Ukrainian domains of Russia, which were plunged into the chaos of civil war between Bolsheviks and anti-Bolsheviks, the Central Powers did all they could to forestall the inclusion of the eastern part of Austrian Galicia into the body of the rising Polish State. The province has a large body of Ukrainian-speaking peasantry; but the towns, through the long centuries of unbroken connection with Poland since the middle of the fourteenth century, had become purely Polish; and particularly the chief city of the region, Lwów (Lemberg), erected by the Austrians into the capital of their Polish province, had always been a stronghold of Polish patriotism and Polish culture in the south-eastern borderlands. It had remained so during the century and a half of Austrian rule, in spite of all that had been done by Austria to turn it into a centre of rising Ukrainian separatism. The possession of Lwów was the key to the whole eastern Galician position, the Ukrainian country population being notoriously and constitutionally passive. Well aware of this, the Austrian authorities, when abandoning Galicia, turned their stores of war material at Lwów over to the nationalist organizations of the Ukrainian *intelligentsia*, and the Poles of Lwów, at the time when all Poland was asserting its freedom, found themselves confronted by a Ukrainian occupation of Lwów, accomplished with the help of remainders of the Austrian troops. Polish counter-preparations, however, had not been wanting, and an armed struggle for the possession of the city began. The city and the province had known terrible days during the World War, when the tides of offensive and retreat had repeatedly rolled back and forward over Eastern Galicia, and a year of severe Russian military occupation of Lwów had been followed by the hardships and privations of the later war-time *régime* of Austria and Germany.

But the worst was to come now. For weeks, the principal buildings and the streets of the city were the object of embittered fighting between improvised Polish armed forces and the Ukrainian occupants. On the Polish side, grey-haired old pensioners fought side by side with university students of both sexes, and even with half-grown schoolboys and schoolgirls. Scores of the latter—now immortal in Polish song and story as " the Eaglets of Lwów "—shed their heroic blood, and many of them repose in honoured tombs in the cemetery of " the Defenders of Lwów." It was a task of superhuman difficulty for the new Polish State, during the very first few days of its free existence, to muster up, out of its scanty rudiments of an army, a rescue force strong enough to come to the assistance of the Poles of Lwów. But such a force, composed largely of fresh volunteers, was got together after all and fought its way into the brave city. By the end of 1918, not only the city of Lwów, but the whole of Eastern Galicia was free from the Ukrainian occupation and reunited to the body of Poland.

The unhappy region, however, had not yet seen the last of war. It was once more to become the scene of a large offensive and of its repulsion from the very gates of Lwów during the coming Polish-Bolshevik campaign.

## II

During 1919, the newly formed Polish Army, powerfully reinforced at last in the spring of the year by Haller's excellently equipped and well organized " blue " army from France, was actively extending Poland's frontiers eastward. Soviet Russia, occupied with domestic war against leaders of counter-revolution in its east, north and south, was not capable of much resistance on her western side ; and the Poles succeeded in recovering a considerable belt of their historical eastern border territory, from Wilno, the ancient capital of the Lithuanian portion of the Monarchy, in the north, to Kamieniec Podolski, that old outpost against the Turk, in the south. Towards the end of the year 1919, an attempt to engage in peace negotiations was made on the part of Russia, and found favour in the Nationalist camp in Poland, in consonance with its traditional maxims. But Piłsudski—with many others who by that time had had sufficient experience of Bolshevism—realized that the Bolshevik rulers of Russia, in any situation short of a crushing defeat, would not consider themselves bound by a treaty with a " bourgeois " Power. The negotiations, accordingly, were broken off, and a state of war continued. Operations, however, were not very active until, in the spring of 1920, Piłsudski took a decisive step towards the realization of his " federalist " conception of a series of buffer states between Poland and Russia. An anti-Bolshevik Ukrainian Government having been formed by a military leader, Ataman Petlura, the aspirations of that Government towards domination over the whole wide expanse of the Ukrainian south of Russia were recognized by Poland, and an alliance entered into with it on the understanding that Poland was to retain Eastern Galicia. Piłsudski's and Petlura's forces, acting in concert, pushed their way into the heart of the Ukrainian regions, and finally entered Kiev, the ancient capital of South Russia, together. It was the moral impression produced by the capture of this historical city that became a factor of strength for the Bolsheviks. Even the non-Bolshevik forces in the country could now be roused : an appeal to the officers of the Old Russian Army appeared over the signature of General Brusilov, the leader of the great Galician offensive of 1916. The Bolshevik forces having, by the same time, disposed of the armies of counter-revolutionary generals in the north and east, the whole impact of enormous numbers could be brought to bear on the Polish front, which proved unable to withstand the pressure. Not only had Kiev soon to be abandoned, but Wilno in the north was quickly in the hands of the Bolsheviks again, and town after town in the north, the centre and the south was taken during the early summer months. The Bolshevik armies were apparently irresistibly rolling on towards Warsaw, while in the south a daring raid of Budienny's Cavalry Corps was menacing Lwów.

Poland's plight became desperate. No military help was to be expected from the western Allies, with their demobilized armies and universal war-weariness among the people. Such assistance as could be offered in the form of munitions and supplies was in danger of not reaching Poland, on account of the unfriendly attitude of both factory and transport workers. A wave of social radicalism had swept Central Europe in consequence of the Russian Revolution, and sympathies with Bolshevism were universal among the working class. Czechoslovakia, in deference to them, refused to permit munitions for Poland to pass through its territories ; and there were serious difficulties of the same sort with the harbour of Danzig. Only Poland's age-long fellow-campaigner against the Turk—Hungary —at that critical moment stood resolutely by her side : herself disarmed and reduced in territory, yet well aware of what was at stake, because just emerging from a terrible ordeal of domestic Bolshevism, Hungary did what she could : she sent a considerable quantity of war material, which in view of Czechoslovakia's attitude had to be transmitted by way of Rumania, but happily reached Poland barely in time to be used in the decisive battles.

12

The appeal to the western Powers, launched by Poland at this juncture, bore scanty fruit, even at the price of heavy concessions in matters affecting Poland's vital interests. By an agreement signed at Spa, Poland had to abandon her claims, territoral and others, at almost all points left open by the treaties, the frontier disputes with Czechoslovakia over parts of Austrian Silesia and over the mountain districts of Spisz and Orawa, south of the Tatra mountains, were settled, after all, without the promised plebiscites and almost entirely in favour of the Czechoslovak pretensions. If the western part of the Duchy of Cieszyn (Teschen) with its rich coalfields and its 150,000 Polish-speaking people was assigned to Czechoslovakia off-hand, this was done not only because of the economic value of the territory and its vital importance to Czechoslovakia as a link between the Czech and the Slovak portions of the new republic, but also because it appeared a foregone conclusion that the whole of Poland would come under Bolshevik rule, and it seemed indicated thus to save at least a strip of highly cultured industrial territory from Communist ruin.

Nor did Poland fare any better where the plebiscite was actually held. It *was* held in the southern border belt of East Prussia at the very moment when the Bolshevik invasion was at its height. Very naturally, a majority population (reinforced, for plebiscite purposes, by Germans from Germany who happened to have been born in that part of the country) voted against inclusion in Poland, and in conclusion, the frontier of the miscalled " Polish Corridor " was only very insignificantly rectified along the eastern bank of the Vistula.

With regard to Poland's immediate danger of absorption into Bolshevik Russia, Great Britain, indeed, offered her mediation. Lord Curzon proposed more than liberal cession of territory to Russia, by drawing up the famous " Curzon line " which was cutting off from Poland, on the eastern side, all districts in the least degree mixed in speech. But the Bolsheviks refused British mediation ; while offering a frontier more favourable to Poland than the " Curzon line," they proposed other terms of peace which would have amounted practically to the abolition of Poland's status as an independent State.

Poland braced herself for a life and death struggle. France came to her assistance by sending her Marshal Foch's Chief of Staff, General Weygand, with a body of other able officers to help in the conduct of operations. But as General Weygand himself has admitted since—the plans for the decisive manœuvre, more daring than anything he thought safe to suggest, were framed by the Polish Command, and the repulsion of the Bolsheviks' onslaught was entirely the work of a huge national effort. The Bolsheviks were so assured of success that they actually appointed a provisional Bolshevik Government of Poland, two of whose five members were Communist leaders of

Polish origin.  The Bolshevik plan for the capture of Warsaw (which would have morally determined the fate of the struggle) followed a memorable historical precedent.  In quelling the insurrection of 1831, the Russians had forced a passage of the Vistula at some distance from Warsaw, and then closed upon the city from the west as well as from the east.  This it was proposed to repeat in 1920, and flank movements to that effect were in progress, while in the centre of the front, the Bolshevik guns were already thundering within hearing of the city.  The foreign diplomats—with the honourable exceptions of the Papal Nuncio (now His Holiness Pope Pius XI) and the Italian Minister, F. Tomassini (who was to write an important work *La Risurrezione della Polonia*, 1925) left Poland's capital.  Evidently, western Europe generally was giving up Warsaw—and with it, Poland's independence—as lost.

At that critical moment, Piłsudski, by an unexpected counter-offensive, thwarted the entire Bolshevik plan.  Withdrawing some of the forces of defence from the centre of his position, he used them to attack the Bolshevik troops which were bearing down upon Warsaw, in their flank and rear from the south. The operation was successful to the extent of severing the unity of the Bolshevik front, and a general retreat of the Bolshevik armies began.

The " victory of Warsaw," as it has since been called, was hailed by national enthusiasm as " the miracle of the Vistula." If a miracle of any kind, it was certainly a miracle of dauntless leadership and unbroken national vitality.  Thousands of volunteers who had gathered from a famished and exhausted country to fight under conditions of extreme privation, had accomplished the miracle.  Western European opinion—with *The Times* in its vanguard—now did not fail to acclaim Poland as the heroic deliverer of the world from a mortal danger to our common civilization, and to draw the perfectly fitting comparison between this great battle and King John Sobieski's gallant rescue of Vienna, and Europe, from the tide of a huge Turkish invasion in 1683.

The victory on the Vistula was completed by another prolonged battle, fought on the banks of the Niemen in September. An armistice concluded on Oct. 18, 1920, was followed by protracted peace negotiations at Riga in Latvia.

The Riga Peace Treaty, signed on March 18, 1921, although the Poles were largely in a position to dictate its terms, bears the marks of compromise, especially in territorial matters. Piłsudski's conception of a chain of small buffer states between

Poland and Russia proved impossible to realize. The White Ruthenian and Ukrainian territories and populations, which would have formed those states, were divided between Poland and Russia. Poland only received as much territory on the eastern border as had been left to her after the second partition in 1793, before the third and final one ; with regard to Eastern Galicia, the Austro-Russian frontier of 1914 (along the river Zbrucz) was adopted. This solution had many inconveniences from the Polish point of view, one of them being that large numbers of Polish country gentlemen and nobles in the outlying parts of the eastern borderlands lost their possessions, which had been outposts of culture in those regions ; another, that the Soviet Government was placed in a position to turn its portions of White Ruthenian and Ukrainian lands into centres of irreden- tism and bases for Communist propaganda in Poland. This was more or less succesfully done, and even predatory raids of armed bands across the frontier became a feature of border life during the next few years, until at last Poland created a separate, strong and efficient Frontier Force, which turned the frontier into a military cordon and made life and property in the border districts safe.

Of other stipulations of the Riga Peace Treaty some economic clauses may be singled out. Soviet Russia resigned all claims to Poland's share in the Imperial debt of old Russia ; it undertook, on the other hand, to pay reparations to Poland to the amount of thirty million gold roubles. Of that sum, nothing has been paid so far. Poland has been more successful—owing to the indefatigable labours of a commission of eminent experts—in recovering part of the numberless objects of art, historical relics, national and private collections, which the old Russia had carried out of Poland since the partitions and which Soviet Russia now undertook to restore. Equipments of factories and of public institutions, evacuated from Russian Poland during the World War, also came under that clause, and as much of them as proved traceable at all, has been recovered.

The Riga Peace Treaty provided for the establishment of normal diplomatic and consular relations between Poland and Russia. In spite of frequent friction and disturbing incidents, due on the one hand to the activities of Russian counter- revolutionaries, on the other hand to Communist propaganda, those diplomatic relations have for over ten years now been maintained unbroken. Poland thereby holds a world record of official relations with Soviet Russia.

The peace with Soviet Russia laid the most important and

necessary foundation for the peaceful existence of the new Poland. But even at that moment the military troubles attendant upon the formation of the new state were not yet over, and the year 1921 was not yet fated to become the first one devoted to peaceful effort.

13

The new Lithuanian State, which had risen into existence under German protection during the World War, had in 1918, under the pressure of the Bolshevik danger, transferred the seat of its Government from the historical Lithuanian capital Wilno, to Kowno (Kaunas), the principal city of Lithuania's northern province. Wilno, which during centuries of union with Poland had become quite as purely Polish as Lwów in the south, had since 1918 been drawn into the vortex of Polish-Bolshevik warfare on the border and had changed hands repeatedly. Co-operation between organized Polish local forces and the advancing Polish army had led to the occupation of the city by the Poles in 1919 and the appointment of a provisional Polish administration for the district. In 1920, during their advance, the Bolsheviks had taken the city ; at the same time, in order to secure the friendly neutrality of Lithuania, they had, in a treaty with the Lithuanian Government, recognized Lithuania's right to Wilno. Accordingly the Poles, when advancing in turn after their victory, were confronted, in the region of Wilno, by the hostile attitude of Lithuanian troops. Shortly before the armistice between Poland and the Bolsheviks, an armistice was concluded with Lithuania at Suwałki, and the line of demarcation, agreed upon there, placed Wilno outside the Polish sphere of occupation. This produced natural dissatisfaction among a division of the Polish army recruited almost entirely in the Wilno district. This division, with General Żeligowski at its head, revolted against the Suwałki agreement and occupied Wilno a few days later. General Żeligowski appointed a provisional Government of the province, which he called " Central Lithuania." During the year 1921, the state of things created by General Żeligowski's action, became the object of various international negotiations. The Bolsheviks, in the Peace Treaty of Riga, expressly left the subject of Polish-Lithuanian territorial relations to determination by direct negotiations between Poland and Lithuania. The League of Nations, on the other hand, endeavoured to effect a settlement. A project worked out by a Belgian arbitrator, M. Paul Hymans, provided for the creation of two self-governing provinces (to be called, in Swiss fashion, "cantons"), and a Lithuania thus organized,to enter again into its historical relation of federative union with Poland. Now it is union with Poland in any shape or form which appears utterly unacceptable to the rulers of the new Lithuania, because it seems to them that, in such a union, the numerical and cultural preponderance of the Polish element would gradually suppress Lithuanian nationality altogether. Accordingly, the Hymans' project was rejected by Lithuania ; when resumed in modified form, without the suggestion of a federation, it naturally failed to find the approval of Poland. In the Wilno district itself, preparations were made to put an end to the provisional state of affairs ; early in 1922, elections for a Provincial Assembly were held, and the assembly resulting from them voted, by an overwhelming majority, in favour of incorporation of the province into Poland without any stipulations for provincial self-government. Such incorporation was accordingly effected, the deputies of the Wilno province took their seats in the Polish Parliament of Warsaw, and the province of Wilno was organized as one of the sixteen administrative units of the new Poland, which it has remained since. The line of demarcation agreed upon between General Zeligowski's troops and the Lithuanian army in 1920 has become the frontier between the Republics of Poland and Lithuania, and was recognized as such by the Ambassadors' Conference in 1923.

Such, in barest outline, is the history of the " Wilno problem," which again and again, in later years, occupied the attention of the League of Nations, owing to remonstrances raised by Lithuania. A diplomatic deadlock arose between Poland and Lithuania, and has so far continued unbroken. While Poland entered into normal diplomatic relations with all other sovereign states, and concluded commercial treaties with many of them, no such relations of any kind (including even postal or railway communication) could be established with Lithuania. Several attempts at negotiations have been made since 1923, under the auspices of the League of Nations and otherwise, but only a very scanty measure of success was attained with regard to such vital matters of economic life as communication in the frontier belt, and transport of timber down the river Niemen, which is the main natural artery of traffic both for north-Eastern Poland and Lithuania. Lithuania has since taken possession of the internationalized harbour of Memel, but, deprived of commercial connexion with her Polish *Hinterland*, she suffers quite as much from economic isolation as does her western neighbour, the province of East Prussia. Under the influence of her original protectress

Germany, Lithuania, contrary to her economic interests, persists in her uncompromising attitude towards Poland. A commercial treaty with Germany, signed in 1928, has turned her relation to Germany almost into one of economic vassalage. In spite of this it is to he hoped that good sense and a proper regard for the vital interests of the people will induce Lithuania in the end to enter into neighbourly relations with Poland. The unchanging view taken of the Wilno issue by all successive Polish Governments is that since Lithuania refuses a return to the historical union of the two countries, the only acceptable delimitation between them can be but the actual one, based as it is on the principle of nationality—the purely Polish city of Wilno with its predominantly Polish-speaking territory being included in Poland, while the predominantly Lithuanian-speaking province of Kowno (Kaunas) forms the body of the Lithuanian Republic.

14

Side by side with the Wilno question it was the *Upper Silesian issue* which stood foremost among Poland's international and territorial problems still awaiting solution after the termination of the great struggle against Bolshevism.

As mentioned before, the question of Prussian Silesia had been left by the Peace Conference to a plebiscite. In consequence of this announcement, the province became a veritable witches' cauldron of political passion and propaganda on both sides. Already in the course of 1919 an armed rising of the Polish country population against the Germans, who were still in full possession, broke out and menaced to plunge the country into civil war. The Allies hastened the dispatch of the International Commission which was to superintend the plebiscite. It arrived in January 1920, accompanied by troops of all the principal Allied armies. While preparations for the plebiscite were going on, the Polish-Bolshevik war reached its critical stage. Rumours of a complete collapse of Poland being actively exploited by the Germans, a second Polish armed rising broke out in August 1920. Its result was that the local German police was replaced by a force composed of Poles and Germans in proportion to their numerical strength among the population. At last the plebiscite took place, in March 1921. Germany with her old-established administrative machinery at her disposal, had been better able to organize and prepare her share in it than Poland, with a newly organized political apparatus and manifold foreign and domestic difficulties could do. The result was that, of the total votes cast all over Silesia, the majority were in favour of

Germany. But in the different districts, the proportion varied, and the question of a division of the province between Poland and Germany became actual. A rumour having spread that only some agricultural districts in the south as well as the merest south-eastern fringe of the industrial territory of the coal mines would be adjudged to Poland, a third revolt of the Polish country population flared up ; a general strike in the coal mines was followed by another armed rising, on a larger scale than the foregoing ones. Bridges and railway junctions serving for communication with Germany were destroyed by the Polish insurrectionists ; the industrial centres of Beuthen (Bytom) and Katowice (Kattowitz) were in their possession since the very first hours of the rising. It was on this occasion that the political leader of the Poles of Upper Silesia, W. Korfanty—the first Polish Deputy to represent Silesia in the German Reichstag in pre-war times—became something like a Silesian dictator. The insurgents pushed their way towards the river Oder ; the taking by them of the important railway junction of Kandrzin (Kędzierzyn) induced the Allied Mission to negotiate with them. A " demarcation line," was fixed by agreement. But the Germans being dissatisfied with this, and their leader, General Hoefer, receiving succour from Bavaria, hostilities were re-opened on their side later in May, and continued in June. The renewed mediation of the Allied Commissioners finally brought all military action to an end in July, 1921.

The division of Silesia in accordance with the results of the plebiscite followed. Poland received not only the purely agricultural districts of the south, but a considerable portion of the industrial area round Katowice. The north-west of the province, with its capital Breslau, remained under Germany, and with these territories, over half a million Polish-speaking country people, massed especially in the district of Oppeln (Opole), were left outside Poland. On the Polish side, on the other hand, some of the towns—especially Katowice itself—came under Poland with a large proportion of German population.

In June, 1922, Polish troops entered the new Polish province. Polish Silesia, like the Wilno province, was organized as one of the new Poland's sixteen administrative units, with the important difference, however, that Silesia received, in accordance with Poland's international obligations, a provincial Legislative Assembly in which the Polish and German population are represented on an equal common basis of democratic suffrage. For the settlement of outstanding questions and of new disputes, an international Arbitration Commission was set up.

Apart from the work of this Commission, a special Minority Treaty which Poland had been made to sign at Versailles, and, finally the ever-open possibility of appeal to the League of Nations, afforded sufficient guarantees of protection to the Germans of Polish Silesia. The safeguards were much less elaborate—and, indeed, turned out to be much less effective—in the case of those Silesian Poles who remained under Germany.

## CHAPTER IV

# TEN YEARS OF THE NEW POLAND

## I

IT was only with the termination of the last Silesian rising, in 1921, that actual warfare came to an end for the Polish people, and the nation's energies could entirely be devoted to constructive effort. All the time, however, while the long aftermath of war on Polish soil was going on, feverish activities in state-building, by way of fundamental legislation, administrative organization, economic reconstruction, and educational endeavour, had been in progress. A State of thirty million inhabitants, coming into being after a century and a half of division, in the midst of general ruin and starvation, and under pressure of open hostility on the part of all the neighbours from without, and of passionate excitement of all social forces within the country, had a bewildering variety and multitude of the most urgent tasks to attack at once. No wonder that Poland, in her first years, is a perfect whirlpool of new laws and decrees, of organization and reorganization of central and local government institutions.

In the way of state organization and post-war reconstruction, Poland had essentially the same things to do as other states either newly born, or reborn, which now emerged on the map of Europe. But her difficulties were immensely increased by the thorough devastation of two-thirds of the country through seven long years of almost continuous warfare on its soil—the ravages being wider in extent and longer in duration than in any other war area of Europe. And the reunion of three territories which had lived for a century and a half within three profoundly different Empires added another factor of intense complexity to the problem. In both these respects —ruin and disunion—the situation of the new Poland is rather to be compared with that of the Yugoslav Kingdom than with that of Poland's more fortunate western neighbour Czechoslovakia, which had neither been divided, nor swept by war.

Taking a wider survey of post-war Europe, we must again admit that the new Poland found herself very much indeed " in the same boat " with the generality of European States, as far as problems of domestic politics were concerned. Coming into renewed existence at this particular moment of history, Poland, of course, could arise in no other form than that of a thoroughly democratic Parliamentary Republic ; and the Republican form of Government was established by Piłsudski's first decrees in his capacity of temporary Chief of State, in 1918. The historical Polish Monarchy had in fact been—and even called itself—a Republic ; and it had possessed a parliamentary system for three centuries. In adopting, at her rebirth, Republican Parliamentary Government in such form as she found it largely prevailing around her, Poland, like other post-war new states, only fulfilled an obvious dictate of social necessity, while at the same time resuming essentially her own historical tradition.

In doing so, however, Poland not only incurred the danger of relapsing into the political errors of her own historical past ; she also came in for her full share in the inheritance of weaknesses which had developed in Europe's parliamentary systems since the French Revolution, and which in our days—quickened, like all other social processes, by the feverish pulse of war time —have reached the dimensions of a universal crisis of Parliamentary Democracy.

This crisis—which the New Poland could not possibly have escaped—is intensified by the fact that side by side with the extension of political democracy there had gone—in the second half of the nineteenth century, and after—a rapid extension of the social functions of the modern state. This, again, was feverishly quickened by war-time developments ; striking as the social insurance legislation in western Europe during the last decades before the War had been in that respect, the expectations with which the ruined masses of post-war Europe looked for practically everything to the magic power of the state, became truly exorbitant.

Even before the War, the two factors just mentioned— Parliamentary Democracy on the one hand, and the growth of State paternalism on the other—had come into collision with each other. Democratic parliaments, while less and less limited in their powers, proved also less and less competent to deal with all the complexities of those vast domains of modern social life which come under the control of most Continental European States in our time. Particularly was—and is

—this true in the matter of finance, Democracy being always ready lavishly to spend on social welfare institutions, but never very willing to face the fact that it has to find the money for the purpose in its own pockets.

In the case of Poland, the familiar incapacity of modern democracies for the formation of strong Parliamentary majorities and efficient governments was aggravated by the utter political inexperience of large sections of the population and the enormous differences in education between the former three sectors as well as between various classes of the community. The other factor, again—the widespread modern European trend towards State Socialism—was bound to be strengthened in the new Poland, firstly, by the absence, in the ruined country, of almost any means to assert private initiative in social and economic matters, and secondly (and more dangerously) by the neighbourhood of ultra-Socialist Soviet Russia. Thus it inevitably happened that Poland displayed both the deficiencies of parliamentary government and the wide reach of modern state action in particularly glaring form.

With regard to the latter factor—that of social activities of the State—yet another motive, peculiar to the Polish situation, has to be taken into account. That motive is the natural impatience and ambition of a nation deprived of state institutions of its own for over a century, and now seeing the State re-arise, if not in its grandiose historical dimensions, still the eighth in size, and the sixth in population, among the States of Europe. The patriotism of the Poles could not but desire to have the reborn Republic fully equipped immediately with all the appurtenances of a great European Power. Institutions were accordingly planned and called into being on a scale which a country thoroughly ruined by war could ill afford. Many were created whose establishment might still have been somewhat delayed ; many others at once assumed dimensions altogether beyond the new Poland's means. The scarcity of experienced administrative organizers in a country emerging from under foreign rule fostered the growth of a huge and unwieldy bureaucratic apparatus. This overgrown administrative organism absorbed many social waifs and strays (chiefly from the land-owning class) deprived of their position and possessions by the convulsions and changes of war time. The tendency towards immoderate growth of administrative institutions and staff, as well as towards uneconomic generosity in expenditure for the sake of national prestige, was a marked feature during the Prime Ministry of the noble-minded Paderewski, whose ardent love of his country and people did not go hand in hand with a sufficient sense of economic realities. Later governments, even when they showed serious goodwill in the matter at the risk of unpopularity, did not always find it possible to simplify a bureaucratic machine once set going. This difficulty of reduction is a common one in post-War European States ; and so is the fact that the "reduced"— ominous new word !—swell the ranks of social malcontents and are apt to become a most undesirable factor in the commonwealth, while on the other hand, ever-new crowds of university graduates make their appearance, asking for government positions in the absence of other fit employment.

Poland, as we see, combines certain circumstances common to all Continental European States of to-day, with peculiarities of her own, working in the same sense. This is what we have constantly to keep in mind in surveying the record of the first ten years of the new Poland's political life. Whatever political, social and economic problems are besetting post-war Europe at any point, all are sure to be present on the Polish scene as well ; at the same time, they are all apt to appear in Poland with an intensity increased by the peculiar historical conditions of the country, and rendered dangerous by its exposed geographical situation.

2

The constructive efforts of the new Poland in dealing with the different issues of administration and legislation, of racial and religious, social and economic, intellectual and moral life, can only be presented successively in discussing separately each of those domains of renewed national existence. Before attempting this, however, it will perhaps be expedient to supplement the historical summary given above of the circumstances of the rise of the new Polish State by a brief survey of the outstanding events of its inner and outer life during the ten years which have now elapsed since its territorial reconstruction was completed.

How thick and fast Poland's problems came jostling each other is perhaps best illustrated by the fact that certain very important measures of social reform had to be passed by the Constituent Assembly even before it had given the new State its definite political shape. Foremost among them stands the *Land Reform Bill,* passed in 1920. Two-thirds of Poland's inhabitants are peasant farmers, and it was only natural that under a democratic franchise, that social class acquired a great preponderance in the Polish political system. The process of land purchase by the peasantry had been going on since the emancipation of the peasants from serfdom, and even before the War two-thirds of the arable land in Poland were in the hands of peasants. The War, and the new political conditions after it, quickened developments forcibly in this as in other fields. In all the Central and Eastern European States around Poland the pressing demand of the peasant element for more land had caused measures of " agrarian reform " to be passed which provided for the more or less drastic break-up of large estates and for the acquisition of the land by the peasants with financial assistance from the State. The quickest and most thorough-going change had been effected in Soviet Russia, where the larger landowners were dispossessed at once, without any compensation, and the well-to-do peasants attacked shortly afterwards. On their invasion of Poland in 1920, the Bolsheviks launched the promise of land for the peasants as one of their most impressive slogans. It was necessary to make a definite offer of the same kind to the Polish peasant on behalf of his own national government, if he was to be roused in defence of the country. Accordingly, the principles of land reform, already voted by the Constituent Assembly in 1919, were now developed into an elaborate bill, laying down a very moderate maximum of land ownership and instituting compulsory sale, under State control, of all the land of the large estates above that maximum limit. That bill, although it was amended in some of its essentials in 1925 and 1927 in favour of slower and more orderly transfer of the land, yet remains, in principle, the foundation of a great social process which has since been going on uninterruptedly under the control of a special Ministry for Land Reform, and which, within the lifetime of a generation, will, no doubt, completely transform the physiognomy of the countryside in Poland.

The year after the Bolshevik war, 1921, the first year in which peace began to reign throughout Poland, was largely devoted to activities dictated by the elementary necessities of life in the new State. Mr. Hoover's memorable mission and other organizations brought welcome relief to the famine-stricken and destitute population. What this relief meant, on the one hand, and how quickly, on the other, the indefatigable industry of the Polish peasant farmer restored normal conditions, is perhaps best expressed by the fact that, in 1921, seven million tons of food had to be imported into Poland, and in the very

next year, 1922, Poland herself became an exporter of agricultural produce, which, in growing measure, she has remained
since.  The conclusion of peace with Soviet Russia was followed
by the return of many thousands of Poland's former inhabitants
who had been driven into the interior of Russia during the
World War as exiles or prisoners.  The return of these masses
from the Bolshevik inferno again necessitated relief activities
on a large scale.  On the other hand, both the temporary
invasion of the country by the Bolshevik armies, and its new
invasion by the returning Polish exiles, now caused a terrible
spread of epidemic diseases, especially of spotted fever, which,
in those two years, had been reaping a terrific harvest of death
throughout Russia.  In her task of stemming the tide of
epidemics, and protecting herself and the rest of Europe against
them by the creation of an emergency sanitary service, Poland
derived a measure of assistance from the League of Nations ;
but the main effort, here as in the Bolshevik war itself, was
her own, and it deserves perhaps to be remembered no less
gratefully that, having saved Europe from a wave of Communist
ruin, she saved it additionally from a wave of mortal disease.

### 3

Apart from activities of relief and rescue necessitated by
the consequences of the War, the year 1921 saw certain events
of fundamental importance for the course of political affairs
in the new Polish State.

In the first place, on the very eve of the day on which the
Peace Treaty with the Bolsheviks at Riga was signed, Poland
received from the Constituent Assembly its definite *Constitution*.
The Constitution, modelled in many particulars on that of the
French Republic, embodied all modern improvements in
democratic state organization, including universal adult suffrage,
both male and female, "scrutin de liste," proportional representation, and an Upper House of Parliament not materially different
in composition from the Lower.  The powers of Parliament
—protected by the personal immunity of its members even
with regard to their extra-parliamentary activities—were made
supreme in the State.  The President, to be elected for seven
years by a joint session of both Houses, was made a mere
figurehead.  Each act of his must be countersigned by a
Minister, and neither he nor the Government were to have the
right to dissolve Parliament.  A provision was indeed made in
the Constitution to create an " Economic Chamber " and so to
balance the powers of the political representation by those of

a body constructed on a Syndicalist foundation and representing professional interests. But that body never came into being, the question of its possible attributions remaining a matter of dispute. The only institution endowed with something like legislative authority, apart from Parliament, was a " Commission of Codification " composed of the foremost legal experts of the country. Its task was to be the drafting of a complete body of codes of law for the new Poland in place of the different legal systems of the three partitioning powers. In view of weighty differences on matters of principle in contemporary legal theory its work on such fundamental tasks as a Civil Code and a Criminal Code made but slow progress, and progress was rendered even slower by Parliament's delays in dealing with its projects.

The ultra-democratic system created by the Constitution could not indeed but heavily handicap most of the organizing, legislative and diplomatic efforts urgently required by the situation of the new Poland. The tendency—so marked in Continental European democracies generally—for a split-up into numerous small fractions was strengthened by proportional representation ; Poland became governable only by coalitions of parties which hung ill together, and whose co-operation had to be purchased by concessions, often in the form of material benefits. Frequent changes of government became as characteristic of Poland as of other modern European Republics, and Ministerial crises, complicated by the squabbles between coalition parties over both programme and personnel, were usually very prolonged. Parties in Parliament, as well as individual deputies, continually interfered with the organization and working of administrative departments ; vital interests of the State which had nothing to do with party politics were drawn into the vortex of political controversy ; on the other hand, it often happened that urgent matters in the sphere of State organization or of international relations were endlessly postponed by Parliament, because they could not be twisted into carrying an appeal to party interest. Lack of understanding for the difficult questions of international affairs and of economic life was, and is, unfortunately a common feature of democratic politicians. Parliament, of course, *did* legislate continually and even feverishly, but for the most part hastily and inconsiderately.

And there was no factor present to check or correct its popular errors. Even the " Supreme Chamber of Control," whose chief was invested with prerogatives greater than those of a cabinet minister exercised only the strictly limited function of an auditing body, examining the way in which the budgetary measures voted by Parliament had been carried out.

The grave defects of the political system as established by the Constitution were only to become fully apparent when the organs of parliamentary government which it provided for came into being. But even during the existence of the Constituent Assembly—protracted till 1922—some of these evils became manifest enough. Poland, like most other Continental European States in the first post-war years—was floundering in a morass of paper money : the depreciated mark currency, inherited from the German occupants of war time, was descending to lower and lower levels of exchange value. A demoralizing instability prevailed in all economic life, including the household of the State. The budget could never be balanced ; it could not even be constructed properly for a longer period than a month ahead ; Parliament kept pressing for expenditure called for by its social legislation ; and the arising deficits could only be met by stamping more and more paper with more and more fantastic figures of millions and milliards, and putting it into circulation.

In order to stem the tide of money inflation, one of the ablest Finance Ministers of the early years, Professor Michalski—the first one to attempt a balanced budget—resorted, in 1921, to the heroic remedy of a general levy on capital, such as was to be discussed soon afterwards, under a Labour Government, in post-war Britain. In Poland, the Capital Levy was actually voted by Parliament, but not without considerable exemptions, which deprived it of much of its efficacy. The inclusion in Poland, soon afterwards, of the rich industrial district of Silesia, kept the currency stable for a number of months ; but inflation, ere long, irresistibly set in again, and much more drastic experiments in national blood-letting were yet to follow before Poland, like the rest of Europe, attained financial stability.

4

The year 1922 was to bring Poland the beginning of normal parliamentary life under the new Constitution. But instead of anything like a normal course of affairs, it brought convulsions and disaster. A more than usually protracted and acute Ministerial crisis in early summer was followed by a highly excited election campaign for the new Parliament. Polish opinion was exasperated by the fact that all the national minorities of Poland, with Germans and Jews at their head, formed an alliance for election purposes ; the Ukrainians of Eastern Galicia largely abstained from voting altogether. Excitement in the Nationalist camp reached its pitch, when at the Presidential election in the National Assembly (composed of both Houses of Parliament) the National minorities came to hold the balance between the purely Polish parties, and it was owing to the support of the non-Polish elements that a nominee of Piłsudski's, Gabriel Narutowicz, a distinguished Professor of Engineering, who had for several months been Minister of Foreign Affairs, was elected President. A week after his election the new President was murdered by a Nationalist zealot, and the country seemed about to plunge into all the horrors of civil war. This was averted by the firmness with which the new Prime Minister, General W. Sikorski, took matters in hand. An ancient fellow-worker of Piłsudski's in the early days of the Legions, afterwards at odds with him over the issue of developing them into a Polish army in the service of the Central Powers, Sikorski had shown his commanding capacity in the war of 1920, and had since occupied distinguished military posts. He now, as Prime Minister, saved the country from chaos and re-established its prestige abroad. The fruit of his resolution was skilfully reaped by the able Foreign Minister, Count Alexander Skrzyński, who, on March 15, 1923, obtained the international recognition of Poland's eastern frontiers by the Ambassadors' Conference. This included acknowledgement of Poland's sovereignty over the Wilno region and the province of Eastern Galicia.

The problem of parliamentary government in Poland, however, still remained without a solution of any permanence. It was in consequence of the impossibility of forming a strong majority of decided complexion that the election of the murdered President's successor had ended in compromise, and the colourless personality of Professor Stanislas Wojciechowski had unexpectedly risen into supreme office. An ancient fellow-conspirator of Piłsudski's in their Socialist youth, Wojciechowski had become an esteemed theoretician and organizer of the co-operative movement, but his political career, culminating so far in a brief tenure of the Home Office, had not been distinguished by outstanding personal initiative. Neither was his Presidency to be known for that quality.

In Parliament, as a natural result of universal suffrage, a large " People's Party," representing the independent peasant-farmer element—the bulk of Poland's population—occupied the Centre of the House, and neither the Right (composed mainly of Nationalists) nor the Left (represented chiefly by the numerous Socialist group) could think of forming a Government without coming to terms with the Peasant Centre. It became an accepted maxim, in fact, that Poland could only be governed by a Centre-plus-Right or a Centre-plus-Left coalition. It is a Centre-plus-Right combination, formed on the basis of a pact between the Nationalists and the Farmers, which becomes responsible for Poland's destinies during the best part of 1923. The shrewd peasant leader Witos once more became Prime Minister, as he had been in 1920. The portfolio of Foreign Affairs fell to the Nationalists and was entrusted to their honoured leader Roman Dmowski—his last, and, it must be admitted, wholly ineffectual, period of official public service. Dmowski's great antagonist, Marshal Piłsudski, in the midst of prolonged disputes over the question of supreme military authority in war and peace, withdrew in disgust from public affairs and went to live in a modest country house near Warsaw.

The Witos Government proved no more able than its predecessors to stop the disastrous progress of paper-money inflation. The mad race of countless milliards of new mark issues continued its irresistible course, and the sufferings of the salaried and wage-earning classes in the towns were steadily increasing. Discontent at last flared up in the form of sanguinary street fights with the military at Cracow in November 1923, and once more, as after the murder of Narutowicz, anarchy seemed imminent. Once more this was happily averted ; but even Parliament recognized now that the most determined steps had to be taken to get the nation out of the currency calamity. A man resolved to take them appeared upon the scene in the person of W. Grabski, and Parliament voluntarily surrendered to him part of its prerogatives in financial matters.

Grabski's measures of financial reform began with a second capital levy, more drastic than Michalski's had been. It was called a " Property Tax " and was to be collected by stages distributed over a number of years ; it would have proved, however, too severe a drain on the nation's remaining resources if carried out to the end ; accordingly, the later instalments were abandoned. Grabski also was responsible for a tax in kind collected among owners of forests, in the shape of timber for the reconstruction of villages—a measure doomed to extreme unpopularity.

It was, however, only after such preludes that Grabski proceeded, in 1924, to avail himself of his new dictatorial powers in order to deal with the fundamentals of the financial problem. Early in the year, the budget was severely balanced by means of large cuts in expenditure, and the printing of paper money was, at last, stopped. The temporary government credit institution which had issued the old paper money, was now reorganized into a *Bank of Poland*. Such a bank —modelled on the Bank of England—had been founded a hundred years before, in the days of Congress Poland : it had exercised a variety of useful economic functions and had done much to develop the industries of Russian Poland. In the later period of Russian rule it had been transformed into a branch of the State Bank of Russia. Now a Bank of Poland was to rise once more, and it was to be entirely a monument of national self-help. The people were appealed to for the capital of the new Bank, which was fixed at 100,000,000 gold francs, and, by a huge effort, provided it entirely through private subscription. The foundation of the Bank of Poland was shortly followed by that of another government credit institution : the " Bank of National Economy," whose task was to be mainly to aid post-war reconstruction and the rise of industries.

The third and final stage of Grabski's financial reform was the official introduction of a new currency, whose unit, bearing the old Polish name of *złoty* (" gilder "), was made equivalent to the Swiss franc and declared equal to 1,800,000 marks of the utterly depreciated old currency.

The domestic effort of financial reform was duly followed by action abroad : Poland funded her debts to the two largest creditor nations of War and post-war time—Great Britain and the United States—and thus asserted firmly her international solvency.

## 5

During the financial reform campaign the Grabski Government had engaged the services of a British adviser, Sir Hilton Young. This eminent expert, while speaking in the most respectful terms of Poland's determination to achieve her financial salvation unaided, at the same time doubted whether the economic strength of the exhausted country would prove equal to the task. His doubts were to be justified by events. He had declared a budget of nearly three milliards of złoty to be too heavy for Poland and had recommended reductions on an unprecedented scale. This, under the circumstances, was unfortunately a counsel of perfection. Under the pressure of political parties, a high level of expenditure was maintained the balance of the budget soon was seriously affected once more ; deficiencies were met by large issues of silver coin and of small Treasury notes ; and thus inflation, in less perceptible forms, once more crept into the system of Poland's currency.

While the effects of currency reform were thus being nullified, the heavy sacrifices entailed by its accomplishment were bringing their aftermath of crisis in economic life. During the mark inflation period, Poland (whose countryside always supplied an abundance of cheap labour) had benefited by the very ruin of her financial system in being able to underbid the old industrial countries of the west by the cheapness of her production. The demand for all sorts of products being very strong everywhere in the first years after war-time devastation and scarcity, there came for Poland, as for other continental countries with an inflated paper currency, a period of booming trade and of large exports. New industrial undertakings (some of them on a very specious basis) were founded continually, and the State was lavish of subsidies for them in the form of loans ; export trade was conducted on an unhoped-for scale, some of it being, indeed, scandalously predatory in character (such as the huge exports of raw timber) and some giving occasion for serious abuses.

Whatever the ominous symptoms, there had certainly been a period of rising commercial and industrial prosperity, even if somewhat hectic and largely fictitious. This, after Grabski's financial measures, ended with a crash, and a heavy, painful and prolonged crisis ensued. The rate of exchange of the new currency turned out to have been fixed at too ambitiously high a level to make remunerative production for export possible under the given conditions of international competition. At home, the spendthrift habits of the inflation period—when millions and millions of paper money had quickly to be changed into merchandize of any kind before they melted away—were replaced by a sobering and depressing consciousness of great impoverishment, and the dearth of living peculiar to countries with a high-priced currency. The upshot of it all was a great slump in trade, and Poland suffered for nearly two years from acute economic depression, with its corollary of unemployment and other evils.

Grabski had deliberately rejected the easier alternative of a large foreign loan as the foundation for the restored currency, because he abhorred the inevitable measure of foreign control which such a loan would entail. His hope, however, was that advantageous foreign loans would be obtainable when Poland

had resolutely reformed her currency for herself. That hope
was disappointed. Confidence in Poland was far from sufficiently grounded as yet in the spheres of international high
finance ; nor were the proper connections established. The
loans which Grabski succeeded in obtaining (in Italy and in
America), were comparatively small ; they were granted on
ruinous terms, and the later instalments of one of them (the
Dillon loan) were never paid into the Polish Treasury at all.
As a guarantee for some of these loans, important national assets
were traded away under highly unfavourable conditions : the
transfer of the monopoly of matches to a Swedish company was
a particularly unfortunate case of this kind.

The international tribunal of the exchanges finally passed
its verdict on Grabski's finance in the middle of 1925. The
Polish *zloty* fell to half its exchange value, and it was at this
lowered level that later Finance Ministers found it expedient
to let it become stabilized *de facto*. The sufferings and sacrifices
to which Grabski's drastic methods had condemned the
population, had borne only very imperfect fruit.

## 6

It is another one of the many proofs of Poland's mysterious
national vitality, as well as a tribute to her constructive achievements in other than economic domains that she should, while
in the very throes of the crisis brought on by Grabski's currency
reform, have made further marked progress in international
recognition and prestige.

Count Alexander Skryzński has been mentioned before as the
able Foreign Minister who, in the spring of 1923, obtained
international sanction for Poland's *de facto* frontiers on the
eastern side. His tenure of office had given him wide experience
of certain notions busily circulated throughout the world as
to Poland's imperialist ambitions and militarist spirit. He
set himself to counteract these misconceptions, and earnestly
endeavoured to do so by a book in English entitled *Poland
and Peace* (London: Allen & Unwin, 1923), and later on, by his
addresses at the Williamstown Institute of Political Science,
and other utterances. Installed again in the Foreign Office in
1924, he availed himself of all opportunities to emphasize
Poland's active concurrence in international efforts to secure
permanent peace. Poland, in the League of Nations, warmly
supported the Geneva Protocol, and after its failure, herself at a
time advanced a project of a similar kind. In 1925, Skrzyński
even went the length of eloquently advocating the Locarno

Treaties, although the question of security and permanence of frontiers in eastern Europe was expressly excluded from them. Poland had hitherto been known to the League chiefly as the object of wearisome and ever-repeated complaints on the part of Germany, Danzig, Lithuania, and the Ukrainians. Skrzyński's eloquent zeal on behalf of all international understandings, even when Polish interests were not protected by them, established a new character for Poland in the League. His attitude was duly rewarded : when Germany was received into the League of Nations and obtained a seat in its Council, he succeeded in securing election to a seat in the Council for Poland as well.

While making all these efforts to stress Poland's co-operation in the promotion of European peace, Skrzyński realized that further progress of peaceful relations between the victors and the vanquished of the World War would diminish Poland's military importance for France and accordingly lessen the support hitherto afforded by France to Poland's military organization and foreign policy. He accordingly made it one of his aims to loosen the new Poland's established dependence on France by building up a system of closer relations with other Powers. His aspirations towards Great Britain, indeed, met with hardly any response. But exchanges of visits with some of Poland's neighbours markedly improved Poland's standing in eastern Europe, where Poland had so far been somewhat isolated ; and a sensational reception of Soviet Russia's Foreign Minister Chicherin in Warsaw seemed even to herald far-reaching changes in Poland's relations in that quarter. Nothing, indeed, came of this promise ; nor did Skrzyński's peaceful policy achieve any success in the equally vital domain of Poland's relations with Germany. The German Government had availed itself of the expiration of the Geneva Coal Convention in 1925 to close its frontier entirely to Poland's exports of Upper Silesian coal, and so created a new and serious, if temporary, economic difficulty for Poland. The impetuous Grabski's counter-measures promptly resulted in a state of " Tariff War " between the two countries, which has continued ever since.

Skrzyński's foreign policy, although unavoidably unsuccessful in some respects, had made him a conspicuous figure in Polish public life, and when Grabski's Cabinet fell over the economic penalties of currency reform, it was a fairly obvious consequence of the usual political deadlock that Skrzyński was called upon to form a Coalition Ministry. He did so on a wider basis than

had hitherto ever been attempted, his Cabinet including even
a representative of his opponents, the Nationalists, in the
important position of Minister of Finance. But Skrzyński's
handling of Poland's vexed domestic problems was to be less
successful than his activities in the foreign field. The support
of parliamentary parties crumbled away from him as his
Finance Minister, Zdziechowski, proceeded, by necessarily
unpopular measures of retrenchment, to re-establish the balance
of the budget and to cement the work of financial reform.

A renewal of the 1923 agreement between the Farmers'
Party and the Nationalists was achieved, Skrzyński's Govern-
ment had to give way in the spring of 1925, and once again a
Cabinet was about to be formed by the peasant leader Witos.

## 7

It was at this moment that the figure of Marshal Piłsudski
once more appeared upon the scene of Poland's destinies.
He had been consistently kept out of office for nearly three years,
and he had of late repeatedly raised his voice against the management of the army by his successors. He had a numerous and
enthusiastic following among the army officers, especially those
who had fought under his command in the " Legions " of the
early war years. Among the civilian population, numbers of
trade unionists were looking up to him, a section of the Socialist
Party having remained faithful to him in spite of his early
departure from rigid Socialist doctrine. The liberal and radical-
minded elements among the city *intelligentsia* were among his
most ardent admirers, and side by side with them there stood a
certain portion of the national minorities, part of the Jews in
particular, who expected concessions to their claims from his
reinstatement in power. In strange approximation with these
groups, there appeared among Piłsudski's followers a part of
the landed gentry and aristocracy, who were opposed to the
Nationalists on account of the political alliance between these
and the Farmers' Party with its programme of agrarian reform.

This social configuration of Piłsudski's following in the
country was to manifest itself soon in political affairs. At the
moment, however, when he decided actively to intervene in the
political situation, it was chiefly upon his faithful soldiers
that he placed his reliance. In the first days of May 1926
nothing but a continuation of the muddle of government by
shifting combinations of parliamentary parties seemed in
prospect, and the usual petty bargaining for ministerial seats
and for a compromise programme was going on. Suddenly,

Piłsudski, having hastily gathered some garrisons of the neighbourhood round him, appeared at the entrance to the city. A memorable conversation between him and the President of the Republic took place on the bridge over the Vistula, and ended in the President's refusal to grant Piłsudski's demands. Thereupon Piłsudski had resort to arms. The troops which the Government could muster in and around the capital, engaged in street fighting with Piłsudski's forces. Other troops, summoned from the provinces, mostly failed to arrive, partly because the railwaymen aided the Marshal's *coup d'état* by a timely strike, partly because the troops themselves largely either hesitated or declared openly for Piłsudski at once. After two days, the capital was in Piłsudski's hands. The Witos Government resigned, and the President abdicated. The country was *de facto* under a military dictatorship, but constitutional forms were observed in the proceedings which followed : the Speaker of the Lower House, acting as temporary Regent, presided over the Presidential elections held by a joint session of both Chambers of Parliament. Piłsudski was elected against a Nationalist candidate. Then there came the first one of the many surprises which marked this stage of his career. He did not accept the election, but nominated a candidate of his own. This candidate, who duly became President, had never before been heard of in politics. His name was Ignatius Mościcki, he was a distinguished scientist, a Professor of Industrial Chemistry, and he had recently become honourably known throughout Poland for his capable management of the large chemical factory at Chorzów in Upper Silesia, which had passed from German into Polish hands with the province itself, and was run as a State undertaking. The nomination of Professor Mościcki for the Presidency must now be admitted to have been a masterstroke of Piłsudski's domestic diplomacy. Never having been active in politics, he had not become an object of enmity to any party, and was not open to attack. The distinction of his past services to the State was universally recognized, and his personal qualities soon made him popular even among Piłsudski's political adversaries. It is not too much to say that his elevation to the Presidency averted what danger of civil war may still have lurked in the country after Piłsudski's success in the capital. But the danger was certainly much less than in 1922, when an earlier nominee of Piłsudski's—in many ways comparable with Mościcki—had fallen a victim to the excitement of the hour. In 1926, the country was evidently as tired as were other countries in Europe of the inefficiency and instability

H

of parliamentary government, and as ready for dictatorial government by a strong hand.

## 8

Poland, then, had fairly easily gone the way of those other states of post-war Europe which had exchanged their parliamentary systems for dictatorships, and among which Italy was the outstanding precedent. But it was soon apparent that a Polish parallel to Fascismo was not to be expected. Something like the Fascist militia, indeed, was developed out of the semi-military organizations of " Riflemen " under the pretext of auxiliary military training ; and decrees drastically limiting the freedom of the Press were issued after a time. But never was the freedom of speech and of political action interfered with to anything like the extent which their control by the Fascist Party reached in Italy. And in other ways, the picture was quite different.

To begin with, no sweeping changes were made in the Constitution of the Republic. The *coup d'état* having been professedly directed against parliamentary misrule, some measure of constitutional reform, reconstructing the entire fabric of the parliamentary system, was pretty generally anticipated. But Piłsudski, although given to periodical outbursts of insulting language on the moral rottenness and intellectual inanity of Parliament, yet proved at bottom to be more attached to the democratic tradition than some of the officers who formed his immediate surroundings and dreamed of purely military rule. By a law passed in June, 1926, only three points in the constitutional relations between the supreme powers in the State were modified, and all of them in accordance with the best models of parliamentary rule, or with obvious requirements of economic necessity. Firstly, the Head of the State was authorized to dissolve Parliament and to order new elections in case of a conflict between Parliament and Government. Secondly, legislation by Presidential decree was provided for, Parliament, however, retaining the right to annul such decrees afterwards. Thirdly and lastly, the period for parliamentary discussion of the budget was limited to four months, the budget after the lapse of that term becoming valid even if not passed by the Houses.

It was under a constitutional system only so slightly amended that the new Government began its activities. A Cabinet was formed under the presidency of Professor K. Bartel, who was to come into office several times again since. Marshal Piłsudski himself was content with the portfolio of Military Affairs ; at a later period, he assumed the Premiership twice for short periods, but resigned it again. As it was understood all the time that he was the determining power in the State, the term a " disguised dictatorship " was devised, not inaptly, to describe the new state of things.

Inconsiderable as the changes in the constitution were, they provided immense relief for the continuation of organizing activities. A multitude of Presidential decrees issued in the first years of the new *régime* at last introduced order into large domains of public life which had been neglected by parliamentary legislation. The long desired stability of Government, which now seemed assured, had a beneficial influence on administrative practice, and the work of all departments became a great deal more efficient. To single out one of many examples only, it was in the new era that the organization of Courts of Law was unified throughout the country by a decree of February 6, 1928. A complete new Criminal Code followed in 1932.

### 9

Together with manifold legislative and administrative progress, the early years of the new era were happily marked by considerable improvement in the *economic situation*.

Germany's refusal, in 1925, to take any more Upper Silesian coal from Poland had created a difficulty : this was overcome by the opening-up of Scandinavian markets for Polish coal exports. The coincidence of the great British coal strike of 1926 with the beginnings of this movement strengthened Poland's chances in the new direction. In connection with this, the idea of creating a purely Polish Baltic port side by side with the unfriendly city of Danzig—an idea born of the difficulties of munition transports during the war of 1920, and fitfully entertained since—was now pushed vigorously towards complete realization. The harbour and town of Gdynia sprang up with truly American rapidity in place of a poor fishing village, and the trade of the new Polish port soon attained the volume of the pre-war trade of Danzig herself. Danzig, on the other hand, looking askance at this rival and even complaining of it to the League of Nations, not only did not lose, but continued to gain and prosper as it never had done under Germany. It became apparent that Poland's export trade would keep both ports amply busy, and the creation of a third one, a river port to collect and distribute cargoes coming down the Vistula, may soon become necessary. Commercial and passenger vessels flying the Polish flag began to appear in quickly increasing numbers in the Baltic. A direct all-Polish railway line connecting the Upper Silesia coal basin with the port of Gdynia, is nearly finished. On the other hand the close and friendly relations between Poland and her ally Rumania are favourable to growing Polish trade activities in the Black Sea ports as well. In this way, the difficulties of establishing normal economic relations with Poland's eastern neighbour, Soviet Russia, and with her western neighbour, Germany, are being compensated by successful reassertion of the ancient importance of Poland's commerce along the north-south axis, and of her access to two seas as the outlets of that commerce.

With regard to economic development within the country itself, the Government successfully resumed the traditional policy of fostering the growth of industries. President Mościcki's able assistant in the management of the great chemical factory at Chorzów, E. Kwiatkowski, became Minister of Industry and Commerce in the new Government, and he not only was chiefly instrumental in promoting the quick construction of the harbour of Gdynia, but he also realized Mościcki's own cherished plan of creating another large chemical factory of the same type as Chorzów ; and the new Chorzów, called " Mościce," at two hours' railway journey from Cracow, came into being with equally marvellous rapidity. Both factories are mainly devoted to the task of supplying artificial fertilizers for Poland's agriculture. The fact of government initiative in that particular direction illustrates the increased wideness of outlook which now begins to manifest itself in Polish economic policy. Whilst former governments gave one-sided attention to industry as, supposedly, the only foundation of greater wealth, it was now realized that industry can only progress with a capacious domestic market at its command, and such a market can only be created by raising the well-being of the agricultural classes which form the bulk of the population. Agriculture, accordingly, now at last begins to receive its due share of government assistance. Side by side with the Bank of Poland and the Bank of National Economy, a third large government institution, the Agricultural Bank, is established in 1927. Reclamation of waste lands, especially in the marshy regions of the eastern borderlands, is taken in hand at considerable expense ; so is the construction of grain elevators on the American model.

The years 1927 and 1928 become a period of constructive investments on the part of the Government on an unprecedented scale. If Poland is in a position to afford them, this is due to

the fact that it became the happy lot of the new Government
to bring the work of Poland's financial reform to a successful
termination. An eminent American financial expert—Professor
Kemmerer—was engaged to assist in the task, and his
recommendations met with a better fate than those of Sir
Hilton Young. The Kemmerer programme having been adopted, a large loan of $70,000,000 was obtained, late in 1927, from
America on more convenient terms than the loans of earlier
years. This was used to enlarge the capital of the Bank of
Poland and thereby ultimately to fix the exchange value of
Polish currency. Another American adviser, Mr. Charles S.
Dewey, became for three years a member of the Board of
Directors of the Bank of Poland, and his services helped con-
siderably to strengthen Poland's standing in the world of
international finance.

Altogether, it was as an imcomparably better ordered and
more prosperous country that the new Poland celebrated, in the
autumn of 1928, the tenth anniversary of the day when the
foundations of the new State had had to be laid amidst universal
famine and devastation. Imposing evidence of large reconstructive developments in all domains was given by the great
National Exhibition held in Poznań in 1929. The vitality of
Poland's productive life as presented by it surprised even
thousands of Polish citizens themselves, whose day-to-day
attention had been engrossed by political controversies, and
who now only learned at Poznań how large a mass of creative
work had been accomplished in a variety of fields not coming
under their habitual observation.

10

In the domain of *international relations*, the comparative
stability of Government induced by Piłsudski's *coup d'état* also
exercised a favourable influence. Cabinet changes occured, but
the portfolio of Foreign Affairs luckily remained for six years
in the same capable hands of A. Zaleski, whose record of
achievements in raising Poland's prestige abroad surpassed
that of his ablest predecessor, Count Skrzyński.

When Piłsudski came into power, the fact was widely interpreted as the beginning of a period of aggressive militarism in
Poland's politics. Rumours of a large anti-Soviet crusade
which was to be engineered by Britain, and of which Poland
was to be the vanguard, were busily circulated, chiefly from
Bolshevik sources. Communist propaganda in Poland (now
more marked than ever) gave abundant ground for friction ;

so did, on the other hand, some desperate acts of violence committed upon Soviet representatives by Russian emigrants on Polish soil. It speaks well for the maturity and moderation with which Poland's foreign affairs were conducted under the new *régime* that all conflicts with Russia were settled by negotiation, normal diplomatic relations continued unbroken, and the volume of trade between the two countries (in spite of the lack of a commercial treaty) increased considerably.

It was no less difficult to maintain such relations with Germany, in view of continuous world-wide German propaganda in favour of a drastic revision of the Polish-German frontier, in view also of active economic hostility, and of constant complaints against Poland to the League of Nations

The quiet but firm attitude of Poland's Foreign Minister, A. Zaleski—the first Polish statesman to preside over the Assembly of the League of Nations—not only succeeded in the difficult task of establishing correct relations of co-operation with the newly admitted German delegation in Geneva under Stresemann, but it also reaped its due of general recognition by securing Poland's easy and undisputed re-election to a seat in the Council. In the field of individual relations between the two countries, M. Zaleski's patient efforts were rewarded after years of most wearisome negotiations, by the conclusion of a commercial treaty with Germany, early in 1930. Compromises were reached on the subject of difficulties seemingly insurmountable, such as the admission of a fixed monthly contingent of Polish coal into Germany, the right of Germans to settle and do business in Poland, the import of Polish agricultural produce into Germany. The value of the agreement is not diminished by the fact that political complications have so far frustrated its ratification by the German legislature.

The earnest desire for peace shown by Poland on all sides was never more impressively manifested during this period than at the dramatic meeting between Marshal Piłsudski himself and the Lithuanian Prime Minister, M. Woldemaras at the Council table in Geneva in 1927. Never in the annals of the League, perhaps, had the problem of peace as the dominant purpose of all negotiations at Geneva been stated with more trenchant directness than Piłsudski stated it on that occasion. An understanding with Lithuania still failed to be reached, but the effect of Poland's attitude on League opinion remained.

Tasks of the utmost complexity were placed before Polish foreign policy by certain tendencies towards new groupings of European Powers which at this time became manifest. While maintaining friendly relations with the three states of the Little Entente—Czechoslovakia, Yugoslavia, Rumania (particularly the last-named)—Poland yet kept the traditional bonds unrelaxed which had for so many centuries existed between her and Hungary. While unable still, after many efforts, to establish neighbourly relations with Lithuania, she succeeded in drawing closer those ties of common interest which obviously connect her with the Baltic States—Latvia, Estonia and Finland. While remaining the loyal ally of France, Poland cultivates her historical associations and recent political connections with Italy and successfully avoids all appearance of being drawn into any combination directed against either of the two Powers. While, in fine, manifesting her sympathy with all efforts to establish closer union among the States of Europe, Poland keeps unimpaired, and develops by new agreements, her excellent relations with the United States of America. Keeping, in this manner, a careful balance between dangerous extremes, the new Poland in this phase of her existence no longer remains a subordinate minor partner in the great game of international politics : she has acquired sufficient standing to afford movements of initiative on her own part. Such a movement is made by her proposal, in the summer of 1930, for a conference between the predominantly agrarian states of mid-eastern Europe— a proposal which bids fair to create an economic basis for friendly understanding between a group of states hitherto divided by political antagonisms.

## II

The first years after Marshal Piłsudski's *coup d'état* were, then, undoubtedly marked by successes abroad and by a prosperous economic situation at home. As time went on, however, certain difficulties, fundamentally involved in the new state of affairs, began to thicken. Such difficulties had from the first arisen over the further conduct of *domestic politics*.

The revolution had been primarily directed against the harmful omnipotence of Parliament in the Polish Constitution. Parliament had itself, under the pressure of dire necessity, resigned part of its financial powers in favour of Grabski in 1923. It now consented, in June, 1926, as mentioned above, to certain modest extensions of the presidential prerogatives in legislative and budgetary matters. But that did not mean that a majority amenable to Piłsudski's rule, or ready for further curtailment of parliamentary powers, was to be obtained in Parliament as constituted under the ultra-democratic franchise. Certain large parties excluded from his Cabinet—in the first place, his old antagonists the Nationalists, secondly, their allies the Farmers' Party, whose leader, Witos, he had unseated, and thirdly, his early associates the Socialists, with whom he now ultimately severed all ties—were all soon in opposition against his rule.

What followed was mainly a precarious spectacle of petty political bickerings. Several successive Cabinets headed by Professor Bartel vainly strained their energies to obtain a measure of co-operation from Parliament in various urgent and important legislative tasks, and a show of parliamentary sanction for the general policy of the Government. The opposition parties in Parliament expressed their hostile attitude by picking holes into the budget at points where primary interests of the State were concerned—such as the appropriations for the maintenance of the Police Force, or for Secret Service activities against espionage and Communism. The framing of measures of fundamental importance—such as a law for the definite organization of local self-government in 1927—were thwarted by the antagonism between Parliament and Government. The dominant issue of a thorough reform of the constitution was being universally discussed ; the country was fairly swarming with constitutional projects ; but it was clear that no conceivable project would rally any imaginable majority of the existing Parliament for its support.

The imposition of a new constitution by decree, or, at any rate, a change of the electoral system by the same method, would have been a way out. Piłsudski, contrary to expectations, continued to abstain from all such action, perhaps because he assumed that another violent concussion of the political system might be detrimental to Poland's prestige abroad and to her economic interests. So it happened that parliamentary elections took place at the time appointed for them by the constitution, early in 1928, and were held under the established franchise.

Naturally, they could not produce a decisive result. Supporters of the Government, indeed, got into both Houses in large numbers, and in each of them formed a solid group larger than any other, under the name of " Non-Party *Bloc* of Collaboration with the Government."

But the *bloc*, with all its numerical strength, could not supply a parliamentary majority to the Government except by combination with some other group.

Now, it had been Piłsudski's contention that there were, after 1926, to be no more coalition governments—that he had made his stand on behalf of " moral regeneration," as against the manifold " unrighteousness in the commonwealth " produced by such political bargains in the past. The elections of 1928 showed that the negative part of his intention was fairly successfully accomplished. Splits had occurred in almost all the larger parties of the old system ; but the chance of getting a majority together, if no Coalition Cabinet was to be formed, still remained dependent on the sympathies and antipathies of the several groups for each particular measure.

If the elements of opposition in Parliament were broken up and disunited, it soon became apparent that the Government *bloc*, although kept in good discipline, was by no means free from inward rifts. Old Radicals from the city *intelligentsia* and staunch Conservatives from the ranks of the land-owning gentry faced each other in the *bloc* and even in the successive cabinets. As a compromise between these widely divergent elements, the *bloc* did, indeed, produce a constitutional reform project of its own ; but there was no possibility of getting it through Parliament. The Government humoured the Conservatives, and weakened the Nationalist opposition, by maintaining good relations with the Church ; it undermined the Socialist position by appointing commissioners to reorganize the Workingmen's Sickness Insurance Offices, which had become sources of Socialist Party funds. But positive measures dealing with large fundamental problems—and there were a number of such problems awaiting solution—were not forthcoming ; nor was there any inducement for the Government's supporters in Parliament to attempt to frame them, in view of the hopelessness of constructive legislation under the given parliamentary conditions.

Parliamentary life, after 1928, became more and more ineffectual ; sessions were only called to be adjourned at once ; even budget discussions did not reach their natural end, to say nothing of other legislation. The several cabinets headed by Professor Bartel (who had earnestly sought co-operation by Parliament) were followed by others under the presidency of faithful old fellow-conspirators and obedient soldiers of Piłsudski's—men who openly defied Parliament. Ministers who had received votes of " no confidence " in Parliament, were reappointed. Parliament, as a matter of fact, had ceased altogether to fulfil any of its traditional functions, and was leading an almost purely formal existence. A Congress of opposition groups, assembled at Cracow in the summer, 1930, served merely to show their utter want of cohesion and their inability to agree on any but a negative programme.

## 12

Apart from the unending conflict between Parliament and Government, other developments in the later years of the new era were bound to create anxiety in those who had expected that it would bring permanent soundness to Polish public life.

The principal disquieting factor was indeed one which was not of Poland's making. It was the serious *economic crisis* which, ten years after the war, was sweeping all Europe and which became intensified by the American slump of 1929. The prosperous economic situation of the first years after 1926, was changed into a highly critical one. Unemployment once more became widespread, as in the days after Grabski's currency reform. An extreme dearth of credit paralyzed all economic initiative ; at the same time the fiscal screw worked stronger than ever, because the State budget was maintained at the level of the prosperous years. The so-called " compressions " attempted in budgetary expenditure had little effect on the State household, but exasperated those affected by them. The crisis not only laid industries low, but it extended, as elsewhere in the world, also to the entire domain of agriculture. Formerly there was comfort in the reflection that Poland, being a largely agricultural country, would get over critical economic periods more easily than the industrial countries hit particularly hard by them. Now the world-wide fall of prices became particularly marked in agriculture, and made production—even in a country of cheap labour like Poland—almost entirely unremunerative. In previous years, a good harvest had been the mainspring of improvement in the economic situation : now, the paradoxical expression " the disaster of a good crop " became current coin in Polish agricultural circles.

In addition to a world-wide economic crisis, Poland also came in for her share in the *political restlessness and uncertainty* which once more began rapidly to increase in international relations. The Locarno Treaties and the Kellogg Pact had seemed to be definite steps towards securing permanent peace ; yet somehow, armaments, and animosities between powerful states, did not diminish. In the case of Poland, it was, of course, chiefly the changed situation of Germany which gave cause for anxiety. The final deliverance of Germany's western border districts from military occupation in 1930, had for its immediate consequence a considerably more aggressive tone with regard to the problem of a revision of Germany's eastern frontiers. Ominous frontier incidents happened one after another, and it was becoming clearer every day that Germany's utmost efforts, in the League of Nations and elsewhere, would in the near future be directed, in the first place, at the abolition of Poland's access to the sea.     This, in the eyes of Poles, can only mean the cutting of the jugular vein of Poland's economic organism, and a fatal blow to her political independence, as it has proved before, in the period of the partitions.     The introduction of prohibitive tariffs on imported foreign agricultural produce, early in 1930, nullified the whole effect of the commercial treaty with Poland, which had just, after infinite difficulties, been concluded. Poland showed the utmost good will by ratifying the treaty on her side ; but ratification by the German Legislature did not ensue, and " tariff war " continued.     At the same time, the persistent and strenuous campaign conducted by Germany on behalf of a revision of the Peace Treaties, found a sympathetic echo in various states not otherwise tied by bonds of common interest to each other ; and the international unrest is being skilfully fomented by Soviet Russia for purposes of its own.

It was then, in a somewhat gloomy atmosphere, both international and economic, that Poland faced new *parliamentary elections* in the autumn of 1930.     Within the country, the prestige won for the Piłsudski Government by the great successes of its first years had suffered through some political mistakes which the military hotheads surrounding the Marshal had unfortunately been allowed to commit, such as wholesale dismissals of political opponents from State posts, and the imprisonment of a number of Parliamentary Opposition leaders on a charge of conspiracy.     As regards Piłsudski himself, his mysterious irresolution on the issue of constitutional reform kept even his admirers in a state of painful suspense.     Still, however, the glamour of his great personality was strong enough among the people to secure victory at the polls once more.     That victory, after a strenuous election campaign and the use of some administrative pressure, was more sweeping than any previous election result in the new Poland.     The beginning of 1931 found the Government *bloc* in both chambers of Parliament securely in possession of unprecedented majorities, fully qualifying it for legislative action even of the widest scope.

It is too early at this moment, while the Piłsudski Government is in posession of this, its crowning opportunity, to discuss the use made of it.     At the moment when these lines are being written, the problem of transition from the " dictatorship in disguise " to new and permanent forms of constitutional life in the Polish Republic is still entirely open. At the same time, the cloud of economic disaster hangs over Poland, as over the rest of the world, more heavily than ever ; and the Lausanne Agreement on Reparations in July, 1932, as well as some subsequent efforts at international understanding have only brought faint and uncertain relief into an atmosphere of political tension in which the relations between Poland and Germany are, unfortunately, perhaps the most immediately dangerous element.

It is to be hoped that the brunt of the crisis, borne by all nations alike, may at least prevent them from rushing into the common catastrophe of a new war. And as regards Poland, the political vicissitudes of her first years, as outlined above, may perhaps warrant a Pole's belief in the vitality of the new State. Whatever destiny may have in store for this tormented post-war world, Poland assuredly has as much ground to look forward hopefully into the future as any of the States of the new Europe which have emerged from the Great War.

## CHAPTER V

# GEOGRAPHICAL ASPECTS AND ADMINISTRATIVE STRUCTURE

## I

POLAND ranks in international relations as one of the " lesser Powers." In consequence of this, the vague notion has taken root in the mind of the average western European and American that she is " a small country." It is not generally realized that the reborn Poland, although much inferior in extent to the historical Polish-Lithuanian Monarchy, still is considerably larger in area and population than most of the new or reorganized states around her—larger, e.g., than either Czechoslovakia or Rumania or Yugoslavia—being, in fact, the eighth state in Europe in point of area (approximately midway between Spain and Italy in that respect) and the sixth in population (with about one-half the population of Germany, or three-fourths that of France).

Another common fallacy arising out of the unfamiliarity of the West with central and eastern European geography consists in the idea that Poland is a country of largely uniform geographical aspect. It is imagined as a country of wide plains, rendered monotonous by extensive agricultural cultivation, thinly sown with poor villages, and only varied by occasional stretches of forest ; the climate is hazily supposed to be very much like that of Russia.

In reality, Poland, bordered in the north by the Baltic and in the south by the Carpathian ridge, includes within her borders considerable variety of landscape. The breezy headlands and sandy, pine-crested beaches of her short strip of sea-coast ; the belt of lakes and woodlands ("the Kassubian Switzerland ") extending parallel to that coast nearby ; the other equally picturesque lake districts, one round about Poznań in the west, and another and larger one in the neighbourhood of Wilno ; the majestic granite chain of the Tatras—Poland's Rocky Mountains—in her south-western corner ; the green slopes of the " Lowlands " north and west of those mountains, with the winding currents and foaming rapids (*Pieniny*) of the river Dunajec making its way through marvellous rock fastnesses out into the plains; the vast stretches of dark virgin forests covering the huge and solitary ranges of the Eastern Carpathians; the equally vast and equally primeval expanses of forest in the plains of the north-east, in the regions of Białowież, of Suwałki, of Wilno; the wide fen lands on both banks of the Pripet river in the centre of Poland's eastern border, with their strange melancholy charm; the " Holy Cross Mountains " near Kielce, an enchanted island of wooded ridges in the midst of Poland's central plain; the diversity introduced into the aspect of that plain itself by the windings of Poland's main river artery, the Vistula, with the steepnesses of its banks crowned by the beautiful ancient walls of such picturesque towns as Sandomierz and Kazimierz in the south, or Płock and Toruń (Thorn) in the north : these are but a few specimens of Poland's manifold appeal to the lover of scenery and the student of Nature.

This variety in the physiognomy of the country is not unconnected with the *weather*, which is likewise much more diversified than is usually imagined. Poland lies on the border between the predominantly oceanic climates of western European countries and the typically continental climate of European Russia and Siberia. The difference between the two kinds of weather finds expression in Poland rather as one between east and west than between north and south. It is in the wide stretches of open country in Poland's eastern regions that the rigour of winters is apt to make itself felt in something like the Russian fashion—while the sea-coast in the north is marked by moderate temperature both in the winter and in summer. Again, while the average rainfall is fairly high, even in the east, it is the west chiefly which is characterized by capricious changefulness of the weather, especially in the transition periods of early spring and late autumn, which, indeed, according to a common saying, add two " Polish seasons" to the normal four of the year.

## 2

To the variety thus represented by the geographical features of the country, there corresponds a similar variety in the physical and tribal characteristics, the customs and mentality of Poland's country people.

Poland being situated at the crossing of two great highways of trade and migration, it is the natural result of countless early and later wanderings and settlements, conflicts and fusions on her territory that a considerable number of strongly distinct types of the white race should appear side by side and in various combinations within her borders. Long heads and round heads, the light-skinned and the dusky, the fair-haired and the dark meet each other and mingle with each other on Polish soil. The Nordic and the sub-Nordic, the pre-Slav and the Alpine, the Dinaric and the Mediterranean type represent only the principal categories, often dovetailing into each other and with many intermediate forms in between. Variety is added to this gallery of human types not only by the manifold admixtures of non-Polish races—to be surveyed in the following chapter—but also by certain marked differences in physical habit between the gentry and the peasantry. These differences even led an earlier generation of historians to the assumption of a foreign racial origin of old Poland's governing class—an assumption not confirmed by the intense and many-sided anthropological research work conducted in Polish lands in our own century.

No less variety than by the differences in physical habit is produced by the widely divergent conditions of occupation in Poland's rural areas. Both economic and political factors have had their share in producing the vast difference which we can observe within the recreated Polish State between the phlegmatic Kassubian fishermen on the Baltic shore and the fiery mountaineers of the Tatras ; between the shrewd and hard-headed, well-to-do farmers of former Prussian Poland and the sleepy, benighted pitch-burners of the eastern fens on the Russian border ; between the lively " Kurpians " of the northern forest, until recently more familiar with the hunter's gun than with the plough, and the handsome shepherd race of the " Hutsuls " on the Carpathian mountain-meadows in the south-east ; between the enterprising and sociable peasant of the neighbourhood of Cracow in the south-west, and the silent and tenacious cottager of the Wilno region on the Lithuanian border ; between the standardized modern industrial worker in the coal mines of Silesia or the textile factories of Łódź, and the unchangingly traditionalist, elemental Masovian peasantry of Central Poland as depicted in the late Ladislas Reymont's great prose epic *The Peasants*[1]. This panorama of Poland's peasant groups is beautifully reflected in the wide range of picturesque peasant costume which can still be admired on

[1] English translation by M. H. Dziewicki, 4 vols. (I, Winter ; II. Spring ; III. Summer ; IV. Autumn). A. Knopf, New York and London, 1925.

such occasions for its display as the " Harvest Home " at the President's summer residence of Spała near Warsaw in August, a most picturesque annual gathering of numerous peasant delegations from all provinces of the Republic.

### 3

The *towns* of Poland show the wide differences between different sections of the country no less manifestly and vividly than the rural districts. Owing to her changing destinies under different systems of foreign rule, Poland is (happily, in this case) still very far from being a country of standardized modern cities. Those of her larger towns which are incrusted with the thickest coating of uniform modern improvements and ugly nineteenth-century *bourgeois* architecture are the cities of the former Prussian sector : Katowice (Kattowitz) in Silesia, Poznań (Posen) in the centre and Bydgoszcz (which the Germans called Bromberg) in the north. But even these have their redeeming features : *Bydgoszcz* (the prosperous centre of large wood industries) enjoys the advantage of a beautiful landscape setting at the confluence of the rivers Brda and Vistula, and is traversed by a canal which relieves the commonplace aspect of its buildings. *Poznań*, side by side with plenty of hideous, if solid, modern Prussian brickwork, contains such ornamental relics of historical architecture as the old Polish town hall and a fine Baroque Cathedral. And *Katowice*, the growing capital of Poland's " black country," offers, by its rapid recent development, abundant scope for the bold and unconventional simplicity of monumental public building in the Americanized style of to-day.

Passing further east, we at once drift away (at least in the former Russian Poland) from the higher standards of material comfort which German rule left established in the western provinces, but we also enter cities with more individual character in their general aspect. This holds true, in a sense not altogether favourable, in the case of *Łódź,* " the Polish Manchester."Grown up, like a huge mushroom, in a few decades of the later nineteenth century, Łódź certainly displays all the familiar vices of jerry-building and slum accumulation at their very worst : it was the most monstrously unhygienic, and remains—without mitigation—the most offensively ugly of Poland's large towns. But its recent progress—especially in the building of schools, social welfare institutions, and working-men's dwellings—has been truly remarkable, and its American career as a city, as well as the curiously composite character of its industrial population—Germans, Jews, and Poles—make it an object of vivid interest for the social and psychological student of modern city life.[1]

### 4

We now move on towards the central river artery—the Vistula. What geographical unity the purely Polish nucleus of the Polish State possesses, it does possess as consisting essentially of the basin of the Vistula with its tributaries. It is also on the banks of the Vistula that both the cities are situated which were capitals of Poland in succession, after its early western centre had been shifted eastward under German pressure.

*Cracow* (spelt *Kraków* in Polish) the capital of Poland from about 1000 till about 1600—once more was her unofficial capital in the later nineteenth century, when there was home rule in the Austrian sector, while Warsaw could scarcely breathe under Russian oppression. Of the part then played by Cracow in Poland's intellectual and political life, some account was given in a former chapter. In the new Poland since the War, with Warsaw as a real capital again, that importance of Cracow has naturally and necessarily been diminishing. Still, Cracow remains one of the most perfectly preserved medieval cities in Europe, and its magnificent monuments of Gothic and Renascence architecture—such as the church of St. Mary and the Cloth Hall in the City Square, the Royal Castle and the Cathedral on Wawel Hill, numerous other churches, public buildings, and private residences ranging in age from 200 to 900 years—illustrate the splendour and dignity of Poland's historical civilization more tellingly than anything else in the country. The University of Cracow, the oldest in Poland, remains the most authoritative seat of learning in the State, and Cracow's atmosphere of tradition and culture will no doubt always be, as it has been in the past, one of the most potent factors of inspiration for national literature and art.

Compared with Cracow, *Warsaw* (called *Warszawa* in Polish) enjoyed a much shorter spell of political importance, architectural development, and cultural florescence. Her elevation to the dignity of capital came only two hundred years after the union of Poland with Lithuania had created an empire of which the centre lay far north of Cracow. And it was only for another two centuries that Warsaw dominated Poland before the partitions. It is, accordingly, to these two centuries—the seventeenth

[1] For a most vivid account of pre-war life in Łódź, L. Reymont's novel *The Promised Land* may be recommended (English translation by M. H. Dziewicki, New York : A. Knopf, 1926).

I

and the eighteenth—and to the styles characteristic of them, Baroque and Rococo, that the ornamental architecture of Warsaw mainly belongs. But much of that architecture is of very great charm indeed : such are the palaces built under the early eighteenth-century Saxon Kings (who also created the beauty of Dresden), and particularly those due to the initiative of that cultured Maecenas of all the arts, the unhappy last King of Poland, Stanislas Augustus Poniatowski. His summer residence, the small palace called *Łazienki* (" the Bath-House "), situated on an artificial lake in a lovely park, is one of Poland's jewels. The reign of " King Staś " (Stanislas), with a blaze of talent and achievement emanating from Warsaw, is justly remembered as another " golden age " equal in cultural splendour to the glorious and more happy Cracow era of the sixteenth century. An afterglow of that golden age of Warsaw still came during the short few years of comparative freedom after the Congress of Vienna ; but after that, there followed long and weary decades of political eclipse, and of repression of all cultural effort. At last, changed again into the capital of a large State out of the mere seat of a provincial Russian Governor-General, Warsaw during the dozen short years of her renewed free existence has made huge efforts to live down all the traces which the cramped Russian period had left behind, especially in the shape of mean, ugly or uncongenial building, and of general squalor and untidiness ; much has been achieved on a monumental scale, in spite of Poland's post-war ruin and poverty, and Warsaw has by this time more than half risen again into a condition worthy of a modern capital city with a fine historical tradition of intellectual subtlety and artistic charm.

## 5

After the two representative cities of Poland's middle region, two outposts of Polish civilization in the east may be singled out as equally representative and certainly not less beautiful. They are Wilno in the north and Lwów in the south.

*Lwów* (called by the Germans *Lemberg*), once the chief emporium of Poland's trade with south-eastern Europe and western Asia, at the same time served for ages as a bastion against eastern invasions, and made herself particularly famous in the seventeenth century by her burghers' valiant stand against assaults by huge armies of Cossacks and Tartars. In modern times, Lwów regained some of her ancient importance when the Austrians made her the capital of their province of Galicia. The World War, after countless sufferings under changing overlordship, finally brought another heroic period for Lwów when her Polish children valiantly defended her against an Ukrainian invasion in 1918 ; and much precious Polish blood was shed again in warding off a Bolshevik attack in 1920. No wonder that, with such an historical record as this, the city is very dear to the heart of the Pole ; but her charms contribute not a little to that popularity. Rich in parks, and presenting a magnificent panorama when surveyed from " Castle Hill," the city, with its three cathedrals of different Christian denominations (two of them of eastern type), breathes the peculiar fascination of a meeting-ground of West and East ; and race mixture has no doubt something to do with the genial and vivacious temperament of her population.

Vivacity is not an outstanding feature in the temper of the people of *Wilno*, but the proverbially generous hospitality and cordial ease of manner characteristic of the Polish-Russian border lends its own peculiar charm to the social atmosphere of that north-eastern city. Its outward aspect, as we regard it from " the Mound of the Three Crosses " or from the crest of one of the wooded ridges which give it a wondrously beautiful setting, has even more romantic glamour in it than that of Lwów. Here, East and West indeed meet and unite before our very eyes : numerous Roman Catholic churches, mostly exhibiting a particularly refined variety of Baroque, rub shoulders with Greek ones, marked by their gaudy-coloured torch-flame cupolas. And the charm deepens and grows in power when we remember the amazing vicissitudes of the city's history, its frequent early ravages by Tartar invasions, its efflorescence when it became the capital of the Lithuanian half of the great Jagellonian Monarchy, its brief blaze of cultural splendour even in the first years of Russian rule, when its Polish University shone with a galaxy of talent both among teachers and pupils —its heroic share in Poland's nineteenth-century armed risings and subsequent martyrdom, its vigorous artistic revival in our own days, when Wilno is the seat of one of the new Poland's most remarkable groups of painters.

These few hints as to the attractions of Poland's principal cities must suffice for the purposes of the present survey ; it would carry us to undue lengths to attempt a detailed account of the manifold attractions of various provincial towns, whether enlivened by gay-coloured country costume, like *Łowicz* near Warsaw, or dignified by ornamental old architecture, like *Zamość* in the province of Lublin, or rich in great historical memories, like those which haunt the castle and cathedral of

*Lublin* itself (where the final pact of the Polish-Lithuanian Union was concluded in 1569), or fascinating to the student of religion, like *Częstochowa* with its famous shrine of the " Black Virgin," the goal of numberless pilgrimages from all parts of the country—or, last not least, renowned for sheer beauty of scenery, like *Zakopane* at the foot of the Tatra Mountains, the health resort called even before the War " the summer capital of Poland," and now better known as a flourishing centre of winter sports. In summer, Zakopane has long had powerful rivals in a number of beauty-spots in the lower regions of the mountain district north, west and east of the Tatra chain— many of them famous for curative mineral waters (with *Krynica* now foremost among them). More recently, the attraction of Zakopane in summer has even more successfully been contested by that of a number of fast-growing Polish watering-places in the north, dotting the short strip of Poland's Baltic coast in the neighbourhood of *Danzig* and of the rapidly developing harbour of *Gdynia*. All these points of beauty and interest on Polish soil will no doubt ere long be duly discovered by the international tourist movement, as they are already being piously visited, year by year, by thousands of Americans of Polish origin who come and go by the Polish steamers plying between Gdynia and New York.

### 6

The changes and chances of history have resulted in the fact that the territory of the reborn Polish State exhibits perhaps more striking contrasts within its borders than almost any political unit in the new Europe. Thus, while Silesia is among the most densely populated regions on the Continent, with an average of 226 inhabitants to the square kilometre, the density at the other end of Poland, among the bogs and woods of the eastern provinces, drops to less than one-tenth of that average. It is a far cry indeed from the forests of industrial chimney-stacks, the expanses of intensely cultivated fields, the network of roads and railways, and the thick-set villages and towns in the west, to the forests of primeval trees, the dreary wastes of marshland, the vast stretches of roadless country, the rare and poor hamlets and sparsely scattered provincial towns of the eastern border. In the west, every inch of ground is a costly possession ; in the east, waste land is still plentiful and accordingly dealt with recklessly. Among the western population, education and organization, under the keen stimulus of struggle against the German advance, have become rooted habits ; in the east, illiteracy and lack of organization still subsist as the sad heritage of Russian rule.  In addition to such wide differences in educational and economic development, the equally enormous differences in mere administrative and legal machinery between the partitioning powers have made the task of State-building in the reunited Poland particularly complex and difficult.  A dozen years of joint existence, even had they been spent under the most normal and prosperous conditions, could bring the population of a country in this condition only a little way towards political consolidation ; a new generation will have to grow up under the new system before a really marked effect in the way of outer and inner unity is achieved.

In the meantime, however, Poland's unification has progressed by strides in spite of political instability and economic difficulties.

While an army for the new Republic, under the pressure of the imminent Bolshevik danger, was being rapidly put together out of various scattered war-time formations, while in the territorial fashioning of the new Poland a federalist and a nationalist conception were still struggling against each other, while Poland's constitution-makers in the Constituent Assembly were weakening the foundations of economic and political consolidation by establishing the principle of parliamentary sovereignty in the widest sense, the necessities of life urgently demanded the creation of administrative order and unity. The troubled and chaotic armistice autumn of 1918 still sees five different Polish Governments in actual existence :  the war-time  Polish National Committee in Paris, a " National " Cabinet in Warsaw and a " Democratic " one at Lublin both claiming power over the whole country, and in addition to these, temporary governing organs in the Austrian and the German sector.  Of these improvised administrations, some, viz., the Lublin Government and the Paris Committee—disappeared quickly when Piłsudski became Chief of State ; others—the separate administrations for the former Prussian province and for former Austrian Galicia—owing to distinct local conditions, continued to exist for years and even evolved elaborate bureaucratic apparatus of their own.  On the whole, however, the organization of central power proceeded quickly, and the Paderewski Government, early in 1919, not only commanded a dozen more or less full-grown Ministerial Departments, but exercised actual authority throughout the Republic.

## 7

Simultaneously with the creation of a central Government and its departments, it was imperative to set up, in all haste, the necessary subordinate machinery for local administration, and for this purpose, to divide the country into territorial administrative units. The delimitation of these administrative units—which were called, in the ancient Polish fashion, *województwa* (or *counties* in the British sense of the term), had to be accomplished quickly, and it came inevitably to represent a compromise between the historical system of Poland's provinces and that more recent division of the country by the partitioning powers, to which the population had become accustomed during a century of foreign rule. The sixteen territorial units, as delimited rapidly in those early days, have so far remained unchanged, and the problem of more adequate repartition into provinces—perhaps fewer in number, larger in size and no longer preserving the boundary lines of the partition period— is one of Poland's tasks for to-morrow. For the time being, amidst the bustle and ferment of the turbulent early years, a working administrative machinery of uniform type had to be set up within the newly created administrative territories. This was done as successfully as was possible under the circumstances, the new organization often making difficult headway against deep-rooted local use and wont. One province only— that of Silesia—received, in accordance with Poland's international obligations, a complete fabric of parliamentary self-government ; another one—the Wilno region—by a vote of its local assembly in 1922 voluntarily declared for unconditional incorporation into Poland ; for a third—Eastern Galicia, divided into three counties—a system of provincial autonomy was devised, and even passed by Parliament, in 1922, but it has not been put into operation.

Apart from such special provisions realized or contemplated in border provinces whose mixed population demands them, the " counties " of the rest of Poland were all of them intended to be not administrative territories only but to possess a certain amount of organized local self-government as well. Only in the counties of former Prussian Poland (Poznania and Pomerania), however, where certain institutions of the Prussian era supplied a ready framework, were county assemblies of a parliamentary type called into being. Both in former Russian and Austrian Poland such arrangements for local self-government remained practically non-existent till 1928. In that year a Presidential decree made provision for the creation of two kinds of local advisory bodies, viz., county councils which are to be composed of delegates of the districts and of the municipalities, and to act as a sort of " county parliaments "—and county committees, which are to consist of a few members, partly officials and partly elected delegates, and to represent something like " county cabinets " with the governors of the counties as their heads.

8

Descending lower in the scale of organization, from the county to the district and the town or village community, we are confronted by a variety of forms of organization, which were developed under the partitioning powers, and have so far resisted unification, being the social units most familiar to the average man of the people and therefore most firmly grounded in his civic consciousness.

The *districts*, like the counties, are, in principle, both administrative territories and local government units in one ; their official chiefs, bearing the time-honoured Slavonic title of *starosta*, combine, in the former Russian and Prussian sectors, the function of central and local government, while in the Austrian sector the latter were in Austrian times in the hands of an elected " District Marshal." In Austrian as well as in Prussian Poland, elected district councils existed before the War ; but the franchise on which they were constructed was socially and nationally unfit for the new Poland ; in Russian Poland, no district councils had been in existence at all. They were given to former Russian Poland in the new era, and being constructed on modern democratic principles, they developed an activity often highly beneficial to the districts in the way of material improvements, but in more than one case financially reckless and ruinous, after the habit of popular representations. In former Prussian Poland, where the old system of district assemblies was calculated to secure ascendancy for the German element, the district franchise was reformed on democratic lines in 1921. In the former Austrian sector, an archaic group franchise had existed which gave predominance to the land-owning gentry : pending the introduction of a new and more democratic one, the districts are temporarily governed by appointed commissioners and nominated committees.

The *cities* and *towns* of Poland received, with Poland's deliverance, the privileges of municipal self-government, which some of them had lost under the partitioning powers. In Russian Poland, in particular, municipal self-government had

not existed under foreign rule : instead of an elective Polish
municipal representation, the towns were governed by imported
Russian Government officials, and the backwardness of many
towns of this sector in matters of public health, education,
and architecture, was due to the fetters which Russian bureaucracy and administrative centralism imposed on all municipal
enterprise.   In the new Poland, city government of the ordinary
European and American type, with a mayor, an elected town
council and a body of aldermen issuing from it, is now the
rule throughout the country.   In the former Austrian sector,
where this kind of self-government had existed for a long
time, the antiquated system of elections for the city councils
has caused (as in the case of the districts) the temporary
suspension of municipal self-government in some cities ; but
the government-appointed commissioners and councils are
admittedly provisional.

On the other hand, some of the larger cities even under
foreign rule—especially under Austrian—exercised through their
organs not only functions of local self-government, but some
of those of the central administration as well ; they continue
to do so, and thus are from the administrative point of view,
in the position of districts.   One of the cities, viz., the capital,
Warsaw, even has the administrative organization and privileges
of a county by itself, quite as Greater London forms a separate
county in England.

The uniform organization of the *village community* is one of
Poland's greatest problems.   Villages are the most conservative
bodies in a nation's life, and two-thirds of Poland's population
are villagers.   In Russian Poland, as in Russia proper, a group
of several villages formed one village commune (Russian :
*volost*) together, with an elected bailiff, aldermen and a council.
The village population thus, under Russia, possessed self-
governing institutions denied to the towns—this being part of
Russia's policy of national disintegration in Poland.   The
Russo-Polish village commune certainly had the advantage of
representing greater numerical and financial strength, and so
being able to maintain a higher level in the management of its
affairs, not only materially, but even intellectually.   The one-
village self-governing communes of Prussian and Austrian
Poland, small and poor, are at an obvious disadvantage in
comparison, and it will have to be (as it is now) one of the
main endeavours of Poland's administrative reformers to break
through the barriers of custom in that respect, and create larger
collective village communes throughout the Republic.

The question of reorganizing and definitely unifying the system of territorial and local self-government passed through several phases, corresponding to the vicissitudes of Poland's Parliamentary politics. A somewhat amateurish bill dealing with these problems, and introduced into Parliament by a Radical Peasant Group in 1926, failed to be passed owing to differences of opinion on essentials between the Government and the authors of the project. Only in the early months of 1933 was another Local Self-Government Bill voted by Parliament, placing these highly controversial matters at last on a uniform footing.

### 9

It was not only the political and administrative, but also the *religious* organization of the country which had to be put on a new basis, and constituted a complex problem.

The vast majority of Poland's population had ever since the tenth century been Roman Catholic, and remained so even after the temporary spread of Protestant doctrines in the sixteenth century.

Through contrast with the Protestant Germans on the one hand and the Greek Orthodox Russians on the other, the association of Catholicism with Polish nationality became particularly close.

The Catholic clergy, side by side with the country gentry, became a mainstay of national resistance to foreign rule after the partitions ; in consequence, the Church suffered a great deal of oppression and persecution at the hands both of Russia and Prussia in the nineteenth century. Austria, being a Catholic Power, behaved differently, at least since her Concordat with the Pope in 1855. The rise of a reunited and free Poland after the World War found the Catholic Church placed in very different legal and economic conditions in the three sectors. The Constitution of the new Polish Republic, while guaranteeing religious toleration to all recognized denominations, acknowledged the traditional importance of Catholicism by granting it a leading position among the religious communities in the country. But in view of widely different political opinions among Poland's legislators and rulers as to the proper relations between Church and State it was only after several years of uncertainty and fluctuation that a *Concordat* between Poland and the Holy See (concluded on February 10, 1925), placed these relations on a settled footing.

To begin with, the administrative division of Poland into ecclesiastical territories was rearranged, and the frontiers of the five large ecclesiastical provinces of the country were so drawn as to obliterate the artificial boundaries set up by the partitioning powers. On the other hand, the dioceses on Poland's border were made conterminous with the territories of the Republic, and new dioceses were established where necessary, so as to make Polish citizens independent of foreign ecclesiastical jurisdiction. The Archbishop of Gniezno (in former Prussian Poland) once more holds the position of Primate, as had been the case almost since the dawn of Polish history ; and once more, as before the partitions of Poland, a Papal Nuncio resides in Warsaw. The Government, under the provisions of the Concordat, has a right of veto on Church appointments, both high and low, and all clergymen are subject to the ordinary courts of justice. In comparison with citizens of the secular professions, they enjoy only one important privilege—that of freedom from conscription for active military service, except in the capacity of chaplains in war time. The teaching of religion is compulsory in all elementary and secondary schools, and Faculties of Catholic Divinity exist in all the universities. The existence and establishment of monastic congregations in Poland is under no Government check whatever, and, in consequence, many of them which were not tolerated by the partitioning powers are again active on Polish soil.

The Catholic Church, in all its secular and monastic branches had been among the largest owners of land and buildings in the old Poland. Much of this property had, in the nineteenth century, been taken away from the Church by Poland's foreign rulers. The Polish State becoming the inheritor of the partitioning powers with regard to former Church property, it was stipulated in the Concordat between Poland and the Vatican that the Polish Republic, by way of compensation for such property of the Church as is now in the hands of the State, is to provide out of Treasury funds for the sustenance of the clergy at least in the same measure as was done by the partitioning powers.

Such landed property of the Church as had not been confiscated by Poland's foreign rulers, is liable, in Poland itself, to diminution under the land reform law, the aim of which is to break up all large estates in favour of middle-sized peasant farms. In view of this, it was expressly stipulated in the Concordat that both parishes and bishoprics, as well as chapters, seminaries, monasteries, and convents are to be left in possession of certain guaranteed irreducible *minima* of land.

Such, roughly, are the present arrangements with regard to

the legal and the economic position of the Catholic Church in Poland. The other denominations represented among the population of Poland are, in the main, the religions of such racial and national minorities as the Germans, the Russians, the Ukrainians and the Jews, and will accordingly best be dealt with in connection with those minorities themselves.

10

Next to the Church, the *Law*, as a pillar of social order, claims some attention.

The new Poland's task in this domain was one of particular difficulty. In the case of other central and eastern European states reconstructed after the World War, the problem was one of extending to new territories a legal system prevailing throughout the main body of the country ; Poland alone had to grow together out of three large portions dominated by three different systems of law. And while those systems were all foreign, there was no national tradition of law to revert to, the Polish law of past ages being unadaptable to modern conditions. Legal notions and legal habits, being backed by the executive authority of the Government, have a way of becoming particularly rooted in the mentality of the people ; at the same time legal unity is vital as an outward expression of political consolidation.

The gravity and urgency of the problem was realized by Poland's Constituent Assembly in the very first months of its existence, and a " Commission of Codification," composed of University Professors and other eminent experts in law, was called into existence for the purpose of drafting codes of law which were to be given legal force by Parliament. This procedure suggested itself as the most appropriate one because the laws of the partitioning powers were all of them of the nature of " code law " (ultimately based on Roman law), and not " case law " of the English and American type.

The labours of the Commission naturally divided themselves into the two fundamental sections of civil and of criminal law, and within each section the work on codification had to be distinguished from that on legal procedure. Special sections had to be devoted to the important separate domains of commercial law and of the organization of judicature. Of the six groups of the Commission resulting from this division of tasks, two had at the end of the first ten years of the new Poland's existence completed its work, viz., those of penal procedure and of the organization of judicature.

Procedure in criminal cases, and the structure of courts of law of all kinds, are now uniform throughout Poland. On the other hand, the activities of the civil law group, covering a very wide field, developed into several distinct sections devoted to marriage, family and inheritance law, to the law concerning real property (including mining law), and to general civil obligations respectively.

It is the working-out of a great *civil code* for the new Poland which presents the greatest fundamental difficulties. The systems in force on the territory of the divided Poland were most widely divergent here.

Austria possessed an extremely antiquated civil code of 1811; Prussia, on the contrary, a very advanced modern one of 1900. In the Russian sector, the central Polish province was governed by a code of its own, going back to the Code of Napoleon and through it to pure Roman law, while in the eastern borderlands Russian civil law was in operation. The fusion of these differences into one system is all the more imperative as civil law enters, perhaps, more profoundly than any other law into all departments of the individual citizen's life. At the same time, Poland has to frame her new laws at a time when the thoroughly changed social conditions of the post-war era are causing a perfect ferment of reconsideration and revision of maxims and doctrines. To single out one capital problem of civil law as an example: the question of marriage law, and particularly of the respective functions of Church and State with regard to marriage and divorce, is most eagerly disputed and cannot easily be dissociated from the major political issue of the relations of Church and State. Such facts were bound to occasion delay in the preparation of the code in its final shape. In the meantime, the clash of three different systems of civil law on Polish soil called most urgently for provisional adjustment. Accordingly, two brief codes regulating private legal relations—one in inter-provincial, the other one in international cases—were drawn up first, and came into operation as early as 1921, before the task of drafting an elaborate and permanent civil code was taken in hand. The complete civil code has not yet emerged from the workshop of the Commission, but some urgently needed minor codes dealing with individual problems of real property, such as a copyright law, a law for the protection of inventions and trade-marks, and law against unfair competition, have been produced, and are actually in operation. In connection with them, we may mention another group of codes dealing with certain portions of commercial law : codes relating to bills of exchange, to cheques, to patents, to warehouses, to joint stock and limited liability companies, were all completed and passed before the first ten years were out, because the economic necessities of daily life clamoured for them.

Another kind of pressure is likely to hasten the completion of codes on certain larger aspects on civil law. In the large and important domain of the law of obligations, for instance, a strong tendency for unification on an international basis is manifesting itself throughout the world. Canada and several European States have already declared their readiness to adopt an international code of obligations when ready. A uniform international code of obligations could become the nucleus of a future " world civil code."

To return, however, to the realities of the Polish situation : it would seem natural that a code of procedure in civil litigations, the necessary concomitant of a code of civil law, could only be finished after the civil code itself. And yet the order was reversed, and a code of procedure in civil cases was ready by 1928, chiefly owing to the active interest taken in this subject by the first President of the Commission of Codification, the late Professor F. X. Fierich of the University of Cracow, who was an authority in this particular field.

In the same way, owing to the presence of eminent experts in the ranks of the Commission, a code of procedure in criminal cases—as has already been mentioned—actually preceded the completion of a code of penal law. In the sphere of penal law, there is, perhaps, even keener ferment and a more violent clash of opposed opinion throughout the world in our day than in that of civil law ; the preventive view of penal law is in conflict with the diehard doctrines of the old punitive school, and the principle of capital punishment is passionately disputed everywhere. Poland, in framing her own code, could not keep out of this turmoil, and accordingly had to wait for several years till a compromise between two different projects, drafted by equally eminent experts, was effected. But by 1930 this was achieved, and the final draft of the penal code was published by the Commission ; the draft of an additional code on misdemeanours was also completed and issued. The code officially came into operation in 1932. The Army has a penal code of its own, mainly based on that of pre-war Germany, and promulgated in 1928.

The work of the Commission is always submitted to the Ministry of Justice and sometimes passes also through the ordeal of examination by the principal legal organizations in the country. Finally, it must receive the legislative sanction of Parliament. Under these circumstances, the end of the labours of the Commission—with all the progress it has made —may not be as near as could be desired : the Commission has already survived its first President, Professor Fierich, who died in 1929. But it may be taken for certain even now, that the body of the new Poland's laws when completed, will be as well-matured and as thoroughly modern in spirit as the laws of any nation in the civilized world.

## II

To the remarks on the new Poland's laws, now in the making, a few words must be added on the apparatus for the *administration of justice*. As noted above, a uniform organization of the courts of law, and uniform systems of procedure in civil and in criminal cases, have recently superseded, all over Poland, the threefold arrangements left behind by the partitioning powers. The Army has also been in possession of a unified judicial system of its own since 1928.

Under the new uniform organization of courts of law, Poland possesses a graduated structure of communal, district, and provincial courts, crowned by a Supreme Court in Warsaw. Trial by jury is to be compulsory in all graver cases. The decisions of the Supreme Court in particularly doubtful instances are to be taken by a special quorum of seven judges to be entered in a " Book of Legal Maxims," which is to have the binding authority of precedent. At this point, then, the codified law of Poland passes into judge-made " case law " of the type familiar in Britain and America. In the inferior courts, facilities for ending a law-suit by conciliation without judgment are offered in all cases of lesser importance.

With regard to administrative control, the courts of the entire Republic are subject to the Minister of Justice ; but legal provision has been made for independence of the individual judges and fixity of their tenure of office, as well as for their dissociation from party politics. All the judges of the higher grades are appointed by the President of the Republic. Only local justices of the peace (an institution which existed under Russia) are to be elected by the population ; and the judges in commercial courts are nominated by the Chambers of Commerce and appointed by the Minister for a term of three years.

A number of courts are concerned with public as distinguished from private law, and must be mentioned separately because of their international and national importance. Such are for international affairs : the Court of International Justice at The Hague (on whose bench Poland is represented by Professor M. Rostworowski, of Cracow University) ; the Polish-German Mixed Arbitration Tribunal in Paris, set up by virtue of the Versailles Peace Treaty ; the Polish-German Arbitration Tribunal for Silesia at Beuthen (Bytom) ; and a Polish-Czechoslovak Arbitration Tribunal agreed upon in 1925. Within Poland, there exists a Supreme Administrative Tribunal for the redress of grievances occasioned by actions of the administrative authorities ; a " Competence Tribunal " for settling disputes between the administrative authorities and the ordinary courts ; and a Tribunal of State (composed of senators and deputies, and presided over by the Chief Justice of the Supreme Court) for the trial of Ministers who are impeached. Members of Parliament, according to the Polish Constitution, enjoy legal immunity not only with regard to their political activities, but to all other actions : they are sometimes extradited, by Parliamentary vote, to the ordinary courts, to be tried for specified offences, or, in other cases, are tried by their peers in a specially constituted Parliamentary Court.

Of the Polish *prison system*, the worst reports have been circulated abroad by hostile propaganda, and it took repeated visits of eminent foreign experts to disprove and refute them. The prisons on Polish soil were taken over by the Polish State from the partitioning powers in overcrowded and partly very backward condition. Uniform reorganization was ultimately achieved only in the form of a Presidential decree of 1928. It included, as its principal improvements, universal provision for medical treatment, educational facilities, and the organization of manual labour. Solitary confinement is now limited to the initial stage of the sentence, and release before the appointed time is rendered admissible in case of good behaviour. The labour of prisoners is paid for both in money (which is being saved up during their imprisonment) and in kind (by increased food rations). Teaching in prison schools is compulsory for the imperfectly educated ; libraries, lectures, radio auditions and instructive cinema performances are provided ; so are opportunities for gymnastics. Well-equipped hospitals exist in all the larger prisons, and infirmaries in all. Apart from household work in the prison itself, prisoners are employed, in increasing numbers, in special workshops organized in the prisons. The output of these has lately risen so rapidly, that it has even given occasion for serious complaints from artisans

and manufacturers against the unfair competition of cheap
prison labour. Particular care has been devoted to the organization of prisons for juvenile offenders ; these, together with the
Juvenile Courts in larger cities, form a thoroughly modern and
highly humanitarian feature of Poland's legal system. Both
juvenile and adult prisoners enjoy the protection of special
Committees of Citizens, which are concerned with their welfare
during imprisonment, and assist them in finding employment
and starting normal life anew after their release.

### 12

Poland having regained her independent existence during a
great war, the *Army* was naturally and necessarily one of the
first organs of the State to come into being ; but, equally
naturally, under Poland's peculiar conditions, the beginnings of
the formation of Polish armed forces in the course of the World
War were desultory and unco-ordinated. Some account of
these early efforts has been given in a former chapter ; the
united Polish Army, hastily shaped out of them under the
pressure of danger to the new-born State, stood a fierce test in
the Bolshevik War of 1920, during which it grew to nearly one
million soldiers. But it was only in the course of the years
of peace which have followed since, that leisure could be found
to give the Army its definite organization.

Conscription is in Poland, as in most other Continental
European countries, the basis of military organization, and
was established as such by a law of 1924. The term of service
under the colours is two years, which tends to become reduced
to eighteen or even fifteen months, especially in the case of
soldiers with a secondary school education. This shortening of the
period of active service is rendered possible by the wide extent to
which preliminary military training, as part of physical education, is practised in the schools. A large Central Institute of
Physical Education superintends the whole of this work, which,
incidentally, has done much of late to raise the standard of the
efficiency of Poland's youth in sports and all kinds of bodily
exercise.

In the field of military training proper, it was no easy task
to set up one uniform Polish type in place of the distinct military
traditions of Germany, Austria and Russia, in which most of
the organizers of the Polish Army had grown up. The experience of the Bolshevik War in 1920 having laid the foundation, a French Military Mission, established in Poland for
several succeeding years, gave much assistance in further

systematic development. At present, the Polish Army is, and has been for several years past, entirely independent of foreign help, and its programme and methods of training, as well as its organization into groups, and its hierarchy of command, can be described as firmly settled.

Apart from its essential task, which consists in the military education of the conscript, it was realized at an early date that the Army in the new Poland would have a large task before it in the way of supplementary adult education. It was only on the occasion of military service that large numbers of illiterates from the more backward and out-of-the-way villages of the former Russian sector, especially from the eastern borderlands, came to the notice of the authorities at all. At the very beginning of the new Poland's existence in 1919, courses of instruction for soldiers were made compulsory throughout the Army, and ever since that time thousands of conscripts, beginning their active service as illiterates, have been leaving it able to read and write. About 100,000 soldiers are profiting, year in year out, by educational courses. Besides the three R's, these courses include the elements of civic education, with the necessary data from history and geography. They are supplemented by soldiers' clubs, which exist in every unit, and offer reading in the form of books and periodicals, also theatrical performances, concerts, lectures, and various social amenities.

For purposes of education for the military profession as such, Poland now possesses a fairly large number of schools for the training of N.C.O.'s as well as " Cadet Corps " (on the level of secondary schools) whose graduates proceed to Officers' Training Schools, differentiated according to the branches of the service. Apart from these, there are officers' courses for the acquisition of special accomplishments, as well as courses preliminary to promotion to the higher ranks. The road to the promotion of N.C.O.'s to officers' rank lies open through an " Officers' School for professional N.C.O.'s." The entire edifice of military education is crowned by a Staff College in Warsaw, with a two years' course for officers aspiring to service on the General Staff.

With regard to the organization of the Army for the purposes of its active service, it can only be stated here in a general way that the obvious prospect of " field warfare " rather than " trench warfare " under Poland's peculiar conditions (as illustrated by the Bolshevik War) induced the organizers of the Army to give the greatest possible measure of independence

K

and self-sufficiency even to such smaller units as regiments. Thus, an infantry regiment in particular, by the provision of light tanks and small field guns as well as heavy machine guns, is rendered fit to conduct isolated operations. Another lesson of the 1920 war consists in the certainty it gives that cavalry—which, in Poland as in Hungary, had been the most favoured and representative branch of the service down the centuries—will remain important for the defence of Poland, even if it should become more or less extinct in the west. Again, in the case of artillery, territorial conditions and the state of the roads forbid, for a long while to come, the use of motor traction in Poland on anything like the scale on which it has, since the World War, become accepted in the western countries. Aircraft, which had its glorious chapters in the wars of 1918–1920,[1] had to be created, under the utmost difficulties, out of nothing, and so had its subsidiary industries ; a " League for Air and Anti-Gas Defence " (*L.O.P.P.*) has become a popular institution among the civilian population, and is supported out of millions of pockets which can ill spare the sacrifice—another striking proof of the feeling of insecurity which, twelve years after the Peace, still hangs over vast regions of Europe.

The Polish *Navy*, so far, consists of about a dozen small-sized vessels, including two destroyers, for service on the Baltic, and a few monitors for service on the larger rivers, on which, indeed, they proved very useful in the war of 1920. The rapid increase in volume of Poland's sea-borne trade and of her commercial fleet will necessitate a corresponding increase of her small Navy for the protection of her strip of sea-coast, unless international agreements at last open up an era of greater security in the near future.

## 13

In connection with the Army and Navy, the *Police Force*, which is organized on a military basis, calls for brief mention. In this field Poland was confronted by one of those grave psychological tasks which are typical of her exceptional situation. While the idea of a reborn Polish Army could not fail to rouse the highest enthusiasm among all ranks of the population, the Army having been associated with some of Poland's most glorious achievements in history, the very notion of the police, on the other hand, had become, during the century of Poland's captivity, distasteful to every Pole, since the police

---

[1] In 1920 the " Kościuszko Squadron " of U.S. airmen did unforgettable auxiliary service to Poland.

of the partitioning powers—and particularly of Russia—was the foremost, and in many ways the vilest, instrument of Poland's oppression. The creators of the Army had but to appeal to a cherished national tradition : although that tradition had been interrupted ever since the last armed rising of 1863—for more than half a century, that is—and professional service in the Armies of the partitioning powers had been more or less boycotted, volunteers for Polish military formations during the World War were easily found, and its end found Poland in possession of a small body of experienced and seasoned soldiers, who were looked up to by the people. In the case of the police, on the other hand, a solidly established prejudice had to be overcome, and confidence in the new Force as well as respect for it had to be created out of nothing. Civic constabularies, hastily organized in war-time in various Polish cities (including Warsaw) when abandoned by the foreign occupants, to some extent paved the way ; but they were improvised and casual bodies, not fit to originate a new tradition. In 1919, a legal foundation was laid for the unification of the Police Force throughout the Republic ; nine years later, 1928, the process was completed by a Presidential decree on the ultimate organization of the Force.

The police is organized on military lines, being composed of privates, N.C.O.'s, subalterns, and staff officers ; administratively, it is subject to the Ministry of the Interior, being distributed over the larger and smaller administrative units of territory (counties, districts, boroughs, communes), while in its executive capacity it acts as an organ of the Courts of Justice and the Public Prosecutors.

There were three factors which contributed to the growth of prestige of the Polish police and to the development of popular affection for it. The first was the fact that in organizing the police, the best and most authoritative system in the world— the British Police—was taken for a model (of which every visitor to Poland is reminded by the cut and the dark-blue colour of the uniforms of Polish policemen). A second and more important fact, imprinted on national memory, is the truly heroic record of Poland's police in its struggle against violence and crime in the first unruly years after the War : many policemen laid down their lives for the cause of law and order in fighting banditism in town and country, solemn services for their souls are reverently held every year, and literature has not stinted them their meed of praise, placing them next to the gallant soldiers who fell in the field. Third, and no less important, there stands to the credit of Poland's Police Force the remarkable development of special schools for the officers and men of the Force in recent years. Together with this, there goes progressive specialization in the functions of different sections of the body : besides criminal police and traffic police, there is a seaside and a river police, a police attending to public morals, and, inevitably, a secret political police fighting both foreign espionage and the worse bane of Communist propaganda.

Midway between the police and the Army there stands a military organ whose arduous and highly responsible service is looked upon with particular favour by Polish public opinion, viz., the *Frontier Corps*. During the first years after the Riga Peace Treaty between Poland and the Bolsheviks, it was part of the Soviets' consistent policy to organize incursions into Poland's eastern border territory by troops of irregulars, whose depredations caused a great deal of distress and unrest. Since 1924–5 the whole of the eastern frontier line, nearly 1,000 miles in length, has been guarded by a special Corps of several brigades, whose characteristic wooden barracks and watch-towers all along the border have become popular symbols of effective protection. By developing educational activities and organizing social amenities, not only for its own soldiers, but for the population of the neighbourhood, the posts of the Frontier Corps have become true " outposts of culture " among the backward and forlorn inhabitants of the vast, sparsely peopled and inaccessible eastern border regions. Sanitary services and social relief are among the benefits conferred by the guardians of the frontier upon their neighbours ; in fact, this picked body of troops nobly and worthily upholds the age-old civilizing mission of Poland in that part of Europe.

An analogous Force for the protection of the southern and particularly of the western frontier (on which incidents with armed bodies of German nationalists have unfortunately become frequent of late years) has been in existence since 1928, and is exercising its functions side by side with the Customs Guard, which is an organization of rather civilian type, as in other European countries.

## 14

It remains to supplement the above outline of the administrative framework of the Polish State by some account of its *foreign representation*. Here, again, everything had to be practically stamped out of the ground at a moment's warning.

The diplomatic career, like the higher ranks of the Army, had been almost entirely closed to Poles under Russia and Prussia ; nor did the Austrian sector supply any considerable number of trained diplomats. At the same time the most vital international interest of the new-born Republic clamoured for representation ; accordingly, a Diplomatic Service was knocked together in the first months of 1919, and before the year was out, hundreds of thousands of cases concerning the rights of citizens of the new Poland in foreign countries had been attended to. The activities of the new Polish Diplomatic Corps had been prepared by preliminary organizations in war-time : the Regency Council established in Warsaw under German occupation, had had its representatives in Vienna, Berlin and (later) in Moscow ; the Polish Committee in Paris had laid the foundation for a Polish representation in London ; and on the neutral ground of Switzerland, of Holland and of Sweden, Polish representatives from both sides of the front had met. During 1919 and 1920 these nuclei were developed into full-grown Legations and Consulates, and new ones established in the more important capitals. The rising international prestige of Poland in later years brought with it the transformation of some of the Legations into Embassies. To-day, there are Polish Ambassadors in London, Washington, Paris and Rome (one at the Vatican and one at the Quirinal), and Polish Ministers in twenty-five other capitals. The Republic, apart from Consular Departments in many of the Legations, possesses twenty Consulates-General and some forty Consulates of other grades, besides honorary Consuls in many cities. The Polish representation at the seat of the League of Nations stands in a category by itself. Candidates for the Diplomatic Service in Poland now receive their training mostly in the Faculties of Law of Poland's universities, and in the Schools of Political Science connected with the Universities of Warsaw and Cracow. The duties of the diplomatic and the consular representative abroad are to-day considerably larger in extent than they were in former times : they cover, in fact, not only the entire field of the nation's political and economic interests, but include the proper presentation to foreign nations of all its productive activities, both material and spiritual. The practice of what is somewhat unfortunately called " cultural propaganda " through diplomatic channels is universal and highly developed in our days, and Poland is making every effort to keep pace in this respect with other Powers, some of whom have brought considerable amounts both of money and of brain-power into play to stir up anti-Polish feeling in western Europe and in America. Among the means employed outside the diplomatic field to spread a better knowledge of Poland in foreign countries, an important place is held by lecture tours of scholars and scientists, and by the creation of chairs of Polish history and literature in foreign universities ; it is among the proudest recollections of the present writer that he has had the privilege to serve as such an " intellectual ambassador " of his country for a time, first in British, and then in American universities.

## 15

From the particular aspects of Poland's administrative structure we may now, in conclusion, turn our eyes to the summit of the fabric, and consider briefly the *supreme executive and legislative powers* in the State.

As related in a former chapter, Poland, since 1926, has been in fact, if not in form, under dictatorial government, and a thoroughgoing revision of the Parliamentary Constitution of the Republic is under discussion. Under these circumstances, all that can be done here is to give a brief account of the order of things as established by the Constitution given to Poland by her Constituent Assembly on March 17, 1921, and of those changes in the system which have actually become law since the *coup d'état* of Marshal Piłsudski in May, 1926. Some of these details have, indeed, been anticipated in the historical outline of political events given previously ; but they are summed up once more at the end of the present descriptive chapter for the sake of convenient reference.

The Constitution of March 17, 1921, drafted by some of Poland's foremost legal experts, but very thoroughly amended in essential points by the Constituent Assembly, bases *Parliamentary Representation* on the principle of universal adult suffrage both of men and women, the voting age being 21 for the Lower and 30 for the Upper House of Parliament. Eligibility begins at 25 for the one and at 40 for the other. The Lower House counts 444, the Upper one 111 members, all of them elected. The mode of election (modelled on the Belgian *scrutin de liste* system) imposes on the elector not the choice between individual candidates who are to represent his constituency, but between several lists of candidates proposed by the political parties. Proportional representation being an essential part of the system, the passage of part of the candidates on lists which command a minority of electors, is secured, and the device of " national lists " besides " district " ones affords further security for the representation of bodies of minority electors scattered over different districts.

In Parliament, the powers of the Lower House (called by its historical name of *Seym* or " Diet ") considerably surpass those of the Upper House, or Senate. An amendment introduced into a *Seym* bill by the Senate—and, according to some interpreters of the Constitution, even the wholesale rejection of such a bill in Senate—may be voted down by an eleven-twentieths majority of the *Seym* ; and the Senate is deprived of the power of originating bills itself, or of appointing Committees to investigate selected problems. Nor has the Senate the right to impeach Ministers ; and a declaration of war requires consent of the *Seym*, but not of the Senate.

The *President of the Republic* is elected (as in France) by a National Assembly composed of the two Houses of Parliament together. His tenure of office is seven years. His powers are strictly limited. Treaties concluded by him on behalf of the Republic with foreign Powers require ratification by Parliament ; all legal acts signed and published by him must be countersigned by a Minister ; he has no right of veto over parliamentary legislation ; he may be impeached by the vote of a three-fifths majority of the *Seym*, and is then made responsible before the Tribunal of State. Ministers are responsible to Parliament, not to the President.

The responsibility of *Ministers* is twofold : collective and individual. Parliamentary responsibility operates in the way common in other countries, resignation being the necessary consequence of an adverse vote in Parliament. The conditions for impeachment of Ministers are the same as in the case of the President. As at present constituted (after some fluctuations), Poland possesses eleven *Ministerial Departments*, viz., those of Foreign Affairs, Home Affairs, Military Affairs, Finance, Justice, Education and Denominations, Trade and Industry, Agriculture and Agrarian Reform, Labour and Social Welfare, Communications, and Posts and Telegraphs. Something like a Department by itself is also formed by the Prime Minister's office and staff.

Under the Constitution of 1921, the President had no right to dissolve Parliament. This important right was given him by a bill of 1926, shortly after Marshal Piłsudski's *coup d'état*. The same bill conferred on him the right of legislation by Presidential decree, subject to subsequent ratification by both Chambers. The bill also limited the time for the *Seym's* discussion of the budget to three and a half months and the Senate's to thirty days, after which the budget, even if not formally passed by the Houses, is to become law in the form proposed by the Government. In case of dissolution of the Chambers before the passing of the budget, the Government is authorized to collect revenue and incur expenditure within the limits of the budget for the preceding year.

Such was the constitutional *status quo* in 1926, which has indeed since been still further modified in practice, but which (at the moment when these lines are being written) still awaits formal modification by a legal change of Poland's Constitution.

## CHAPTER VI

## MINORITY PROBLEMS

### I

WHEN the World War brought the question of a thorough rearrangement of the map of Europe up for discussion, it was recognized as an axiom that the principle of *nationality* would have to serve as the general foundation of these changes. This was natural in view of the dominant developments of the era preceding the War. The nineteenth century had been the age of the growth of modern nationalism. The great idea of democracy, striving towards realization in all parts of the European Continent in consequence of the French Revolution, implied not only equality of rights as between the individuals of any given community, but also, by an extension of its application, equality of rights as between national units in the comity of nations. This democratic tendency to grant to smaller and politically dependent nations equality of opportunity with the great and free ones, was reinforced by the powerful movement of romanticism in early nineteenth-century European literature and thought : it was one of the principal aspirations of romanticism to awaken interest and respect for all the varieties of national self-expression in art, and to raise the poetic and artistic manifestations of the common people to equal estimation with the individual productions of cultured artists. The study of folk-poetry and folk-lore became an important contributory factor in the development of the sense of nationality.

But far more important than these intellectual currents were certain hard facts of social evolution which affected especially the growth of nationalism in eastern Europe. The emancipation of large peasant masses by the abolition of serfdom led, first, to the gradual acquisition of property by the peasant farmer, and then to a struggle for social privilege and for the higher education which was the road to it.

As a result of this, we witness the emergence of a class of peasant-born *intelligentsia*—at first in the shape of clergymen, afterwards also of teachers, lawyers, doctors and other professionally educated laymen—among large and hitherto mostly inarticulate peasant races. The new class, ambitious for leadership, gave a political voice of its own to a people which had so far been paternally governed by country gentlemen of another stock, and the outside world was made aware, to its surprise, of the existence of another nationality of which it had not heard before, but which had apparently for hundreds of years lived obscurely on the soil.

It was in this way that national differences became multiplied or at least intensified, and that new problems and conflicts arose in out-of-the-way parts of Europe during the later nineteenth century. Keeping this origin of new national movements in mind, we shall also understand why the task of rearranging Europe on the basis of nationality, when undertaken by the peacemakers after the World War, did not prove at all so simple in practice as the simplicity of the formula had made it appear. It remained to be discovered by statesmen unfamiliar with the local history of the regions concerned, that, in consequence of repeated territorial changes in past ages, districts of mixed race and speech were a frequent phenomenon on the Continent, differences of social rank or of religious tradition sometimes adding emphasis to the difference of nationality and increasing the gravity of the problem. Apart from the existence of these mixed districts, it was also perceived that in some cases it would not be feasible to carve a nationally homogeneous political unit out of a larger composite fabric, because such a unit was obviously unfit to lead an independent life, either on account of its small size, of its impracticable territorial configuration, or of its economic structure.

In view of these complications, sometimes, the plebiscite was resorted to as an ultimate means of asserting, by majority vote, the principle of nationality; in other cases, compromises were entered into either with economic necessities or with territorial traditions of the past. In this manner, the break-up of the most composite and variegated Empire of pre-war time, viz., Austria-Hungary, gave rise to a Czechoslovakia in which the total of non-Czech elements—Germans, Slovaks, Hungarians and Poles—surpasses the Czech population; to a Yugoslav kingdom of three nations in place of the old national unit of Serbia; to an enlarged Rumania with considerable proportions of non-Rumanian population in its border provinces.

## 2

Poland's case was a similar one. In order not to disappear again too soon between the two millstones of Russia and Germany, the rebuilt Polish State had to assume a shape somewhat reminiscent of the Poland of past centuries, although not equal to it in size.

This once admitted, it was unavoidable that in place of the terrible problem of a dismembered and oppressed Poland which had haunted Europe's diplomatic chancelleries so long, the problems of a reunited Poland should in turn occupy the attention of that new world forum, the League of Nations. Poland does not by any means stand alone in the post-war world in having serious problems of mixed national composition to grapple with, nor are those problems new to her own historical experience. The old Polish-Lithuanian Monarchy had struggled for nearly two centuries with the task of welding Poland and Lithuania into a political whole ; it had been obliged, for over a century, to resort again and again to armed expeditions to enforce the loyalty of the German burghers of Danzig, highly profitable as the connection with Poland was to them : it had seen the Ukrainian Cossacks change from a tool of Polish border policy into a cause of ruinous domestic trouble and foreign war ; it had vainly striven to harmonize Eastern with Roman Christianity within its frontiers, and ultimately furnished, by these religious complications, a pretext for Russian intervention.

With all this, however, the task of dealing with non-Polish elements within Poland's political system was in past centuries made comparatively simple by the fact that this was still the era of dynastic policies and unawakened national aspirations. The populations of whole provinces, according to the views then prevailing all over Europe, were so much passive human material for Empire-building ; the nobility of the Lithuanian and Ruthenian lands of the Monarchy were attracted by the prospect of equal political privileges with the governing class of Poland, and, sharing them, in due time adopted Polish culture and speech.

It was a totally different situation by which Poland, coming into renewed existence in our democratic age, found herself confronted in those very same eastern provinces which had been her principal " minority territories " in the past. And in addition to the portion which she regained of these, Poland in acquiring, on the western side, her section of Silesia, was enlarged by part of a province originally Polish indeed, but subject for many centuries to the strongest German influences and thickly scattered with compact groups of Germans in the towns. With national susceptibilities roused to a feverish pitch everywhere after the War, Poland, with roughly one-third of her citizens non-Polish in speech and race, had indeed, in this question, one of her largest and most difficult political tasks before her. And the difficulty was not lessened by the fact that she was made to sign, at Versailles, a somewhat humiliating special convention guaranteeing the rights of minorities within her borders, and that afterwards, besides the watchful protection of the League of Nations, frequent visits of foreign journalists and politicans kept the cause of the minorities in Poland constantly before the world's eyes. After the few short years which have elapsed since the territorial consolidation of the new Polish State, Poland's record in the matter of fusing her national minorities into a working political whole with the Polish majority is certainly far less satisfactory than her constructive achievements in other fields. But this will not be wondered at by those who realize to some extent the gigantic dimensions and terrible urgency of the tasks of economic reconstruction, administrative organization, and social legislation which Poland has had to shoulder during these same first years of her new existence. And it must also be considered that the restless fluctuation of shifting parliamentary coalitions which produced Poland's numerous early Cabinets, as well as the unstable tenure of local administrative office under these conditions of parliamentary government, were not at all favourable to the maintenance of any consistent line of minority policy. On the whole it may be said that before Marshal Piłsudski's *coup d'état* in 1926 the prevailing tendency was to devise the legislative and administrative means for the assimilation of the national minorities to the body of the Polish population, while since that time the dominant aim seems to be rather to conciliate them by liberal treatment of their claims to distinctness in social and cultural arrangements. If definite steps towards provincial self-government of some of the minorities have failed so far to be taken, the reason is to be sought in the atmosphere of passionate excitement which still surrounds all national problems in post-war Europe, as well as in the connection which exists between Poland's minority problems and the very gravest aspects of her international situation.

3

The minority group which is numerically the most important in Poland, is constituted by the *Ukrainians*. Some account of the historical antecedents of the Ukrainian problem has been given in previous chapters. The province known in modern times by its Austrian name of " Eastern Galicia " had since the dawn of Polish history—as far back as 1000 A.D.—been a bone of contention between Poland and the old South Russian Empire, which centred round Kiev. It was alternately under the rule of Polish monarchs and of South Russian territorial princes of the same Rurik dynasty which ruled the Kiev State. This territorial dynasty becoming extinct in the middle of the fourteenth century, the province was definitely included in Poland and remained part of it for four centuries, until the partitions. On her border, provinces to the east and north, whose population partly spoke the same dialect (represented by the Ukrainian language of to-day) and partly White Ruthenian, were added to the Polish political system in the later fourteenth century. In consequence of the spread of the Roman Catholicism and of Polish culture in those provinces as well as of the expansion of Polish institutions to them, the borderlands, in the course of centuries, assumed a purely Polish complexion as far as the aristocracy, the gentry and the urban population were concerned. Polish colonization of the countryside was conducted but fitfully and never became a systematic development ; the bulk of the country population, accordingly, retained its racial distinctness and continued to speak its dialects, which were akin to Russian.

The difference in language and in social status between the Polish and non-Polish elements in the border provinces was reinforced by a difference in religion. Roman Catholicism, advancing eastward, found established in those lands the eastern European type of Christianity, which had originated in Byzantium, and which afterwards developed into the National Church of Russia. This difference in religion meant much more than distinctions in creed and ritual. Eastern Slav alphabets (the old Church Slavonic, modern Russian, Ukrainian, Serbian, Bulgarian one), based on Greek instead of the Latin letters of the European west, which Poles and Czechs had adopted for their languages ; the Greek tongue, and in later stages the ancient Slavonic, in place of the cosmopolitan Latin of the west ; Byzantine vestments, rites, church architecture and religious art, all of them in acute contrast with the outward trappings of religion common to western Europe : such were the visible symbols of a profound spiritual difference which separated the petrified, hierarchical Greek culture of the Byzantine Empire, lying at the foundation of eastern Christianity, from the living, adaptable internationalism of the Roman Catholic civilization, uniting the western European world of the Middle Ages into a true League of Nations. This deep difference, grounded in religion, afterwards found political expression in the contrast between the absolute monarchy of Russia and the parliamentary system of Poland : the gulf fixed between Polish and Russian mentality since their historical beginnings, deepened with time, and it is only a natural consequence of this development that the Poles, in later times, came to occupy a somewhat isolated position among Slavonic nations by their thorough aversion to every idea of Slavonic unity under Russian protection.

Let us, however, return to the problem of the Greek Christians in the eastern border provinces of the historical Polish-Lithuanian Monarchy. In spite of the intense penetration of all the lands of the monarchy by Roman Catholicism, it became evident in the course of the fifteenth and early sixteenth century that the absorption of the entire populations of Poland's vast eastern and south-eastern borderlands by the Catholic system could not be considered as practical politics. In view of this, the Jesuits, that most potent factor working for Christian reunion in the Catholic fold during the era of the Counter-Reformation, devised a compromise in the form of the " Uniat Church " for Poland's eastern provinces. That Church, definitedly created at the Synod of Brześć (Brest) in 1596, retained the ritual and outward apparatus of Greek Orthodoxy, but owned allegiance to Rome. It was intended to serve the ends not only of religious unity with the west, but of political cohesion within Poland's political system : the eastern Christians of the border provinces were now definitely withdrawn from the orbit of the Russian Church, which was becoming a political instrument of Tsardom.

The Uniat Church, throughout the later centuries of the old Poland's existence, served its original purposes indifferently well ; it would have done so even better if Uniats and Disuniats had not continued to exist side by side in the eastern provinces, and if the jealousy of Roman Catholic prelates and magnates had not kept Uniat dignitaries from their due share of political privileges.

It was only in recent times, however, with the modern growth of a distinct Ukrainian nationalism, that the Uniat Church was to become the Church militant of a national movement opposed to Russia and Poland alike.

4

During the period of Poland's division and subjection, the fate both of Ukrainianism and of the Uniat Church was very different under the different partitioning powers.

Something has been said in a previous chapter of the way in which Austria fostered Ukrainian nationalism so as to turn it into a political force counterbalancing the Polish element in the province of Galicia, and ultimately even turning the area of Galician self-government into a perpetual battle-ground. In consonance with this policy, the Uniat Church, in the Austrian sector, enjoyed the protection and favour of the Government.

Russia's Ukrainian policy was exactly the reverse. It was in the Russian sector that Ukrainianism, as a national movement had had, early in the nineteenth century, its literary hero in the person of the poet, Taras Shevchenko. But Russian imperialism never allowed Ukrainian separatism to manifest itself in any other way than as a harmless interest in the rich folklore and popular art of the southern regions. Politically, the Ukrainians were treated as an inseparable branch of the great Russian stock, which was indicated even by their Russian official name of " Little Russians." The Uniat Church was gradually suppressed in favour of Russian orthodoxy, a beginning being made as far back as the 'thirties of the nineteenth century by the apostasy of a Uniat bishop, Semashko, and a body of clergy who followed his example. In later decades, the country people who clung to their Uniat tradition—especially in the centre and the north-east of the border belt—were cruelly persecuted by the Russian authorities ; even massacres of whole congregations during service happened from time to time until nearly the end of the century. The devotion of the Uniats to their cause was stimulated by secret missions of clergymen from the Austrian sector. The moral fruitlessness of religious persecution—so often demonstrated in history—was made magnificently manifest when, in 1905, during the short " False Dawn " of constitutional life in Russia, religious tolerance temporarily prevailed, and immediately 200,000 Uniats, forcibly registered as Greek Orthodox, declared their Uniat allegiance. But it must be admitted that large masses of population remained in the Orthodox fold, into which a whole generation had summarily and arbitrarily been transferred in the 'thirties.

With regard to the relations between the Ukrainian and the

Polish element, the difference between conditions under Austrian and under Russian rule had the paradoxical effect that, while under Austria political antagonism developed between the Poles and the Uniat clergy as the vanguard of Ukrainian nationalist opposition, under Russia the community of persecution produced a certain amount of sympathy between Polish Catholics and Ukrainian Uniats on the border. But whatever kindly feelings grew up on the common ground of political and religious suffering, they were thwarted by the rooted old social enmity between the poor Ukrainian cottager and the Polish landlord in the manor. When the fire of Bolshevism touched this age-old fuel of class animosity, a terrible " blaze " of savage peasant riots flared up in all the border districts formerly governed by Russia, and ruthlessly consumed the property of Polish landlords as well as the lives of many of them.[1]

## 5

Such were the antecedents of the new Poland's rule over her Ukrainian minority. The delimitation of the eastern frontier by the Riga Peace Treaty in 1921 placed within Poland's borders the whole of what had been Austrian Eastern Galicia, and of the former Russian territories adjoining it on the northern side, the predominantly Ukrainian-speaking province of Volhynia, together with Ukrainian districts in some neighbouring ones. The number of Ukrainians in Eastern Galicia is, in round figures, three millions out of a total of five, in Volhynia and around it well over a million.

Throughout these provinces they are in a majority ranging from two-thirds and less to three-fourths and more of the population. The Poles everywhere form an appreciable minority, rarely falling beneath 20 per cent. in any neighbourhood ; in some districts of former Eastern Galicia they are in the majority, particularly in its principal city, Lwów, which is 85 per cent. Polish.

Polish rule found those profound differences in existence which have already been hinted at as arising between the two sectors of Ukrainian territory out of the different methods of Austrian and Russian policy. The Galician Ukrainians, well organized politically and educationally, in possession of an educated class of lay leaders, were prepared for active and

[1] See *Blaze* (Polish, *Pożoga*) a vivid and most pathetic account of these events by the distinguished Polish woman writer *Mm. Sophia Szczucka*, herself the daughter of a country gentleman in Volhynia and witness of what she describes (English translation, Allen & Unwin, London, 1925).

persistent opposition to Polish administration : they began it by a war in 1918 (for which retreating Austria had left the weapons in their hands) and have since continued it by a variety of means, from boycott of parliamentary elections to tactics of obstruction in Parliament itself, and from attempts upon the lives of Polish Government representatives to campaigns of open violence in the countryside, such as the epidemic of rick-burning and general sabotage in 1930, which had to be drastically suppressed by military force.

The Ukrainians in Volhynia, in spite of active propaganda conducted from former Galicia, have to a large extent remained nationally inert, being not only without an educated class so far, but in fact largely illiterate. The Uniat Church cannot play its part among them because, in consequence of decades of Russian anti-Uniat policy, they are mostly Greek Orthodox. This implies an attachment to Russia, recently transformed by Bolshevik propaganda even into sympathies for the Soviets. The opposition of the Volhynian peasantry to Polish rule has not been active, like the Galician Ukrainians', but their sullen passive resistance has caused many a serious difficulty.

Three factors in the Ukrainian situation have made Poland's handling of it a particularly arduous task. The first of them consists in the continuance of Germany's pre-war policy of material and moral support to the Galician Ukrainians' anti-Polish efforts. This makes itself felt particularly whenever the Ukrainian problem in Poland comes up for international discussion, whether in the League of Nations or elsewhere. Ukrainian nationalism is also supported—for somewhat different reasons —by Czechoslovakia, who, by her acquisition of the Ukrainian-speaking districts on the southern slopes of the Carpathians (in former North Hungary), has stretched out an arm towards Russia along the southern border of Poland's Ukrainian province.

The second factor, which also strengthens the Ukrainian position, is constituted by the relation between the Uniat Church and Rome. The ambitious head of the Uniat clergy in Galicia—Archbishop Szeptycki (descended of a Polish noble family, and appointed in Austrian times with a view to conciliation) has succeeded in finding particular favour with the Vatican by holding out to it the prospect of the reunion of the whole of Russia with the Roman Church. The same prospect, it will be remembered, was skilfully opened up by a Russian Tsar of the sixteenth century, and then caused the Vatican to induce a King of Poland to stop midway on his victorious progress into Russia. Now it is productive of displays of

L

special sympathies of the Vatican for the Uniat Church, which are, of course, immediately exploited by the Ukrainian leaders in a political sense.

But graver than both the above-named, there is a third factor which so far looms indistinctly if gigantically in the background, but may in the near future come decisively to the fore. This is the existence of a large Ukrainian Republic adjoining Poland's Ukrainian possessions across the Soviet border. Vast Ukrainian-speaking lands lie there (some of which belonged to the old Polish Monarchy) ; they stretch as far across the south of Russia as the Don and almost to the slopes of the Caucasus ; if erected into an independent State, they would form a large thirty-million unit including huge stretches of some of the most fertile soil in Europe, containing rich mineral resources, commanding the enormous water-power of the river Dnieper (now in course of electrification), occupying geographically a key position for trade, and possessing access to the Black Sea. No wonder that these territories are the favourite subject of Ukrainian nationalists' dreams of a great state, with the ancient capital of Kiev for its centre. A large portion of these lands was constituted by the Bolsheviks as a " Ukrainian Soviet Republic " (with Kharkov for its capital), forming one of the larger units in the Federation of Soviet Republics, which has replaced the Russian Empire. Professing to respect the principle of the " self-determination of nationalities," the Bolsheviks made a great display of the " Ukrainization " of the entire public service in that Republic, granting amplest scope to the use of the Ukrainian language in all branches of administration and education. In reality, it soon became apparent that strong centralist pressure on the whole system from the Russian capital remained, as under the Tsar, the order of the day. However, " Ukrainization," once proclaimed as a principle, has continued to develop even against the wishes of the Russian rulers, and in spite of their efforts to " get rid of the spirits which they called up," like the sorcerer's apprentice in Goethe's ballad. Now this may not mean much as long as the whole Soviet Union is a hell of economic distress and political tyranny, but when these evils relax, the Ukrainian Soviet Republic may one day assume the attractive colours of a rallying centre for what would then become the *Ukraina irredenta* on the Polish side. The Soviet Ukrainian Republic, then, must be considered as a standing warning signal for Poland, plainly indicating the truth that this period we live in is the very hour of Poland's historical opportunity with regard to her Ukrainian possessions : to produce a state of contentment and loyalty among her Ukrainian population is the best and only safeguard against the contingency hitherto but dimly adumbrated by the state of things across the Soviet border.

## 6

After numerous vicissitudes in the international treatment of the Ukrainian problem in the early post-war years, and after the recognition of Poland's sovereignty over her eastern provinces by the Ambassadors' Conference in 1923, the task of devising a scheme of provincial self-government for the domains inhabited by the Ukrainian minority remained as undefined, and as much of a puzzle for Poland's politicians as ever. In spite of its gravity and admitted urgency, no system could be determined on which would at least in a tolerable measure have satisfied both Polish and Ukrainian requirements. Every plan of a united apparatus for provincial representation and autonomous administration of the whole territory awakened concern in the Poles for the destinies of what would then be the Polish minority of the province ; on the other hand, plans of self-government organized by sections were met by the Ukrainian objection that they would, by the break-up of the Ukrainian element, nullify all its aspirations towards adequate representation, and would, besides, lead to endless friction and bureaucratic complications in the working.

While all such projects were being discussed, the territory in question remained—and has until now remained—organized, like the rest of Poland, into administrative units called by the old Polish name of "województwa" ("counties"): Eastern Galicia consists of three such counties, those of Lwów (Lemberg), Stanisławów and Tarnopol, and Volhynia forms another.

Within the counties, the Ukrainians possess the rights generally granted to national minorities in Poland : together with all the undiminished rights of the ordinary Polish citizen, they have, as a national group, the right to use their own language, not only in the inner and outward life of their organizations, but also in their official relations with local public authorities and courts of law. They also have the right to state-supported elementary schools in all localities where the parents of at least forty children of school age ask for instruction in the Ukrainian language. Besides these purely Ukrainian schools, there are others in which half the teaching is done in Ukrainian and half in Polish : these are established in places where, apart from the demand for teaching in Ukrainian on behalf of at least forty children, instruction in Polish is asked for on behalf of at least twenty. Altogether, the Ukrainians in Poland have 804 purely Ukrainian, state-supported public elementary schools; in 2120 elementary schools one-half of the teaching is in Ukrainian, and one-half in Polish; and in 1722 Polish schools Ukrainian is one of the subjects taught. Besides, there are seven government-supported Ukrainian secondary schools. The Ukrainian educational organizations, (mainly the large society called *Prosvita*—" Enlightenment ") support another 15 private secondary schools, but only 31 elementary ones, in view of the ample provision of elementary schools by the State. A Ukrainian University still remains a *desideratum*, as it was under Austria; plans for one, ever since Austrian times, have always encountered the opposition of the Polish element, not indeed against the idea in itself, but against the localization of the University in the city of Lwów, or what seems still worse to the Poles—against the change of the Polish University of Lwów into a bi-lingual one. Pending the debates on the location of the Ukrainian University, some headway has actually been made with the training of a staff for it, Poland's oldest University, Cracow, having lately admitted a number of Ukrainians among its lecturers. Many hundreds of Ukrainian students pursue their studies in Polish universities—mostly preferring Warsaw or Cracow to Lwów—and considerable numbers also study at Prague in Czechoslovakia. Extension university courses are being conducted in Ukrainian at Lwów itself by Ukrainian educational organizations; a central body for the promotion of Ukrainian research work in Poland exists in the *Shevchenko Society*.

## 7

After this brief account of the actual state of affairs, something remains to be said of the possible future of the political struggle. In order to form an estimate of it, some attention must be paid to questions of political tactics and of other than nationalist policies. Under Austria, the Poles in Galicia, in the later pre-war stages of the Ukrainian problem, found it politically expedient to enter into an alliance with a section of the Ukrainians which did not share the tenets of modern Ukrainian nationalism, but considered their people as a branch of the Russian nation. These " Old Ruthenians " of pre-war time have been succeeded by similar Ukrainian allies of the Poles in the new Poland, particularly a peasant party calling itself the " Bread-makers " (*Khliboroby*), and pursuing social and economic rather than political aims. The operation of such Polish measures of social legislation as the Land Reform Bill, calculated to increase the number of peasant proprietors, has been extended to Eastern Galicia, much land has in consequence passed into the hands of Ukrainian peasant owners, both through sale under the Act and through purchase in the open market, especially from that large land-owning body, the Uniat Church. Colonization of eastern territories by Polish ex-service men was for a time conducted by the Government, but not on a large scale, and without great success.

The political alliance of the Poles with the non-nationalist Ukrainian Peasant Farmer Party cannot be said to have had a very marked influence on the general trend of Polish Ukrainian relations. Neither has another recent venture—the formation of a Ukrainian " Party of Conciliation "—had much success so far. Sooner or later, the Ukrainian problem in Poland will doubtlessly reach a stage in which ever-strengthening ties of common interest will bring the Ukrainian minority to come to terms with the Polish Government ; and it is to be confidently anticipated that advancing prosperity in Poland's Ukrainian provinces, promoted by their connection with the large economic unit of the Polish Republic, will make it gradually more easy to arrive at a working compromise between Polish sovereignty and Ukrainian claims of provincial self-government.

### 8

In connection with the Ukrainians, it is convenient to deal with the other outstanding national minority of Poland's eastern border provinces—the *White Ruthenians*, who occupy in the north-east somewhat like the position held by the Ukrainians in the south-east.

When Poland was united by dynastic marriage to the principality of Lithuania in the fourteenth century, that principality was a large conglomeration of territories which, besides Lithuania proper, contained the vast adjoining lands of the White Ruthenians and stretched even far southward into the " Red Ruthenian," or Ukrainian, domains. White Ruthenian was even the official language of the Lithuanian Grand-Ducal Court, and remained so for a time after the union with Poland. In the succeeding centuries of that union, the social process was the same here as elsewhere : the nobility and gentry becoming Polish, the peasant people retained their old language and habits. With regard to religion, the Greek Orthodoxy of Moscow had made some progress in White Ruthenian lands ; on the other hand the advance of Roman Catholicism was more successful here than in the south, being backed by the reception of Roman Christianity on the part of the entire Lithuanian people. The later Polish device of the Uniat Church, described above in its working among the Ukrainian element, played its part among the White Ruthenians as well and, in the nineteenth century, after the partitions of Poland, suffered the hardships of Russian persecution. The modern White Ruthenian national movement, originating in the course of the nineteenth century, was somewhat divided in its very beginning, in accordance with the old religious and cultural divisions. The western portion of the White Ruthenians, largely Roman Catholic, and permeated with Polish civilization, sought Polish support and sympathy for its endeavours to register and dignify folklore traditions, and to elevate a peasant dialect to the position of a literary language. On the other hand, the large eastern section of the White Ruthenians, Greek Orthodox in religion, naturally inclined towards Russia. It was only in the period of revolutionary stirrings and constitutional liberties in Russia, about 1905, that the White Ruthenian movement became distinctly political, and demands for provincial autonomy were first heard of.

The end of the World War found the White Ruthenians divided, as before, in their cultural and political sympathies, with the important difference that those with a Russian tradition now became strongly tinctured with Bolshevism. In consequence of the Riga Peace Treaty, the White Ruthenian lands, like the Ukrainian ones, were divided between Poland and Russia. A fairly large White Ruthenian Soviet Republic was established under Poland's elbow, with Minsk for its centre, boasting even a White Ruthenian University, and Bolshevik propaganda among the White Ruthenian population on the Polish side was intensely conducted from that Soviet White Ruthenia. Accordingly, the politicians representing the one million White Ruthenians of Poland in the Polish Parliament, often became a cause of trouble by their pronounced Bolshevik sympathies. The White Ruthenians in Poland are in possession of the same rights as the Ukrainians with regard to the use of their language in public relations, and are provided with schools in a similar way : there are 26 purely White Ruthenian Government-supported elementary schools, and others in which the teaching is one-half in Polish and one-half in White Ruthenian. Of the four White Ruthenian secondary schools (conducted by private organizations), one is located in the city of Wilno. While the White Ruthenians constitute a real problem for

Poland—though one of much less magnitude than the Ukrainian one—there is properly speaking, no problem of a *Lithuanian minority* within Poland. The Lithuanian element in Poland, distributed mainly along the frontier between Poland and Lithuania, amounts to an insignificant fraction—a bare 0·2 per cent. of the population (total, 74,000 according to the census of 1921). The city of Wilno, Lithuania's ancient capital, rendered Polish by centuries of political union, according to German war-time statistics, does not possess more than something over 2 per cent. Lithuanians among its inhabitants. The Lithuanians, ever since the baptism of the nation through Poland in 1386, have been solidly Roman Catholic, which created a strong bond of union between them and Poland, unlike the religious differences in the case of other minorities. The Polish-Lithuanian issue of to-day is not a problem of domestic, but entirely one of foreign policy, and in that aspect has been dealt with in a former chapter.

### 9

Apart from the two compact national minorities of Poland's eastern border—the Ukrainians and the White Ruthenians—there remains, scattered all through the eastern provinces, a not inconsiderable number of *Russians* of central or " Great Russian " stock. They represent the residue of a fairly intense, official and unofficial, colonization of the border provinces by Russia during the century of Poland's captivity. Some Russians had property in those lands and clung to it ; some had held office under the old Russian *régime* and have managed to obtain employment under the Polish Government or local authorities ; some only came during or after the War, escaping from the clutches of Bolshevism. Of the latter category, many made a living of some sort in Warsaw, although European capitals further west became more important centres of the emigrant movement.

Altogether, the Russians in Poland are not significant enough in numbers to become a serious factor in Polish domestic politics. Owing to their scattered distribution over the territories, they did not succeed in obtaining a larger representation than one solitary deputy in Parliament ; and the only occasions when the Russian element was heard of at all, were the diplomatic incidents caused by the attempts of emigrant Russians upon Bolshevik representatives in Poland. In some of these cases, the Polish Government, for the sake of maintaining peace with the Soviet ʃneighbour, was obliged to refuse further shelter on Polish soil to active opponents of Bolshevik rule.

The Russians in Poland represent not only their nationality, but also the *Greek Orthodox Church* to which they belong. That Church suffering from dire persecution under the Soviets, the Polish State offered a welcome refuge to a section of it. Although the Russian Church had been the willing tool of Imperial Russia's anti-Polish policy in the period of Poland's oppression, fullest religious toleration has been accorded to it in the new Polish Republic, on the same basis as to other Christian denominations. The Church was declared self-governing ("autocephalous") within the borders of Poland : this was a measure fully justified by reasons of State interest, as it was necessary to preclude all possible interference in Poland's affairs abroad by a reborn Russian National Church in the future. The measure, besides, had for precedent the self-governing Greek churches in various eastern countries. In spite of this, resentment was roused among the zealots of the one and indivisible Russian State Church of pre-war time, and a fanatical priest even murdered the Archbishop appointed by Poland. Soon, however, it was patent to everybody that Poland meant well by the Russian Church within her borders : the creation of a Greek Orthodox Divinity Faculty in the University of Warsaw contributed to the raising of the standard of education (hitherto deplorably low) among the Greek Ortho-dox clergy ; and Poland's good intentions received the sanction of a synod of the higher clergy of the Eastern Church in Poland (the first since 1791) and of ceremonious visits from patriarchs of some venerable Greek Orthodox centres of the Near East. Recently, a legal dispute arose between the Roman Catholic and the Greek Orthodox Church in Poland over the revindication by the first of numerous church buildings in the eastern border-lands which had been turned over, under Russian rule, to the latter: it is probable, however, that a compromise will be found to prevent producing ill-feeling among the Greek Orthodox congregations of the eastern provinces by too sweeping a dispossession of their Church. Even more recent attempts of the Vatican to make the eastern provinces of Poland the centre of a distinctly Russian section of the Catholic Church, are viewed with some concern by Poland.

10

Before we quit the eastern border and its complicated national and religious conditions, it will be well to point out that the above survey does not by any means exhaust the variety of racial and denominational elements which are met with there. To illustrate that variety, another few examples may be quoted which are not important numerically or politically, but interesting as evidence of historical migrations and of the resulting intermixture of races. There are, first of all, the *Armenians* in Eastern Galicia, settled there since the early Middle Ages and now entirely Polish in speech and habits of life, but retaining their unmistakable physical type, their shrewd business sense, and, last but not least, their religion : the Armenian Church, with its archaic ritual and language, and its ancient style of architecture owns allegiance to Rome. The city of Lwów is the seat of the Polish Archbishop of that Church, and the occupant of that seat has, in recent generations, always been as well known for his ardent Polish patriotism as his Uniat colleague in the same city for leadership in the Ukrainian national movement.

As a second example of this category, the *Karaim* communities of certain eastern Polish towns (Wilno, Troki, Łuck and Halicz) are worth singling out, although they have dwindled down to a very few thousand people. They attract the particular attention of oriental scholars by representing, in race, speech, and religion, a unique blend of the Jewish stock, from which they are originally derived, with Turkish elements.

A third and final example of this kind must not be omitted, being proudly familiar to nearly every Pole, viz., the Polish *Tartars* of the Wilno region. The Tartar invasions, devastating Poland periodically since the early thirteenth century, occasionally left a sprinkling of Tartar colonists behind. These were drawn into the orbit of the political life of the Polish-Lithuanian Monarchy as far back as the beginnings of the Union, and they remained loyal to Poland throughout the vicissitudes of her fortunes : the exploits of a volunteer body of Polish-Tartar cavalry were one of the heroic features of Poland's war against the Bolsheviks in 1920. To-day, an eminent judge and other respected professional men in the city of Wilno, while purely Polish in language and culture, profess the Islamic faith ; and Wilno's Mohammedan mosque, among its numerous Christian churches and Jewish synagogues, is an additional touch of glamour in the romantic atmosphere of that fascinatingly beautiful city.

## II

From the eastern border we now transfer our attention to the western frontier regions of Poland, in order to deal with another serious minority problem, viz., that of the *Germans* included in the new Polish State. There were over a million of them in Poland at first ; but considerable numbers of these, being either Prussian officials or colonists planted on the Polish soil by Prussian Government support, have left the country since, and the census of 1931 recorded a considerably lower figure.

The German minority in Poland is chiefly to be met with in three distinct provinces : Poznania, Pomerania, and Silesia.

The struggle of the province of Poznań (Posen) against Prussia's Germanizing efforts during the period of Poland's captivity has been dealt with in a former chapter. The deliverance from the Prussian yoke in 1918 was followed by a great exodus of Germans, especially from the city of Poznań itself, which now has the highest percentage of purely Polish population among all the towns of Poland. The seaside province of Poland, or rather what remains of that historical province in the shape of the so-called " Polish Corridor," was noted in German Imperial geography before the war as a " danger zone " because of its overwhelming majority of Polish inhabitants and its representation by Polish deputies in German parliamentary bodies. That Polish majority has, of course, become even stronger since the War ; only four towns of the region had a majority of German inhabitants even in 1921. In the country, however, here as in Poznania, a considerable amount of land remains in German hands, especially in the form of larger estates.

In the Polish portion of Silesia, the towns retain a more considerable proportion of German population, and large industrial undertakings (including the coal mines), as far as they are not State property, are mostly in German hands.

Outside these three territories, accumulations of German population exist in a few isolated districts, where German immigrants form " islands " among the surrounding sea of the Polish population. Most important among those islands, the large industrial city of Łódź, " the Polish Manchester," built up largely by German and Jewish enterprise in the course of the nineteenth century, consists also to-day predominantly of these elements among the employers, while the working people are Poles of the neighbourhood. There are, besides, rural colonies of Germans in former Eastern Galicia, where Austria deliberately set them up after the partitions, and in Volhynia, where a similar attempt was made by Russia. The old-established Galician settlers had, even in Austrian times, partly become assimilated to their Polish surroundings, those in Volhynia have only recently returned on their soil, after having been driven forth into the interior of Russia during the War.

In the western provinces delivered from Prussian rule, it was the natural and deliberate aim of the Germans to continue, under the new conditions, the process of colonization of Polish land by German settlers which had been forcibly conducted in the Prussian days. Poland, on the other hand, as naturally, used every means in her power to diminish the volume of the German element on the land and prevent its further infiltration. The expulsion from Poland of those German inhabitants who had opted for German citizenship aroused much ill-feeling in Germany and led to reprisals against the Poles under Germany : an agreement in this matter was only arrived at in 1925. The further question remained open of whether new German settlers were to be admitted to Poland in the further future, and German citizens to be allowed to establish new business undertakings within Poland's frontiers ; on this, after much dispute, a compromise was reached in the Polish-German commercial treaty of 1930.

Wherever the Germans appear, in the new as in the old Poland, they manifest not only the habits of industry, thrift and orderliness peculiar to their race, but also the sense of discipline and co-operation characteristic of all their collective endeavours.

It is due to these qualities that the German minority in Poland, resolutely opposed to Polish rule and considering itself the vanguard of renewed German penetration, has been able to make most efficient use of the political and other rights which Poland granted to this as to other minorities. The small but compact group of German deputies (ten at first) in the Polish Parliament had to be reckoned with as a force of opposition by every Polish Government, and during the elections of 1922, the Germans even were chiefly instrumental in arraying all the various national minorities of Poland in one solid *bloc* for electioneering purposes. They have also maintained, with admirably organized consistency, a running fire of complaints against Poland's treatment of her German minority in the Press and in the League of Nations ; that fire always grew stronger when the purposes of Germany's international action required it, and it was busily exploited by German diplomacy for these purposes.

In the matter of schools, the Germans in Poland are much better provided for than the Poles under Germany. They have 658 Government-supported public elementary schools, besides

221 private ones, some of the later using public school buildings. Besides these, there are 9 schools mixed in language (one-half Polish and one-half German), and German is taught wherever asked for on behalf of at least 18 children of any given school. There are 7 governmental and 3 municipal German secondary schools. The city of Łódź, with its excellent German schools, German theatre and German University Extension Lectures, and similarly another important textile manufacturing centre, the Silesian town of Bielsko (Bielitz), also a predominantly German community, and similarly well provided with German institutions, are both of them convincing instances of the liberalism of Polish rule in the matter of the cultural needs of Poland's German citizens.

12

As we have seen, a difference of religion was added to that of nationality in Poland's eastern borderlands, and increased the intensity of conflicts. Similarly, the contrast between Poles and Germans in the western border provinces was intensified by the religious difference. *Protestantism* in Poland, while making some headway among the intellectual *élite*, had never gained much ground among the masses and ultimately been rejected by the nation at large, because popular instinct repudiated it as " a German creed." In the nineteenth century, when Protestant Prussia assumed the leadership of modern Germany and at the same time developed its anti-Polish programme, the Polish-German antagonism in Prussian Poland became strictly identified with that between Catholics and Protestants, and in Silesia the reawakening of the sense of Polish nationality even had its actual source in a Catholic religious movement. The connection between this aspect of Polish patriotism under Prussia and the " struggle for culture " waged by Bismarck's Government against the Catholic Church in Germany has been mentioned in a former chapter ; but Polish nationalism under Prussia, while remaining as essentially Roman Catholic as ever, soon dissociated itself from political alliance with the German Catholic Centre Party.

It was only in the Austrian part of Silesia and in large historical centres like Warsaw and Wilno that old established communities of purely Polish Protestants existed and were led by Protestant clergymen of Polish nationality. It was from these groups also that, in the new Poland, a desire emanated to emancipate Protestantism in Polish lands from German influences. This desire found strong expression at a conference and a Lutheran Synod which met in Warsaw in 1922 for the purpose of placing the relation of Polish Protestantism to the State on a definite basis. The Polish sections of the various Protestant denominations (chiefly Lutheranism and Calvinism) were ultimately made self-governing within Poland, in the same way as the Greek Orthodox Church in Poland was made self-governing. But both denominational and national differences made it impossible to create a united supreme representation of the Protestants in Poland. Only on 1926 was the constitution of a " Council of the Evangelical Churches in Poland " resolved on, and in 1928 that Council at last came into being.

After all these efforts, however, the fact remains there that, of the one million Protestants in Poland, 70 per cent. are Germans in the western provinces, and there the traditional identity of the contrast between Pole and German on the one hand with that between Catholic and Protestant on the other hand persists in full force.

## 13

If, now, we survey the German minority territories of Poland for active manifestations of the continued friction between the German and the Polish element, we find that such conflicts are most acute neither in the central province of Poznania, where the historical supremacy of the Polish element has been thoroughly re-established, nor in the sea-side province, which always had an overwhelming Polish majority, and whose inclusion in Germany is demanded from outside on other grounds than those of population—but on the volcanic territory of coal-mining *Silesia*.

The Polish province of Silesia, composed of the south-eastern part of former Prussian Silesia and of the eastern section of Austria's Silesian province, was constituted, in accordance with international agreements, as a self-governing territorial unit with a provincial legislative assembly of its own. In spite of adequate representation of the Germans in that assembly, the international Commission set up in Polish Silesia for the settlement of disputes has always had its hands full, and the halls of the League of Nations in Geneva have often resounded with discussions of Silesian affairs. German employers exercised pressure on their Polish workers both with regard to their vote at elections and to the choice of schools for their children, and endeavours to secure for the Polish population its due freedom of action in these matters provoked angry German complaints in the international forum. German organizations professing legitimate cultural and legal aims (like the German National Alliance in Poland) conducted political activities with a final view to detaching Silesia from Poland. Other and more secret organizations of the militant type so common in post-war Germany occasionally committed acts of violence. Such violence was exercised, on the adjoining territory of Prussian Silesia, even on the persons of a university lecturer and a company of theatrical artists from Poland. On the Polish side, an association of those who had taken part in the Silesian rising of 1921, kept the tradition of armed conflicts alive. Excitement on both sides rose to a high pitch in the heated general atmosphere of German-Polish relations during 1930. There was a plentiful crop of frontier incidents, and disturbances resulting in destruction of property and loss of life occurred in greater numbers and more violent form than before. This is all the more deplorable as the economic fabric of Silesia on both sides of the new border had in the meantime, as will be seen from a later chapter, tolerably adjusted itself to the new political conditions.

## 14

A discussion of German minority problems in Poland cannot be concluded without some reference to Poland's relations with the Free City of *Danzig*. This city, it will be remembered, was not included by the Versailles peacemakers in the political territory of Poland, to which it had belonged for more than three centuries, but constituted as a city republic under international control. The sovereignty of the city of Danzig, however, was limited in favour of Poland in a number of points : Danzig has no foreign representation of its own, she is included within the Polish customs boundaries (although with a separate customs administration) ; both Poland and Danzig are represented in the council administering the Port of Danzig ; Poland herself administers the railway lines and also has a postal service of her own within Danzig.

This somewhat complicated system of combined administration inevitably led to disputes, which frequently occupied the League of Nations. Danzig, as will be seen from a later chapter, at once began to profit economically through her connection with Poland as she had never profited by her position under Germany. Even when a Polish port began to be developed out of the neighbouring fishing village of Gdynia, Danzig's prosperous development continued, thanks to the rapidly growing volume of Poland's sea trade. In spite of this, Danzig, being largely governed not by burghers of the city, but by imported Prussian officials, continually endeavoured to loosen the Polish connection and extend the limits of her self-government, with an ultimate view to reunion with Germany. At times, the strength of the Socialist element in the Senate of the Free City seemed to be directing its policy into the channel of economic interests and, accordingly, of a better understanding with Poland ; but Nationalist currents again and again got the upper hand. Latterly the question of the future status of the City of Danzig has been included, by German propaganda, in the programme of a revision of the frontiers between Poland and Germany, the restoration of Danzig to Germany being demanded together with the restoration to her of the " Polish Corridor." This grave international issue, however, connected as it is by many intimate threads with the problem of the German minority in Poland, does not properly come within the scope of the present chapter.

### 15

Poland shares with several adjoining countries—Hungary, Rumania, and south-western Russia—the peculiarity of having, among her minority problems, a *Jewish Problem* of extraordinary magnitude and complexity.

The problem is fundamentally one of numbers, the proportion of Jews to the rest of the population being much larger in these countries than in western European lands. The origins of this disparity lie far back in history. In the early Middle Ages, Jewish bankers and merchants had contributed a good deal to the economic development of the new western European Monarchies. When these had reached a certain degree of economic growth and independence, reaction against the Jewish monopoly of finance and business set in. Groups of persecuted and exiled western European Jews began to seek refuge, among other eastern countries, also in Poland. Polish rulers received them hospitably and allowed them to settle on liberal conditions of self-government. This was not prompted solely by motives of generosity : those who invited Jewish colonization as they had invited German colonization before, realized that the Jews were bringing business experience, enterprise, and capital into an undeveloped country. The liberal conditions of communal self-government under which the Jews were allowed to live in Polish towns, extended even to nation-wide organization : a sort of Jewish Parliament existed in the old Poland's later centuries and legislated in Jewish affairs down to the eighteenth century. This very liberalism, however, itself unconsciously sowed the seeds of future conflict. It prevented fusion between the Jews and their Polish hosts : keeping Jewish communities united, it also kept them separated from the Poles. Not only did a more exclusive Jewish monopoly of trade arise than anywhere in western Europe—a monopoly which has largely continued to exist until our own days—but the Jews remained sharply distinct from the Poles in local habitation, in dress, manners and customs, and even in speech. The " ghettoes " or purely Jewish quarters, still existing, in medieval fashion, in many Polish cities, are a strange world indeed to the visitor from western Europe. More amazing even than the sight of the Jews in their black cloaks, with their long beards and the screw-like locks hanging down from their temples, is their unwavering adherence to the ancient regulations of the Mosaic law affecting every detail of their daily life, from birth to death, from prayer to business, from marriages and meals to quarrels and fasts. The language spoken by the Jewish masses of eastern Europe as their *lingua franca*—the " Yiddish " or *jargon*—a mixture of German and Hebrew—is also an inheritance of past centuries : it has a literature of respectable age to which some writers of great talent—mostly born in Poland or Russia —have added splendour and given world-wide renown in recent times.

In the divided Poland of the nineteenth century, the Jewish problem developed differently according to the different policies of the partitioning powers. Under Austria, where the Jews obtained real equality of rights, a large measure of assimilation between educated Jews and the Polish educated class was effected, but the unfettered growth of the Jewish power over trade was also promoted. In Prussian Poland anti-Semite tendencies of the Government, practised semi-officially, kept the Jewish element within bounds ; at the same time, the rapid industrial progress of western Germany after the Franco-Prussian War attracted Jews from the purely agrarian province of Prussian Poland, while in that province itself a strong sense of economic organization among the Poles, acquired in the struggle against German encroachment, furthered the growth of a trading Polish middle class. Hence the fact that the percentage of Jews among the population of Prussian Poland dwindled down to a minimum of 1–2 per cent. and remains at that level even now, in strong contrast with the other provinces.

Under Russia, nineteenth-century developments added strong influxes of Jews from the east into Poland to the historical Jewish immigration from the west. The barbarous persecution of Russia's Jews by the Tsarist Government, by limiting, *inter alia*, the right of Jews to live in Russia proper, forced upon Russian Poland large masses of Russian Jews. Especially in the eastern border belt a congestion of Jewish population developed in the provincial towns, with its necessary concomitants of horrid squalor and atrocious misery. Such eastern towns as Pińsk accumulated—and retain—Jewish majorities to the extent of 80–90 per cent. of the total population. It was in these congested districts of the east, as well as in the crowded and equally miserable " ghettoes " of the larger cities of central Poland, that both Jewish national separatism and revolutionary social radicalism were bound to run riot among the younger generation. While in western Europe the beginnings of modern Zionism were developing on intellectual foundations under the quickening impulse of certain symptoms of nascent anti-Semitism in cultured social relations, under Russia a much more rapid growth and greater violence of instinctive Jewish feeling among the wretched masses of proletarian Jews was fostered by such horrors as the frequent *pogroms* encouraged, or even organized, by the Tsarist police. No wonder that Jews figured prominently in all Russian opposition parties, from the mildly liberal " Cadets " to the rabid Bolshevik Socialists, who were ultimately to become the instrument of historical retribution.

Both in Russian and Austrian Poland, the national programme of constructive economic effort, described in a former chapter as characteristic of Polish life in the last pre-war decades, had necessarily been directed against Jewish trade in the interest of building up again a commercial middle class of Polish race. Slogans of boycott of the Jewish traders were launched again and again ; a boycott movement of particular vehemence was started by the Polish Nationalist Party in Russian Poland when, at the Duma elections of 1912, a candidate of the Jews was returned by the city of Warsaw.

Even more violent reaction was called forth in the later stages of the World War by evidence of Jewish war-time profiteering, as well as by the anti-Polish attitude of the Jewish border population in the new Poland's wars against the Ukrainians and the Bolsheviks. Anti-Jewish riots took place in the first year of the existence of the new Poland ; grossly exaggerated accounts of them in the foreign Press described them as *pogroms*. These reports were authoritatively corrected by the findings of two international commissions of inquiry, both of them headed by distinguished Jews—Sir Stuart Samuel from Great Britain, and Mr. Henry Morgenthau from

M

the United States—it was established, in particular, that only such Jews had been the actual victims of violence as had manifested active enmity to the new State.

16

It was under these unfavourable auspices of fresh excitement that the new Poland came into her historical inheritance of a large and grave Jewish problem. Her Jews number over ten per cent. of the population, and form a total of over three millions. Scattered over the whole country, they range in density from one per cent. in the west to ninety in some towns of the east ; the large cities of Central Poland (Warsaw, Cracow) have well over thirty, those of the eastern provinces (Wilno, Lwów) about forty per cent. of them.   Socially, Poland's Jews present a wide scale of variety, from the cultured and conventionally dressed Polish-speaking Jew scholar, lawyer, doctor or business man of western cities to the squalid, miserable, exotic-looking, Yiddish-speaking small trader in ghettoes, country towns and villages.   In ideas, there is an equally wide range, from enlightened religious indifference to unlettered orthodox fanaticism, and from the passionate nationalism of the Zionist to the revolutionary fervour of the Communist conspirator.

In view of a minority not limited territorially to any section of the country, self-government of the type of provincial autonomy was obviously impracticable in the case of the Jews. At the same time the special treaty safeguarding the rights of minorities, which Poland had been made to sign, applied to the Jewish minority as well.  This opened up a fertile ground for quarrels about legislative and administrative problems, when universal suffrage in the new Poland carried a strong group of more than thirty Jewish deputies into Parliament.  During the first few years of Poland's new existence, that group maintained a united front and an unvarying attitude of clamorous opposition against every Polish Government.  Demands were raised for such extended privileges of self-government as no sovereign state could ever grant to a minority, and one scattered all over the country, too—demands which, in fact, frequently amounted to what would have been, in Mr. Morgenthau's words, "the creation of a Jewish State within the Polish State."  But even subjects fit for discussion, in an atmosphere of political realities, turned out to be vexed questions indeed.  A few of these may be singled out as examples.  Thus, the claim of Orthodox Jews to be allowed to trade on Sundays because they never do business on Saturday, might appear to be fair, yet would at bottom have meant highly unfair competition with the Christian trader, since it is just Sunday which is the average customer's only really free day. Again, the admission of crowds of poor Jews leaving Soviet Russia with its unbearable conditions of existence, would have seemed, to an outsider, to be a dictate of common charity : yet Poland, deprived of any outlet for her crowded and rapidly expanding population, and already afflicted with a plethora of proletarian Jews in some parts, had no choice but to be uncharitable in this instance. This, of course, gave occasion for world-wide Jewish complaints, although, after all, a considerable number of Jews from Soviet Russia succeeded in settling in Poland.

More prolonged and intense ill-feeling was roused by certain measures which Poland—not at all alone among post-war countries in this respect !—at one time began to take in order to limit the access of Jewish students to her universities. The immoderate influx of students from all ranks of society into the universities was a marked social phenomenon even before the War ; since the War, it has assumed unheard-of dimensions in Europe and become extended to America as well. In Poland, the Jews were the element of the population whose number among university students grew more quickly than that of students from other sections—partly perhaps because it was a point in the programme of Zionist Jewish nationalism to make the Jews a nation in the full sense of the word again by developing rapidly their educated class—and partly just on account of war time increase in wealth among the Jews, and successful evasion of military service on the part of their young men. Thus, there was a time in the later years of the War when the medical faculty of the University of Cracow had seventy per cent. Jews and only thirty per cent. Gentiles among its students. Such disquieting figures impressed Polish imagination all the more as the Poles' endeavour to become, on their part, a nation in the full sense of the word again by building up a commercial middle class, made very little headway against the practical monopoly of trade which the Jews held in the towns. Now, with hardly any gain in the sphere of commerce, there appeared to be growing loss of ground in the sphere of the academic professions. It was against this prospect that the barrier of the *numerus clausus* was to be erected, the percentage of Jews in the universities to be kept at the same level as the percentage of Jews among the population at large. After short and only partial operation these regulations were abandoned : the outcry raised against them did harm to the interests of Poland abroad, and

Jewish students mostly found the means to finish their education
in foreign universities, and afterwards satisfied all requirements
for recognition of their foreign degrees in Poland. Unlimited
freedom of access to the universities was restored to the Jews,
with the result that in most Polish universities their percentage
is between two and three times as high as that among the
population at large.

## 17

Many were the efforts made by successive Polish Governments
to induce the Jewish Parliamentary Group to abandon its
propaganda against the Polish State abroad. At one time, in
1925, a pact between the Jews and the Government of the day
was even spoken of as concluded. But it was only under the
rule of Marshal Piłsudski, since 1926, that the tension between
Poles and Jews began visibly to diminish. This was partly due
to the fact that the greater liberalism of the Marshal's Government towards the national minorities was also extended to the
Jews, which made the Marshal's person and system popular
among them. But partly the cause of decreasing friction lay
in certain developments within the Jewish community itself.

It had been observable from the beginning that the tone of
perpetual opposition and loud protest had been characteristic
rather of the Jews born under Russian rule and brought up in an
atmosphere of political persecution and revolutionary unrest,
than of the Jews of former Austrian Poland, who had enjoyed
full civic liberty for decades, and had mostly lived in peace
with their fellow citizens. It was, however, not along this
regional line that political cleavage among the Polish Jews ran
when it came. Real division of attitude was called forth by the
fortunes of Zionism. The high tide of Zionist hopes during and
after the War had carried Jewish nationalism in Poland to the
fantastic level of Utopian demands. With the disappointments
that the later course of Palestinian affairs brought in its train,
the interest of the Orthodox Jewish masses in the nationalist
programme began to fade, and not only aspirations in Palestine,
but aspirations in Poland were recognized by them as unreal.
It began to be felt, that since the Polish State had evidently
" come to stay," it was only by loyalty towards it, and peace
with the Polish element, that Jewish interest in Poland could
be successfully advanced. Such was also the advice urged upon
Poland's Jews by the well-organized and influential community
of Polish Jews in America, among whom even a special Committee to promote better relations between Jews and Poles in Poland

was recently formed with the concurrence of leading Polish citizens of the United States.

With such developments proceeding, the Zionist leaders in Poland no longer could incite the masses to unflagging political opposition, and the decay of their authority was made manifest by the elections held under Piłsudski's rule in 1928 and 1930. The united Jewish Parliamentary Group dwindled down to a mere handful, and prominent Jewish politicians made their appearance in the ranks of the Government *bloc*. The process is likely to continue, and the day is perhaps not far distant when there will not be a distinctly " Jewish Party " in the Polish Parliament, any more than there is, or has been, or is likely to be, any " Catholic Party."

In the meantime, the Jews of Poland, besides the full rights of Polish citizens, are enjoying, in accordance with the old Polish tradition, a considerable measure of local self-government within their religious communities.

These Jewish religious communes, called *cahals*, formerly were completely independent of each other in matters of religious administration, but now they are united into an association under the supreme authority of a Jewish Religious Council. The communes are governed by the local rabbis with the assistance of elected committees, the central council consists of 34 lay members and 17 rabbis. A certain amount of control is exercised by the Department of Denominations in the Ministry of Education both over the composition of the council, the selection of rabbis, and the administration of the communes. A State-supported Jewish Theological Seminary exists in Warsaw. Local Jewish charities and social welfare institutions are subsidized by the Government as well as by provincial and municipal authorities in the same way as Christian ones. The Jewish religious communities are indivisible administrative units, but within the Jewish population, especially in the larger western cities, a religious division is to be observed between the strictly Orthodox Jews of the old type and the " progressive " elements which do not adhere to the Mosaic law in all its formal rigour : the two sections have each its own synagogues and rabbis. Among the strictly Orthodox section, it must be added, the rabbis exercise unofficially the authority of judges in civil cases : most legal disputes between Orthodox Jews are brought before the rabbi, and many of them never come before an ordinary court.

With regard to educational facilities, it must be stated that most Jewish children attend the public Polish schools. In these, the children of Orthodox Jewish families are freed from writing, drawing, and handicraft lessons on Saturdays, in accordance with their old religious laws. Where there are larger numbers of Jewish children, they are grouped together in separate schools or classes, in which no lessons at all are held on Saturdays, and Jewish teachers only, as a rule, are employed. In all schools, the teaching of Jewish religion is provided for, and, in the case of sufficient demand for it, also the teaching of the Hebrew language.

Purely Jewish elementary schools are supported, to the number of 385, by Jewish organizations ; about 40,000 Jewish children (one-seventh of the total) receive instruction in them. There are also 24 Jewish secondary schools, supported by Jewish societies and communities ; in 17 of these schools the language of teaching is Hebrew, in 7 Yiddish. Thus, the conflict between the claims of the ancient classical and the modern colloquial tongue for recognition as the Jewish national language unavoidably finds expression in Jewish educational effort on Polish ground.

The above selection of facts from the modern history of the Jewish problem in Poland may convey some idea of its wide bearings and extraordinary complexity. Nevertheless, the present writer ventures to agree with the opinion uttered in a discussion of his own paper on " Poland and the Problem of National Minorities " at the British (now Royal) Institute of International Affairs, as far back as 1922, by a distinguished British Jew, Mr. L. C. Wolf, who then said that " The Jewish problem in Poland was, in the long run, solving itself." In fact, this as well as the other national minority problems of Poland, given favourable conditions of international peace, domestic stability, and economic progress, are sure to give place gradually to harmonious co-operation between fellow-citizens of different race. In the case of the Jewish problem, additional relief may come through opportunities for emigration from the congested border districts into Russia, when something like normal conditions will have been established in that country and the great tasks of its economic development will attract commercial and industrial enterprise from abroad. A spontaneous eastward movement of Polish Jews under such favourable conditions would not only redress the balance of nineteenth century Russian policy, which created some of Poland's Jewish difficulties, but it would also mean a further evolutionary stage, under more fortunate auspices, of the historical process started by the medieval migration of western European Jews into Poland.

18

The above account of Poland's minority problems must be supplemented by a few data concerning the fate of *Polish minorities in other countries*.

The number of Poles living outside Poland is estimated at about seven millions. Nearly one-half of these live in the *United States of America*.

The history of Polish emigration to the United States being essentially a pre-war process, now practically closed by the American immigration laws, it has accordingly been dealt with in the chapter on Poland's pre-war fortunes. There also, some mention has been made of the emigration of Poles to other parts of the American continent—*Canada* and the *South American States*. To these countries, Poles continue to emigrate from the new Poland—to South America even in growing numbers—but here also Polish emigration has recently been confronted by increasing tendencies to limit admission, and these outlets, like the United States, may soon become closed.

On the other hand, post-war developments have opened up a new outlet for Poland's overflow of population, much nearer home. Poland's great western ally, *France*, depopulated by war-time losses and irrevocably addicted to birth control, began willingly to absorb hundreds of thousands of Polish emigrants, at first as factory workers and farm labourers, then as settlers. At present, numbers of small tradesmen and independent farmers form part of the Polish population of northern French mining towns and villages, and the social evolution of the new Polish colonies in France seems to be proceeding exactly along the same lines as formerly that of the United States. That new Polish emigration is also becoming similarly important in volume : the Polish element now definitely settled in France, approaches one million, and the saturation point of this new territory for Polish colonization has apparently not yet been reached. Even now it may without exaggeration be said that the north of France is to as large an extent Polish as the south of France is Italian. The organization of Consular protection, educational facilities, religious service, and social welfare work, for the transplanted and largely bewildered masses of Polish emigrants in France has made very satisfactory progress of late ; but here, as in America, assimilation of the younger generation to the new surroundings is a widespread and inevitable process.

Of the long and varied history of Polish emigration to another vast territorial reservoir, viz., *Russia* both European and Asiatic, and of the part played by the large Polish " diaspora " in the pre-war Russian Empire, something has been said in a former chapter. Of this " diaspora," augmented by war-time exiles and certainly well over two millions in number at one time, large portions flowed back into Poland, under conditions of unspeakable misery and in a state of utter destitution, in 1921–3, when an official " repatriation " movement was conducted under the provisions of the Riga Peace Treaty. " Repatriation " added considerably to the new Poland's economic and social difficulties, but it saved hundreds of thousands of Polish people from the common fate of Russia's population under Bolshevik rule. Even after mass " repatriation," however, a considerable residue of Poles remains in Russia and has to share that fate. The Polish population of the region of Kiev alone is estimated at half a million ; of the numbers of Poles scattered over the vast expanses of northern European Russia and of Siberia it is difficult to form even an approximate estimate, although Polish Consulates now exist in a number of important cities both on the European and the Asiatic side. Even with the protection afforded by them to those who are legally Polish citizens, the Polish population of Soviet Russia cannot, generally, be expected to fare better under Bolshevism than the Russian people itself. Economic dispossession and distress coupled with political and religious persecution are the main factors of that existence. The large estates, and the industrial and mining undertakings formerly owned by Poles in Russia, are lost to their owners. A few concessions more recently granted to Polish business groups, and a Russian-Polish Trade Corporation (*Sovpoltorg*) lead an uncertain and precarious economic existence and employ a number of Polish working-men and managers. Politically, the Poles under Russia are subjected to the sharpest repressive measures as soon as there is any complication or friction in the relations between the Bolshevik and the Polish Government. Besides, they are exposed to unresting Communist propaganda backed by every means of official pressure and exercised chiefly on the young people. With regard to religion, the Poles being almost in a body Roman Catholics, it is Polish clergymen largely who represent the Roman Catholic Church in Russia : they are one of the principal objects of Soviet Russia's unceasing anti-religious campaign ; ever since the imprisonment and trial of Archbishop Cieplak and the execution of Monsignor Budkiewicz in 1923, Catholic Polish clergymen have been among the regular inmates of the dreadful Bolshevik prisons, and many of them are now dying a lingering death in that terrible place of deportation—the Solovetsk Islands in the Arctic Sea. The imprisonment both of clergymen and of prominent laymen from among the Polish community in Russia was frequently used, in the early post-war years, as a means of pressure on Poland in order to cause her to deliver up imprisoned Communist propagandists in exchange for these Polish victims of Soviet rule.

With such practices as these openly conducted, Bolshevik Russia continues to make a pretence of realizing the principle of national self-determination within the Soviet Union. A border district largely inhabited by Polish people has even been proclaimed a Soviet Polish Republic, and named after the deceased Communist leader Marchlewski, who was a Pole by birth : the object of the erection of this " model republic " of course was to set up a radiating-centre of Communist propaganda among the Polish people under Poland's very elbow. Both in that district and elsewhere in larger centres of Polish population under Russia, Polish schools are supported by the Soviet Government. Like the Russian schools, they are made strictly subservient to the preaching of Communist party doctrine to the young, beginning with Communist nursery rhymes and ending with Communist organizations of youth in imitation of the Boy Scouts and Girl Guides of western Europe.

### 19

The situation of *the Poles under Germany* is not so calamitous as that of those Poles who have the misfortune to live under Bolshevik rule. At the same time, the plight of the Polish minority in present-day Germany certainly compares unfavourably with the treatment of the German minority in Poland.

The Poles under German rule, even after the inclusion of pre-war Germany's Polish provinces in the new Poland, outnumber the Germans in Poland. They certainly far surpass a million in number, although large portions of them are concealed in German census returns under provincial headings, and many, no doubt, are registered as Germans under the pressure of their employers. The permanent Polish population of Germany is largely distributed over the north-western part of Silesia, which was left to Germany after the plebiscite, as well as the districts immediately adjoining the Polish provinces of Poznania and Pomerania. In all these regions, the population in question mostly consists of peasant farmers. Apart from them, there are considerable bodies of factory workers and miners in the industrial centres of western Germany, particularly in the

Ruhr basin. The Polish miners' community in Westphalia amounted to about 100,000 even before the War, and was nationally well organized at the time. Since the War, and the Ruhr occupation, a part of that accumulation of Polish workers has been absorbed by the mines of northern France ; but a considerable portion remains in Germany.

Besides these bodies of Polish agricultural and industrial labour permanently resident on German territory, there has always been, since long-ago pre-war times, a large floating population of temporary emigrants who came over from Poland as hired workers for the harvest season and returned to their country for the winter year by year. Their number may likewise be put, even before the War, at more than 100,000 ; it was swelled considerably during the War, Polish workers being engaged in hundreds of thousands to work in Germany's factories in place of those who were at the front. After the War, those workers were discharged, and strong movements have been breaking out again and again in favour of keeping Germany entirely clear of Polish immigrant labour. But these movements were always countered by economic and social necessity : the large landowners of eastern Germany in particular, although animated by extreme nationalist fervour, are too strongly affected by " the flight from the countryside " of the native German element not to appreciate the convenience of the ever-flowing supply of cheap labour from Poland. They continue, accordingly, to welcome it. These Polish rural labourers, representing the landless and destitute surplus population of Poland's villages, had no choice but to submit to merciless exploitation by their foreign employers ; and this exploitation was intensified, after the War, by the fact that for a long time their legal status in Germany was not regulated by any international convention. Such a convention, preceded by preliminaries in 1925 and 1926, has been definitely in existence between Poland and Germany since 1927, and under it, the " seasonal workers " enjoy a fair amount of Consular protection in such matters as passports, transport arrangements, employment contracts, and insurance. No schools, however, are provided for their children.

With regard to schools for the permanent Polish population of Germany, it is in this respect that the difference between the fate of Germans in Poland and Poles in Germany is most glaring. The Poles under German rule are under the double disadvantage: firstly, of not being territorially united but distributed over several provinces far apart from each other, and secondary, of having no special treaty for the protection of minorities to base their claims on, such as Poland was made to sign at Versailles concerning the minorities within her borders.

In consequence of those two basic facts, and in spite of a certain improvement produced by a Prussian School Bill in 1928, the proportion of Polish schools in Germany to German schools in Poland is highly unsatisfactory : of German schools in Poland there are (as was stated above in its place) well over six hundred, of Polish schools in Germany less than one hundred ; and to the ten public German secondary schools in Poland there does not correspond a single Polish secondary school in Germany.

The Polish element in Germany, disciplined through struggle —especially the well-organized industrial workers' community in Westphalia—is combating these educational disadvantages by strenuous self-help : private Polish educational courses are maintained in about sixty emigrant centres, and adult associations for cultural purposes are supplementing their work. All these activities are superintended and assisted by an " Association of Poles in Germany " with its headquarters in Berlin ; and the work of such Polish organizations would bring forth even more fruit in the field of education if it was not interfered with by administrative chicanery, and sometimes even by judicial unfairness in cases which come before the courts.[1] Owing to their territorial distribution, it is not possible for Germany's Polish citizens to obtain proper representation either in the Reichstag or in the Prussian Parliament, and there to seek legislative remedies for their grievances. It is only to be hoped that the League of Nations, so often kept busy with the complaints of Germans from Poland, will in due time pay proper attention to the situation of Poles under Germany as well ; in fact, that it will proceed ultimately to establish equality and reciprocity in the treatment of minorities as a universally binding principle.

Less space than to the condition of the Poles under Germany need here be given to the situation of Polish minorities in the smaller countries surrounding Poland. In three of these countries—*Lithuania, Latvia and Rumania*—sweeping measures of " Land Reform " were passed in the early post-war years with a view to strengthening the native peasant farmer element against the land-owning gentry mostly foreign in blood. This

---

[1] A hasty death sentence passed and carried out in 1928 in the case of a Polish working man named Jakubowski, who was given no proper opportunities to plead his innocence in his own language, called forth loud protests even among the Germans.

land-owning gentry, besides the Baltic Germans in Latvia, and the Hungarians in Rumania, was largely represented by old-established Polish noble families in certain portions of all the three countries. It was they, accordingly, who to a great extent bore the brunt of the agrarian reform measures. Similarly, in the field of educational organization, efforts were made to counteract the foreign influences of the cultured gentry by giving the language of the people as predominant a position as possible in the school system. Here, again, the rights of minorities were curtailed.

Amicable negotiations between Poland and her neighbours Latvia and Rumania have, at least to some extent, softened the rigorous operation of the land reform laws with regard to the Polish land-owning element in both countries ; as regards education, the generally higher level of culture of the Polish element has enabled it more or less successfully to assert its rights in that domain.

Success in either respect, unfortunately, seemed barred in Lithuania, with its animosity over the Wilno question and its persistent refusal to enter into normal diplomatic relations with Poland. As a matter of fact, the Polish land-owning class was ruthlessly reduced to the legal limit of eighty local acres per estate, and often chicaned by administrative persecution into selling even out of that pittance. But in the field of education, the age-old cultural ascendancy of the Polish element proved too strong to break. In spite of the suppression of over three-fourths of the Polish schools in 1927 and 1928, the activities of a large Polish educational association continued irrepressibly to promote private teaching in the Polish language ; large numbers of young Polish people are reaching the higher stages of the educational curriculum without losing their sense of Polish nationality ; and even among the Professors of the Lithuanian University of Kaunas (Kowno) a number of distinguished scholars and scientists of Polish origin are testifying to the importance of Polish civilization for Lithuania. At the same time, a number of Polish Press organs are maintaining their activity through all phases of persecution, and Polish economic organizations—an agricultural co-operative, an insurance society, a credit-bank—are safeguarding the material interests of the Polish minority. Such atrocious abuses as the ill-treatment of Polish political prisoners in Lithuanian prisons, and the acts of violent *sabotage* committed on the premises of Polish organizations, now belong—it is to be hoped—for ever to the past ; voices in favour of an attitude of conciliation are more

and more frequently making themselves heard, even in Lithuanian quarters, and both the Poles in Lithuania and the Polish
State may perhaps look forward to better relations in the near
future.

The situation of the Polish minority in *Czechoslovakia* differs
essentially from that in the countries just discussed. The
solid body of nearly 150,000 Poles cut off from Poland by the
division of the Duchy of Cieszyn (Teschen) in former Austrian
Silesia in 1920, is composed entirely of peasant farmers and
coal-miners, and the immigrant elements which have swelled
the Polish population of Czechoslovakia during and since the
War, belong to the same social strata. Accordingly, land
reform could not affect the Polish minority here, as it did in
other States. It must, however, be regretfully stated that
even in this friendly Slavonic country, closely related to Poland
by race and historical development, the Polish element had
certain causes for grievance. Administrative appointments,
from the first, were calculated to impart, artificially, a Czech
character to the Polish-speaking Silesian districts. Czech schools
were established everywhere side by side with the Polish ones,
and in some cases Polish schools were closed. Similarly, the
Protestant National Church of Czechoslovakia was favoured as
against the Roman Catholicism of the Poles. Finally, both in
1920 and 1930, undue pressure was brought to bear on the Polish
population during the census. To such measures the Polish
minority successfully opposes its well-organized economic and
educational forces. Polish elementary and secondary schools,
as well as cultural societies and co-operative and credit associations, are strenuously active ; and two Polish deputies, voicing
Silesian complaints in the Prague Chamber of Deputies, have
obtained a certain amount of redress. Czechoslovakia, under
the enlightened rule of its philosopher-president Professor
Masaryk, is treating its large German minority with wise and
truly statesmanlike liberalism ; it may confidently be expected
that the community of manifold vital interests, both political
and economic, which exist between the Czechoslovak Republic
and Poland, will prove a weighty factor to induce the Prague
Government to change its Silesian policy thoroughly and thereby
to remove one of the obstacles in the way of harmony and
co-operation between the two neighbour States.

This account of conditions under Czechoslovakia brings our
survey of the principal Polish communities outside Poland to a
conclusion. A number of other countries—such as Denmark,
with 12,000 resident Polish emigrant workers, or Palestine,

with some 40,000 Polish-Jewish colonists—might still be mentioned. Some of them—as, for instance, Manchuria, with its large and vigorous Polish colony at Harbin—are beginning to play a part of some importance in Poland's international trade relations. The fate of others—such as the 100,000 Poles in Canada, the 200,000 in Brazil, or the 40,000 in the Argentine —is not easy to predict at this moment. One thing, however, must, under the existing conditions be described as certain, viz., that mass movements of emigration will, for a long time to come, have to be reckoned with as a social and economic necessity for the rapidly growing population of Poland. Colonies may become as vital a requirement for Poland as they became for Germany in the second half of the nineteenth century. Efforts to settle Polish rural colonists in the north African possessions of France have been tried, and may in the future become more successful than hitherto ; and even such distant regions as the Portuguese colony of Angola have recently been envisaged as outlets. It is a task of obvious importance for the Government of the reborn Poland both to watch carefully over the interests of existing Polish communities outside Poland, and to direct wisely the creation of new ones ; for they may all become sources of strength and support for the new Republic, quite as some of them were for the oppressed and divided Poland of pre-war time.

## CHAPTER VII

# ECONOMIC LIFE

## I

As indicated in a previous chapter, it is a pathetic peculiarity of Poland's modern destinies that the period of her division and captivity was at the same time that of some of the greatest social and economic changes which came over the face of the civilized world. The industrial revolution and the progress of democracy, those two basic facts of nineteenth-century social development throughout Continental Europe, could not fail to leave their imprint even on a community in Poland's abnormal political position. The dawn of the century found Poland, fresh from the catastrophe of the partitions, still essentially in the old feudal condition of a country of large landowners and of masses of peasant serfs, with trade decayed in the impoverished towns and hardly any industries in existence. The close of the century left her in possession of a powerful class of small farmers growing in prosperity and in a sense of social importance ; with strong modern industries built up especially in Russian Poland ; with a Polish middle class once more evolving in the towns, with industrial labour organizing for the conquest of political rights, and with a quickly increasing *intelligentsia* fed by influxes both from the old landed gentry and from the newly emancipated peasant masses.

The legacies left behind by these pre-war results of social evolution to the free and reunited Polish State in the field of social and economic policy can be summed up in three problems of dominant magnitude.

Firstly: how is the accomplished social emancipation of the peasant class to be given its necessary economic corollary in the form of a redistribution of property in *land*, without a ruinous effect of the great change on the general level of agricultural prosperity ? In fact, how is this prosperity to be enhanced in order to meet the needs of a rapidly growing country population, in the midst of what is more and more clearly manifesting itself as a world-wide crisis of agriculture ?

Secondly : how, in view of the power of older industrial
countries over the world's markets, are those *industries* to be
developed which, in a densely populated country, are an essential condition of economic well-being ?   How, indeed, are those
once flourishing industrial centres to be maintained which,
through their separation from Russia and Germany respectively,
have lost their original economic bases ?

And thirdly : how is Poland once more to become that
prosperous emporium of international *trade* which she was in
the Middle Ages, and which her geographical position obviously
qualifies her to be ?   How, in particular, are the energies of her
town population to be directed anew into trade channels, so
as to diminish the overweight of an economically unproductive
*intelligentsia* ?

Here, indeed, are problems to tax the capacities of the greatest
social politicians—problems all equally urgent, and all rendered
equally difficult by the given post-war conditions of economic
crisis and social unrest.   The landless (or almost landless)
peasant, the destitute industrial worker, the university trained
professional man unfit to make money by his work, in Poland,
as elsewhere in Continental Europe, stand in acute opposition
to those mainstays of the Capitalist order—the landowner, the
manufacturer, and the tradesman—and they clamour for
provision out of the coffers of the State under the form of " social
insurance."   These coffers must be filled by draining, through
severe taxation, the resources of renascent capitalism in a
devastated country ; and the result is that instead of a prospect
of slowly growing wealth, the country is confronted by the danger
of advancing pauperism.

It is with this dilemma that Poland, like many another State
in the Europe of to-day, has had to grapple ; and in order to
show in some detail to what effect she has done so, it will obviously be expedient to adopt the division of problems outlined
above, because within its framework the main social issues fall
into line with the fundamental economic ones.   In dealing
first with agriculture, then with industry, and last with trade,
we shall at the same time be discussing the social categories of
peasant and landowner, working-man and manufacturer, city-
dweller and city trader, respectively.

2

Of the technical conditions and social aspects of *agriculture*
in Poland, enough has been already said to show that the tasks
of reform to be attacked after war-time ravages and after the

reunion of three sections of the country widely different from each other in agricultural progress, were enormous indeed.

To begin with the *social problems* of agriculture, one of them, above all, concentrated the attention of Poland's legislators and administrators upon itself in the first years of the new Poland's existence : the problem of *agrarian reform*, that is to say, of the more equable distribution of property in land. Something has been said in a former chapter on the political conditions under the pressure of which legislative action in this matter became one of the earliest and most urgent necessities in the life of the new Poland as well as of some neighbouring post-war States. Here it will be our task to consider mainly the economic aspects of the question.

The disproportion between the enormous size of a number of large estates, and the pitifully small farms of a struggling and quickly multiplying peasantry was an obvious social evil, which called for remedy. On the other hand, the break-up of large centres of agricultural production in favour of a network of peasant farms was, economically speaking, a dangerous proceeding—very much what, in industry, an attempt to return from a system of large factories to one of small artisans' work-shops would have been. How to render justice to an evident social necessity and at the same time not to lower the standard of agricultural production, has since constituted the dilemma of land reform in Poland and elsewhere.

As related before, the principles of land redistribution were laid down on very radical lines in a resolution of the Constituent Assembly passed as early as July, 1919, and in its bill voted at the height of the Bolshevik invasion in 1920 ; and their application, especially by governments in which the Peasant Farmer Party was a dominent force gave ground for a good deal of complaint. It was only by a bill of 1925 (with some additional legislative acts in the same year and in 1927) that the land reform scheme was recast into a less radical mould. To begin with, the principle of compulsory sale of portions of the larger estates was replaced by that of purely private transactions in land, with the Government only controlling the total extent of these transactions and sanctioning them. In the second place, a serious attempt was made at last to finance the whole scheme, and an apparatus for the purpose was created soon afterwards by the foundation of a Land Bank. At the same time, provision was made to secure the existence of the rural labourers, thrown out of employment by the breaking-up of large estates. Finally, it was recognized for the first time that not only large estates

N

were in need of " reform," but something must be done as well
to improve the status of the peasant farms, some of which, in
consequence of continued sub-division among numerous children,
are uneconomically small, and divided into scattered strips of
land, too. The original Land Reform Bill having fixed a
*maximum* of land ownership, to which larger estates were
gradually to be cut down, the necessary corollary to this would
have been the determination of a *minimum* of land constituting
a workable farming unit, which must not be sub-divided
further. Such a minimum has not been fixed so far, although
the idea of the " farming unit " was propounded very con-
vincingly in a " Land Code " project, drafted by the late Professor Jaworski of Cracow. The bill of 1925, however, established
a connection between the process of parcelling-up the large
estates and that of rounding off dwarf-sized peasant farms, and
so linked up the important work of land reform with the no
less important task of what is called " commassation " of
scattered peasant fields. It was only by the combination of
these two ideas that land reform justified its claim to being
considered as leading to a real improvement of the country's
agricultural organization.

Under the provisions of the law of 1925, over 5½ million acres
of land now belonging to large landowners are to be parcelled
up, while nearly 10 million acres are to remain in the owners'
possession in the shape of *maximum* units of 450 acres each. In
the case of the border provinces, where Polish landed property
is protected for political reasons, the *maximum* limit is higher ;
and estates devoted to some specialized form of agricultural
industry or high-quality production, are to be free from the
operation of reform.

A survey of the actual working of the land reform scheme
during the first ten years brings out the following salient facts.

Immediately after the passing of the first Land Reform Bill,
there was a rapid rise in the demand for land on the part of
small farmers, and in the supply of it by large owners who, under
the terms of the original bill, were threatened by compulsory
expropriation. After 1921, the peasantry, who at first had
profited by the famine conditions in the towns, became impoverished, and accordingly, the figures of sale and purchase
of land rapidly fell during the next few years. In 1925, the
passage of the new Land Reform Bill gave a new stimulus to
land transfer, and another process of rapid growth of peasant
proprietorship is observable ; credit facilities being offered by
the Government to peasant buyers, the total of transactions

under Government control rises much more quickly and is much larger from the first, than that of voluntary sales. The figures of 1921 are surpassed by one-third in 1928 ; since that year, the economic crisis has had a strongly depressing effect on the process of land reform : the lack of capital, the dearth of credit, and the unprecedentedly low level of market prices for agricultural produce keep the demand for land almost at the zero level.

### 3

" *Commassation* " (as it is called in eastern Europe) has been mentioned above as an element of land reform equal in importance to the transfer of land from large to small owners. The chequerwork produced by scattered peasant possessions is still a characteristic feature of the Polish countryside from the point of view of land ownership. It is the result of manifold causes connected partly with serfdom, and partly with the conditions which arose after its abolition ; and reform in this respect is rendered particularly difficult both by the stubborn conservatism and the ingrained diffidence of the peasant class. The problem being common to Poland and the neighbouring agricultural countries, its importance was realized even in pre-war times by the partitioning powers ; but only Prussia, by attacking the task resolutely as far back as 1821, succeeded in accomplishing it almost in its entirety. Under Austria, an Imperial law of 1853, and a Galician provincial bill of 1899, dealt with the subject, but very little headway was made. Russia was very late in approaching the problem at all ; but it must be admitted that the Stolypin Government, in its desire to win the support of the peasantry against the revolutionary *intelligentsia* of the towns, acted very strenuously in the matter. Under Stolypin's decrees of 1906–11 considerable progress was made with the commassation of peasant fields, especially in the provinces of the Polish-Russian border, where a Polish country gentry and a non-Polish peasantry confronted each other. In Russian Poland proper, the initiative of the community itself had long preceded that of the Russian Government, and a good deal had been accomplished even before Stolypin. Altogether, the reunited Poland inherited over 28 million acres of peasant land requiring measures of commassation, and situated almost entirely in former Russian and Austrian Poland.

Owing to the complicated state of pre-war legal arrangements in these matters in the three sectors, it took several years before a uniform " Commassation Law " for the whole of Poland was worked out ; and this, like the Land Reform Bill, was amended in 1925 and again in 1927.

In view of the fact that commassation always raises the quantity of agricultural production, the Polish law treats it as a measure of public welfare and accordingly authorizes the local Land Offices to proceed with it at the request of only a small fraction of the owners concerned, and sometimes even without any such request. The fees for the necessary surveying activities are made payable by easy instalments, and the work is always undertaken with the aim of leaving each owner in possession, if possible, of one connected area of land, or at least of a consolidated unit of land of each category (building, arable, pasture, forest).

Since the passing of the Commassation Law, the acreage of land property rearranged under it grew rapidly from year to year, each year doubling the figures of the preceding one. It rose to 1¼ million acres in 1930, the total dealt with up to that date in the new Poland amounting to five million acres, or more than one-fifth of the total area which was originally in need of such rearrangement. At the rate of progress which so far has remained uninterrupted (even during the recent economic crisis), and with the growing experience and skill of the official personnel, it can confidently be anticipated that in another 20–25 years the labours in this domain will be completed and the wasteful dispersion of farm lands in Poland will be a thing of the past.

There is one other minor field for reforming activities left over as an inheritance of the great historical transition from peasant serfdom to peasant ownership. This consists of *rights to use pasture and forest land*. Such rights with regard to the landlord's property were often left to the peasants when released from serfdom, and have now gradually to be bought off by equivalent plots of land. The law in this respect, entangled in the meshes of different pre-war arrangements in the three sectors, was only rendered workable in 1927, and since that time the progress in freeing land from such rights of others than its owners has been more marked. Altogether over 168,000 properties were so freed between 1919 and 1930, and the area of land given in return for rights amounts to nearly 1¼ million acres. To this must be added some 60,000 acres of common lands (mainly pastures) broken up into individual allotments.

These figures complete the picture of the enormous change in conditions of land tenure which is passing over the face of the new Poland. The ideal of transforming the entire countryside into a network of middle-sized, workable peasant farms, and of thereby raising the prosperity of millions of rural population, may still be very distant, and the rapid multiplication of that peasant population itself certainly interferes very seriously with its ever becoming fully realized. However, Poland is progressing in that direction, and no thoroughgoing change of land policy is contemplated. At the same time, it is being more and more fully realized that apart from mere redistribution of land, technical improvements must keep pace with the reform of ownership conditions if land reform is not to spell economic disaster.

### 4

Among the achievements of the new Poland in the way of technical progress in agriculture, the promotion of *drainage* of fields is perhaps the most important.

Poland inherited from the partitioning powers an area of about 2½ million acres of fields which had been drained. There remained within the frontiers of the new Republic nearly 50,000,000 acres requiring drainage, and nearly 70,000,000 requiring irrigation. In many cases the regulation of river beds and brooks would be an indispensable preliminary condition of field drainage. A State Fund for financing drainage operations was created in 1925, and augmented to nearly ten times its original amount in the course of the next four years. Until 1925, only about 7500 acres a year had been drained in the new Poland ; after 1925, the figures increase rapidly, and for 1928, the amount is already 120,000 acres. The actual work is being organized by local draining associations, of which some 600 exist in Poland now, while before the War there had been no more than 100. There are 46 enterprises conducting drainage operations, and half a dozen experimental stations devoted to them. The main area for future work of this kind on a large scale consists of the extensive marshes in the province of Polesie, in the centre of the eastern border belt, along the river Pripet and its northern and southern tributaries. These marshes are the largest in Europe, covering over 4,000,000 acres of ground. Their utilization for normal agriculture would mean an enormous addition to the wealth of Poland. Preliminary research with regard to the huge task is far advanced ; but serious progress with the work itself can only be made if foreign capital comes to Poland's assistance ; and inasmuch as the regulation of rivers is part of the task, and all the rivers concerned flow into the Dnieper, and with it into the Black Sea, the correlation of

Polish enterprise with corresponding work on the Russian side
of the border would be a condition of success.   This, however,
is almost impracticable in the present state of Russian affairs.

## 5

Having singled out drainage as the domain of technical
improvement in which progress has been most marked, it remains
to say something of the working of those *moral factors* which
must be brought to bear on the system if the workers themselves
engaged in agriculture are to rise to the height of their task.
Among such factors, two are of prime importance for the
prosperity of a country gradually endowing its peasant masses
with land :  they are, the co-operative organization of farmers
and their scientific agricultural education.

*Agricultural co-operation* had received a powerful stimulus in
nineteenth-century Poland from political persecution at the
hand of the partitioning powers.   It was in Prussian Poland
that the struggle for the Polish land against the German colonizing campaign knit country gentry and peasant farmers most
effectively together in a large " Central Economic Society "
which lifted the quality and quantity of agricultural production
in the Prussian sector to the high level maintained by it.   It
was there also that under the name of " Patronate of Agricultural
Circles " an excellent credit organization for small farmers was
built up under the leadership of Roman Catholic priests.   In
Russian Poland, again, in the middle of the nineteenth century,
when an " Agricultural Society " was the only Polish organization allowed by the Russian Government, that society for a
number of years became the radiating centre of the best national
effort in the economic, social, and even, vicariously, in the
political and intellectual field.   Under Austria finally, the
" Galician Agricultural Society " uniting chiefly larger owners,
and side by side with it, a network of " Farmers' Circles " and
of Farmers' Co-operative Credit institutions connected with
them, had decades of highly useful work behind them, when the
War came.

All those old-established organizations emerged from the War
with their capital and apparatus largely destroyed, but strenuous efforts both from above and from below were soon made
to revive their activities, as well as to create new centres.   At
the same time, it became the obvious task to combine old
sectional organizations into new large units embracing the
whole area of the reunited country.   This was by no means
easy, in view of differences in local conditions, and of strong

local jealousy directed against every appearance of " centralism." Nevertheless, a good deal of headway was made. In 1927, 4,100 local Farmers' Circles all over Poland, comprising 120,000 members, were united within the Central Agricultural Society and the Central Association of Farmers' Circles. The total number of agricultural co-operative organizations in the new Poland rose from 364 in 1924 to nearly 600 in 1929. Whether large or small, agricultural co-operatives mostly have the form of warehouses for the sale of agricultural produce on the one hand, and shops for the purchase of articles necessary to the farmer on the other. Collective bargaining in selling and the exclusion of middlemen in buying—those two principal aims of all co-operation—have been most successfully achieved by the large associations of western Poland, with the schooling they had received before the War through struggle with the Prussians. Dairy co-operatives deserve to be singled out as a particularly important section of the agricultural co-operative system. Here again it is former Prussian Poland which takes the lead : its co-operative steam dairies are models to the rest of the country. The example is being eagerly followed by former Russian Poland, where the number of dairies grew from 70 to 300 in the three years 1924 to 1927. Owing to co-operative dairy enterprise, Poland's exports of butter jumped up from 1,000 tons in 1922 to 15,000 in 1929, and the success was achieved of entering the British market, where Polish butter now holds an established position.

The work of all types of organizations promoting agricultural co-operation is receiving material assistance and administrative support from central and local government authorities, with the Ministry of Agriculture at their head. Central executive organs have been formed to bring the weight of professional opinion to bear on the Government's decisions in matters of agrarian policy. Home Rule in agrarian matters is to be exercised by " Agricultural Chambers," which before the War had existed in Prussian Poland only, and which, under a law of 1928, are being organized in other parts of Poland as well. Poland's agricultural organizations are represented in the International Institute of Agriculture at Rome and at all international agricultural conferences and congresses. One such congress of late years was held in Warsaw ; and the conference of delegates of the predominantly agricultural powers of central and eastern Europe, held in Warsaw on the initiative of Poland's Foreign Minister in 1930, is another manifestation of Poland's active share in the treatment of international problems of agriculture.

## 6

*Agricultural education and research* in Poland before the War had had important centres of their own, even in the darkest days of captivity. An Agricultural College at Marymont, near Warsaw, had been founded long before the resolute Russification of Russian Poland began ; in later days, self-governing Austrian Poland created an Agricultural Academy at Dublany near Lwów, a secondary School of Agriculture at Czernichów in the Cracow district, and an Agricultural Department (now a Faculty by itself) in the University of Cracow.

These were antecedents not to be despised, and it was on the basis of an established tradition that the new Poland could build. After a dozen years of organizing activities, Poland is in possession of four Faculties devoted to Agriculture and Forestry in the Universities of Cracow, Lwów, Poznań, and Wilno. In Warsaw, there is a complete Academy of Agriculture as a separate institution of university rank.

On the secondary school level, there are now seven State-supported agricultural schools in the country, and one supported by a special foundation. There are also three secondary and two higher schools of gardening, two schools of dairy-farming, six colleges for the training of teachers of agriculture, and half-a-dozen large private institutions for the education of women in all branches of rural household science.

Agricultural schools on the elementary school plane now aggregate a total of 115, of which two-thirds are for boys, and one-third for girls. They are all connected with experimental farms. In the more advanced parts of the country, particularly in the western provinces, winter courses of agricultural education for young men of the farming class are doing very useful work. The large numbers of pupils leaving these schools—about 4,000 a year—introduce a very desirable element of culture into the life of out-of-the-way Polish villages. Culture in the village is also promoted by the educational activities of Farmers' Circles, and by those of travelling agricultural instructors—of whom there are about 750 in the Republic. The device (borrowed from America) of prizes for the best accomplishment of certain definite tasks in crop-raising or stock-breeding is also proving a great stimulant of technical advance in peasant farming : in 1929, there were 53,000 young people of the peasant class taking part in such competitions. Finally, the practice organized by certain university extension agencies, of sending young peasants for periods of practice to model farms in Denmark, may be mentioned as productive of good results.

*Agricultural research* in Poland found a home in the large Agricultural Research Institute at Puławy, established in 1917 on the foundation of a similar Russian institution, and afterwards fused into one large whole with another institute which had existed under German rule at Bydgoszcz. The Institute, composed of sixteen sections altogether, was superintended in its early years by Professor Emil Godlewski, a plant physiologist of great international reputation. Apart from the Institute, the Chairs, Departments, and Faculties of Agriculture in Poland's universities are active centres of agricultural research, and valuable investigations into the problems of plant physiology and bacteriology, of seed-testing, stock-breeding, of the chemistry of plants and the composition of the soil, of artificial fertilizing, of agricultural machinery, and, last not least, of the comparatively new and rapidly developing science of agricultural economics, have been accomplished in those new Polish workshops of research and filled hundreds of volumes during the last dozen years. The influence of this large bulk of research work on agricultural practice has been considerable, and might have been greater still if lack of capital had not stood in the way of its application throughout the country. It is not to be forgotten, after all, that all these efforts were made in a country whose agriculture had been more thoroughly ruined by the War than that of any other land in Europe.

## 7

During the World War, Polish agriculture had suffered the loss of over a million and a half of farm buildings ; the live stock was reduced by one-third ; of the area of arable fields, 20 per cent. still lay fallow in the first post-war years ; in addition to all this, large portions of the country had been drained of man-power, partly by conscription, partly by enforced war-time emigration.

In spite of these enormous upheavals and devastations, the indefatigable industry of the Polish farmer redressed the balance with amazing quickness. In the first year of real peace for Poland, 1921, the ruined and famished country was still obliged to import seven million tons of food without being able to export any ; but in the very next year, it had already become a food-exporting country, and has remained so, on an increasing scale, ever since. All the arable land was under cultivation again within the very first years of regained peace ; farm buildings have largely been reconstructed, and the quantity of live stock now is considerably above the pre-war level. Improvements in the way of use of high-quality seeds, of the application of artificial fertilizers and the introduction of machinery are in progress to a much greater extent than could be expected in a country deprived of capital and enjoying very scanty credit. Agricultural industries, like the production of beet-sugar, were in a flourishing condition again within the first ten years of the new Poland. The whole of Polish agriculture, indeed, with the acquisition of considerable new outlets for export, seemed to be entering on a great era of advance, when the world crisis, by its repercussion in Poland, put a stop to these developments.

A few selected details may serve to illustrate these general statements.

In the domain of *grain farming*, to begin with, Poland is above all a producer of *rye*, and only in a much smaller measure of *wheat*. Her rye crop, in the years from 1925 to 1929 (the last "good years" before the crisis) averaged 62,000,000 quintals (over one-fourth of Russia's and four times that of the U.S.A.), her wheat crop only 16,000,000, or, roughly, one-fourteenth of either that of Russia or of the United States and one-tenth of Canada's.

As far as rye is concerned, Poland is, on the whole, self-supporting : within the five comparatively normal years 1923 to 1928, the excess of exports over imports was over 200,000 tons. The increase in output of rye during the period was considerable (from an average of 180 to one of 190 kilogrammes per head of the population), but it did not find expression in exports, the rye being mostly grown for home consumption and largely kept within the country by measures of economic policy.

In the case of *wheat*, imports during the same period surpassed exports by more than 350,000 tons, It must be noted, however, that the trend of wheat cultivation in Poland, particularly in the central provinces, has generally been upward : the output per head of the population rose from 40 to over 50 kilogrammes between 1922 and 1928.

For *oats*, as for wheat, imports are generally somewhat larger than exports ; while *barley* is emphatically an export article, the balance in favour of exports amounting to over 460,000 tons, in the period under review.

The categories of agriculture so far enumerated provide the raw material for certain *agricultural industries* which are most fitly discussed here. There is, first of all, the time-honoured occupation of the miller. Of the 20,000 *flour mills* in Poland (of which four-fifths were active in 1926) only a small section could be classed as industrial establishments (mostly steam mills, and to be found mainly in the western provinces) the rest being old-fashioned watermills, or (in much lesser number) windmills. The recovery and progress of the industry after the War was somewhat impeded, in the new Poland's early years, by legislative regulations interfering with fine-flour production in the interest of bread prices in the towns. But in the era after 1926, when the interests of agriculture received more consideration, these restrictions were gradually removed.

Next to the mills, the *breweries* of Poland call for brief mention. There were about 500 of them before the War. They had a hard struggle to recover from War-time devastations, the more so as Polish legislation considerably restricted the brewing of all stronger grades of beer till 1925. Even after that year, beer containing more than $2\frac{1}{2}$ per cent. of alcohol was treated on an equal footing with whisky containing as much as 40 per cent., and the bar against its sale on Sunday prevented the domestic market for beer from developing normally—which was, perhaps, not quite in the interests of real temperance.

The pre-war *per capita* consumption of beer in Poland being estimated at about 8 gallons annually, and the post-war average having only reached 2 gallons in 1928, it is easy to see, what possibilities of development are before the breweries as a purely domestic industry of Poland.

8

The remaining main items of Poland's large-scale agricultural production are sugar-beet and potatoes, both of them also providing the raw material of important agricultural industries.

The cultivation of the *sugar-beet* and the production of sugar from it occupied, in pre-war times, a very prominent place in the economic life of some parts of Poland, especially of the south-eastern borderlands both under Russia and Austria, to some extent also, of certain large estates in the Prussian sector ; 87 sugar factories were active then on the area of the Poland of to-day, and they produced over half a million tons of sugar per annum, or $6\frac{1}{4}$ per cent. of the world's beet-sugar production.

The War, apart from the total destruction of 24 factories and of the ruin of beet cultivation, led to an utter collapse of sugar consumption in the home market, while in the foreign markets cane-sugar won a predominant position.

Nevertheless, recovery was very quick. Sugar-beet cultivation after the War increased very rapidly, the increase finding expression mostly in the extent of the area under cultivation rather than in intensity of yield : the pre-war area of cultivation was reached in 1925–26 and surpassed since, but the output both of sugar-beet and of sugar, even in 1927–28, still lagged somewhat behind the pre-war figures, and consumption has only recently exceeded the pre-war level. Of the 24 factories destroyed, 15 were rebuilt ; a number of those in former Prussian Poland which had produced only raw sugar before, were developed into refineries, and others were modernized in their methods of production, chiefly by the introduction of electric power and by transport improvements.

Within a few years after the War, two large associations of Poland's sugar producers, a western and an eastern one, were formed, and they became instrumental in obtaining foreign credits, while a " Sugar Industrialists' Bank " established at Poznań organized the entire sale of the product. The producers also organized both a research institute devoted to problems of the industry, and experimental studies concerning sugar-beet cultivation. As a result of it all, Poland's production of sugar in 1929–30 had risen to over 900 million tons and was surpassed only by the U.S.A., Czechoslovakia, Soviet Russia and Germany.

All the efforts to raise production, however, did not save the Polish sugar industry from its share of difficulties arising out of the world crisis of over-production in recent years. The problem of disposing of Poland's annual output of sugar became an oppressive one, and here as in other fields, foreign markets could only be held by taxing the domestic consumer.

## 9

The *potato*, which, together with rye bread and cabbages, remains the staple food of large masses of the poor peasantry in Poland—has since the War shown heavily decreasing figures of production, especially in the western provinces, owing to the tariff war with Germany ; sugar-beet, in the west and elsewhere, frequently took the place of potatoes. The result was a considerable decrease in the *per capita* output of potatoes (from 10½ to 9 kilogrammes per head of the population between 1922 and 1928), but the quantities produced in comparison with other countries are still considerable : Poland, with an annual average of 265 million quintals, produces one-fifth of the world's crop and her self-sufficiency in this domain is perfectly assured.

The production of *spirit from potatoes* had long before the War been a flourishing agricultural industry in Poland ; almost

every estate of any size possessed its own distillery, and excellent
food for cattle was an important by-product. Two-thirds of
the potato spirit produced before the War in Polish lands were
exported. Of the pre-war output, only about one-fourth had
been reached by the end of the first ten years of independent
Poland, and the export markets were almost entirely lost. In
1924, a Government Spirit Monopoly was introduced in Poland
as one of Grabski's fiscal measures. The monopolist management of the industry did not succeed in opening up avenues for
export, and it kept the market price of the product inconveniently
high, owing to the heavy costs of Government administration.
The use of spirit in industry is still imperfectly developed in
Poland, only 18 per cent. of the total production being absorbed
by industries. The consumption of spirit in the form of liquor,
on the other hand, has been decreasing by leaps and bounds
since the coming of the crisis—perhaps one of the few desirable
social effects which the crisis has had, but unfortunately at the
same time a cause for serious concern to the agricultural spirit
producers on the one hand and to the Government (of whose
budget the spirit monopoly was a mainstay) on the other.

Passing over the production of starch and some minor potato
industries, we may summarily remark that Poland's possibilities
in this field are far from being exploited to the full of their
capacity, and, in a coming period of more normal international
trade, great developments in Poland's potato industries are
likely to take place.

### 10

Having surveyed the principal domains of large-scale agriculture severally, we may now for a moment consider some of the
*general economic aspects of agricultural production.*

The total balance for grain of all sorts shows a net surplus in
favour of exports only if we take the years 1925 to 1928 under
consideration, and this chiefly owing to the bumper crop of
1926 ; while for the preceding years—which include the bad
harvest of 1925—the surplus is on the import side.

Of the total exports of all kinds of grain, the lion's share went
to Germany, which consumed over nine-tenths of Poland's
exported rye, and four-fifths of her exported wheat. Similarly,
among the countries from which Poland imported cereals,
Germany stands head and shoulders over the rest, in spite of
the state of " tariff war " between the two Republics.

As regards output, there is a considerable difference between
Poland's west, which had learned useful lessons from its German

rulers, and the east, where extremely primitive methods of agriculture still very largely prevail : the harvests in the west, in spite of rather poor soil, are from 50 to 100 per cent. higher than in the eastern provinces. Again, there is a marked and very natural difference between the productiveness of farming on large estates and on small peasant farms, the former being superior to the latter in the case of grain, by 20–23 per cent., and in the case of potatoes, by 14 per cent. Finally, it must be stated that the increase of area under cultivation has been largest (as noted above) in the case of the sugar-beet, while in the case of grain it has not been strong enough to reach pre-war dimensions again : wheat, rye, barley and oats after the first ten post-war years, still covered 10 per cent. less ground than in 1914.

## II

To the above account of arable farming in Poland, a few remarks may now be added on *gardening* and some other specialized forms of tillage of the soil.

Both flower and vegetable gardening, together with the corresponding branches of technical education and with horticultural industries, stood fairly high in the pre-war Austrian sector, and particularly in Prussian Poland. Under Russia, the protective tariff policy and the possibility of large vegetable exports into the interior of the Russian Empire promoted mainly extensive market-gardening. Since the War, higher horticultural education has had its established centres in the Agricultural Faculty of Cracow University and in the Agricultural Academy of Warsaw, and secondary and lower schools of gardening exist in a number of towns, including the town of Zaleszczyki in the happy south-eastern corner on the Rumanian border, long known for its apricots, peaches, and other fruit of southern type. There are a number of experimental stations conducted by the Government ; horticultural societies promote gardening by organizing shows and courses of instruction, as well as publishing periodicals. The consumption of home-grown fruit is being somewhat artificially stimulated by heavy duties on such imported foreign fruit as oranges and bananas, which have become a luxury to the average Polish citizen. In spite of these and similar restrictions, Poland remains a large market for foreign fruit—e.g., for Californian and Australian apples— because her own climate, on the whole, does not favour the cultivation of high-class products of the kind. The severe and prolonged winter of 1928–29 destroyed large numbers of fruit trees all over the country.

*Seed Culture* in Poland, as a special occupation, is of recent origin. Until towards the end of the nineteenth century, Polish lands were dependent largely on foreign sources (chiefly German) for high-class seeds. In the new free Poland, landowners and commercial firms, have been competing with government-supported experimental and research institutions in the endeavour to raise the standard of all kinds of field and garden seeds, and the happy interaction of expert knowledge and empirical practice in this respect is yielding good results. It is with a view to further progress in this respect that highly specialized and experimental estates are exempted from the operation of the great social scheme of land reform.

*Meadows* in Poland still are largely in a natural condition, without systematic cultivation, and for *pastures*, land is used which cannot, for some reason or other, be brought under the plough. The meadows are, accordingly, often marshy stretches of land in the valleys of large rivers, while pastures consist of steep and stony slopes in the mountains. Meadows and pastures cover altogether about 17 per cent. of Poland's total area, and the relation of their extent to that of tilled land is one to three ; but five-sixths of them require drainage and other improvements. Of the efforts made in the way of drainage generally, some account has been given above.

## 12

Next to fields, meadows, and pastures, *forests* make up a large portion of the vegetable covering of Poland's soil : they occupy over 23 per cent. of her surface. Of these forests, over one-half are included in large private estates, while nearly one-third belong to the State and only less than a tenth to small farmers. The exploitation of forests by private owners had in the past often been reckless, suggesting itself as the easiest means of paying off heavy debts or making up for a shortage of income from agricultural crops. The landowners of the new Poland cannot, unfortunately, be freed from the same reproach which burdens the account of their forefathers ; during the first ten years of the new independence, the forest surface became diminished by 3 per cent. of its total acreage in 1919. There were, indeed, compelling reasons for such uneconomic exploitation.

First of all, a heavy " forest tax " was imposed by the State on the large owners, and levied in kind for purposes of reconstruction of the wooden buildings in the country after the war. Another motive for quick and prodigal exploitation was supplied by the fact that, in the original Land Reform Bill of 1920, a clause had been rashly included which announced the wholesale nationalization of all privately owned forests. The clause was not, and could not be, carried out ; but it had its harmful effect on private forest administration.

Of the large quantities of timber felled in the forests, about one-half has been used—uneconomically again—for fuel : eastern Poland still uses almost exclusively wood, and not coal, for heating. Of the portion of the timber not used for fuel, about one-half was used for various purposes within the country, and one-half exported. Large timber exports, in answer to the ample demand from abroad, were a favourite device of some of the new Poland's early Governments for improving her trade balance : unfortunately, vast quantities of this timber were exported in the raw, which may have been a temporary necessity, but was certainly most wasteful. Only in recent years, with the erection of many new saw-mills, has over one-half of the exported timber been leaving Poland in the form of boards : this proportion, however, is still far from satisfactory.

The domain of forest administration was one of the many into which order was introduced by the Piłsudski *régime* after 1926, when Parliament no longer hampered such constructive efforts. Two Presidential decrees, issued in 1928, laid down certain maxims for the rational management of the State forests and of the major privately owned ones. Progress towards " rationalization," which indeed had begun before that date, has been very marked since ; there is, particularly, a notable advance to be recorded of late in the systematic replanting of forest land and in careful cultivation with a view to maintaining a high standard of quality among Poland's typical forest trees. An industrial establishment for the preparation of high-class pine-tree seeds at Kłosnów (formerly under Prussia) is displaying intense activity.

With this renaissance of afforestation certain adverse happenings have unfortunately interfered recently. The mass appearance of insect parasites ruined some 175,000 acres of pine forests in the former Prussian sector. The terrible frosts of the severe winter of 1928–29 (mentioned before in connection with horticulture) left large masses of forest trees all over Poland lifeless and fit only for the axe.

With all such handicaps, however, intelligent appreciation of Poland's forest resources and reasonable dealing with them are steadily making headway. Apart from legislation, important contributions to this are being made by educational effort, through the three Forestry Departments in Polish universities, through a number of lower schools for the training of foresters, through a Committee for Experimental Research in Forestry, working under the Ministry of Agriculture, and through the labours of individual scientists which are devoted to forestry problems and are appearing in the form of numerous monographs and manuals.

It is perhaps the crowning outcome of this growth of intelligent interest in forestry that the State has lately accorded a great deal of protection and support to a widespread movement for the preservation of natural beauties, and particularly of forest scenery, in intact condition. Poland has followed the great example of richer and larger countries (like the United States of America and the Union of South Africa), in turning wide tracts of state-owned forest into " *reservations* " which are to remain entirely inviolate. Such reservations exist in the large forests in Poland's north-east (Białowież), in the Tatra Mountains in the south-west, and in the eastern portions of the vast Carpathian range. By agreement with Czechoslovakia, a belt of virgin forest in the hills is to extend as a common " National Park " on both sides of the border between the two States, and the frontier between them, once fiercely disputed in that particular region is to be merged in it. This act, accomplished in 1932, establishes a fine precedent for the settling of international frontier disputes in a truly civilized manner.

## 13

In connection with the above account of Poland's timber resources it seems appropriate here to make brief mention of the *wood industries* of the country.

As said before, exports of raw timber were a more or less necessary evil of Poland's earliest years ; later, the *saw-mill industry* recovered and became active. In 1927, Poland had over 1600 saw-mills, of which 1300 were provided with motors, while of the rest one-half used water-power, and the others were out of action. These saw-mills are mostly small affairs ; but in spite of its decentralized condition, the saw-mill industry is one of Poland's important economic assets, employing 50,000 industrial workers, that is to say, one-tenth of the country's industrial population, and surpassing in dimensions even the old and well-developed saw-mill industry of Sweden.

The saw-mills supply the material for a number of further wood industries, such as, above all, the *furniture* factories. The furniture industry—centring largely round the city of

Bydgoszcz, in former Prussian Poland, exported its products on a large scale, even overseas (to America and Australia) during the last years before the crisis (exports being doubled in quantity between 1924 and 1928). Altogether, the export of wood and wooden articles from Poland constituted, in 1928, one-fourth of the total exports of the country in value.

This large export bill included a considerable proportion of the output of Poland's *factories of matches*. The Grabski administration, in 1924, included the establishment of a match monopoly among its drastic fiscal measures. The exploitation of the monopoly was turned over to a Swedish-American concern. But it was soon realized that this hasty contract was very unfavourable to the material interests of the Polish State. In 1931, the conditions of the match contract were essentially amended, and it was made the basis of a loan to Poland.

Next to the manufacture of matches, among Poland's larger wood industries, there stands the manufacture of *paper*. In the case of this, as of many other industries, there was in pre-war times a marked difference between the Austrian and Prussian sector on the one hand and the Russian on the other. Under Austria and Prussia paper factories were few, and these produced only the coarser kinds of paper, while the high-quality product was provided by the industries of the inner provinces of the two Empires. In Russian Poland, on the contrary, the industry flourished : a dozen factories produced over 60,000 tons of paper a year, of which a large portion was sold all over Russia.

In the new Poland, the industry, fostered by drastic tariff protection (which was even strongly resented by the publishing trade), quickly increased in volume, especially after the reform of the currency. This progress was stimulated also by a rapid growth of demand, and the result was that while production increased tenfold (from 15,000 to 150,000 tons) in the first ten years, yet imports more or less maintained a level of over 30,000 tons. These imports cover the need in the best qualities of paper, which the Polish industries are not yet fitted to produce. When it is considered that the *per capita* consumption of paper in Poland, although rising very fast with the spread of education, is still only one-sixth of the British or German average, it will be seen that the future prospects before Poland's paper industry are very large indeed.

### 14

From the vegetable resources of Poland's national household we now turn to her *animal wealth*.

Side by side with Poland's vegetable exports, the export of animals and animal-food articles is a factor of growing importance for the national economic system. The crisis caused by over-production and fall of prices in the domain of agriculture has, in some of its phases, reacted favourably on stock breeding in Poland : potatoes, e.g., fetching no adequate prices in the market, were often and widely used by farmers to feed quickly-growing numbers of pigs. On the other hand, the difficulties more recently experienced by stock-breeding nations in western Europe in the way of making their production pay have neces-sarily found their echo in Poland : hence the keen struggle conducted in order to secure the highest possible contingent of pig and other animal exports in each commercial treaty con-cluded between Poland and the neighbouring States in the last few years. The domestic market has not had much effect on the situation, meat being still a rare article of food among Poland's rural masses and only fats being in considerable demand in addition to the staple articles of bread, potatoes and milk : hence the striking fact of considerable imports of animal fats from abroad into an essentially agricultural country.

Our survey of Poland's live-stock economy will fitly begin with the *horse*—traditionally a most popular animal among a nation which conducted its almost ceaseless wars against eastern invaders for centuries largely on horseback. Pedigree horses were a favourite luxury with the Polish as with the English country gentleman, and some of the larger privately owned studs in pre-war Poland reached a very high level of quality. They were, of course, almost completely destroyed in the course of the Great War, and the dawn of the new freedom found Poland almost completely deprived not only of pedigree, but of ordinary working horses. It was the army which, under the pressure of immediate needs, first began to remedy this situation systematically. The territorial conditions of the eastern borderlands being such that cavalry must play a large part in warfare there, horse-breeding for military purposes had to be promoted in haste. The foreign occupants had left three provisional studs behind in Central Poland : these were regrouped and increased by occasional purchases. The un-expected return, in 1919, of over 200 pedigree horses, evacuated into Russia from Warsaw in 1915, and brought back, under most adventurous conditions, by a well-known racing man, meant a very lucky windfall. Pedigree stallions being, under post-war conditions, generally beyond the means of the private owner, the entire domain of horse breeding naturally got under State control, and is administered by a special Government Office which forms part of the Ministry of Agriculture. The Government keeps three studs and eight stallion stations in the country, and it lends reproductors from them to private breeders.

The small and unsightly, but extremely enduring breed of peasant farmers' horses which was characteristic of large areas of pre-war Poland has reappeared in masses, and the ennobling of this common stock is one of Poland's tasks for to-morrow, the more so as the disappearance of the horse in favour of motor traction is certainly not a near contingency in the Polish countryside. Poland now has considerably over 4,000,000 horses in place of the pre-war 3½ millions ; her army as well as her agriculture cover their needs in horseflesh entirely within the borders of the country, and tens of thousands of horses are exported every year.

## 15

In the case of *horned cattle,* the situation at the end of the War was as desperate as in the case of horses : the recovery, on the other hand, has been even more complete, and the systematic improvement in the quality of the stock much more marked. As far as can be ascertained with the help of the imperfect statistics of the early post-war years, the increase in quantity between the first real peace year in Poland, 1921, and the year 1927, when a census of cattle was taken, amounted to 6–7 per cent, which is not exorbitant ; but the milking capacity, on a moderate estimate increased in the same period by 50 per cent. This was chiefly due to considerable improvement in the feeding of cattle.

There are two breeds of cattle peculiar to Poland : the red and the black-and-white. The red breed has the advantage of being native to the soil and therefore well adapted to climatic and other conditions ; the black-and-white, predominant in the central plains and the western provinces, is the outcome of systematic crossing of the Polish stock with Dutch and North German. With regard to both breeds, efforts to raise the milking capacity have recently yielded very gratifying results, especially on large estates in the western provinces.

The latest total figure available for horned cattle in Poland (June, 1930) is 9⅓ million head, being over one-half of Germany's total and twice the total of Czechoslovakia.

*Pigs* have always been a most popular form of live stock both with large landowners and small farmers in Poland : this is accounted for by the fact that pigs, different in this respect from horned cattle, are easy to keep, especially with the help of Poland's abundance of potatoes, and they are highly prolific.

The present number of pigs in Poland is over six millions, being one-half of the official figure of Russia, but only somewhat over one-fourth of Germany's total. The export figure is about one million and a half *per annum*, this including exports in the the form of meat and bacon.

The Polish breed of pigs, according to experts, shows considerable traces of crossing between the domestic stock and the wild boar, which once was a very common animal all over the country, and at present still is fairly frequent in the eastern Carpathian regions. Crossings with imported foreign breeds considerably improved the quality of the Polish breed even before the War. Since the War, much has been done to raise the level of pig-breeding not only on large estates, but on small farms. There is no doubt that with the progress of land reform on the one hand and of agricultural co-operation on the other, pig-breeding will occupy a more and more important position among the different branches of Polish rural production and export trade.

In connection with these prospects, a few words may be added here concerning the *meat and fat industries* in Poland, since they deal chiefly with pork. Before the War, it was Austrian Poland chiefly which was known for its pork products : " Cracow sausages " had a wide market in Central Europe. Production, however, was not conducted on an industrial scale, and it was only in the later years of the first post-war decade that several factories of meat products arose in different parts of Poland. Important progress has been made above all in the production of *bacon*. Only two bacon factories existed in pre-War Poland (in the Russian sector), and those had been closed during the War. It was only in 1926 that bacon production was revived, and access to the British market gained in hard competition with Denmark, Holland and America. By 1928 Poland possessed twelve bacon factories, new ones were forming, and the exports of bacon to England continued even when the crisis had set in.

*Poultry farming*, like pig-breeding, being practicable both on larger estates and on small farms, constitutes an important factor in Poland's export trade. In this domain, the ravages of the War were made good with particular quickness : the number of all categories of fowl within the first ten post-war years became twice what it had been before the War, and it is now estimated at 60,000,000. Poultry farmers and exporters have organized into large associations, and Poland has made a creditable show at three post-war international dairy-farming congresses in Europe and America. Among forms of exports, it was the export of *eggs* which soon became a particularly flourishing branch of Polish trade : within the five years of 1922–27 it rose from 5,000 to 70,000 tons.

Without stopping to consider such comparatively minor items of Poland's rural economy as the breeding of sheep, goats, rabbits, and pigeons, a word may be added concerning the keeping of *bees*. In this sphere, a modest Polish parish priest in the period of Poland's division between foreign powers, Father Dzierżon in Prussian Silesia, contributed in an epoch-making way to progress by his studies on the life of bees (published in German scientific periodicals), and by the invention of the "cupboard hive," divided into compartments. The War, in this as in other fields, meant vast wholesale destruction ; but the number of hives has, by this time, reached the pre-war level again and, in some parts of Poland, even surpassed it. A central society of bee-masters has been formed, a body of inspectors and organizing instructors are at work, there are some twenty biological stations devoted to the observation of the life of bees, and several co-operatives are serving as centres for the sale of honey, wax, and the apparatus for rearing bees.

Nor must it pass unmentioned that the production of mead, time out of mind one of the favourite strong drinks of the Pole, has also been revived.

## 16

*Fisheries* have so far occupied much less than their due position in Poland's national household. Of Poland's total consumption of 90,000 tons of fish annually only somewhat less than one-fourth originate in Polish waters, the rest being imported and consisting largely of British and Norwegian herring. Of the Polish fish again, 11 per cent. come from the sea, being caught along the short strip of Poland's sea-coast while 47 per cent. are supplied by rivers and lakes, and 42 per cent. produced systematically in ponds. Of the total of Poland's fish output, only $6\frac{1}{2}$ per cent. are exported (chiefly salmon and eel).

Of inland lakes Poland possesses an area of about half a million acres ; the larger lakes, however, are situated mostly in the eastern part of the former Russian sector, and fishing in them remains in a backward and primitive condition. Much more has been done to promote rational pisciculture in the

rivers coming down from the Carpathian mountains in former
Austrian Poland, where Anglers' Societies look after the systematic reproduction of the salmon and trout stock : two breeding
stations on the river Dunajec, one at Nowy Targ and one at
Nowy Sącz, were founded in the new Poland and can boast
of a considerable output (1½ million fertilized grains of roe in
1928).

The raising of carp in private fish-ponds has an old tradition
in Poland, going back to the fourteenth and even the thirteenth
century. At present, an area of about 140,000 acres of ponds
produces something like 10,000 tons of fish per year, many new
ponds having been created since the War, especially in the
former Austrian sector. Chairs of Fish Lore in the Agricultural
Faculties of the Universities, and government-supported
experimental stations, by the sea-board and on the shore of one
of the larger lakes serve the cause of progress of Poland's
fisheries.

If, with such advance in production, fish, in modern Poland,
has not yet become a popular article of consumption, it is
because the organization of transport, storage and sale, owing
to lack of capital, does not keep pace with the rise in quantity
of the output. Thus the bulk of the sea fish caught on the
Polish coast still goes by the traditional pre-war trade-route of
Danzig to the interior of Germany, instead of being distributed
over the new Polish *Hinterland*.

That Poland, with her still very large forests, is a promised
land for the lover of *game*, may be assumed to be one of the
few facts fairly widely known about the country. Here again,
the War had meant sheer destruction. The bisons, kept in
some reservations, disappeared entirely ; the elk, the beaver,
the lynx, the wild cat, even those more common inhabitants of
the Carpathian region, the bear and the boar were on the verge
of disappearance ; partridges, pheasants, deer, had vanished in
many parts of the country. It was only a game-keeping law of
1927, published in the form of a Presidential decree, which
saved the remainder of Poland's game from destruction. Elks
and beavers have reappeared in greater numbers (two couples
of Canadian beavers being imported to make a new start);
harts and deer are fairly abundant again, and boars have even
become a nuisance in the hillside districts. The latter is
emphatically true of *wolves*, which make their appearance in
considerable numbers in the north-east, the east, and the south,
and are being combated as a pest by societies organized for the
purpose with government assistance.

17

After the plant and animal wealth of Poland, we proceed to consider her *mineral resources*, which at the same time takes us from the sphere of agriculture into that of *industry*, and from problems of the country, transfers us to those of the *town*.

In 1929, when " Ten Years of the new Poland " were celebrated by a great national exhibition at Poznań, comprising several imposing industrial pavilions, Poland could boast that in place of the 500,000 industrial workers on her territories before the War, and of the mere 130,000 of the first post-war year, she was giving employment to nearly 600,000 ; that she had developed her domestic market sufficiently to counterbalance the loss of the pre-war Russian markets for her textile products, and had gained entrance into enough new foreign markets for her coal and iron to be able to weather a " tariff war " with Germany, her chief former client for these exports. The rude blast of the world-wide economic crisis has since tarnished the splendour of these solid achievements of the first ten years ; but the fact that Poland has " come to stay " as a serious factor in the world's industrial system remains as permanently established in these days of widespread unemployment as it had become in the more prosperous years.

That fact stands secure chiefly because it is based on Poland's possession of some of the important natural resources for industrial development. The most vital one of them—*coal*— is at Poland's disposal in super-abundance. It is generally realized in Poland now that the inclusion, in the reconstructed Republic, of the Polish-speaking portion of coal-mining Silesia was essential for the real independence and economic life of the country. The allegation that Poland would prove unfit to maintain coal production in the Silesian basin at the high level to which pre-war German management had developed it, was quickly belied by the facts. Since the taking over of the Silesian districts in 1922, Poland's annual output of coal— with one set-back only, due to the beginning of the " tariff war " with Germany in the middle of the period—showed a continuous rise, until, in 1928, with over 40 million tons, it had nearly reached the figure of 1913 again. Parallel with this advance, there went an even more rapid increase in the consumption of coal within the country : between 1924 and 1927 alone, domestic consumption rose by 37 per cent., reaching, in 1928, a level of 23½ million tons. Even at that moment, 17 million tons of coal remained to be disposed of by way of export. Until 1925, Germany was the chief foreign consumer of Polish coal, being obliged, under the terms of the Geneva coal convention, to take half a million tons of coal per month off Poland's hands.

When this convention expired and was not renewed, Polish coal began to make its appearance abroad. The northward outlet on the sea being available, Scandinavian markets were naturally the first to be entered. The position obtained in them for Polish coal in 1925, was strengthened in 1926, during the British coal strike. Ever since, these markets have remained divided between the new and the old source of coal supply : Poland's exports to Scandinavia in 1928 (the last year before the world crisis) considerably surpassed those of the British strike year.

### 18

Another hopeful feature is the high quality of technical equipment and organization which characterized the coal mines of Silesia under Prussian rule, and which, under Poland, has remained unimpaired, and is receiving unwearied and competent attention. The National Institute of Chemical Research in Warsaw is devoting a large part of its energies to the problems (now so prominent in world-wide attention) of the industrial transformations and economic utilization of coal. The production of *gas* is, indeed, still imperfectly developed over large areas of Poland ; but *coke* has long been an important product of the Silesian coalfields and remains so under Polish rule : in 1927, no less than 1,800,000 tons of coal were used for coking in that region, and both the high quality of the coke and the efficient utilization of a variety of by-products are well-known features of the Silesian coal industry.

Of course, the picture of the coal situation in Polish Silesia would be incomplete without the grave shadows which entered into it even before it was darkened altogether by the present world crisis. The position won by Polish coal in the northern and other foreign markets was held not only through the highly efficient technical organization of the Silesian mines, but also, to a large extent, through the low cost of production, that is to say, essentially, the comparatively low wages of the Polish worker. Apart from fairly good housing arrangements inherited from the pre-war period, the standard of life of the Silesian coal-miner was, and is, certainly a regrettably low one, his economic difficulties being increased by the fact that families are generally very numerous. A resolute policy of wage

increase, on the American model, is rendered impossible not
only by the fierce competition in the European markets, but
also by the fact that the Government exercises control over the
domestic prices of coal and keeps them down in the interest of
the towns, and by the further fact that the very advanced
labour legislation of Poland (winning frequent praise from the
International Labour Office in Geneva) subjects mining capital
to an uncommonly heavy pressure of taxation in favour of social
insurance institutions.   It is, in fact, largely due to drastic
taxation of the Silesian industries that Polish Silesia has been
able, during the very first years of its new existence, to build
not only some of the finest hospitals and other social welfare
institutions, but also some of the most magnificent schools, the
best roads, and the finest administrative buildings which Poland
has to show to the visitor.   The difference in this respect is
very striking indeed when we cross former Russian frontier
into the adjoining coal basin of Dąbrowa Górnicza, where things
are still in a much more primitive and backward condition.
An all-round amelioration of the living condition of Poland's
miners can only be hoped for if co-operation and international
adjustment at last takes the place of the present war of competition between Europe's different national coal-mining syndicates
—a contingency to which the universal pressure of the crisis is
perhaps bringing us nearer than is generally realized.

19

*Iron* is the usual neighbour of coal in economic surveys.
Iron ore is to be found in various parts of Poland, but it is for
the most part low-grade ore, the percentage of iron contained
in it being rarely higher than 36.   This does not make the
working of the deposits very remunerative, and the production
of iron ore in  Poland accordingly remained, as a rule, far
below the pre-war level, surpassing it only in the boom year,
1928, with a record figure of 699,000 tons of ore, as compared
with the pre-War average of less than half a million.   At its
best, the production of iron ores from Poland's mines could
supply barely one-tenth of the requirements of Poland's iron-
works, which had developed into considerable industries both
in Russian Poland and in Prussian Silesia, in the neighbourhood
of the coal deposits.   High-grade ores were, and are, being
imported into Poland from Sweden and some other countries ;
the importation of scrap-iron from Germany also constitutes
an important item, and a quantity of 165,000 tons of it had to
be secured by special agreement.

" Iron is either a beggar or a king "—that classic saying of Andrew Carnegie's certainly holds true of the varied fortunes of Poland's iron industry.  The end of War found it, of course, in a state of beggary, the occupants having practically dismantled and carried away the entire machinery.  Recovery pursued a more or less steady course till 1923, after which there came a violent slump caused by the blow which Grabski's drastic reform of the currency inflicted on industries.  An upward movement began once more in 1925, but the line of renewed ascent only became steep in the years 1926–28. The world crisis raging since 1929 brought another and even more heaving slump with it, and Poland's iron industries are largely kept alive now by Soviet orders connected with the Five Years' Plan.

Within this period of ups and downs, progress had been made from 700,000 tons of steel in 1919 to 1,300,000 (almost twice the original quantity) in 1928.  And the progress was not merely progress in output, but also in organization.  The industrial groups of Prussian Silesia and of Russian Poland respectively, which in the early days of political re-union had faced each other as strangers and foes, were fused into one syndicate in 1925 ;  new ore bases were secured, connections between the foundries and the metal industries on the one hand, and between the foundries and the mines on the other, were established ; export problems were successfully attacked; with the difficult problem of raising the standard of iron consumption within the country, some headway was made.  Poland's consumption of iron is a striking example of the difference in conditions between the west and east within the reunited country :  from 63 kilogrammes per head and year in Silesia it drops to the average of 1·41 in the eastern provinces.  Yet there is the hopeful fact to be placed on record that the absorption of Polish iron by those eastern provinces rose from 2,000 tons in the first half of the year 1926 to 9,000 tons in the first half of 1928.  When the present world crisis is over, the Polish iron industry may confidently anticipate a steady and healthy increase of demand in that domestic market which is its firmest foundation.

20

Besides iron, one other metal must be singled out as an important item on the list of Poland's mineral resources.  As a producer of *zinc*, Poland occupies the third place among the countries of the world, after the United States and Belgium. The zinc mines, situated among the coalfields in the south-west of former Russian Poland and in Silesia, had a period of rapid progress in output during the years 1923–28, and with a production of 160,000 tons of pure zinc in 1928 (one-fourth of the United States' and four-fifths of Belgium's) were approaching the pre-war figure. At the same time, however, the import of zinc ores from abroad was also increasing quickly, and Poland became more and more dependent on foreign ore for her zinc foundries. The reason for this was that Polish ores (as in the case of iron) are low-grade ones, and the critically low price of zinc in the world market made it less and less worth while to work Poland's zinc deposits. The zinc crisis (which preceded the general economic crisis by several years ) affected Poland's industries heavily, and only the cheapness of nearby coal fuel and the cheapness of labour helped it to make head. Zinc is an important item on Poland's export trade bill, 90 per cent. of the country's production of zinc being exported, and zinc exports standing third in value after those of coal and timber. Prospects for the Polish zinc industry began to brighten when, at the end of 1928, the electrolytic method of production of zinc from ore was introduced, which made it possible to work even low-grade ores (such as are found in Poland) profitably. At present of course, the general crisis affects this as it does other industries.

In connection with zinc, it must be mentioned that zinc ores are also the source of a most valuable other element, viz., *cadmium*, of which they contain occasionally as much as 1 per cent., and which is used both in dye production and for alloys with copper and with lead. Of cadmium, Poland was the only producer in the world until deposits of it were recently found in the United States and in Tasmania.

21

In connection with the above brief account of Poland's metal resources, something may perhaps at once be said about her *metal industries*.

In the pre-war period, Russian Poland could boast of well-developed metallurgical industries of various type. Polish metallurgy commanded the vast markets of European and Asiatic Russia, even after Russia had begun to develop metal industries in her own inner provinces. All over the Russian Empire, iron bridges were built, boilers, motors and agricultural machinery were supplied by certain well-known Polish firms of Warsaw, Sosnowiec, Lublin, and other places in Russian Poland. To mention one striking instance only, it was the present writer's memorable experience to see the largest bridge on the Asiatic continent, viz., an iron bridge of eighteen arches over the river Amur near Habarovsk completed by functionaries of the Warsaw firm of K. Rudzki in the later years of the war, when Warsaw itself had already been separated from Russia for good.

These flourishing metal industries of Russian Poland were thoroughly ruined by the war, the plant of some of them being bodily carried away into Russia, and what remained, being often confiscated and carried off by the Germans in turn. Of the equipment of factories transferred during the Russian retreat of 1915 into the interior of Russia, a certain portion has, with infinite pains, been recovered at the hands of the Bolsheviks under the terms of the Peace Treaty of Riga. In the meantime, the Polish Government had endeavoured, by state orders and by organized control over production and sales, to promote a revival of the metallurgical industries. The abnormal conditions of the inflation period for a time favoured quick industrial progress, and new large metallurgical factories even came into being in former Austrian and Prussian Poland, such as an engine factory at Poznań and one at Chrzanów near Cracow. The painful process of currency reform hit some of the new and the revived undertakings very badly, but a number of them remained in existence, and on the tenth anniversary of her existence, the free Poland possessed no less than 900 metallurgical industrial establishments of factory size, employing a total of 120,000 workers and producing over 900,000 tons weight of articles.

## 22

Next after coal and iron among Poland's mineral raw materials there ranks *oil*.

It was a Polish mining engineer—originally a modest chemist, Ignatius Łukasiewicz who, in 1853, gave the initiative for the exploitation of the oil wells on the northern slopes of the Carpathians, in Austrian Poland. It was he, incidentally, who also invented the kerosene lamp, that faithful companion of the family life of several generations.

The Polish oil industry progressed but slowly till 1884, when the introduction of mechanical drilling and, at the same time, the establishment of a protective tariff by the Austrian Government, gave it a new start. The efforts of a great patriot, Stanislas Szczepanowski, to base the further progress of the industry on the savings of Austrian Poland's population proved fruitless, and the industry got under the control of foreign (largely Belgian and French) capital. But the industry itself progressed rapidly, the output rising at the rate of nearly 100 per cent. a year, and reaching, in 1909, its *maximum* of 2 million tons—then 4 per cent. of the world's production of oil. Soon after this, the wells of Borysław and Tustanowice in the eastern Carpathians, which had provided the bulk of the product, began to show signs of exhaustion, and, the oilfields not having been systematically extended by new drillings, the output fell considerably in a few years. The War brought it down to less than one-half of the maximum attained in 1909 ; and it was all the new Poland could do in her first ten years to keep it from further disastrous decline and more or less stabilize it on a level of 700,000–800,000 tons a year. Considerable technical improvements were introduced in the working of the wells ; investigations with a view to extending the oilfields further west along the slopes of the Carpathians are now being conducted, in organized fashion, by the State Geological Institute ; but the intense drilling activities which would be required and to which a new start was given in 1928 by the foundation of a company with government assistance for the purpose are hampered by lack of capital and discouraged by recent abnormal conditions in the world's oil business.

A side-issue of oil production which was developed into importance in the new Poland since the War, consists of the utilization of " *earth gases* " which usually make their appearance together with oil. From these gases light gasolene is obtained through cooling processes or with the help of brown coal, and the remaining gaseous matter is used for fuel. Separate fields producing only gas and not, so far, any oil, have been opened up in the western Carpathian lowlands, particularly near the town of Krosno, which is entirely heated with earth gas. Further east, the gasfields of Daszawa have proved highly productive ; special pipe systems distribute the gas fuel from them over a wide area, while the light gasolene obtained from it in the first stage is absorbed by the rising motor-car traffic of Poland.

The *oil distilleries* of Poland—a branch of industry built up on the exploitation of the oilfields—were specially protected by the Government, both through a prohibitive tariff on foreign oil, through a veto against the export of raw oil, and through a price policy calculated to secure the sale of Poland's export surplus of oil abroad (these exports amounting to about 40 per cent. of the total production). Poland's oilfields, however, proved insufficient to feed the distilleries to their full capacity, and stagnation in the distillery business ensued. In recent years, a state-supported factory of mineral oils at Drohobycz was developed along several different lines of production (e.g., that of paraffin and of lubricating oils). All the distilleries of Poland are now united in one syndicate.

One of the greatest difficulties which the oil industry of the new free Poland had to face, consisted in the organization of exports. While before the War the Galician oilfields had an assured market in the other provinces of the Austro-Hungarian Monarchy and to some extent in Germany, now they found themselves confronted by the competition of American and of Rumanian oil in all these markets. The distilleries of Czechoslovakia and other " Succession States " being anxious to attract raw oil from every available source, and Poland, on the other hand, endeavouring to keep the whole of her raw oil output at the disposal of her own distilleries, some compromise between these opposed tendencies became necessary, and Poland began to export half-distilled oil which is being turned by Czechoslovak, Hungarian and other distilleries into the finished product. The loss of the German market through the tariff war with Germany after 1925 was partly compensated, as in the case of coal, by the opening-up of Scandinavian markets accessible through Poland's outlet on the sea.

Domestic consumption began to increase steadily since the reform of the currency, and shows a particularly striking advance with regard to motor oil, owing to the progress of automobile traffic : the use of Polish motor oil in Poland was quadrupled between 1924 and 1928.

In concluding this rapid survey of Poland's oil industries, it seems worth mentioning that a reserve of the oil resources of the country is constituted by the large and unusually thick layers of *bituminous slates* (in the Carpathian Mountains) from which oil could be obtained, but which there has been so far no attempt to work.

## 23

Among other mineral resources of Poland than the capital items of coal and oil, *salt* occupies a place apart. The ancient salt mines of Wieliczka and Bochnia near Cracow, which have been worked since the twelfth century, and in which crystalline salt is found in the form of solid salt rock, are a great natural curiosity of Poland, much visited by tourists. Besides them, the country possesses twelve salterns, for the most part situated in the eastern portion of former Austrian Poland. All these having been in government hands before the War, the Polish State inherited them, and salt became one of the Government monopolies of Poland.

Some of the salt mines and salterns were taken over by Poland in a state of decay and neglect, and the total production at first was below the country's own needs. In 1919–20 Poland still had to import more than 40,000 tons of salt from Germany ; but since 1923 she became herself a salt-exporting country, and by 1928, her exports had risen above the 40,000 ton mark. In the same year, the total output of Poland's salt-works was already more than twice that of the last pre-war year ; a salt mine in former Prussian Poland, which had only begun to be worked since the War, alone yielded nearly 100,000 tons a year. Of the salt thus obtained in Poland, about 60 per cent. is being consumed as table salt, while 30-35 per cent. is used in industry, chiefly for the manufacture of soda and chlorine.

Impressive as the figures of production are in the case of salt, they are even more striking in the case of a mineral closely related to salt and considerably more important industrially, viz., *potassium salts*, which are a principal component of the manufactured artificial fertilizers used by modern argiculture. Deposits of potassium salts are known to exist in several parts of Poland ; but only those near Kałusz and Stebnik in the eastern part of former Austrian Poland have so far been worked systematically.

Their exploitation was begun in 1911 by a Company formed with the assistance of the Austro Polish Provincial Administration in spite of the counter-efforts of the powerful German " Kali Syndicate." In 1921, production was resumed after the ravages of the War, and soon rose in truly startling progression : from 15,000 tons in 1921 to 359,000 in 1929. The year 1928 marked an epoch in the development of the industry, the Government showing its interest in it by a large addition, out of state funds, to its capital. This made new investigations possible, and unexpectedly rich deposits were discovered, some of them near the old ones. Poland, which now produces 2 per cent. of the world's output of potassium, may in the near future rise much higher in the scale.

### 24

Having passed in review some of the industries utilizing the principal mineral resources of Poland, we may now turn to those which put other natural resources to use. Among such, the group of *electrical industries* occupies a high place in every modern community. In the new Poland, the conditions of the production and distribution of electrical energy were regulated by a law of 1922. By subjecting this entire domain to central government control, the law paved the way for rational consolidation of the electric-power supply in a few large overland stations, in place of the uneconomic, numerous, small local works. A few large stations, serving wider areas, have come into existence, foremost among them being that of Gródek (in the northern portion of former Prussian Poland), which feeds, *inter alia*, the rising port of Gdynia. Other large power stations are still in the sphere of projects. The dream of Poland's noble-minded first elected President, Professor Gabriel Narutowicz (killed in 1922), of utilizing the uncurbed water-power of some of Poland's rivers in their descent northward from the slopes of the Carpathians for the production of electric power on a large scale, has so far remained unfulfilled through lack of capital. Recent negotiations with the Harriman concern for the electrification of a large part of western Poland broke down. As things stand, Poland's production of current is still on a comparatively low level : in 1928, it was only one-twelfth of that of Germany, and one-sixth that of the British Islands. The industries producing electrical machinery (with the recent large addition of wireless apparatus) show a much better rate of progress.

## 25

Poland's *textile industries* have perhaps a greater tradition behind them than any other form of industrial activity within her borders. In surveying, in a former chapter, the hundred years of Poland's captivity, mention has been made of the rapid growth of the city of Łódź, which came to provide the whole of the vast Russian Empire with its popular textile products. During the War, the industries of Łódź were thoroughly ruined both through systematic despoliation of the factories by the German occupants, and through large losses of outstanding debts in Russia. The large Russian markets being irrevocably separated from Łódź, recovery within such a comparatively small State as the new Poland seemed impossible. Yet the trade boom of the first post-war years (heightened by paper-money inflation) helped the Łódź factories to make a new start, in spite of the lack of capital. By 1923, the production of woollen stuffs had only reached one-half of its pre-war volume ; but that of cotton goods had risen even beyond the pre-war level. The slump subsequent upon currency

P

reform in 1924 brought heavy unemployment to Łódź, reaching the figure of 90,000 in 1926. Since that year there was marked improvement again, aided both by a good crop in Poland and by orders from Soviet Russia. The year 1928 brought a new crisis, which deepened as the world-wide depression set in.

Such, in outline, is the history of the vicissitudes through which the textile industry has so far passed in the new Poland. If we ask for its prospects, there is, first of all, the fact to be noticed that the industries of Łódź have adapted themselves to the needs of their new markets, that they are thoroughly modernized and rationalized, and that, on the other hand, the consumption of cotton and woollen goods by Poland's population has not yet reached the pre-war level : if brought to reach it again and to surpass it, domestic consumption alone would keep Łódź busy to its full capacity, at least as far as cotton goods are concerned. Furthermore, there are export possibilities to be considered, some of which Łódź had actually succeeded in developing before the world crisis : in 1926, Rumania was absorbing large quantities of Łódź products, and other and more distant markets, as far away as Persia, China, the Far East, and South America, had been reached.

Apart from Łódź, Poland possesses several textile centres of minor importance : foremost among them Bielsko (Bielitz) in former Austrian Silesia must be mentioned. Different from Łódź, it had specialized chiefly in high quality woollen cloths, and had played almost the same part in the Austro-Hungarian economic system as Łódź in the Russian Empire. Of less importance, there are the textile manufactures of Białystok in the north-east of former Russian Poland (constituting 8 per cent. of the bulk of Poland's textile industries), the jute factories around Czestochowa, and the linen manufacture of Żyrardów (the latter controlled by French capital, and of late deliberately allowed by it to decay). Finally, the rapid development of the manufacture of artificial silk at Tomaszów Rawski in the Łódź district must be singled out as an item deserving notice not only on economic, but also on sociological grounds. It is surely a sign of our times, indicative not only of economic possibilities but of changes in social life and manners, that the production of artificial silk in Poland should have jumped up in eight years from a mere ton per month in 1920 to a monthly average of over 2,000 tons in 1928 ! The mention of this truly amazing development, however, has transferred us from the sphere of textile industries proper to the wide and varied domain of the chemical ones.

## 26

Before we turn, however, to chemical industries in the strict sense of the word, one industry may yet be mentioned which is conveniently placed here, because, like the textile industries, it provides the raw material for certain parts of clothing, viz., the *leather industry*. Such tanneries as existed in Poland before the War—mainly in the Russian sector—provided mass articles of a coarse and heavy kind for the Russian markets. In the new Poland, the development has necessarily gone not in the direction of an increase of mass production, but of raising quality to a higher level within narrower quantitative limits. The industry lying in ruins after the War, a new beginning was made by government control of raw hides for distribution among the factories, and by closing the frontier against leather imports. The common " boom " of the inflation period followed ; recovery from the subsequent slump was aided by renewed import restrictions in 1926 and 1927, but another crisis set in, somewhat earlier in this industry than in others, because of the dearth of raw material and of the strength of competition, particularly on the part of small country tanneries, working in a primitive manner and producing cheap if inferior leather. There were, even in 1927, nearly 1000 tanneries in Poland employing up to five persons each, against a mere 100 employing over twenty. As the general crisis deepened, the leather industry was further affected, and many tanneries had to close down. The position of the industry was rendered more difficult by its dependence on the import of certain categories of hides—for instance, South American horned cattle hides for sole leather, the hides of Polish cattle being unfit for the purpose—and in the case of calf hides by the absurdity (due to Poland's lack of capital reserves) of reimports of Polish hides bought up by foreign speculators in Poland during the season when they are in the market. In spite of these difficulties, the strong foundation provided by constant and growing demand assures the continued progress of the industry.

## 27

Poland's *chemical industries* have been mentioned before as possessing foundations in large natural resources, such as the deposits of potassium salts. The scientific exploitation of these resources in the new Poland was originated during the War, by the establishment of an Institute for Research in Industrial Chemistry at Lwów. With the promotion of its organizer,

Professor Ignatius Mościcki, to the Presidency of the Republic in 1926, the institute, now transferred to Warsaw, widened its scope and became the dominant national institution in the field of applied chemistry. Its work with regard to the industrial chemistry of coal has been mentioned before.

Besides the foundation of the institute, Professor Mościcki won fame in the history of Poland's industries chiefly by his highly efficient management of the largest chemical factory in the country—one of the largest in Europe—viz., the nitrate factory of *Chorzów* in Silesia, which was taken over by Poland in 1922, and after some litigation before international courts, is now securely established in her possession. The nitrates produced by Chorzów are used as artificial fertilizers for poor soil and are, accordingly, a product of capital importance for a predominantly agricultural country like Poland, whose territories include large stretches, of sandy land. In fact, the Chorzów factory is the principal and most powerful link between industry and agriculture in the economic structure of the country. Taken over by Poland under extremely difficult conditions, the factory soon began to flourish under Professor Mościcki's administration : thanks to the introduction of a number of mechanical improvements (some of them of Professor Mościcki's own invention), the figures of production rose in steep ascent from 40,000 tons in 1923 to 150,000 tons in 1928. This success encouraged Professor Mościcki, when he had become President of the Republic in 1926, to proceed to the foundation of a second state-owned factory of the same kind : it was built near the town of Tarnów in former Austrian Poland, and called *Mościce* after the name of its founder. In the meantime, however, the world-wide wane of agricultural depression had reached Poland ; with the unprecedentedly low level of market prices for agricultural produce which now prevailed, it became unremunerative to use artificial fertilizers on Polish soil, and both Chorzów and Mościce were obliged to restrict their production considerably. The consumption of artificial fertilizers by Polish agriculture, however, is bound to rise again in more prosperous times and to increase considerably beyond all figures of the past, with the progress of agricultural education and co-operative organization. The future of this branch of industry in Poland, accordingly, would seem to be assured by the natural conditions themselves under which it originated.

Domestic consumption has also been, so far, the sole objective of an industry which may conveniently be mentioned here because it utilizes various chemical products, viz., the *glass industry*. The reunion of Polish lands, together with the requirements of post-war reconstruction, gave a powerful impulse to this industry, which before the War had been well-developed in Russian Poland only, while the Austrian and German sectors had received their glass mainly from the factories of Bohemia, Prussian Silesia, and Saxony. The somewhat rank and uncontrolled growth of glass-works in the new Poland, often without expert superintendence, caused a number of failures, but 68 establishments survived and remained active in 1928, over two-thirds of them being united in a Producers' Association. The raw materials for glass production are all to be found in Poland in abundance, some of the chemicals only being imported from abroad. The demand in a country devastated by war naturally ran at first, almost entirely, in the direction of ordinary window-glass for mass consumption : the more refined and specialized branches of production for decorative and technical use had little chance to develop. Still, those who visited the National Exhibition at Poznań in 1928 had ample opportunity to admire Polish-made glass wares which did not at all yield in elegance to high-class foreign work.

## 28

Similar, but even more remarkable results have been achieved under somewhat analogous conditions by a group of industries also advancing from mere utility towards decorative functions, viz., the *printing industry* with all its ramifications in the way of reproduction of drawings, maps, posters and the like.

The demands of a newly organized State on the printing-press were enormous and manifold, ranging all the way from the production of paper money—of whose disastrous dimensions in the early years something has been said before—to government publications of every kind and to school-books for those large sections of the country which had used mainly German and Russian text-books before the War. Apart from the large paper-money printing works of the State—whose activities, soon after their transfer from Bydgoszcz to an imposing new building in Warsaw, could fortunately be considerably reduced —the central and local authorities, both civilian and military, soon began to keep a great number of printing presses busy in their service, and some of those official printing offices, being assured of permanent support, could afford, without particular risk, to overstep the legitimate limits of their activities and engage in competition with private printing presses : in 1927 a decree had to be issued which set up barriers against such undesirable developments.

Apart from presses serving the needs of public authorities, there are some others which are placed in a privileged position by mass articles used in connection with the working of public institutions. Foremost among this category, there stands the firm of *Książnica-Atlas*, which holds practically a monopoly of school text-books and maps throughout the Republic. The firm (which is closely connected with an association of secondary school teachers) can boast of having made extraordinary technical progress in cartography : the maps and atlases issued by it (under the superintendence of the distinguished geographer Professor E. Romer) satisfy the highest requirements by the precision of their design and the neatness of their execution. The development of the mechanical apparatus of this firm is a favourable specimen of the progress in technique brought about by the rapid growth of demand in the new Poland. In other cases, this progress, owing to its very quickness, was unsystematic and planless, and pursuing too many different directions at once, without the requisite experience, did not lead to really efficient specialization. To remedy this, a " School of Graphic Industries " was organized in 1926 in Warsaw in place of the desultory courses of former times. That school now occupies a stately building of its own, and is training hundreds of pupils. For efficiency in organized production, the presses of some of Poland's great newspapers—particularly that of the *Illustrated Daily Courier* at Cracow—must be singled out ; for artistic beauty, illustrated books printed in Poland for some great Warsaw, Cracow and Poznań firms (such as the firm of the late Jacob Mortkowicz) have repeatedly of late years won foreign recognition at international book exhibitions.[1]

## 29

The present survey has not, so far, covered a number of industries which may now conveniently be dealt with together, because they possess a firm common foundation in popular demand due to the fact that they provide elementary necessaries of life in the way of clothing and housing.

The *clothing industry* existed before the War principally in the form of a " home industry " in Russian Poland. In place of

---

[1] E.g., the *Salon International du Livre d'Art*, held in Paris in June, 1931 ; see the special issue of *The Times Literary Supplement* devoted to it (June 25), p. iv, " The Polish Section."

this, the huge and universal demand for articles of clothing in the early post-war years gave rise to thirty-odd new shoe factories, more than a dozen factories of clothing, several factories of linen, and some new hat factories, besides the half-dozen old ones, which revived. Minor and supplementary branches of the industry—such as the production of umbrellas also shared in the benefits of the boom period. The sequel— a slump in 1924 and 1925, and considerable recovery on more healthy foundations, from 1925 to 1928—was the same as in the case of other industries. In the present instance, a lowering of tariffs in 1924 (in the interests of the consumer), severe restriction of imports from 1925 to 1928, and readmission of imports in 1928, were additional factors in the situation. It is the shoe industry of Czechoslovakia and the linen industry both of that country and Austria, which make their competition particularly felt in Poland. Poland's own capacity for export in this domain, on the other hand, has lately shown signs of developing : Warsaw shoes (which always were an article of repute for their elegance) have found their way abroad, and the large Polish exports of ready-made clothing to Britain even became an object of discussion in the House of Commons.

The *ceramic industries* contributory to building may be mentioned next. The reconstruction of Poland's *brick-kilns* after the War was accomplished, in spite of considerable difficulties, within the first ten years, and some progress was made with the introduction of machinery. By 1928, the pre-war average of 2 milliards of bricks per annum was nearly reached again ; but arrears of about 30 per cent. remained unsold, because of the slow progress of building activities in the country. In the case of pipes for field draining and of tiles for roofs, demand developed at an even slower pace. Much quicker progress was made in the *cement industry*, which, starting in 1919 with one-seventh of its pre-war output, had in 1927 surpassed the pre-war total by one-seventh. One-fifth of the cement produced in Poland was by that time being exported, in spite of severe foreign competition.

The *building industry* in the proper sense of the word was perhaps the slowest of all to recover, in spite of the enormous housing shortage caused by war-time stagnation. Poland started her new post-war existence with a housing problem of even more monstrous dimensions than most other European countries, because of the wholesale destruction of dwellings in the countryside, throughout the eastern provinces. The quick growth of population soon caused conditions of distressful congestion in the cities, particularly in Warsaw, which, almost at a moment's warning, had to become transformed from the administrative centre of a province of Russia into a capital of a thirty-million State, with all the apparatus of national sovereignty. Lack of capital and of long-term credit facilities hampered building activities, while a " Rent Restriction Act," protecting tenants, discouraged enterprise. This was amended after a number of years, but the other obstacle remains in full force. The State, with a thousand urgent tasks on its hands, did what it could to assist private initiative, and the credits granted by the Bank of National Economy are still practically the only source of capital for building activities in the country. Provincial and municipal authorities could do but little, for lack of funds.

The result of such conditions is a certain disproportion which cannot fail to strike the foreign visitor even while he remains in the capital of the country : Poland is making fairly good progress with the erection of public buildings, some of them even unexpectedly large and sumptuous ; and collective homes for various categories of public functionaries are arising in considerable numbers at public expense ; but private building activity lingers sadly behind, and the problem of dwellings for the masses in all populous centres still remains in a more or less deplorable condition. Silesia with its industrial wealth and sound pre-war tradition in the matter of working men's houses, is perhaps the only large exception to this general aspect of things. And some of the summer resorts, both by the sea-side and in the mountains, are in a more favourable situation with regard to building, because Poland's prohibitive passport policy fosters their development. In the cities, apart from the economic difficulties already outlined, some particularly severe building regulations interfere with building progress. They were to some extent a necessity as a barrier against jerry-building, which showed a dangerous rising tendency, especially in the inflation period. But neither very solid and elaborate architecture nor highly mechanized and rationalized building industries are in accordance with the present economic status of the country. The need to pitch the aims lower if crying requirements are to be satisfied within reasonable time, was recognized, in 1931, in a notable utterance of the Prime Minister, who declared that if the present generation could not afford to leave " a Poland of brick " behind, it would at any rate, do its best to build up " a Poland of wood."

The idea of returning to wood as the building material for

mass dwellings, even in the towns, may partly have been suggested by the fact that the reconstruction of homes after war-
time devastation in the Polish countryside had made, on the
whole, much more progress than housing activities in the towns,
and this comparatively satisfactory state of affairs in the
country was due to the fact that thatched wooden cottages are
still the prevailing type of village architecture in Poland.

## 30

Having devoted some attention to the particular branches of
industry, it remains to say a few words about the *organization
of Polish industries*. The difficulties in this respect were of a
particularly complex nature, and could only be overcome after
considerable time. Industrial development in the three pre-
war sectors of the country having been unequal and essentially
different, the industrialists in the different parts of the reunited
country were strangers to each other in person, in mentality,
partly even in speech (those of Silesia being mostly Germans).
In Prussian and Austrian Poland compulsory associations of
producers in the form of " Chambers of Commerce and Industry "
had existed since the middle of the nineteenth century, while
there were none in Russian Poland. There, on the other hand,
a large and powerful " Industrial Association," with many
subordinate sections comprising the different branches of
industry, had come into existence and been very active. This
Association considerably extended its range in 1919, and became
even a great power in Polish politics (where it was known by the
popular name of " The Leviathan.") But the separate organizations of the former Austrian and Prussian provinces, although
induced in course of time to co-operate with it, could not be
brought to consent to fusion. On the other hand, the extension
of a compulsory network of " Chambers of Commerce and
Industry " to the whole of the Republic was a slow task. It
was partly due to the pressure of the economic crisis that, in
1930, Chambers of Commerce and Industry became universal
in Poland, and, in 1931, a united all-Polish Association of
Industrialists came into being.

It was also the pressure of post-war economic conditions
which promoted another form of industrial organization.
In Poland, as elsewhere in Continental Europe, industrialists
of the same branch in many cases formed " syndicates " or
" cartels " for the sake of eliminating wasteful competition,
of regulating prices, and of dividing domestic and foreign markets
between them. Of late years, when exports were rendered more

and more difficult by the tariff policy of all European Powers, and the State, in the interest of Poland's balance of trade, was obliged to foster exports artificially by offering material advantages to exporters, the accomplishment of that task became only possible by encouraging the formation of organized groups of exporters of one branch. The State, accordingly, became a great promoter of the formation of industrial " cartels." Experience has already proved that such " cartels " (like the trusts in America) are occasionally apt to exercise their power in a manner inconvenient to the State and oppressive to the consumer. In spite of some manifest abuses, however, the promotion of " cartel " organization by the State continues to be considered as favourable, on the whole, to economic progress from the point of view of the consolidation of production. A " Cartel Law," organizing State supervision, was passed in 1932.

## 31

*Labour conditions* in Poland are another subject which claims consideration in a discussion of Poland's industries. Something has been said on this subject before, in connection with one of the largest industries of Poland, viz., the coal industry. Here it remains to give a comprehensive account of the state of *labour legislation* and *social insurance* in the new Republic.

In the very first year of the existence of the new State (1919) a bill was passed which made the *eight hours' working day* universal and compulsory. The time being reduced to six hours on Saturdays, the legal weekly total is 46, and this may only be extended in exceptional cases of urgent necessity, or in undertakings working continuously. By one of the numerous exaggerations of social doctrinairism which mark Polish labour legislation, the time limit is also applied to the work of the owner himself in his own shop or workshop.

*Labour Contracts* were regulated by a law in the form of a Presidential decree in 1928, the principal provision being that of a fortnight's notice in case of dissolution of the contract.

A system of *factory inspection* was organized in 1927, an inspector being appointed for every administrative district in the Republic. Special protection is extended, by a law of 1924, over minors and women working in industry, and arrangements for the infants of working women are compulsory in each larger undertaking.

*Labour exchanges* exist in three forms : those conducted disinterestedly by social organizations, those run for profit as private undertakings (which require to be licensed anew each year), and, thirdly, the labour offices of the State, which serve also for unemployment registration. To the organs of State assistance in the matter of employment there belongs also the large State *Emigration Office*, whose principal task it is to protect the would-be emigrant against exploitation by the agents of shipping companies and of foreign employers of indentured labour—these activities having been, before the War, a domain of rank abuses of all sorts.

Among the social insurance institutions the foremost one is that of *Sickness Insurance Offices*, established by a law of 1920, at the rate of one per district, with ampler provision in the case of large cities. Everybody doing hired work in any contractual capacity is subject to compulsory insurance against sickness, the contributions being divided in equal portions between the employer and the employed. Free medical treatment in case of sickness is guaranteed for periods extending from six to nine months, and pecuniary assistance to the family, as well as part of the funeral expenses in case of death, is included in the insurance benefit. The system having been made very comprehensive—it includes even rural labour, in spite of the long distances of manors and farms from the official places of treatment !—the Sickness Insurance Offices soon became rich institutions, equipped with large buildings, up-to-date medical apparatus, and efficient professional service ; at the same time, owing to the vast numbers of clients, treatment unavoidably was (and is) very summary, individual attendance being rendered practically impossible by the crowds of patients ; inevitably also, a large bureaucracy developed round the Offices and kept growing like a snowball. It was perhaps another necessary outcome of the social character of these institutions that their governing bodies became strongholds of the Socialist Party and they themselves served as sources of political campaign funds for the Party. With all these accumulated evils in the working of the Sickness Insurance Offices, the Piłsudski Government began to cope at last by appointing Commissioners for their supervision and reorganization. The year 1931 sees a scheme under way according to which the number of Offices is to be diminished and their bureaucratic machinery reduced. How far this will bear fruit, remains to be seen ; it is to be hoped that the reorganization will promote the sound ends of popular medicine and hygiene. As it is, the Sickness Insurance Offices have undoubtedly had the good effect of making recourse to medicine common among the working class for a wide range

of ailings which formerly were neglected and kept the standard
of general health among the masses lamentably low.

*Unemployment insurance* is organized in Poland on a basis
of contributions from employer and employed, as well as from
the Treasury. It becomes claimable after five months' continuous employment and is paid during a maximum of thirteen
weeks per year to the amount of 30 per cent. of full wages in the
case of unmarried and 50 per cent. of married workers. Although considerably inferior, as we see, in its dimensions to the
post-war growth of the system in Britain, unemployment
benefit has, owing to the recent crisis, become a nearly unbearable strain on the resources of the new Polish State, and a
reduction of the social services generally is now in view, as being
one of the obvious means of relief in the distress both of the
Treasury and of private capital in these days.

It may be added that *brain workers*, as distinguished from
manual ones, have a *Pension Fund* of their own, which also
insures them against unemployment and incapacity to work,
and guarantees rents to their families in case of death.

*War invalids*, and the families of those who fell in the War,
are provided for by a law of 1921, which, besides pecuniary
assistance and medical treatment, covers such items as the
supply of artificial limbs and the schooling in handicrafts which
invalids are fit to practise. The employment of invalids by
private industrial undertakings at the rate of one to every
fifty workers is made enforceable by law, and the State has
provided for a large number of War invalids by granting them
licences for the sale of products of the tobacco monopoly.

The system of compulsory insurance in Poland—a very wide
system, as will be seen from the above—has even been extended
to *real property*, the insurance of buildings against fire having
been rendered obligatory since 1927, and that of movables,
crops and live stock having been placed within the power of
regional authorities.

### 32

It is a well-known fact that the development of industries
means the decay of *handicrafts*. The somewhat forced industrial
progress of Poland's early years could have no other effect, and
the handicrafts of the different pre-war sections, unable to
organize and adapt themselves to the new conditions, were a
more or less passive prey of events until 1927, when the Government of Marshal Piłsudski drafted and passed a uniform Industrial Law for the whole of Poland, which included a measure of

protection for handicrafts. That law not only placed the organization of the craft-guilds and the admission to the ranks of apprentices, journeymen, and masters on a firm foundation, but it also provided, by the compulsory organization of " Chambers of Artisans," an instrument of collective defence of the interests of handicrafts. The volume of the class thus protected is not unimportant even in the midst of recent industrial developments : according to the estimates of the Ministry of Industry and Commerce, there are over 300,000 artisans' workshops in Poland, and nearly 900,000 people at work in them. For the well-being of this large stratum of society, capital was even more vital than legal protection. The Government realized this, and legal organization was soon followed by the grant of credits to artisans' co-operatives in the different sections of the country. Both these co-operative organizations and the Chambers of Artisans mentioned before were modelled, for the whole of Poland, on the institutions of this kind which had existed in the Austrian sector before the War. Pre-war Galicia also supplied precedents for such social activities as the creation of hostels for apprentices, of educational institutes, and of artisans' clubs. The large Home for Apprentices at Cracow, founded by a Jesuit priest (Father Kuznowicz) and modelled on the British and American Y.M.C.A.'s is justly famous all over Poland.

In spite of all efforts, a number of handicrafts in Poland are evidently doomed even now to gradual disappearance. The turners, wheelwrights, and harness-makers, whom industries are superseding, may within appreciable time be followed even by tailors and shoemakers. The passionate gregarious demonstrations of shoemakers in Polish cities in 1931 against the establishment of branches in Poland of the great Czechoslovak shoe factory of Bat'a were assuredly, in their obvious futility, a sign of the times. On the other hand, the growth of certain industries carries the rise of ancillary handicrafts with it : thus the motor-car repairing workshop, common in western countries by this time, will no doubt soon become a frequent and familiar sight in Poland.

### 33

To the handicrafts in the towns, there corresponded, since immemorial times, the *arts and crafts and domestic industries of the country folk* in the villages—their occupation during the long leisure period of winter, and a source of additional income to them. These village home industries differed according to

the raw material supplied by the neighbourhood, and in the use
of ornament the different styles characteristic of regional groups
found their expression. It was rather artists and folklore
students than practical business men who took interest, in pre-
war Poland, in these time-honoured activities of the peasantry.
In Austrian Poland however, where, under home rule, public
funds for subsidies were available, the economic aspects of
village industries became prominent with the foundation of
schools for smiths, locksmiths, furniture-makers and toy-makers,
potters, wood-carvers, basket-makers, weavers and lace-makers
in the several localities which were the traditional centres of
these different trades. The school of wood-carving at Zakopane
acquired a particular renown for its art products ; the ornamen-
ted style of wooden house architecture and furniture peculiar
to the mountaineers of Zakopane became fashionable all over
Poland about the end of the nineteenth century, and has retained
much of its popularity to' this day.

In the new Poland since the War, after some isolated efforts,
a foundation for permanent government protection of the
village industries was laid by a law of 1924, and a special fund
was created for the purpose. Besides the Government, a
number of local societies for the promotion of village industries
became active. It was their merit that the artistic value of
work hitherto known only in a small district—such as that of
the coloured webs of the Wilno region—became known to wider
circles. By the creation of Bazaars of Folk Products, the sale
of such local work all over the country was organized. A Central
Association, through its travelling instructors, is making local
centres acquainted with improved foreign methods of work in
their respective lines. Propaganda abroad for the proper
appreciation of Polish folk art as manifested in pottery, woodcarving, and weaving, has not been very effective hitherto ;
but some successes have been achieved at international exhibitions, and Polish hand-made " kilims " (rugs and wall-hangings),
in particular, have gained a considerable number of admirers
and purchasers in many foreign countries.

### 34

It has been thought fit to give a somewhat detailed account
of the particular industries of Poland—at least of the principal
ones—in spite of the fact that such a presentation made a
certain amount of repetition inevitable. In almost every
branch of industry, in fact, the outline of development is
essentially the same : war-time ruin is followed by a boom in the

inflation period, and this in turn by a slump after the reform of the currency ; then, a steady upward movement on a more solid foundation sets in, to be interrupted in turn by the depression due to the present world crisis.

In illustrating this typical development by the fate of different industries severally, it was intended to show that the differences in their development matter quite as much as the resemblances.

Poland's industrial history in the first ten years of her re-newed existence might, by a superficial observer and wholesale generalizer, be taken to represent nothing else than a typical case of post-war economic nationalism. In the unsettled and far from peaceful atmosphere of Continental Europe after the World War, most of the states newly built up out of the wreckage of Austria-Hungary and parts of the two adjoining Empires, felt ill-assured of their freshly-regained political independence and endeavoured to provide a firm economic foundation for it by making an imaginary self-sufficiency their aim. Hence the irritating tariff barriers cutting up the economic body of the Continent and shutting off comparatively small territories ; hence the almost universal practice of fostering industries artificially, by state credits, even in countries which had so far been mainly agricultural, and of promoting industrial exports at the expense of the domestic consumer ; hence the general futility of post-war commercial treaties, the dearth of credits, and the permanently abnormal condition of trade. But as soon as the political system of post-war Europe will have acquired a fair degree of stability, international economic relations will necessarily be resumed on a large scale, and with their return, the artificial structure of many national industries will tumble down.

There is undeniably a large measure of truth in such a picture of the present state of affairs in Central Europe. To mention one instance only—if the commercial treaty between Poland and Germany, concluded after so many difficulties in 1930, were at last to be carried into effect, the decay of some Polish indus-tries now living on the absence of German competition would be the immediate consequence.

It will, however, I venture to hope, have become apparent to the reader of the survey of Poland's industries given in this chapter, that quite a number of the principal industries of the country are firmly established on a natural basis of good and abundant raw materials within easy reach in the country ; that some of these industries, as well as some others, have an assured future before them in view of the growing capacity of the home market ; and finally, that some neighbouring countries, industrially less developed than Poland, stand in the same relation to her as she does to Germany, and this gives Poland chances for export which are certain to keep many of her industries alive in any case.

## 35

Given such prospects, there can be no question of a return of Poland to the status of a purely agricultural country. Such a return, moreover, is rendered impossible by that root factor of economic development—the *increase of population*. Poland belongs to the countries with a still unabated and uncommonly high birth-rate. With a net increase of population by nearly half a million a year, she is not provided with outlets for it in the shape of colonies, and the possibilities of emigration are very limited : what France and Latin America have lately been offering in this respect, does not at all make up for the recent loss of access to that former large reservoir of Europe's population surplus—the United States. Again, agrarian reform, which is to provide land and means of livelihood for the peasantry, will have exhausted its resources in soil within a generation : the large estates which kept crowds of landless rural labourers employed, will be gone, and the pressure of masses of village proletarians on the towns will become stronger than ever. Under these circumstances (which are common to Poland and a number of other countries), the maintenance of industries within the country is not merely an arguable line of policy, but a hard economic necessity.

To this it might be opposed that the intensification of agriculture is a better and more natural remedy against population difficulties than a forced growth of industries. It has, I trust, been made sufficiently clear in the first section of the present chapter that agricultural progress has of late received at least as careful attention in Poland as industrial development.

Certain international factors must, however, be reckoned with as limiting Poland's purely agricultural prospects. Even if we disregard the resolute opposition of some of Poland's neighbours (especially Germany) to large imports of Polish agricultural products—this being obviously only one of the many symptoms of temporary unrest and diffidence in post-war Europe—there yet remains the more important fact that such agricultural producers on a gigantic scale as Canada, the United States, and, above all, Russia, are once more beginning to make their appearance in the world's markets in full force. From being crushed underneath the steam-roller of such colossal competition, a comparatively small agricultural unit like Poland can only save itself by a variety of activities, which must include industrial as well as agricultural developments.

From whatever point, then, we may look at the problem, the conclusion appears inevitable that, in the case of Poland, as in the case of many other newly industrialized countries, industrialization is not a nationalist fad but, within reasonable limits, a condition of independent existence. The change of Poland and of other states in a similar position from predominantly agricultural countries into countries of mixed industrial-agricultural aspect is a fact which will permanently count in the world balance of industrial production and distribution in the future.

### 36

From industry it is natural to turn to *commerce*. In fact, the commercial aspects of both industry and agriculture have already repeatedly been touched upon in the foregoing sections of the present chapter. Here, it remains to say something on the organization of commerce and on the commercial policy of the State.

Commerce in post-war Europe is still a highly debatable subject.

The break-up of old economic units by the political reconstitution of the eastern half of the Continent, the tariff barriers placed across accustomed trade routes both by land and water, the universal high fever of protectionism and the almost universal practice of dumping—all these things mean a violent break with established traditions, and it will no doubt take some time until commercial relations have become adjusted to the new political conditions.

In the case of Poland, the break with tradition is more complete than elsewhere. As has been pointed out in the introductory historical chapter, the old Poland was a country of flourishing trade in the Middle Ages ; but the shifting westward of the centre of gravity of European trade in the early modern era, together with the indifference to trade of Poland's agrarian ruling class, caused a decay of commerce from which the Poland of the nineteenth century, made subservient to the different economic policies of three Foreign Powers, naturally did not recover.

There was little, then, in the legacy of the immediate past which could be built upon in framing a commercial policy for

Q

delivered and reunited Poland. There was little also in the nation's mentality to serve as spiritual equipment for the task. The country gentleman, whose ways of thinking were anything but commercial, had, after all, been the model type of Pole to the other classes ; there was very little of a Polish commercial middle class in existence ; commerce had become practically the monopoly of countless small Jewish traders, who had things in the towns, and, still more so, over vast areas of the country, very much in their own hands. The Jewish publican of the village was usually both the squire's privileged commercial agent and the peasant farmer's universal provider ; and the great wholesale dealers were also largely Jews. The only sector of the country in which this state of things had undergone really marked changes before the World War, was Prussian Poland.

In the new Polish State, the devastations and general impoverishment of war time were followed by the moral corruption of the inflation period, during which speculative purchases and gambling in foreign currencies became a universal habit. The clash of conflicting tariff policies along the new frontiers encouraged widespread smuggling ; on the other hand, the State, in Poland as well as elsewhere, displayed an immoderate and harmful disposition to fetter commerce by a mass of regulations —this being, on the one hand, the automatic continuance of war-time state control of all economic life, and on the other hand, the only means to squeeze out of a thoroughly impoverished community the fiscal revenues needed to fulfil the manifold social tasks which the democratic masses of to-day expect to be performed by the state authorities.

If there were far too numerous regulations hampering the development of commerce, this does not mean that a great many of them were not urgently needed. To begin with, the new Polish State found itself confronted by the obvious necessity of placing commercial relations within the country on a uniform footing. As stated in a former chapter, the commission for the codification of the new laws of Poland very properly considered the framing of codes regulating business relations as one of its most pressing tasks, and a number of important and indispensable legal measures in that field were among the first fruits of its labours. If even in these codes of law widespread popular notions about " post-war profiteering " found expression in a way which unduly interfered with the growth of legitimate trade, this was still more marked in the sphere of taxation : the oppressive " turnover tax " made the rise of larger commercial undertakings extremely difficult.

Under the circumstances, commerce, which did not have the same strong natural foundations as industry, could not, even after the stabilization of the currency, progress very quickly. The percentage of Polish citizens engaged in commercial pursuits is still a mere 3·8 (as compared with Germany's 12) ; and among them, small traders are an overwhelming majority.

Poland's share in the world's commerce, after the first ten years of her new existence, had not yet reached 1 per cent. The rapid growth of the harbour of Gdynia will no doubt soon raise that figure to a considerably higher level. Gdynia alone certainly means more in that respect than the thirty-odd commercial treaties which Poland succeeded in concluding with Foreign Powers during that first decade. The universal passion for high tariffs makes " scraps of paper " of commercial treaties very often and very soon ; the " most-favoured-nation clause," being usually included in the treaties has become an almost meaningless convention ; and the fact that Poland has not been able so far to enter into treaty relations with her two principal neighbours, Germany and Russia, speaks very eloquently of the unfavourable influence of political insecurity on economic conditions in post-war Europe.

### 37

In the sphere of actual organization of trade within the country, there are certain definite achievements to be recorded. A bill of 1921 (amended by Presidential decrees in 1924 and 1928) laid a common legal foundation for the creation of *produce exchanges*, which were a basic condition of commercial unity and independence, the three sections of the country having formerly gravitated commercially towards the exchanges in the capitals of the several partitioning powers. The new Polish exchanges were organized as closed corporations under government supervision, this being exercised through Commissioners of the Ministry of Industry and Trade. Exchanges for transactions in agricultural produce were established in the four principal cities (Warsaw, Cracow, Lwów, Poznań), timber exchanges at Bydgoszcz and in Warsaw, a meat exchange in Warsaw. There was also a textile exchange at Łódź, but it had to be closed owing to trade depresion. On the other hand, the rising provincial centre of Katowice in Polish Silesia received an agricultural exchange of its own, and is likely to assert its commercial importance more and more in the near future.

Next to the new produce-exchanges, certain old-established *associations of merchants* must be mentioned as passing into a new stage of their existence with the rebirth of Poland. Cracow, Poznań, and Lwów had their time-honoured " Congregations of Merchants," some of them dating back to the fifteenth century ; and in the pre-war Russian sector, organizations of Polish merchants had had a flourishing development during the brief spell of constitutional freedom after 1905. In the new Poland, a number of local organizations and regional unions were soon added to the old associations. A Congress of Polish Merchants had been held in Warsaw while still under German occupation, in the last months of the War ; later on, a nation-wide Association of Polish Merchants was created and developed favourably. Yet the older and the newer societies lacked co-ordination until another Congress, in 1925, ended in the creation of a Supreme Council as the joint representation of all merchant associations in the Republic.

Side by side with voluntary associations, the official " *Chambers of Industry and Commerce* " are doing their work. Such Chambers, as have been mentioned before, had existed under Prussia and Austria, but not under Russia ; by a Presidential decree of 1927, their organization was extended to the whole of the Republic, and rendered obligatory and uniform. Their functions are manifold, and they are legally open to further extension, which might very usefully take some of the many economic activities now conducted by the State, off its hands, and decentralize them with proper regard to local conditions. As it is, a variety of achievements in the way of organizing local exhibitions and conventions, of conducting educational courses and publishing commercial periodicals, of assisting in the development of foreign trade relations, of the sale of products of folk art, of tourist traffic—stand to the credit of the older and the new Chambers of Commerce in Poland. They have extended their protection over the new produce exchanges and stock exchanges, some of which they were instrumental in creating.

It was under their ægis also that a number of commercial schools grew up, including the four institutions of university rank which now serve to train business leaders for Poland, viz., the Commercial Colleges of Warsaw, Cracow, and Poznań, and the Foreign Trade College at Lwów.

Turning now from commercial organizations within the country to the problem of promoting the new Poland's *foreign trade*, we find that in this respect little was done during the first years —chiefly because the early Governments, in their anxiety to prevent social revolution on the Russian model, were guided in their economic policy above all by consideration for the consumer in the towns, and looked unfavourably on exports of any kind, particularly on exports of food.   In industrial exports, as has been stated before, almost fantastic successes were achieved at the time through the cheapness of Polish articles caused by inflation ;  but these successes were not followed up by proper organization and did not last long.   It was only after the definite stabilization of the currency and under the pressure of the tariff war with Germany that the organized promotion of exports was taken in hand.   A National Export Institute was created, on whose council authoritative representatives of agriculture, industry, and commerce are sitting, and whose correspondents supply information from abroad.   Certain important and elementary domestic tasks which had to be accomplished in the interests of export trade—such as the standardization of export articles and the development of transport facilities —received the attention of the Institute ;  it had a hand in the establishment of direct connections between Poland and oversea countries, and it has an advisory voice with regard to the revision of commercial treaties as well as in the conclusion of new ones.   The least amount of success has so far been achieved in the direction of drawing a part of the profits from transport, mediation, insurance and the like, in Poland's foreign trade (import as well as export trade) into the orbit of Polish enterprise :  the mediation of foreign commercial agencies and foreign transport services still remains a dominant feature, chiefly owing to the lack of the capital required for the development of Polish activities in that domain.

The fact that Poland's export trade is still to such a large extent under non-Polish control accounts for certain imperfections of Poland's foreign trade policy from the point of view of national interest.   A country still so largely agricultural should export mainly agricultural produce, meat and timber, and import industrial articles.   Instead, Poland continues to import serious quantities of food and of raw materials, while exporting large quantities of mineral products (coal) and timber, less considerable quantities of agricultural produce and meat, and certain industrial articles whose export is, in part at least, somewhat forced and artificial.   Besides this imperfect adjustment of export trade to the condition of the country, it must be mentioned that *transit trade*, for which Poland by her geographical situation is particularly fitted, has not, so far, been developed to any appreciable degree.   The continued *dearth of credit* in Poland—a consequence of the financial difficulties and mistakes of the early years—is another handicap in the way of foreign trade relations. However, the rapid growth of Poland's sea-borne trade—from 7·3 per cent. of her exports in 1922 to 67 per cent. in 1932—shows that spontaneous progress in that direction is not lacking, and Poland's future part in the world's commercial relations is likely to be of some importance.

## 38

Among the means of reviving and promoting trade in post-war Europe, annual *fairs* held in important commercial centres have become a popular institution. Organized at first to meet the urgent demand for merchandise of all sorts in the famished, war-stricken countries, they have proved to be of more general usefulness, especially in a reunited country like Poland, where they helped long-separated provinces to become acquainted with each others' resources and economic possibilities. The Poznań Fair, held in 1919 for the first time, established a conspicuously successful precedent, and the " Eastern Fairs " at Lwów, organized annually since 1921, have followed it up worthily. In 1928, a Fair at Wilno was added to the record. Possessing all the attractions of exhibitions, these Fairs act as a stimulant not only to trade, but also to tourist traffic.

The Poznań Fair, having extended its activities to the inter-national field, was recognized by the International Chamber of Commerce as one of the six largest periodical Fairs of Europe. A set of large permanent buildings was created for the Fair. After this, it was natural that Poznań, westernmost of Polish towns, distant only by five hours' railway journey from Berlin, became the chosen site of the great *National Exhibition* which was organized to commemorate the tenth anniversary of the new Poland's existence. National in scope, it necessarily became in practice largely the work of the strenuous and discip-lined people of Poznań and proved indeed a triumph of the organizing capacity and the habits of co-operation which they had acquired in their hard struggle against Prussianism. The Exhibition, besides presenting Poland's economic life—both industrial and agricultural—in all its aspects on a very extensive scale, gave in its large Government Pavillion an excellent survey, in the form of admirably constructed statistical diagrams, of the whole range of the manifold activities of the new Polish State in the way of administration, education, and social welfare. In the same manner, the constructive achievements of local government organs and of the larger municipalities were amply illustrated. A large building was filled with well-selected treasures of contemporary Polish Art. Besides all this, the

Exhibition contained an abundance of material illustrating the natural beauties, the economic resources, the dwellings, dresses, customs, and folklore peculiarities of almost every district of the new Poland, with inclusion of all the more important Polish emigrant settlements abroad and overseas. The organizers of the Exhibition achieved the record (very rare indeed in such cases) of having all the thirty-two sections completely ready for inspection on the day of opening, which was May 16, 1929. In the course of the five months during which it was open, the Exhibition, besides 4½ million individual visitors and twenty official missions from other States, was visited by about 180 excursion groups from abroad and about 120 conventions and congresses, both national and international, which met within its walls. If the individual attendance of tourists from the western countries was not what it might have been, yet the Exhibition richly repaid the labours of its organizers as a unique achievement in popular education on a large scale: it gave to vast numbers of Poland's own citizens (and of Poles settled abroad, especially in America) a comprehensive object lesson of the utmost interest in the resources and achievements of the reborn country, and thereby meant a great advance in the building-up of renewed national unity and civic consciousness.

### 39

The subject of trade cannot be dismissed without brief reference to that important rival which in modern societies has arisen to private commerce in the shape of *co-operative organizations*.

Co-operatives in Poland have a respectable record to look back upon. As mentioned in a former chapter, they did service, with singular success, as a weapon of organized opposition to the inroads of German colonization in Prussian Poland ; they also were the principal means of the gradual economic strengthening of the peasant-farmer class in the Austrian sector. The wholesale destruction of Polish national wealth by the War and by money devaluation after it did not spare the capital of the co-operative societies : the accumulated capital melted away, and the confidence of the masses in co-operative organization was thoroughly shaken, just at the time when the impoverished nation would have needed co-operative effort more than ever as a means of rebuilding prosperity. A new co-operative education of the people was necessary. It was undertaken— one of the new Poland's Presidents, Profesor Stanislas Wojciechowski, being among the principal educators. At the end of ten years, a membership of $3\frac{1}{2}$ millions, and a capital of 600,000,000 złoty, eloquently testified to the renascence of the co-operative movement ; 16,000 co-operative societies, one-half of them united in large associations, were by that time active in Poland. This development was not brought about without considerable assistance from the coffers of the State in the form of loans from State Banks ; and it did not reach a definitely healthy stage without the breakdown of a good many makeshift post-war co-operatives, fathered by sheer need but established on weak foundations—and without sensational unmaskings of some fictitious co-operatives, which had served as cloaks for the dishonest practices of impostors. The purgation of Poland's co-operative system from such excrescences necessarily took time, and its consolidation is still in progress.

*Credit co-operatives*, fundamentally the most important, are organized in two groups, representing the two types which are distinguished after their German inventors Schultze-Delitsch and Raiffeisen. Each group has a large bank for its centre ; but within the groups there are sub-divisions, represented by associations of societies homogeneous either in language (Polish, German, Ukrainian), in denomination (Christian, Jewish), or in political creed (Nationalist, Socialist). Thus have political divisions inevitably reacted on economic organization. Credit co-operatives play a particularly important part in the countryside, where they act as banks for the small farmer. Their present membership amounts to 2·6 per cent. of the population.

*Agricultural co-operatives* have been dealt with in the section of this chapter devoted to agriculture. What they mean for the population of the countryside is represented in the life of the towns by *co-operatives of consumers*. These developed with feverish quickness in the distressful first post-war years : their growth was fostered by the State through the grants of all sorts of privileges. In the later years of the first decade the trend was more towards consolidation than towards further expansion. The total number in 1929–30 was over 6,000, more than one-half of these societies belonging to the industrial territory of Silesia. Besides their obvious economic tasks, these co-operatives, like the Farmers' Circles, devote a considerable amount of energy to adult education : 80 books were published by the Consumers' Co-operatives in the course of 10 years, and a large number of educational courses were conducted, the principal association keeping about 60 travelling instructors in its pay. An important channel of educational influence on the masses is provided by the existence of *Army Co-operatives*, through which the co-operative spirit wins apostles in the most remote villages in the persons of ex-service men. From sale, the consumers' co-operatives have some time ago passed on to *production*, by running mills, bakeries and small factories of such necessaries as soap and the like. They also were taught by financial disasters to invest portions of their capital in real estate, which strengthened their position.

*Building co-operatives*, in view of the post-war housing shortage, were as urgent a necessity in the first years as consumers' co-operatives. The building co-operatives were also favoured and fostered by the State : a special fund for building credits was created as far back as 1919, a bill of 1921 provided for the cession of state-owned areas to building co-operatives, another one of 1922 freed all new buildings from taxation for fifteen years ; and a plan for the extension of towns was created in 1922 and refashioned in 1925 and 1927. Building co-operatives received loans to the amount of 90 per cent. of building costs, and the legal foundations of co-operative building enterprise were not always determined with sufficient clearness. Speculation in building plots was not infrequent, and the result of it all was a certain diffidence towards building co-operatives among the general public.

With all their shortcomings, however, due to the material and moral conditions of post-war time, the building co-operatives as well as the other co-operative societies of the new Poland must be admitted to have made important contributions to the reconstruction of the nation's prosperity in town and country.

### 40

*Communications* are a subject closely connected with economic life, being largely created by its needs, and are therefore considered in this chapter.

In this as in so many other domains of her new existence, Poland was confronted by enormous tasks of readjustment. During the century of division and foreign rule, as far as there was any active policy of developing communications in the country at all (which was by no means continually and universally the case), the object of such policy was in the case of each sector to link it up with the Empire to which it belonged, and not with the other two sectors. Regions along the new frontiers were deliberately neglected in the matter of communications, especially under Russia. The several communication policies of the partitioning powers, tending to disunite Poland still further, were bound to be particularly marked in the sphere of railway communication, since railways—a point to remember !—only began to be built nearly half a century after the partitions of Poland. And besides different aims of policy, there were considerable differences in its intensity : after a century and a quarter of foreign domination, Poland was left with a fairly thick network of railways in her Prussian section, a much less liberal allowance of them in the Austrian one, and the mere elements of a railway system in the Russian portion. And Russia, besides her general slowness in railway construction and the deliberate neglect of her border districts in this matter, also cut herself off from the rest of Europe by adopting a different gauge for her railways—broader than the one common to all other countries on the Continent.

The differences between the three sectors of Poland in the matter of roads were analogous to those in the matter of railways. And as regards waterways, it was only in the Prussian sector that any advance was made beyond what had been created by Polish initiative during the era of canal-building in the later eighteenth and early nineteenth centuries.

To begin with *roads*, it was always a considerable drawback to the development of Poland's road system that the large plains of the centre and the north are very poor in stone, and the transport of stone from the quarries along the mountain ridges in the south greatly increases the cost of the building and preservation of roads. Poland's 126 quarries of to-day, many of them primitive and inconveniently situated, are far from supplying the quantities required for road-building and street-paving, while the manufacture of clinker as a substitute for stone is only in its beginnings. The result of such conditions is that the majority of roads in Poland are still without stone superstructure. These are mostly the roads of the former Russian sector, which also differ from those in the other parts of the country by their breadth : with characteristic Russian recklessness in the matter of space, roads in the Russian Empire, if devoid of solid superstructure, were made as broad as twenty yards, while those under Prussia and Austria rarely exceeded six or seven yards in breadth.

At the moment of Poland's deliverance, her territory included some 26,000 miles of highway, a network considerably surpassing that of the vast area of European Russia, but equal only to one-fifth of Germany's. To this, over 3,000 miles of road were added during the existence of the new Poland. The greatest amount of road-building was done in the rich industrial province of Silesia, and there also the roads are best in quality, many of them being provided with a surface of asphalt.

In order to raise the standard of quality of Poland's existing roads, and to make better progress with the building of new ones, the Polish Government intended to follow the example of those of some Western European States by creating a " road fund." But the motor-bus traffic, which was to serve as the chief source of revenue for the purpose, proved too weak to bear the burden of additional taxation. As things stand at present, it seems that without ample assistance from foreign capital the huge problem of providing a network of adequate roads for Central and Eastern Poland cannot be solved satisfactorily or soon.

### 41

Of the *railways*, which began to be built on Polish territory about the middle of the nineteenth century, some lines have retained their pre-war importance, such being particularly those from Warsaw south-westard to the coal-basin, from Cracow to Lwów, and from Toruń (Thorn) to Danzig. Other lines, mainly those leading eastward into Russia and north-eastward into the Baltic countries have lost in importance in view of the fact that Poland's own exchange of products with Soviet Russia is insignificant, while transit trade between Russia and Central Europe is conducted almost exclusively over the head of Poland, through Lithuania and East Prussia. It is along a different transit line, at right angles to this one, that Poland may in the near future expect to develop really animated traffic : when the direct railway connection between Silesia and the port of Gdynia, now being quickly completed with the help of French capital, is ready, it will probably serve not only for its principal purpose—as the main artery for Poland's coal exports—but also as the highway for transit from Czechoslovakia and Rumania northward to the Baltic.

Poland, having inherited from the partitioning powers over 10,000 miles of railways, has so far not been able to add quite 500 miles of new ones, and the problem here, as in the case of the roads, is one to be solved only by an influx of foreign capital. With her own resources, Poland was barely able to make head-way with the reconstruction of the many railway stations, bridges and sectors of lines which had been destroyed by the War ; of all these, about four-fifths had been rebuilt by 1930. As things stand now, Poland's railway network is three and a half times as thick as that of European Russia, but three times less thick than that of Germany. As in so many other respects, so in this regard also there is a marked difference between the west and east of the country, the length of railway lines per 1,000 square kilometres being, on an average, more than 100 in the western provinces, about 50 in the centre, and less than 30 in the east. The rolling stock, which was naturally very poor both in quantity and in quality after the War, was trebled during the first ten years, and both engines and passenger cars manufactured in Poland are not inconspicuous among it.

The working efficiency of Poland's railways was put to a hard test at the very beginning, in 1920, when an army of a million men was put into the field against the Bolsheviks, and transport services had to be performed for it under quickly shifting conditions of advance, retreat and renewed advance, the front ultimately extending over the whole eastern frontier of Poland, many hundreds of miles in length. This test having been withstood successfully, a high standard has been uniformly maintained since, in spite of cramping material difficulties. If the quickness of express-train traffic in Poland is still below the western European average, this is largely due to the imperfect solidity of the substructure of railway lines in many parts of the country.

Poland's railways—all of them in the hands of the State—were at first run at a deficit, in view of the huge tasks of reconstruction which had to be grappled with. That deficit was increased by the immoderate growth of railway *personnel*, the State railway system serving as another outlet for Poland's growing surplus of population ; and the large expenditure on social insurance services for the numerous railway employees added its share to the burden. The system, in a word, suffered from all those weaknesses of a state-conducted bureaucratic apparatus which are familiar to the observer of Continental European affairs. These defects were realized and widely discussed in Poland : " commercialization of the railways " was repeatedly declared to be the aim of the Government ; but it was only in 1928, by a resolute all-round 20 per cent. increase in personal tariffs, that balance was established in the domain of passenger traffic. [1]By that time, happily freight traffic (particularly coal transports) had raised the total revenue from Poland's railways by 100,000,000 *zloty* per year above working costs, and with such a surplus in their hands, the Polish railway adminis-

---

[1] All State functionaries, whether civil or military, retain the privilege of travelling at half price, and Parliamentary Deputies have a free ticket on all lines.

tration was enabled to do much more in the way of reconstruction and new construction than had been done in any previous year. Since that time, of course, the general economic crisis has had its inevitable adverse effect here as elsewhere.

*Motor-bus traffic* has of late developed in Poland as a substitute for railways in those parts of the country which do not possess them. Over 1500 motor-bus lines were in existence in 1930, and progress had been very rapid for the last three years. In 1931, certain Government projects calculated to raise the standard of safety and comfort as well as to extract revenue from motor-bus traffic for road improvement, caused a set-back and widespread stoppage.

*Motor-car traffic* increased at the same quick ratio as motor-bus traffic : the volume of both has nearly trebled since 1927. Still, the total number of motor cars in Poland remains considerably inferior to that of western countries : it was little more than one per thousand of the population in 1931, as compared with Germany's one per hundred. But the number is rising quickly, in spite of high tariffs, which have had the effect of inducing foreign firms to establish assembling plants on Polish soil, and even of calling the beginnings of a Polish motor-car industry into being.

### 42

Passing from communications by land to *waterways*, we may begin by a few data concerning Poland's *sea-ports*.

The harbour of *Danzig*, as explained in a former chapter, is not included in Polish territory proper, Danzig being a Free City, but Poland has a share in the administration of the harbour : the Harbour Council is composed of representatives of Poland and of the Free City in equal proportion. Danzig, although often chafing against Polish rule, had flourished under it during three centuries ; when included in Germany after the partitions of Poland, the port was eclipsed by Hamburg and entered on a period of decay. The Polish connection, renewed in different form since the World War, once more became an occasion for continual protests and active opposition on the part of the German nationalists who govern the city : but once more also it brought growing prosperity to the people of Danzig. The course of that prosperity was not interrupted even when Danzig's persistent policy of *chicane* compelled Poland to start building a harbour of her own at Gdynia in the same bay. The two harbours together, with Gdynia quickly grown to the size of a respectable port, are not sufficient to cope with Poland's sea-borne exports and imports : for a large portion of these (305,000 tons of imports in 1928) the German harbours of Hamburg, Bremen, Stettin, and Königsberg are still used. As regards Danzig herself, Poland did much for her development: the railway network within the territory of the Free City was enlarged by nearly one-third in the first ten years ; large sums were spent on the regulation of the lower Vistula ; the Polish State guaranteed a $4,500,000 American loan for the building of a new basin within the harbour ; the length of quays was increased by nearly a mile and a half with Poland's financial assistance ; and this process of growth is steadily continuing. The capacity of the port, which did not surpass 3,000,000 tons a year before the War, has risen to 8,000,000 tons recently. The number of ships entering and leaving the port was about 3000 a year before the War, and twice that number in 1930, and their total tonnage in the same period rose from 1,000,000 to more than 4,000,000.

The fishing village of *Gdynia* within sight of Danzig, was selected as the site of a new, purely Polish port in 1921, but the building of the port on a large scale only began in 1926. In 1932, the volume of Gdynia's shipping had reached 3600 ships, with a total tonnage of about 5,000,000 higher than that of most Baltic ports, including even Stockholm and Copenhagen. Gdynia so far is used chiefly for exports, while Danzig serves both for exports and imports ; but imports by way of Gdynia are also increasing rapidly. Among its exports coal is the dominant item, far surpassing everything else taken together. But the possibilities for the export of sugar, meat and grain by that route are growing with the development of the harbour. It is with regard to timber exports only that Danzig is likely to hold its present monopoly. Gdynia is also growing in importance as a centre of passenger traffic, especially between Poland and North and South America, while Danzig's passenger traffic is diminishing.

Poland's *commercial fleet*, a creation of the last few years consisted on January 1, 1931, of 29 vessels, whose total register tonnage approached 60,000. They were in possession of four companies, one of which, financed by the State, owned one-half of their number. The other three companies specialize in traffic with Britain, America, and the Scandinavian countries respectively. Regular steamship connections are now established between Gdynia and Le Havre, Gdynia and London, Gdynia and New York, Gdynia and Rio de Janeiro, as well as with the principal Baltic ports.

*Inland navigation* in Poland, like her navigation by sea, is only in its beginnings, chiefly because the waterways of the long divided sections of the country have not yet been properly linked up with each other, and the regulation of the navigable rivers has not made sufficient progress ; also for the additional reason that railway-freight rates have not been duly co-ordinated with those for water transport and compete with them successfully by their cheapness. Three companies for inland navigation exist in Poland, one of them being financed by the State. Between them they own about 150 steamers and motor-boats, besides which there are over 1300 barges of various kinds. Most of this craft plies on the Vistula and on western Polish waters, such as the river Warta, flowing through Poznań. The rivers, and the eighteenth- and early nineteenth-century canals of Poland's eastern provinces now suffer from a decay of traffic as compared with earlier periods. The fact that some important rivers are, in part, frontier rivers and, in the case of others, the new political frontiers cut across their course, necessarily interferes with the development of navigation. Thus, the use of the Niemen for transports of timber and other exports of Poland's eastern provinces is rendered impossible by Poland's unsettled relations with Lithuania.

### 43

The *air* has recently become a pathway of communication equal in importance to land and water. In Poland, airlines have since 1929 been definitely established between Warsaw and the principal cities of the country, as well as between Warsaw and a number of foreign capitals, from Paris to Bucharest. A direct connection by air between the shores of the Baltic and the Mediterranean is now provided by the airline from Gdynia to Salonika. The efficiency and safety of the Polish air service is actually greater than that of railway communication : there is, so far, not a single mortal accident on record. The company in whose hands the service is centred, is almost entirely controlled by the Government. The number of air ports, represented in 1927 by the modest figure of 21, is quickly on the increase.

*Telegraph* and *telephone* stations, as well as *post offices* in Poland are still relatively few and far between in the eastern provinces ; hence the comparatively low figure for the whole country : about 4000 offices of each kind, which means an average of 12 per 100,000 of the population. With the heavy snowfalls not infrequent in winter, and the violent storms

occasionally sweeping the country in summer, overhead lines
are apt to suffer. Underground telephone cables so far exist
in modest dimensions only ; a line from Warsaw to Łódź was
completed in 1930, and others are soon to follow.

*Wireless telephony and telegraphy* is spreading rapidly in
Poland. There are *seven broadcasting stations*, those of Warsaw
and of Katowice being particularly powerful. The number of
listeners is continually increasing, especially in the country,
where the radio provides a welcome link with the outside world,
and where the instructive talks for farmers—a constant feature
of the Polish wireless programme—are duly appreciated.

By lectures, recitals, and concerts, the radio in Poland is
doing a great amount of highly useful work in the way of popular
education in art, literature, history, natural science, civics,
political economy and practical affairs.

There are five *radio-telegraph* stations in Poland, including
one in Warsaw for Transatlantic communication, and one at
Gdynia for communication with ships on the waters of the
Baltic.

The telegraph and telephone in Poland are entirely in the
hands of the State (being administered by a special Ministerial
Department) ; the broadcasting stations are controlled by a
" Polish Radio Company " in which the State is a large share-
holder. There are state-owned factories of telegraph, telephone
and wireless apparatus, and a State Radiotechnical Institute
is being created.

## 44

In conclusion of the present survey of Poland's economic
life, it seems fair to add some account of Poland's *financial
organization*. The history of Poland's currency has been given
in outline in a former chapter ; here, something remains to be
said of the *banking system* and of *credit institutions*.

The abnormal conditions of the inflation period were much
the same in Poland as in other Continental European States
after the War. The country was filled with a mushroom growth
of small speculative banks and ephemerous joint-stock companies, while capital had melted away into a tide of worthless
paper-money, and long-term credits became an obsolete institution. After the introduction of the *zloty* currency in 1924, the
normal habits of saving and investment quickly began to
return among the population and the reconstruction of credit
seemed under way. This development was interrupted by the
fall of the new currency in 1925. The ensuing financial crisis

was weathered by some banks only with the aid of State credits. Many credit institutions disappeared, and the accumulation of capital was checked. It took some time after the renewed stabilization of the currency—this time on a more reasonable level—before confidence was reawakened, and saving in the form of bank deposits once more became an established practice. Even then, many people preferred to keep their savings in the banks in the form of dollars rather than in *złoty*, and large masses of capital were still deposited abroad. Improvement, however, was indisputable : the State Banks began to resume long-term credit operations ; the surviving private banks were reorganized on sound lines ; they began to attract savings and to enjoy foreign credits, and they were no longer dependent on the State Banks for financial support. In spite of the extreme impoverishment of the country and of the hard burden of taxation required to defray the cost of the manifold social services of the modern State, definite if slow progress in the accumulation of capital was made in Poland from 1926 to 1929. A law of 1928 put the organization of banks on a uniform and definite legal basis. Steady progress seemed guaranteed by the condition of state finances as well : the firmness with which the budget was kept balanced after 1926, maintained the currency in a condition of satisfactory stability, and even after the advent of the world crisis, the *złoty* remained strong enough not to be affected by the financial disasters in Austria and Germany during 1931 and by the fall of the pound sterling. At the same time, the drastic and unpopular economies in State expenditure which were required by the considerable falling-off of revenue during 1930–31, were more easy to carry out under a semi-dictatorial Government unhampered by parliamentary criticism ; and the reserves accumulated in the Treasury during the " good years " 1926–29 helped to cover the deficit which inevitably made its appearance in the course of the crisis. While thus the finances of the State remained well-founded, the lack of money in circulation, the scarcity of capital and the dearth of credit were more keenly felt during the crisis than before, and Poland still remains one of the countries with the highest official discount rates and private rates of interest in Europe.

## 45

Among banks, pride of place is naturally due to the *Bank of Poland*. As mentioned in a former chapter, it was created in 1924 on a basis of private subscription among the citizens of

R

Poland. Its original capital consisted of 100,000,000 *zloty* paid up for 1,000,000 shares of the nominal value of 100 *zloty* each. That capital was increased by 50,000,000 *zloty* after the American loan of 1927. The Bank, which has over 50 branch offices in the larger towns of Poland, is legally independent of the State. In return for the exclusive privilege of issuing banknotes which is granted to the Bank, the State has an open credit at the Bank to the amount of 50,000,000 *zloty*, free from interest. After a year of restricted activities and uncertainty, due to the collapse of the *zloty* in 1925, the Bank entered on an era of favourable development in 1926 ; the most important stages of this were the legal stabilization of the currency on its new and lower level in 1927, and the American loan of $70,000,000 in the autumn of that year, which brought half a milliard *zloty* in gold and in foreign currencies into the coffers of the Bank. Ever since that time, the Bank's stock of gold and foreign currency has been well above the statutory *minimum*. The amount of paper-money in circulation has so far always been considerably smaller than could be desired in the interests of economic life, and the practice of accumulating Treasury reserves in the Bank (a practice which proved useful in times of crisis) restricted it still further. However, after the inflation calamity, it was wiser to keep the country on a short allowance of money than to expose it anew to the old danger. The Bank's credit policy could only become somewhat more liberal in 1927 and 1928 ; at the same time, the favourable growth of other credit institutions in these years diminished the percentual share of the Bank in the task of financing the country's economic life. The favourable developments, which found outward expression in a lowering of the Bank rate and a rise in the dividend paid by the Bank to its shareholders, were checked by the world crisis of 1929. After three years of that crisis, the Bank of Poland, thanks to the cautious financial policy of 1926–29, still stands firm, while all around Poland states are going bankrupt in various ways.

Side by side with the Bank of Poland, there arose, in 1924, the Bank of National Economy (*Bank Gospodarstwa Krajowego*). It was built up on three banks of a similar type in pre-war and war-time Austrian Poland, and its aim was to perform those services of financing reconstruction and economic development in the country which private capital, ruined by the War and by inflation, was incapable to accomplish. Building activities of all sorts were to be promoted in the first place. Seventy per cent. of the original capital of the Bank came from the Treasury ; to this, as time went on, considerable private deposits were added. Hampered at first in its activities by the consequences of the currency crisis, the Bank, after three years of existence, had become one of the principal factors in the country's economy : most of the reconstruction work done in the towns in particular, was due to its assistance ; many public buildings devoted to social service in Poland's cities would never have arisen without it.

The rural areas of the country, as indicated before, were less favoured by Poland's early government than the towns. Gradually, however, it was realized that the great social change which was coming over the country through land reform, could not proceed on a sound economic foundation without the provision of adequate credit facilities for the small farmer. It was to this purpose that a *State Land Bank* was to be devoted, the creation of which was decreed as early as 1919, but which exists in its present, fully developed form only since 1928. Its main purpose is to finance the purchase of land by small farmers, and to assist them in introducing improvements on their farms as well as in paying off debts to private creditors. In 1928, the Bank (whose capital had increased rapidly) issued bonds for the special purpose of financing soil improvement. The Bank's short-term credits, issued primarily to agricultural co-operatives, increased twentyfold between 1924 and 1928 ; the Bank also took in hand the sale of artificial fertilizers from the state factories, and the administration of state funds allocated to agricultural purposes.

Besides the three State Banks, Poland possesses a *Post Office Savings Bank*, modelled on the analogous institutions of other countries, and intended to collect and utilize small savings all over the country, as well as to facilitate money transfer without payments in cash.[1] The Bank was founded in 1919, but it only began to flourish after the definite stabilization of the new currency in 1925. Between that year and 1928, the savings deposited in it increased tenfold : from 1927 to 1928 alone the increase was fourfold. The accumulated savings were invested in stocks and bonds, and thereby agriculture, industry and building activities received ample assistance. The practice of payment by cheques of the Bank made rapid progress, likewise increasing by 1928 to three times the dimensions of 1925. In the same years, the Bank's activities were considerably extended by the foundation of a number of branch offices in

---

[1] Bank cheques are still very little used for private payments in Poland, and are an unfamiliar instrument to the masses of the population.

France for the use of Polish emigrant labour there, whose savings now began to flow into the country through that channel.

The activities of the four State credit institutions thus outlined may appear to the foreign observer to have a somewhat makeshift character and to represent undue intrusion of government action into certain legitimate domains of private finance. But it must be emphasized that, with the scarcity of private capital in Poland and its ruin by the War and by post-war developments, the new Republic really had no other choice, and, given the circumstances which forced its hand, the organization of the State Banks was effective as well as necessary.

## 46

On *private banking* in Poland it is naturally impossible to offer more than a few general observations here. Of the unfortunate and abnormal conditions of banking in the inflation period enough has been said before. A few large and respected pre-war banks succumbed to it ; of the surviving ones, some were irremediably shattered and fell into decay. Some, like the Commercial Bank (*Bank Handlowy*) in Warsaw regained their position through considerable influxes of foreign capital ; a very few only—like the *Bank Spółek Zarobkowych* at Poznań (the main instrument of pre-war resistence to Prussianization) weathered the crisis by their own unaided strength.

There followed a period of comparative prosperity under the more or less normal currency conditions after 1925. At first, indeed, the public favoured the State Banks rather than private banks : savings in the former, during the first year of the new era, grew twice as quickly as in the latter ; also, savings at first were preferably made withdrawable without notice, which compelled the banks to keep large reserves of cash unutilized. And dollar accounts were (and remained) more popular and common than accounts in *złoty*. At the same time, the strenuous reduction in the number of banks and bank offices in Poland (from 834 in 1923 to 296 in 1926) not only cleared the atmosphere of unhealthy elements, but also diminished the ratio of administrative expenses in relation to capital (from 3 per cent. in 1925 to 1 per cent. in 1927). In 1926, the transition from deficits to income was once more achieved ; in 1927, the public had sufficiently regained confidence in the private banks to deposit 35 per cent. of its savings in them, while only 19 per cent. flowed into the State Banks. Foreign capital also began to make its appearance in larger quantities ; its total share gradually came to amount to 28 per cent. (the figure for 1931). Credit activities were reviving by 1928 : 50 per cent. of the short-term credits obtained in the country came from private banks, while formerly the State Banks had played a predominant part in that field. The private banks, although still far inferior in capital to the State Banks, became less and less dependent on them. Together with these favourable symptoms, there went progressive concentration of capital in a few strong institutions : of the 29 banks combined in the National Association of Poland's Banks, the four largest ones had, by 1928, attracted more than one-half of all the savings.

The world crisis interrupted this prosperous development of the Polish banking system, as it interrupted economic progress in so many other domains.

During 1930 and 1931, bankruptcies, even of seemingly strong and well-organized banks, occurred in Poland, as they did in other countries.

The communal and district *Savings-Banks* were a form of credit organization particularly favoured by the small investor in Central and Eastern Europe before the War, and they accordingly revived especially quickly when permanent stabilization of the currency seemed achieved.

In one year alone—1927—the savings accumulated in them were doubled. Their legal position was strengthened, and the foundation for their uniform progress throughout Poland laid, by a Presidential decree of 1927 which replaced the different laws of the three partitioning powers in this regard ; in former Russian Poland, the scanty and undeveloped pre-war organizations of this type had already been replaced by a thicker network of new Polish ones since the beginning of 1925. By the end of 1928, there were nearly 300 communal and district Savings Banks all over Poland, in comparison with the 200 of 1926. When the crisis of 1929 came, these Savings Banks were not as immediately affected by it as were the private banks ; with the authority of local self-governing bodies behind them, they enjoyed greater confidence on the part of the public, and they deserved it by being much more circumspect in their credit policy and generally averse to speculation. There was even, in 1930 and 1931, a strong movement among the public in favour of transferring savings from private banks to municipal and provincial Savings Banks, and the cellars of some of the latter became choked with dollar bills. It was only in the later part of 1931 that the further progress of the crisis made itself felt in this quarter as well ; there were occasional runs on Communal Savings Banks, and they began, in their turn, to suffer drainage of their resources.

### 47

*Stock Exchanges* were practically non-existent in Poland when the War ended : even the Warsaw Exchange (which had been founded in 1817) held only private meetings and issued no official quotation-list. Official quotations were re-established in 1921. In the subsequent years, Poland's currency calamities occasionally necessitated drastic restrictions of exchange activities, and unofficial " black exchanges " became seething centres of speculation in foreign currencies in all the larger urban centres. With the coming of more settled currency conditions in 1925, the official exchanges resumed the freedom of their activities and their importance. Poland now has six of them (in the cities of Warsaw, Poznań, Cracow, Lwów, Łódź and Wilno), foremost among them being the Warsaw Exchange, whose quotations are the determining factor in Poland's money-market. The organization of exchanges was placed on a uniform basis by a law of 1921, in which the Austrian exchanges were taken for a model. One of the features of the Austrian system, viz., the principle of compulsory exchange membership for all stock-brokers in a given city, was modified in favour of more liberal regulations in a Presidential decree of 1925. This decree, however, maintained the standard of requirements established by the law of 1921 as qualifying for admission to the profession of certified stock-broker. Supervision over each exchange is exercised by a Government Commissioner, who has even a right of veto on all resolutions of the elective Committee which administers the exchange.

A subject closely related to banking and exchange is that of the capital invested in *joint-stock companies*. The feverish industrial boom of the inflation period gave rise to a plethora of joint-stock companies, most of them based on unsound foundations. This tide subsided with inflation itself, but the impulse to organize large-scale undertakings on the extended platform of the new re-united Poland remained.

In connection with this, it was an obvious and urgent necessity to create a uniform law relating to joint-stock companies, in place of the three different laws of the partitioning powers in these matters. This was ultimately accomplished in 1928, when a code dealing with the subject was made law by Presidential decree. In the meantime, a new growth of joint-stock companies, more solid than that of the inflation period, was proceeding. While before the War, only 327 joint-stock companies had existed on the present territory of Poland (of these 221 in Russian Poland), the figure in 1928 was 1410 ; but the capital of the new companies, in consequence of war-time losses and post-war impoverishment, was (in terms of gold francs) only about one-fourth of the pre-war average per company. Here, however, as in banking, a tendency towards concentration of capital in stronger concerns became marked in due time. With regard to distribution over the different industries, coal and iron heads the list with only 53 companies, but with more than half a milliard *zloty* of capital ; textile industries stand next ; food industries (including the important item of sugar factories) come third, and oil occupies the fourth place. There follow, in order of financial power : metal and machine industries, electrical industries, chemical industries, communication and transport, mineral industries.

With regard to the important question of the share of foreign capital in Poland's industries, the figures according to the most recent statistics available (the Polish Statistical Year-book for 1931) were as follows :

| | |
|---|---|
| Gaswork, Waterworks and Electricity works | 75·6% |
| Ironworks | 65·4% |
| Mining | 51·9% |
| Chemical industries | 40·6% |
| Communications and telephones | 29·3% |

The average for the whole of Poland's industries is 33·3%, or exactly one-third of the capital invested. Apart from this, 67 companies are active in Poland which have their management in other countries ; among these, German and French companies stand head and shoulders above the others. Of the total foreign capital invested in Polish joint-stock companies in 1931—the bulk of which was estimated at about 150 million dollars— equal shares, viz., over 25 per cent. in each case, belonged to France and Germany respectively, while the American contribution amounted only to 21 per cent., the Belgian to 9 per cent., the British to less than 5 per cent., and the Austrian to 4 per cent.

## 48

To complete this survey of financial organization, it remains, after banks, stock exchanges and joint-stock companies, to add a few particulars concerning *insurance companies*.

In pre-war Poland, hundreds of agencies of foreign insurance companies were active, but only a few native ones ; and these had not reached the masses ; while the country gentleman generally was a good client of insurance institutions, the small farmer, in the early years of the century, was only beginning to grasp the importance of insurance. To improve this state of affairs, many insurance companies were founded in the first years of the new Poland ; foreign capital had a considerable share in them. While of the old pre-war companies many suffered ruinous losses through the depreciation of paper-money, of the new ones a good many survived owing to a judicious investment policy. The State, like other European States of to-day, was bent on conducting extended social insurance activities of its own, and accordingly hampered the growth of private insurance companies. The private companies were placed under very strict government supervision, with a special " Insurance Control Office," for its organ. A Presidential decree regulated not only the range of activities of private insurance companies, but also their investments, the administration of their funds, and the important problem of reinsurance. Thus, the protection exercised by the State over the interests of the insured went very far indeed in Poland.

The number of private insurance companies in Poland after the first ten years was 112 : of these, 11 were large mutual insurance societies, 21 had the form of joint-stock companies, and 91 were smaller institutions. Among the categories of insurance, it is insurance against fire which still considerably predominates over the rest. Life insurance (which really is a form of saving) is only gradually advancing. As mentioned before, private insurance companies have a powerful rival in the State, which conducts insurance institutions analogous to the private insurance companies. Of these five, two are regional, and two have specialized in particular categories of insurance (life and fire).

The largest of the five, the " General Mutual Insurance Institute " (*P.Z.U.W.*) conducts its activities all over the Republic, and is one of the largest institutions of its kind in Europe. Its domain is the special one of fire insurance, and a wide *clientèle* has been secured for it by two Presidential decrees of 1927, which made the insurance of all factory buildings in Poland (and in Warsaw also of dwelling houses) against fire compulsory, and at the same time confined the possibilities of fire insurance in private companies to fixed and very narrow limits. With regard to farm buildings, the introduction of

compulsory insurance against fire by " local option " of district
authorities was made possible, and between 1927 and 1929
fifteen districts in former Russian Poland (where the principle
of compulsory insurance existed before the War) had actually
introduced it. The State Insurance Institute is extending its
activities to other categories of insurance (e.g., the insurance of
harvest against hail), and bids fair to become a privileged
competitor too strong for private companies to oppose. Even
the nationalization of the entire insurance apparatus of Poland
is considered a possible contingency of the near future. A new
and lucrative government monopoly would thus be created.
In pre-war Russian Poland—as mentioned before—insurance
against fire was compulsory. Recollections of the peculiar
" paternalism " of this Russian policy, which aimed at " educating " the peasant masses into economy by administrative
pressure, have combined in the new Poland with the influence
of the modern western European spirit of State Socialism, which
also tends to " make the people virtuous by Act of Parliament."
And the two tendencies together have resulted in Poland's
insurance legislation, making it an extreme example of the
invasion of large domains of economic life by state control.

### 49

A survey of the new Poland's economic life like the one attempted in the present chapter would have been impossible, or at least
very difficult, if the State had not created for itself certain organs
whose task it is to observe the course of economic development
and to register their observations.

Foremost among these organs, there stands the *Central
Statistical Office* of the Republic. Founded in very earliest
days of the new Poland's existence, in 1918, and composed of
over 400 workers now, the Office, besides conducting current
statistical work and publishing its results in annuals, organized
a number of great statistical surveys either in connection with
international statistics or by way of illustrating particular
problems of legislation and administration. Among statistical
undertakings of the former kind, the most important are
periodical censuses. A census of the population of Poland,
accomplished under considerable difficulties with the help of a
volunteer body of university students, was taken in the first
year after the Bolshevik War, 1921, and it included the registration of towns and villages, of buildings, dwellings, farms, live
stock, as well as statistics concerning common ownership of land,
the number of workers in each profession, and the number of

orphans. A new census was taken in December 1931 : preparations for it were considerably hampered by the economic crisis, and its range had to be limited. The surveys of the second category mentioned above—those connected with particular problems—were the following : (1) a survey of the larger estates in the country for purposes of land reform legislation, 1921 ; (2) a registration of all state servants, 1923 ; (3) a survey of all cultivated land ; (4) a new census of live stock, 1927. The continuous statistical activities of the Office, besides its year-books and two periodicals, are represented, so far, by thirty volumes of systematic statistics of Poland, eight volumes of labour statistics, a register of towns and villages, an annual of town statistics, foreign trade reports, a three-volume album of statistical diagrams, and the like.

Statistics giving only a purely quantitative image of conditions, they must be supplemented, for purposes of economic policy, especially at times of crisis, by a more reasoned survey of the inter-relations of economic factors. To serve these ends Poland organized, in 1927, a Commission for the Investigation of Conditions and Costs of Production and Exchange.

It was composed both of administrative officials and of men of business and economic experts ; it examined industrial undertakings throughout the country, and published fifteen volumes of reports, divided according to branches of industry.

To the labours of this Commission, which was a temporary institution, there were added, in 1928, the permanent ones of an *Institute for the Examination of Trade Conditions and Prices*, organized on the model of similar institutions in many other European States. Its objects of study are those constant oscillations in the course of trade and in the movement of prices, which constitute the principal determining factor of economic policy. The materials collected and presented by the Institute are, accordingly, of the highest value both for the rational conduct of production in all its branches and for those planning and regulating activities of the State which, after the era of extreme *laissez-faire* doctrines, are once more becoming a marked feature of economic life.

In addition to the fundamental work done by the institutions described, the highly important aim of educating the whole nation into deeper understanding for, and more vivid interest in economic affairs, is being served by a number of *economic periodicals*, mostly either published by business organizations or subsidized by the State ; some of them, like *The Polish Economist* (published in English by the Ministry of Industry and Commerce) appear in foreign languages. The more serious organs of the *daily press* are also devoting an increasing amount of space to economic information and engaging the services of better and better experts for the appreciation of current economic events and problems. If, to these popularizing factors, we add the gradual influence of the respectable amount of research work in economics accomplished by the teachers of the subject in Poland's universities and by the growing ranks of their pupils, it will certainly not be vain to express the confident hope that an increasing measure of sound economic sense will enter into the judgments of the new Polish democracy both on national and international problems. When introduced into the national consciousness, it will usefully counter-balance that exaggerated national sentiment which was the natural inheritance of a century of political persecution, and which all too often served as the only criterion in dealing with those problems. That strong admixture of economic sense to popular thinking on political and social matters is, indeed, " a consummation devoutly to be wished," not only in Poland, but in other European democracies of to-day ; it is vitally needed to provide the foundation for that concerted international action which alone can get the modern world out of the grave and universal crisis of our days.

### 50

Allusions to the crisis have continually been cropping up in the pages of this chapter. No wonder, for the chapter is being written while that crisis is apparently reaching the height of its intensity ; and it might well be objected that the destructive effects of the crisis have rendered a large portion of this present account of the new Poland's economic life antiquated and futile. The facts and figures illustrating the overcoming of manifold initial difficulties and the steady and sometimes rapid growth of production in the later years of the new Poland's first decade— all break off at the year 1929. The picture which I have been able to give generally does not extend beyond that year ; and what systematic information is available on developments after that date presents things under a thoroughly changed aspect indeed. In fact, the very essence of former economic endeavour—the promotion of production above all—is rendered pointless by those disastrous conditions of world-wide over-production which seem to be the main constituting factor of the present crisis.

However, to those who look below the surface, the crisis

has long ago revealed itself as arising essentially, not out of over-production, but out of imperfect distribution and undeveloped consumptive capacity through vast regions of the world of to-day. In the light of that truth, the above account of the new Poland's economic struggles and first achievements may, after all, not have been written entirely in vain, and not appeal to merely historical interest. For it will have shown to the western European and American reader the image of a nation which illustrates, by its post-war fortunes, certain worldwide problems of our time. Poland, more thoroughly ruined by war than any other country in Europe, then reconstructed politically out of three sections which had lived under entirely diverse economic conditions, made resolute if not always welljudged efforts to achieve organic economic unity. These efforts had to be directed at the difficult aim of producing within a country hitherto predominantly agricultural, that balance between industrial and agricultural development which Poland's material resources warrant, and which the growth of her population makes necessary. The mutual diffidence which pervades the post-war political system of Europe, and which finds economic expression in tariff barriers, worked together with the excited ambition of a newly resurrected nation, and the two dispositions jointly fostered the growth of Utopian notions of national selfsufficiency. It must be added that the Poles were driven to seek refuge in such notions by the comparative lack of interest and assistance on the part of nations which might, with profit to themselves, have aided Poland in her economic reconstruction during the most difficult early years. This lack of interest (partly due to ignorance of Poland's possibilities) proved, however, a blessing in disguise, inasmuch as it kept Poland from becoming burdened with debts, which would have made the impact of the crisis of 1929 more heavy, as they did in the case of Germany. As it was, the crisis affected Poland more lightly than it did some other and more prosperous countries ; firstly because, the industries of the country being less fully developed, less damage could accordingly be done by the great trade depression ; and secondly, because in a country still predominantly agricultural, it is always more easily possible, even through a critical period, to provide the necessaries of life in the way of food for the masses of a population accustomed to live on a modest level of material comfort, like the country population of Poland.

It is an old experience that there is rarely any evil out of which some good may not arise. The present crisis, whatever further phases of economic unsettlement it may yet lead us into, will perhaps have the good effect of ultimately doing away, in many European countries, with the delusion that the economic existence of political organisms rigidly partitioned off from each other, and self-supporting within their several boundaries, is practicable in the world of to-day and to-morrow. Those delusions once broken, the European scene and the whole world in the coming period may see forms of international economic co-operation for which the best economic thought has been vainly longing so far. In that case also, the possibilities of Poland both as a centre of various kinds of production and as an important channel of trade communications may come to be more widely realized than hitherto. And then also the proudest form of national capital, which Poland possesses in abundance—the enduring and indefatigable industry of her hard-working peasant stock—may find opportunity to be more profitably applied, and receive its well-deserved meed of world-wide appreciation.

## CHAPTER VIII

# EDUCATION AND RESEARCH

I

SOMETHING has been said in a former chapter on the long and not inglorious educational tradition of the old Polish commonwealth : stress has been laid, in particular, on the great achievements of Poland's oldest University, Cracow, in that glorious fifteenth century, when the immortal astronomer, Nicholas Copernicus, was among its pupils. Even in the sixteenth century, when it became the fashion among young Polish nobles to attend foreign universities (first Padua, then Paris), Cracow, on her part, attracted such foreign celebrities as the German humanist Conrad Celtes ; the Swiss, Rudolphus Agricola, and the Spaniard, Pedro Ruiz (Roysius) ; besides these, there was also an Englishman on the roll of its Latin lecturers at the time— Leonard Coxe of Salisbury, from whose pen we possess a Latin oration on the state of the University in 1525.

If the splendours of Renascence Polish education and scholarship are somewhat dimmed by the subsequent Jesuit monopoly of education, which in the seventeenth century degenerates into mere verbalism of Latin elocution and old logical formulas—the eighteenth century is marked by another great educational revival. The supremacy of the Jesuits in education is successfully contested by another order, the Piarists, and Stanislas Konarski, an ornament of their ranks, becomes the great reorganizer of Polish education on modern lines. A model public school set up by him under the name of *Collegium Nobilium*, and side by side with it a military academy in Warsaw, founded by the last King of Poland, count among their pupils some of those who afterwards endeavour, by judicious political reform, to ward off the impending ruin of Poland. The greatest step in advance is made when the possessions of the Jesuit order, on its dissolution by the Pope in 1773, are utilized to endow a national system of secular education under state control. The renowned *Educational Commission* of Poland is really the first Ministry of Education in Europe, and its school programmes and text-books win the admiration of students of to-day by their modern spirit.

The study of the mother-tongue, and instruction in natural science, now come into their own in Polish education. Under the auspices of the Educational Commission a fiery young priest and budding statesman, Hugh Kołłataj, thoroughly reforms and modernizes the decaying University of Cracow ; and a Jesuit college which had existed since 1580 at Wilno, receives, by similar reform, the status of a modern university.

Thus the old Polish State, when it succumbs at last to violence at the hands of its neighbours, goes down to its grave in a blaze not only of herioc resistance and of equally heroic, if belated, political and social regeneration, but also of revived and creative cultural effort. It is but the harvest of the noble seed sown in the eighteenth century if, during the very first decades of Poland's captivity, the reorganized University of Wilno lives through a true golden age, becoming equally famous by its teachers and by its pupils : the great historian Lelewel is among the former, Poland's greatest poet Mickiewicz among the latter. And Wilno has a worthy counterpart in the sphere of secondary education in the shape of a great public school at Krzemieniec (in the south-eastern border province of Volhynia), which, like the University of Wilno itself, has, after many decades of eclipse, been happily revived in the new Poland after the World War.

2

Of the story of Polish education during the century of division and foreign rule enough has been said in the chapter dealing with the period, to illustrate both the efforts made in the Russian and Prussian sectors to resist the wholesale suppression of the national tradition, and the reconstruction of a complete Polish school system under the more favourable conditions of provincial home rule in Austrian Poland.

When the World War came and turned Austrian Poland and large portions of Russian Poland into an area of combat, the Austro-Polish school system was very thoroughly shattered at the outset by the destruction or military appropriation of school buildings, and by the dispersion of teachers and pupils. Slow and painful recovery only began in Western Galicia when, by the end of the first war year, the front was definitely shifted eastwards. In Russian Poland, at the same time, German and Austrian military occupation had produced a condition of comparative stability, and the occupants thought it wise to grant certain concessions to the large Polish population in the rear of their armies. Concessions in the field of education were considered politically most harmless, while being known at the same time to be particularly welcome to the Poles. Accordingly, the Austrian sector of occupied Russian Poland (with Lublin as its administrative centre) soon received a Polish school organization resembling that of Austrian Poland proper. In the German sector of the occupied territory (centring in Warsaw) the growth of private Polish secondary schools, which had begun in 1905 under Russian rule, was allowed to start again, and a very popular move was made by permitting the re-establishment of a Polish University in Warsaw, almost exactly a hundred years after it had entered on its first brief period of existence. Some other Polish academic institutions were set up anew—an Engineering College, an Agricultural and a Commercial one,—and a provisional Department of Education, originally organized as a section of a Citizen's Committee, was, on its re-establishment, endowed with official powers, and became the nucleus of a Ministry of Education. The teachers of Russian and Austrian Poland co-operated in the work of consolidating the new Polish educational apparatus by holding joint conventions in full war-time, in 1917 and 1918. Nor must it pass unmentioned that those Poles from Russian Poland who were driven into the interior of Russia, displayed corresponding activities. Polish schools of all kinds were organized in Russian towns ; even Polish University courses were for a time conducted in the cities of Kiev and Moscow, a periodical devoted to research was published at Petrograd, and a society of research workers held regular meetings in Moscow and published its proceedings.

While Russian and Austrian Poland were thus preparing the material for a reunited system of national education, Prussian Poland, untouched by the war but helpless in the grip of German power, could do nothing in the matter until, at the end of 1918, defeat and revolution in Germany, and, soon afterwards, the expulsion of the Germans from Poznań, gave freedom of action to the province. A Department of Education was soon organized and took over the magnificent German school-buildings abandoned by their staff. Children waiting to be taught were plentiful, but Polish teachers were scarce.

Such was the situation in the three parts of Poland when the Warsaw Education Office, in the closing months of 1918, could at last assume the authority of a Ministry of Education. It took several years, however, before that authority was ultimately extended over the territories where independent local educational administrations had come into being ; before some working harmony was evolved out of the discordant systems of educational legislation left behind in the different parts of the country by the partitioning powers ; and before the truly desperate conditions which prevailed in 1918 with regard to school-buildings, personnel, and educational materials had markedly improved.

### 3

It is one of the minor ironies of Poland's renewed existence, that she is fated to organize her public life in a period of world-wide ferment, in which all established traditions and recognized certainties of political and social thought and practice are called in question. Education is a domain in which this unsettlement and restlessness are particularly pronounced. The post-war world is fairly swarming with projects and counter-projects of most thorough-going reforms with regard to the structure of the school-system, the subject-matter of teaching, and the pedagogical methods. No wonder, then, that Polish education found it impossible to escape a vortex of constant changes. Even the outward history of the " *Ministry of Public Instruction and Religious Denominations,*" as the supreme educational authority of the country is officially called, is one of almost continuous reorganization. The most important among the many structural modifications which it underwent, was, perhaps, that of 1928, when the wish to identify the higher grades of elementary with the lower ones of secondary education was emphasized by uniting the elementary with the secondary school section of the Ministry. Vocational schools have another section to themselves, while universities are controlled by one which also superintends and promotes research activities. Art (with literature, music and the theatre) had originally a separate Ministry to itself, and after the first few years only became the object of a section in the Ministry of Education ; during the economic crisis after 1929, this section—significantly enough !—dwindled into a sub-section. In the section devoted to denominations, Catholicism—the religion of two-thirds of the population—has a section to itself, while all the other Christian denominations are jointly in charge of another, and non-Christian denominations are grouped together under a third.

Apart from the official apparatus of the Ministry, which is doing the day-to-day administrative work, a consultative body has recently been created in the shape of an *Educational Council,* which is to be composed of delegates and representatives of all the more important institutions and organizations in the country concerned with, or interested in public education. It is to this

s

body of about one hundred men, meeting at regular intervals in the capital, that all the larger issues of educational reform and reorganization are to be submitted for discussion.

Immediately subordinated to the Ministry are the governing offices (*Curatoria*) of the educational districts, into which the country was divided in 1921 ; the province of Silesia (included in Poland only since 1922) forms a separate district and enjoys, in accordance with Poland's international obligations, a high measure of self-government in educational matters. Otherwise, the educational districts do not coincide with the counties : the number of districts has in 1932 been reduced to eight, or exactly one-half that of counties. In the case of the " inspectorates." however, into which the educational districts are further sub-divided, the area is always conterminous with that of the smallest territorial unit of political administration. Neither the inspector (who in some parts of the country presides over a " Circuit School Board " ) nor, *a fortiori*, the *curator* of the large educational district, are in any way subordinated to the political administration. All endeavours to incorporate the management of schools in the general administrative machinery have so far failed, being resented by educationalists as an intrusion of political authorities into the self-governing sphere of the school. Thus, the administration of the schools is a separate network of public services covering the whole country, and controlled exclusively by the Ministry of Education. Its control is exercised through the district *curators* and their staff, except in the case of universities and art schools, which are in direct dependence on the Ministry.

The vast majority of schools in Poland, as in most other countries of Continental Europe, are supported by the Government and by local government authorities out of the rates and taxes. Education, according to a paragraph in the Constitution, being universal and free in principle, the fees which are actually levied on students of all kinds of government schools are comparatively low, even in the universities, where, however, the sums thus obtained have been sufficient to meet the crying needs of the first years in the matter of housing, by the construction of houses for professors and students in the university cities. The expenditure on education has since the stabilization of the currency generally equalled about 15 per cent of the total of Poland's budget, this being the highest quota devoted to any public service apart from national defence. Within the educational budget, nearly nine-tenths of the State's contribution go as salaries to teachers and administrative personnel ; the scanty *quota* remaining for material needs of the schools and for the construction of school buildings is supplemented by appropriations from provincial and communal revenues. Poland's requirements in the sphere of elementary and secondary education being largest and most urgent in the first period of her new freedom, the universities (at least the older ones) were necessarily much less favoured, and for such purposes as the promotion of adult education, of pure research, and of art, it has not been possible to spare more than a mere pittance of about 4 per cent of the total expense on education. This made itself felt all the more keenly, as private munificence in these matters—sometimes exercised very generously by large landowners before the War—has become a rare phenomenon, owing to post-war impoverishment.

4

Having surveyed the outward structure of the educational fabric in its totality, we may now proceed to examine its constituent parts severally. In doing so, it seems appropriate to begin at the bottom of the educational ladder.

*Pre-school education* in nineteenth-century Poland, like so many other cultural activities, had had its origin in private initiative under foreign rule : the first *Kindergarten* was organized by a charitable society in Warsaw in 1840. Some of Poland's prominent educational thinkers and writers in the early nineteenth century devoted a good deal of attention to the problem, and in the early twentieth (1903) a " Society for Pre-School Education " was formed in Warsaw ; but unfavourable political conditions reacted even on this branch of education and cramped its growth. When the pressure relaxed during the War, much private initiative was shown ; the new State, on coming into being, was obliged, for economic reasons, to limit itself to the creation of a few model institutions, leaving the bulk of the work to local authorities, societies, and individuals. Important assistance was forthcoming from the Church, *kindergartens* being frequently conducted by nuns. After the first ten years, the number of *kindergartens* in Poland had grown from 100 to over 1400, the greatest advance being noticeable in the city of Warsaw and in the province of Silesia. The *kindergartens* mostly consisted of two sections, for children from four to five and from six to seven years of age respectively. Their educational methods are calculated, on the one hand, by an appropriate choice of games and occupations, to develop bodily and mental efficiency, on the other hand, by exercise in the open air, to promote health. The *kindergartens*, especially in large industrial centres, such as Łódź, are a source of relief for mothers working outside the home, who are unable to look after their children throughout the day. The personnel of *kindergartens* is trained in seven state-supported and seven private seminaries ; one of the state-supported ones (Warsaw) has a three years' course. The programmes of these institutions resemble those of elementary school teachers' training colleges ; both in their teaching and in the practice of Polish *kindergartens*, modern educational doctines, such as those of Madame Montessori in Rome and Dr. Decroly in Brussels, are being considered and utilized.

### 5

Passing to *elementary school education*, we enter the region of inevitable differences between theory and practice.

The complete educational curriculum in the form to which the population of Poland had become accustomed under the three partitioning powers, and which was more or less common to Continental Europe generally, consisted of four (or five) years of elementary school, followed by eight years of secondary school and four (or five) years in the university. For those who did not go to secondary school and university, there existed a three (or four) years' additional course in the larger elementary schools, after which the road lay open for them either into apprenticeship and employment or into vocational schools more or less on the level of higher secondary schools.

By those who organized education in the new Polish State after the War, the need of raising the standard of elementary education among the masses of the people was felt more keenly than any other. Under the spell of the democratic idea, which found expression in the common European slogan *l'école unique*, and which has the American system of elementary school and high school for its avowed model, it was decided to introduce a universal and compulsory elementary school curriculum of seven years (from the age of seven to that of fourteen) for all children in the country, and the principle was proclaimed by decree as early as 1919. The realization of the project would imply the extension of all elementary schools in the land to the proposed limit, a task far beyond the means of Poland in her first years. On the other hand, it would imply the curtailment of the traditional secondary school curriculum by its first three years in favour of the extended elementary school course. Against this, the voices of secondary school teachers and university professors were raised in protest : the traditional secondary school of eight years was defended as an indivisible whole, giving the necessary *modicum* of liberal education to those who are to enter the universities and to become the intellectual *élite* of the nation. The issue became manifest as one between two different conceptions of the social aims of public education in a modern democracy : a higher level of elementary education among the masses on the one hand, adequate training of a class of leaders on the other. Unfortunately, the issue also stood revealed as one between the conflicting class interests of the college-trained elementary school teachers on the one hand and the university-trained secondary school teachers on the other, and this naturally added fierceness to the dispute which soon began to rage round the problem.

For some time, little was actually done, owing to want of means and the pressure of other and more urgent tasks. But when the comparatively prosperous years 1927-28 made the construction of a larger number of elementary schools possible, the Government decided in favour of district schools of the seven-year type : such schools began accordingly to be founded, while some of the smaller old-fashioned village schools were abolished. At the same time, a beginning was made with the strict identification of the teaching programme in the last three years of elementary school with that of the first three years of secondary school. These preliminary measures were at last followed up by a *School Reform Bill* of 1932, which expressly distributes the years of the school curriculum among the different grades of schools. A common universal foundation of seven years' elementary school is now established as the rule. The shortened secondary school stage is to be subdivided further, the last two years of it being devoted to special preparation for a chosen branch of university study (arts or sciences). The new system is to come into complete operation within a few years, but economic difficulties will probably delay, or even considerably modify, its realization. In spite of the experience of western countries, then, which tells against the *école unique* and in favour of a lengthening of the secondary school stage, Polish educational policy in its fervour for " democratization of culture," is now resolutely embarked towards the still distant goal of seven years of elementary school for every boy and girl in the land, at the cost of drastic curtailment of secondary school education. In thus deliberately placing new ideals of quantity above the old ones of quality in education, Poland does not, of course, stand alone in the democratic world of to-day : in exactly the same year, 1932, which sees the passing of the Polish School Reform Bill, an analogous measure is announced, not without the accompaniment of serious protests, in the neighbouring Republic of Czechoslovakia.

## 6

After the principles of reorganization, let us now consider plain statistical facts, as ten years' constructive effort in the new Poland left them. The number of elementary schools in Poland in 1929-30 was 26,539.[1] The number of complete seven-year schools of the new model type was 2617, or, roughly, one-tenth of the whole, the rest being still mostly smaller village schools with provision for a maximum of four years' regular teaching.

It may be added here that of the 26,000 elementary schools only a little more than 1000 are supported by private bodies, the rest being State institutions. It should also be noted that there is in Poland a certain number of special schools for blind, deaf-and-dumb, and mentally undeveloped children ; the provision of them, however, especially as far as mentally undeveloped children are concerned, is still far from adequate. An " Institute for Special Education," founded in Warsaw in 1921, conducts the training of teachers for such schools.

The attendance of all children between the ages of seven and fourteen at school was made compulsory by a Government decree of 1919, but for a number of years the authorities were not in a position to enforce the principle. Conditions only improved after the decree had been reissued in more explicit form in 1923. Through gradual extension of the operation of the rule, all children of school-age came ultimately under its operation before September, 1929.

Actual attendance, between 1921 and 1928, had risen from 66·2 per cent, to 92·8 per cent. of the total number of children of school age ; it had been over 90 per cent. from the very beginning in the western provinces (where attendance at school had long been enforced under German rule); it still remained under 75 per cent, even in 1928, in the eastern border provinces, where Russian rule had established no such tradition.

The number of registered school-children in Poland in 1928-29 was 3,638,000 ; the succeeding years brought a large and rapid increase (reflecting the early post-war growth of population), and the number is expected to overstep the six-million mark by 1940. Under the Polish law, every community in which there

---

[1] Of these, 4735 were schools for the children of national minorities, the language of teaching being Ukrainian in 3,126 of them, German in 777, Yiddish in 356, Hebrew in 209, Lithuanian in 148, and White Ruthenian in 77.

are more than 40 children of school age is obliged to provide and maintain accommodation for a school, the State on its part undertaking to supply teachers and teaching appliances, also to help the poorer communities by loans or subsidies towards the erection of school buildings. With the quick growth in numbers of school-children which is now in progress on the one hand, and the pressure of the economic crisis on state finances on the other, it has of late become more and more difficult to realize the programme of universal education to the full, especially in the eastern provinces.

Another difficulty arising out of the same two factors of over-population on the one hand and lack of means on the other, consists in the unduly high proportion of pupils which falls to the share of each individual teacher in Poland. The average of pupils per teacher had fallen from 56 in 1921 to 47 in 1926, but is still far from satisfactory.

The subjects taught in a full-grown seven-year elementary school in Poland are : religion, the mother tongue, history, geography, arithmetic with geometry, the elements of natural science, drawing and singing. Great stress is laid on instruction in civics ; also on the development of bodily efficiency, both by instruction in handicrafts and housekeeping and by gymnastics and games. Libraries for the children now exist in almost every school ; special periodicals for school-boys and school-girls have a wide circulation ; school workshops of various kinds, school kitchens, and in some cases also chemical and biological labora-tories, have been organized in a number of schools. Charities for the poorer children, and modest meals during school hours are being provided for—especially in many of the city schools—by the co-operation of " Parents' Committees," which also serve as the means of contact between the school and the home.

### 7

The training of elementary school teachers before the War was the work of Teachers' Training Colleges, the average level of which was that of the upper forms of secondary schools. The emergencies of war-time and of the early post-war years brought many persons into the teaching profession who had had no special preparation for it at all. To these, opportunity was given, by the organization of summer holiday courses, to supple-ment their educational training so as to be able to pass the prescribed examinations. Apart from such temporary measures, systematic efforts are being made to raise the standard of teachers' education. This it is definitely proposed to do now by

the abolition of the old teachers' colleges and by giving each
candidate for elementary school teaching the benefit of university
instruction.

This purpose is served by Educational Institutes ( " Pædagogia " ), to which only students are admitted who have a
complete secondary school curriculum behind them. The
" Pædagogia " are conducted on university lines, and their
programme includes a wide range of subjects connected with
education, including even philosphy and sociology ; it extends
over two years.

Every teacher, whether coming from a training college of the
old type of from a " Pædagogium," has to pass an examination
in the practical aspects of education after the first two years of
his professional work. A select class of teachers acquires higher
qualifications in particular subjects at specialized " Superior
Courses for Teachers."

At present, the Teachers' Training Colleges of the traditional
type still predominate over all other forms of teachers' education
in Poland. There are over 200 such colleges in Poland, some
thirty of them serving the needs of the national minorities.
Slightly less than one-half of the colleges are private foundations,
all the rest (as well as the three "Pædagogia" so far established)
being supported by the Government.

The colleges are filled with a crowd of over 30,000 students,
and some of the colleges have of late years been obliged to close
their gates against the further influx of candidates, because the
number of positions available in the profession was far exceeded
by that of applicants.

The total number of elementary school teachers in Poland is
now over 70,000, women being in the majority among them.
The teachers are organized in several professional associations
somewhat different from each other in their political platform.
The " Teachers' Union," which is by far the strongest among
them, built an enduring monument for itself by creating a magnificent large sanatorium for tuberculous teachers at Zakopane in
the Tatra Mountains—a fine example which has since been
followed by a number of the other professional groups in the
country.

8

*Secondary education* in Continental Europe, out of being the
privilege of the few, has lately, with the progress of democratization, become the birthright of the many. In pre-war Poland,
this social progress was most marked in the Austrian section,
where secondary schools and universities were filling more and

more with peasant sons who came straight from the country, and a new educated class, largely of peasant origin, was growing up. With the re-union of the country and the establishment of a uniform national school system, the tendency was bound to communicate itself to the other parts of Poland as well. The secondary schools throughout the new Poland are crowded with boys and girls from the ranks of the peasantry and the town proletariat, and State action and private initiative taken together are unable to satisfy the growing demand for secondary education.

This difficulty, which is essentially social and economic, is accompanied by difficulties no less grave with regard to cultural and technical problems in the organization of Poland's secondary schools.

Long before the War, Europe's secondary schools had begun to abandon the old standards of classical education : natural science, modern foreign languages, and the mother-tongue and its literature had been gaining more and more ground at the expense of the traditional Greek and Latin. The universal post-war ferment in educational ideas quickened the process. In the new Poland, there are only a very few secondary schools left in which Latin is taught from the first form onward, and Greek taught at all. In most of the schools which include Latin in the curriculum, the teaching of it begins in the fourth form and goes on for the remaining five years. Types of secondary schools are distinguished according to basic groups of subjects. The three principal types have mathematics and natural science, the mother-tongue and Latin, and Latin with Greek and classical culture, for their respective bases. At least one foreign language is taught in schools of every type, but the general trend of educational opinion is in favour of teaching two.

The foreign language or languages, being (within limits), optional, there was, in the first years of regained freeedom, a tide of preference for French and English by way of reaction against the long domination of German. French, as usually on the Continent of Europe, was largely preferred to English. Of late years, there has been a marked return to German, which, in Poland's geographical situation, is naturally felt to be most immediately needed in practical life. Russian, two decades ago still compulsorily familiar to man, woman and child over a vast portion of Poland, is becoming an utterly unknown tongue among the younger generation. On the whole, the regained freedom of public use of the mother-tongue and of teaching in it throughout a large united area of thirty million inhabitants, the disappearance of official pressure in favour of a foreign language in school, and, last not least, the greater difficulty of travelling abroad in the hard post-war days—all these factors, some of them lucky and some unlucky, co-operate to bring about a state of things in which Poles generally will perhaps no longer keep their nineteenth-century European reputation of being particularly good linguists.

The fact that it is no longer the country gentleman's manor, nor even the professional townsman's house, but the peasant's cottage which produces the bulk of the educated class, also has something to do with the change.

To a certain extent, however, this change is also due to new methods of teaching. Here, again, Poland is but following the course of certain movements of reform which began to stir the educational atmosphere in Europe even before the War.

It was partly a consequence of the modern ascendancy of natural science over the humanities in the sphere of general culture that stress began to be laid in education rather on the development of active intelligence than on the accumulation of facts in the memory. Modern schools accordingly—not in Poland alone !—are apt to neglect memorized knowledge— including historical data, or the vocabularies of foreign tongues— and to attribute chief importance to items of actual interest and to the independent discovery of such items by the pupil's own effort. In the domain of natural science this finds expression by the widespread application of laboratory and experimental methods in secondary school teaching, in that of the humanities —less fortunately—by impressionist and selective treatment of the historical material. The result is a certain contempt for the age-old store of human experience, a certain glibness in the delivery of independent judgments on questions which have occupied great minds in the past, a certain ingenuous freshness in the handling of life's problems without regard to previous solutions of them. All this may have the advantage of giving greater scope than ever to youthful initiative, but it certainly has in it all the dangers of unhistorical thinking on the great European issues, which are all steeped in history. These dangers Polish education as well as Polish public life has not avoided, young people being now generally in the ascendant in the public affairs of Poland as much as of other Continental European countries.

Let us return, however, from these sociological generalizations to the subject of Poland's secondary schools, and offer a few illustrative figures in conclusion.

In the school year 1929-30 (the latest one for which statistics are available at the time of writing), Poland had 759 secondary schools giving a liberal education, and the number of pupils in them was over 200,000, of whom more than one-third were girls. Of the schools, 272 only were supported by the State, and 487 by private institutions.

The number of teachers employed in the schools was over 10,000 ; of these, nearly 4000 were women : the growth in numbers of women among secondary school teachers, even in boys' schools, has recently been marked. It remains to be added that most of the secondary schools of Poland are day schools, and only a very few—mostly owned by religious owners or other organizations—conduct their educational activities in the collegiate fashion of English public schools. Among secondary schools of the collegiate type, the old Jesuit school at Chyrów in the Carpathians and a secular school for selected pupils recently established, on the basis of a revived eighteenth-century foundation, at Rydzyna in former Prussian Poland, deserve to be singled out for the comprehensiveness of their programme and the high quality of the instruction which they offer.

### 9

In the sphere of *vocational education* the new Poland has had to attack particularly large constructive tasks. It was partly the consequence of the disproportionately important position which literature, art, and history held for long periods in national mentality during the century of foreign rule, that schools providing liberal education became more numerous and more popular in pre-war Poland than technical or commercial ones ; partly also this was due to the undeveloped state of Poland's industry and commerce, and—last not least—to the policy of the partitioning powers which either (as in the case of Germany and Austria) did not favour technical and commercial education in their Polish provinces because they desired to keep them in the condition of agricultural countries, or (as in the case of Russia) were not eager to supply a variety of educational opportunities at all.

Long before the War, however, Polish society itself had become aware of the importance of industrialization, and efforts were made to provide ampler means of technical and commercial training for the future workers in industry and trade. In self-governing Austrian Poland, a number of industrial and commercial schools of higher and lower grade were created towards the end of the nineteenth and early in the twentieth century out of public funds ; under Russia, private initiative endeavoured to supply what could not be organized officially : a technical school founded by the enlightened bankers Wawelberg and Rotwand in Warsaw has continued to do its useful work in the new free Poland.

The reborn Polish Republic has, from the beginning of its renewed existence, devoted unceasing attention and effort to the development of vocational schools of all kinds ; and the same is expressly declared to be one of the chief aims of the new School Reform Bill of 1932. What has been achieved so far, amounts to a very wide extension indeed of technical and commercial education, and in the present state of institutions providing this kind of instruction it is, in fact, a serious question whether they have not run ahead of Poland's general economic development and are not turning out more skilled workers in those domains than can be assured of finding proper employment within Poland in the near future.

Naturally, within this branch of education, differentiation takes the place of the comparative uniformity of general elementary and secondary schools, and there are a great many more various types of institutions. Broadly speaking, four large groups may be distinguished. There are first of all, the *technical schools* proper, which may again be subdivided into schools for the training of *industrial workers* and of *artisans*. To these must be added the schools devoted to *agriculture* and *gardening*, with their various dependent occupations. Both industrial and agricultural schools represent a considerable variety of levels, from that of the higher forms of elementary to that of upper secondary school. The large class of *commercial schools*, on the other hand, predominantly belongs to a category corresponding to the higher forms of secondary school. Third, there stand, in a group by themselves, the *vocational schools for women*, preparing for household occupations and such handicrafts as dressmaking or the arts of ornament. Fourth and last, there is the numerous and varied group of *continuation schools*, for young people already at work in industrial or commercial establishments. These courses, mostly in the nature of evening classes, are calculated for pupils under eighteen, who do not possess more than an elementary school education. They usually offer a three-years' curriculum, specialized, in larger industrial centres, according to the pupils' professional interests and requirements. Apart from continuation schools, *school workshops* are also provided in connection with some elementary schools, as a beginning of technical instruction, or as a substitute for it where unattainable in fuller form.

Technical schools generally requiring a certain amount of expensive apparatus (workshops, laboratories, materials for experiments), there are not many of them conducted by private organizations : the vast majority are government-supported. The proportion is entirely different in the case of the commercial schools : of these, one-tenth only are governmental, the remaining nine-tenths being supported by private enterprise or social organizations. Of the other two categories—artisans' schools and vocational schools for girls—roughly about one third are supported by the State. The continuation schools are, as a rule, municipal, but enjoy more or less ample susidies from the Treasury. So do many of the private commercial and industrial schools, a source for these state subsidies being supplied by a supertax on the fees for the state licences issued to all owners of factories and to patentees.

The total number of institutions and organized courses providing vocational instruction in Poland had risen from 707 to 1269 on the eight years between 1922 and 1930. Of the latter total, 753 served the needs of industry and mining, 360 those of commerce, and 37 those of agriculture and gardening. The number of pupils, having nearly doubled in the course of the new Poland's existence, amounted, in the school year 1929-30 to nearly 85,000 or something like 43 per cent. of the number of pupils in secondary schools of the non-vocational type. The proportion is characteristic : the traditional preference for a liberal as contrasted with a practical education is still very strong, and it assuredly has a certain foundation even to-day in the fact that industry and commerce offer as yet a comparatively limited range of opportunities to trained workers in Poland. It must be observed that the vocational schools are doing their best to impart, besides technical instruction, as large a measure as possible of general education in such subjects as history, literature, foreign languages, and the theoretical branches of natural science. In the School Reform Bill of 1932, further endeavours have been made to encourage vocational studies and raise them in popular estimation. A definite improvement, however, is only to be expected as a consequence of the expansion of Poland's industry and trade in the future. A reversal of the present numerical relation between those receiving a liberal and those receiving a vocational education would certainly indicate economic progress and give a more normal character to the occupational structure of the Polish community. However, the problem in its present state is not limited to Poland ; it is more acute even in some other Continental European countries, and partly also in America. Everywhere, its centre of gravity lies not so much in the sphere of this or that type of secondary education as rather in the new attitude of the masses towards university education and the profound changes which the universities are consequently undergoing.

10

Of Poland's *university* traditions, and particularly of the long and glorious record of her oldest university, Cracow, something has been said in previous chapters. There was also occasion to mention the brief but intense period of splendour of the University of Wilno at the beginning of the nineteenth century, and even the more short-lived efflorescence of academic life in Warsaw in the sixties of that century.

The lights of Wilno and of Warsaw having been put out by Russian oppression after the two armed risings in Russian Poland, the later decades of the nineteenth century gave a new academic importance to the Austrian sector of the country, as possessing the only Polish seats of higher learning and organized research that were left to the nation. As has been mentioned before, Cracow University now entered on a new period of intellectual leadership in Polish lands. Polish effort in research received a centre in the Polish Academy established side by side with the University at Cracow, and the University itself became a rallying-centre not only for scholars and scientists from all parts of Poland, who occupied chairs in it, but also, in increasing measure, for Polish students from all the three partitioning empires. It was particularly from Russian Poland that students began to flock to Cracow in large numbers at the beginning of the twentieth century, when the boycott of Russian schools was taken up in all earnest by Polish youth. Beside Cracow, the Austrian sector possessed a full-grown University at Lwów, and institutions of university rank for the teaching of engineering (in several faculties), of agriculture and forestry, and of veterinary medicine, in the same city. The higher schools of painting and sculpture at Cracow, and of music at Cracow and at Lwów, must also be mentioned, although none of them had university status in those days.

It was with this inheritance of academic institutions, from the age of captivity, then, that Poland entered on her new era of regained freedom. Already during the last decades of the pre-war period, as has been stated before, a wave of " democratization " had set in, and the universities of Austrian Poland became crowded with the sons of peasant farmers. It was to be foreseen

that the same movement would extend to the other large areas of
Poland after reunion ; it was certain at any rate, that a hunger
and thirst for education would be as marked among the masses
after the ruin and neglect of war time as the hunger for bodily
food and for other material necessaries of life. This indeed soon
became apparent. On the other hand, nothing seemed
impossible to the nation, in the way of reconstruction, in its first
enthusiasm over the miracle of regained independence ; and
hardly anything that could be planned seemed great enough
for the new large thirty-million State. The stimulus of
paper-money inflation was added to other impulses : it
made the realization of any plan on a large scale seem delusively
easy.

It was under the joint action of these combined forces of real
demand and Utopian reconstructive fervour that an almost
mushroom growth of universities, as of so many other institutions,
characterized the early years of the new Poland. Not only were
the Universities of Warsaw and of Wilno revived in full war time,
but the former Prussian sector, which had not had a university of
its own, was hurriedly provided with one (built up on the material
foundation of a German " Academy " at Poznań), and Warsaw,
being the capital, was hastily endowed with several other
academic institutions besides the University. All these new
higher schools were soon filled with students, and remain more or
less overcrowded to this day. What is, perhaps, even more
remarkable, the old universities, in former Austrian Poland, not
only did not show any decrease in attendance, but soon had more
than twice their pre-war number of students.

While thus the foundation of a number of new universities was
justified by immediate experience, it proved, after some time, the
source of serious difficulties. To begin with, the new universities
drained the old ones of their reserves of personnel in the shape of
young lecturers and assistants, who were candidates for
professorial posts. Most of these young men receiving chairs in
the new institutions, a general scarcity of appropriate candidates
for university chairs in Poland became the result, and the situation now causes grave concern to many faculties, which are vainly
looking out for adequate successors to old and often highly distinguished teachers. What is even worse, the numerous institutes,
laboratories, and libraries in Poland's universities are proving,
in these days of financial stringency, a burden too heavy to bear
for the Treasury. All academic institutions, with insignificant
exceptions, being government-supported, reasons of economy
make it imperative to keep their maintenance allowances and

their staff on a *minimum* level, which is far beneath the material requirements indicated both by the number of pupils and the aims and conduct of research work. If, under these circumstances, tasks of mass education are accomplished and creditable research work is done, this is achieved at the cost of labours often truly heroic on the part of the ill-paid and scantily assisted teaching staff. The only means of material improvement in the present situation would seem to consist either in the abolition of chairs which fall vacant, and the closing down of entire departments and faculties, or in a substantial increase of the students' fees. The latter course would place a majority of Poland's university students outside the pale of academic education at once ; for that majority, in spite of the facilities now offered by large student hostels, cheap dining rooms, sickness insurance institutions, convalescent homes, Government scholarships and convenient loans from relief societies, still barely manage to pay the present, very moderate fees. Yet both an increase of fees and a material reduction of the present fabric of university institutions in Poland will apparently prove inevitable if the system is to weather the present crisis at all. And again, Poland is by no means alone among the Central European States in having to face such bitter necessities.

## II

The organization of those Polish universities which were left in existence after the century of foreign rule was the same as that of the other universities of the Austro-Hungarian Empire ; that is to say, they were universities of the Continental European as distinguished from the English model. The college—whether in the English or the American sense of the word—was unknown to their structure. The universities were institutions for special training in certain branches of learning, the special branch being chosen by the student on entering the university ; they were not concerned either with the student's general culture (of which the foundations were supposed to have been laid in secondary school), nor with moral education (which was left to outside agencies). Teaching and study were conducted under the traditional conditions of " academic freedom " (extending, on the professor's part, to the choice of material dealt with in his lectures, and on the student's part, to selection from among the courses offered and to attendance at them). The two aims of preparation for a professional career and of a certain amount of training in special research were combined in the system of studies ; the capacity for independent research was supposed to be attained when the candidate, after passing the examinations prescribed, was leaving the university with the degree of *doctor*—the only degree which the universities conferred. In the case of some faculties—notably that of medicine—the degree was at the same time the foundation for admission to professional practice ; in the case of others, it was not essential for professional work, the door to this being opened by examinations different from those for the degree and partly non-academic.

This system, in the main, became the ruling one in all the universities of the new Poland. Certain modifications, however, were introduced. Thus, on the model of western countries, another degree was introduced preliminary to that of doctor, viz., the degree of *master*. This becoming henceforward the normal conclusion of university studies and being the condition of practice in such professions as secondary school teaching or law, it was at the same time made more easily attainable to the general body of students by a gradual system of examinations, extending over the whole of the four or five years' curriculum. The doctor's degree, raised above the master's and to be attained only after it, is henceforward to be reserved for capable research workers only and to be severed from all connection with professional qualifications. Analogously, in the sphere of academic study of engineering, a degree of " doctor of the technical sciences " has been introduced as a mark of distinction for trained research workers, while the degree of " engineer " remains the one which indicates average academic preparation for professional practice.

The detailed regulations concerning requirements for the new master's degree, while facilitating university study considerably by an " instalment " system of examinations, at the same time imply a considerable limitation of the old " academic freedom " of students in the conduct of their studies. On the professors' side, " academic freedom," besides the presentation of their subjects in lectures and at class meetings, also applies to the administration of university affairs. The universities enjoy a larger measure of self-government than any other kind of schools ; this self-government is exercised through academic bodies (the Faculty with its Dean at its head, the University Senate presided over by the Rector, both Rectors and Deans being elected from among the professors for one year at a time). The professors' freedom in the matter of teaching has already undergone considerable limitation in practice by the examination requirements ; the time-honoured privileges of the universities in the way of

T

self-government are also, through a Bill passed in 1933, being replaced by greater dependence on the Ministry of Education. The universities, thus under the new conditions of mass education, are to lose their old character of free homes of higher study and original research, and are being driven into the position of training-schools for professional men, with a strictly defined function within a thoroughly state-controlled educational system. Such developments in the sphere of academic education were bound to seem the reverse of desirable to those who are attached to old liberal ideals ; but once again, in this domain as in others, the tendencies manifesting themselves in Poland are tendencies common to many other countries in our time.

12

To the above account of tendencies of development, let us now add a few salient facts and figures concerning the present state of Poland's universities.

Of academic institutions recognized as being of university rank, Poland at present has eleven, all of them state-supported. They are :  the Universities of Warsaw, Cracow, Lwów, Wilno, and Poznań ; the Engineering Academies of Warsaw and Lwów ; Academies of Agriculture in Warsaw, of Mining and of the Fine Arts at Cracow, and of Veterinary Medicine at Lwów.   Each of these institutions is composed of several Faculties, the Universities all possessing Faculties of Divinity, Law, Medicine and " Philosophy " (the last-named one now mostly divided into a Faculty of " Humanities " and one of " Science " ), and occasionally some others—the Engineering Academies, both of them, including Faculties of Civil and of Mechanical Engineering, of Architecture, Chemistry and Electricity.   Apart from these " Academic Schools," as the law calls them, there are a number of higher schools of academic type, but without full academic privileges. These are :  the Higher Schools of Commerce at Warsaw, Cracow Lwów, and Poznań, a " Free University " of the University Extension type in Warsaw, a State Institute of Dentistry in Warsaw, and a denominational (Roman Catholic) University of three Faculties in the city of Lublin.   These institutions are not entirely supported by the State, but mostly subsidized out of state funds.

The total enrolment of students in all the academic institutions of Poland for the school year 1930-31 amounted to 48,000. Of this total, 34,000 were men, and 14,000 women.   It is the rapidly increasing number of women students which contributes a great deal to the serious state of congestion in the universities.

And it is the growing competition between men and women for employment which is an important source of economic difficulties. But women outnumber men in Poland by nearly 7 per cent., according to the latest census, and the invasion of all spheres of professional life by women must therefore be looked upon as a social necessity which has " come to stay." There is hardly any profession in Poland now (except that of priesthood) which is not open to women and has not been entered by them ; although it must be admitted that in some of the academic professions women are still comparatively scarce—there is, e.g., only one woman among the Professors of the University of Cracow (Mme. H. Willman-Grabowska, Professor of Sanskrit), and the promotion of women to higher and more responsible positions in the Civil Service has not, so far, been practised to any large extent.

Among the branches of study chosen by the students in Poland's universities, " philosophy " (that is to say, humanities and natural sciences) and law stand foremost, being embraced each by about one-fourth of the total number of students. This is to be explained by the fact that these two faculties open the door most immediately to comparatively secure if poorly paid employment by the State (in secondary school teaching and in administrative service). It must be added that positions in the teaching profession being more unreservedly open to women than employment in the Civil Service, more than one-half of the women students choose philosophy, and only one-seventh law. Next after law and philosophy in the favour of students there ranks, at some distance, engineering (this again being chosen much more often by men than women) with somewhat over one-sixth, and medicine, with less than one-tenth of the total body of students (including, in the case of medicine, one-twentieth only of the women students). One tenth of the total is also the proportion of those who choose the academic study of commerce ; in this case, however, the women contribute nearly the same proportion of their own number. Agriculture and forestry take the last place among the more important branches of study, being chosen by a mere one-twenty-third of the total number of students at present (probably because positions for university graduates in agriculture are becoming scarce through the progressive break-up of large estates by land reform).

The teaching staff of the eleven academic institutions of university rank in Poland amounts roughly, to about one thousand professors and lecturers, with not quite twice that number of graduate assistants. The proportion of less than two assistants to one professor speaks eloquently of the difficulties under which university work in Poland is being conducted.

## 13

Outside the universities, there lies the large field of *adult education*—a domain in which in the nineteenth century, with the advance of democracy, great progress was made, especially in Britain, in the Scandinavian countries, in Germany and in the United States. Poland, with the systematic school education of her people deliberately neglected or turned into an instrument for the destruction of national tradition by the partitioning powers, developed, during the century of her captivity, some powerful organizations of adult education. Under Prussia a Society for the Establishment of Popular Libraries was founded as early as 1880 and has continued its activities ever since : the celebration of the fiftieth anniversary of its work, taking place under the happier conditions of a free Poland in 1930, gave occasion to survey its highly creditable record. Under Austria, where political conditions were more favourable even in the later decades of the partitioning period, a variety of agencies pursued the aims of popular education. Foremost among them stands the " People's School Society " (*T.S.L.*) founded by the poet Asnyk in 1891, and maintained in the new Poland. Besides usefully supplementing the work of public organs in founding schools in out-of-the-way corners of the country, the Society has done much to promote the spread of knowledge among the people by the publication of cheap popular literature. In the sphere of adult education proper, the Universities of Cracow and Lwów on the one hand, and the educational sections of trade-union organizations on the other, conducted University Extension courses on the western European model. Under Russia, where Polish initiative in educational matters had been most effectively barred by political oppression, the unrecorded, and often heroic, efforts of self-sacrificing individuals and secret societies were followed, during the brief dawn of constitutional freedom after 1905, by activities of a large organization called " The Mother of Schools " (*Macierz Szkolna*) and by several university extension courses, all of which, however, were suppressed when reaction again set in.

In the new free Poland, adult education was recognized at once as being no less necessary and important than the creation of a school system. So many grown-up citizens entered on their life in the new State with an education left imperfect through the unfavourable conditions of foreign rule, that wide activities in the field of adult education were an obvious and imperative task of national reconstruction. A special Department of Adult Education was accordingly created in the new Polish Ministry of Public Instruction, and local self-government organs showed laudable zeal on their part in this domain.

Educational courses for adults—generally courses of four years' duration, conducted by elementary school teachers—now exist in most of Poland's larger cities; Warsaw possesses a particularly well-organized institution of the kind. In the country-side, such courses are usually organized by district or country councils, and take the shape of "winter schools." Apart from such courses, which are necessarily elementary in their teaching, there are a number of University Extension organizations of various types; besides large centres of extension teaching in the principal cities, and a "Correspondence College," they include several "Village Universities" on the Danish model, which are eagerly supported by "Circles of Village Youth" and exercise a widespread influence through their *alumni* and *alumnae*. In many villages of Poland, cultural endeavour of this kind has now found homes in the form of "People's Houses," which usually contain libraries and club rooms, as well as halls for theatrical performances, social entertainments, and national celebrations. For the use of the instructors who serve such institutions, a number of publications—including several periodicals—are issued with the help of government subsidies. Of the highly important work in adult education done by the Polish army among its conscripts, due mention has been made in a former chapter; similarly, of the good services recently rendered to adult education—especially in the country-side—by that highly popular institution, the Polish Radio Company.

To complete the picture, it must be added that special courses of instruction are organized for school teachers in order to prepare them for their tasks in the sphere of adult education. In connection with this it may be mentioned, as part of the adult education policy of the Government, that courses of supplementary instruction for teachers of all grades, for administrative and public health officers, and for other professional men in public service, are conducted, with every assistance from the Government, in various parts of Poland at convenient periods of the year, mostly in holiday time. They incidentally serve the twofold good purpose of extending the citizens' knowledge of their own recently reunited land, and of promoting personal acquaintance among workers in the same field in the different sectors of the country Of late, the experiment of holding vacation courses for foreign students in Poland, in order to make them acquainted with the history, geography, and national life of the country, has been tried with good success.

In Poland, as elsewhere in these days of specialization, the work of the adult education worker is developing into a profession by itself ; an entire academic department for the training of such " social educators " has been organized in the " Free University " of Warsaw and is doing true pioneer work. It is perhaps not necessary for the purposes of the present survey to give a detailed presentation of the interplay of central and local government action with the activities of educational societies, political parties, churches, trade unions and private foundations in the conduct and control of adult education in various forms and branches. Suffice it to say, by way of illustration, that at a World Conference on Adult Education held at Cambridge (England) in the summer of 1929, Poland was represented by no fewer than thirty delegates of widely different educational bodies. It was the proud privilege of the present writer, as their common spokesman, to be elected one of the Vice-Presidents of the World Association for Adult Education, in express recognition of the importance of Poland's achievements in the field.

## 14

" The true university, in these days, is a collection of books " ; this saying of Carlyle's, justly taken for the motto of that excellent series, *Everyman's Library*, cannot fail to be present to all organizers of education in our era.

Poland's inheritance in the matter of *libraries* was a worthy part of her cultural tradition.

Apart from various ancient convent libraries, the library of the University of Cracow, called into being with the reorganization of the University itself in 1400 (more than half a century before the invention of printing), has ever since been the most important library of Poland ; it contains the most precious treasures in the form of old MSS. and incunables, as well as the most complete collection of modern Polish printed books. No wonder that it could serve as the workshop for the creation of the monumental, comprehensive *Polish Bibliography*, begun in the later nineteenth century by its then chief librarian K. Estreicher, and now continued by his son.

Besides the *Jagellonica*, as Poland's " mother library " is usually called, there arose, in the sixteenth, seventeenth, and eighteenth centuries, a number of book collections of considerable importance, mostly founded by Poland's kings and nobles. Pride of place among these libraries is due to a particularly large and rich one, collected in the eighteenth century by two bishops, the Załuski brothers, and presented by them to the nation. This splendid library, located in Warsaw, was, in the period of the partitions, transferred in its entirety to Russia, where it became part of the groundwork of the St. Petersburg Public Library. It is one of the gratifying results of the new Poland's victory over the Bolsheviks in 1920 that, under the provisions of the Riga Peace Treaty, a large portion of the Załuski library is being restored to Poland and will here, in turn, form the groundstock of a new National Library in Warsaw. On the same occasion, it may be mentioned in passing, an unusually valuable collection of etchings (120,000 in number), collected by that great lover of art, the last king of Poland, has returned from Russian into Polish possesssion.

In the nineteenth century, in spite of adverse political conditions, a number of other important libraries were founded on Polish soil—several of them in Warsaw in connection with institutions of higher learning and research ; the library of the University of Warsaw (Russianized after 1863) was transferred to the interior of Russia during the World War, but is now being restored to Poland, like the Załuski Library. During the period of emigration after the insurrection of 1831, valuable Polish libraries were established abroad,—one of them in Paris, where it still remains, and one at Rapperswyl near Zurich in Switzerland, whence it has recently been moved to Poland, to form part of the new National Library in Warsaw.

The new Polish State, having organized a special Library Department in its Ministry of Education, took stock, by means of a questionnaire, of the library resources within its borders. The questionnaire was answered by 22,531 public libraries in Poland. Among these, the five largest ones, situated in the cities of Warsaw, Cracow, Poznań, Lwów and Wilno, and mostly connected with the universities, number from 300,000 to 800,000 volumes each. Besides them, it was decided to create a new National Library in Warsaw: founded by Presidential decree in 1928, it has been growing up since, and already counts over 500,000 volumes. A Bibliographical Institute has also been established and has conducted, since 1927, a systematic registration of all periodical and non-periodical publications appearing in Poland, as well as of publications issued abroad in Polish or on subjects connected with Poland. Problems of the organization and working of libraries are being discussed in a *Library Review*, appearing since 1927.

Besides the public libraries, there are some private ones of great importance—mostly founded by aristocratic families—which are open to the public and render great services to research. Foremost among these are the Krasiński, Przeździecki and Zamoyski Libraries in Warsaw, the Działyński Library at Kórnik near Poznań, and the Raczyński Library at Poznań itself, the Czartoryski Library at Cracow, the Ossoliński and the Baworowski Libraries at Lwów, and the Wróblewski Library at Wilno. Some of these—notably the Czartoryski Library—are combined with valuable art collections and historical museums. Several among the great private libraries have, in the new Poland become national property—foremost of all, Kórnik, with its priceless treasures in the way of early Polish printed books.

Apart from libraries of Polish origin, and mainly composed of Polish books, there are in Poland's possession some considerable book collections of predominantly foreign character, left behind by Poland's foreign rulers. Such are the former German libraries at Poznań, Bydgoszcz, and Toruń, as well as the Russian library at Łuck in Volhynia, all of them now under Polish administration and being supplementarily stocked with Polish books.

A hunger for reading has been manifested particularly by the population of the eastern border provinces, in which books and libraries were scarce in pre-war times. Much energy and outlay have been devoted to the needs of these provinces, and they are now provided with a network of popular libraries, which are being eagerly used. Less satisfactory progress has been made, owing to want of means, with the provision of new buildings for the existing large libraries in the interior of Poland. Poland's most venerable treasury of books—the *Jagellonica* of Cracow—still housed in an exquisitely beautiful but entirely inadequate fifteenth-century building, which was in the old days the residential college for the University's professors and students, is sorely in need of more appropriate accommodation ; but means to construct the new building, for which plans and site are ready, cannot be found in these critical times.

Next to the libraries, the *museums* of Poland must be mentioned as important institutions of education and research. Like the libraries, many of them owe their existence to the passion for collecting, and the public munificence, of some of Poland's enlightened nobles in the eighteenth and nineteenth centuries. Thus, the Czartoryski Museum at Cracow (with a fine select gallery of pictures by old masters), the Ossoliński Museum (one of Poland's foremost research workshops) at Lwów, and others. Among museums not founded by private initiative, but public from the outset, the National Museum at Cracow (containing, among other treasures, the huge canvases of scenes from Polish history by Matejko) still stands foremost ; it is to be surpassed in size and wealth by a National Museum in Warsaw, now being built up. In Warsaw also, pre-war Museums of National Science, Industry, Agriculture and Archæology have grown up into important national institutions. A similar position is occupied at Cracow by the rich and valuable museum connected with the Polish Academy. At Lwów, apart from several Polish Museums, public and private, the Ukrainians possess two museums of their own. Among smaller provincial towns, apart from such academic centres as Poznań and Wilno, which have museums of importance, it is the summer resort of Zakopane in the mountains and the town of Tarnopol on the south-eastern border which can boast of rich collections of great interest for regional and folklore study.

## 15

*Physical culture* is occupying a place of increasing importance in the educational curriculum of modern states. The English-speaking countries had led the way in these matters, and Continental Europe, long before the War, had begun to follow their example. Games, in particular, as a form of physical exercise, began to gain the upper hand over gymnastics ; and semi-military organizations of youth, like the Boy Scouts and Girl Guides, became quickly popular everywhere. In Poland, the movement in favour of outdoor games had made considerable progress long before the War, especially at Cracow, where an enlightened and philanthropic Professor of Medicine, Dr. H. Jordan, founded a park with playgrounds for children. During the last pre-war years, the Boy Scouts organization rapidly took root in Poland and became very popular. After the War, physical culture became one of the essential components of the educational programme for the free and united nation.

In Poland's elementary and secondary schools, a period of half an hour every day (or, in rarer cases, an hour every day) is set apart for physical exercise of a systematic sort ; besides, games and outdoor sports are organized as far as possible in the free afternoon hours. Participation in the physical exercise periods included in school hours is compulsory, and only pupils of imperfect health are exempt on the ground of a medical certificate. In the universities, games and sports are voluntary. Opportunities for them are provided by " Academic Sport Associations " (*A.Z.S.*), subsidized out of the fees paid by the students. Unfortunately, owing partly to the poverty of the majority of students, and partly to their preoccupation with other social activities (including party politics), sports are only practised seriously by some 10-15 per cent.of the total student body.

The equipment of Poland's schools for physical culture is, in spite of considerable efforts made by all successive Governments, still largely inadequate. Gymnasia existed in connection with most of the larger schools under Germany and Austria, and they are included in the plans of all new schools which are being built in Poland. But many of the older schools, even large ones, especially in former Russian Poland, are still without accommodation for physical exercise ; of the existing gymnastic halls only one-half are provided with the proper apparatus ; and of the private schools, only one tenth are at all satisfactorily equipped for physical education. In spite of serious difficulties in old and congested cities, the municipal administrations are doing all they can to provide playgrounds for schools. The efforts of central and of local government bodies are supplemented by a number of private organizations. Foremost among them stands the Y.M.C.A. Having rendered excellent services to the Polish Army in its early years, the American Y.M.C.A. afterwards transferred its activities to the civilian population, and it became transformed, on civilian ground, into a purely Polish organization working on the American model and with the technical assistance of individual American experts. The institution now has three large and active centres in Poland, in the cities of Warsaw, Cracow, and Łódź, of which two—Warsaw and Cracow—have by American munificence (with considerable contributions from the local communities) been provided with houses of their own, containing all the features of typical Y.M.C.A. buildings. These Y.M.C.A.'s offer ample opportunities to numerous groups of young people (mostly of school age) both for gymnastics and games in their excellently-equipped halls, and for swimming in their admirable covered swimming pools. They have become important centres of sportive activities among the young people, and models, in many ways, for Polish institutions of a similar kind.

It is largely owing to Y.M.C.A. influence that besides football, which had been very popular among Poland's young people even before the War, the games of volley-ball and basket-ball became well known and are great favourites at present. Of other popular sports, mountaineering, swimming, rowing, lawn-tennis, and above all ski-running must be singled out as markedly increasing in popularity of late years.

Apart from the Y.M.C.A., the Boy Scouts Movement must be mentioned as another important subsidiary organization combining noble moral aims with physical culture. The movement has made very rapid progress in the new Poland, and the Polish Boy Scouts and Girl Guides organizations now rank as second in importance in Europe after the British ones. An international conference of Girl Guide leaders held in Poland in 1932 has borne impressive testimony to the efficiency and prominence of Polish organizations of this type.

Since 1926, much has also been done by the Government to promote physical culture in schools under the form of preliminary military training. Although destined primarliy to facilitate the later service drill of the conscript soldier, this " Military preparation," movement ( " P.W." )—analogous to similar movements in some neighbouring countries—has done much, incidentally, to promote bodily vigour and suppleness, as well as a healthy love for outdoor life, among Poland's young people.

Instructors in physical exercise were scarce when the new Poland began her free existence ; and those who were available, were either imperfectly prepared altogether, or behind the times in their ideas and training. One-third of the secondary schools had no physical instructors at all. The crying need for well-trained instructors was met, first by shorter supplementary courses for the old instructors, then by the systematic education of new ones through a university curriculum extending originally over one year, later, over two. At present, four universities of Poland possess fully developed departments for the training of physical instructors, and about 1000 graduates in physical education, including 40 per cent. women, have already come out of these departments. As a central organ, there exists an " Institute of Physical Education " at Bielany near Warsaw, with a magnificent new building, one of the best of its kind in Europe. Control over the whole apparatus of physical education in Poland's schools is exercised by a special " Physical Culture Section " in the Ministry of Education.

Of the attitude of Poland's young people towards physical exercise it may summarily be said here that it is one of rapidly growing eagerness, not free even now from the besetting dangers which have become so marked in other countries.

On the whole, however, such large areas of neglect in the past remain to be made up for that the movement is still in a state of healthy and altogether desirable progress and expansion, and it is only to be wished that the material means to promote it may be more abundant in the near future.

In connection with the above survey of the part played by gymnastics and games in Polish education, a few particulars illustrating the *progress of sports* in the new Poland may not seem out of place here.

In 1919, the total membership of all sportive societies in Poland registered in the State Institute of Physical Education was 43,200 ; in 1932 it is 223,900. The number of regular courses for physical training, which are conducted in the country, has during the same time grown from 11 to 201 ; and the number of summer camps, which was 12 in 1922, was 43 ten years later. Playgrounds for outdoor games were only 91 in number in the Poland of 1919 ; in 1932, there are 706 of them ; the number of stadiums has increased from 75 to 631, that of swimming-pools from 25 to 82, of boating clubs from 20 to 70, of cycle racecourses from 1 to 12, of lawn-tennis courts from 97 to 557, of rifle ranges from 158 to 679, of race courses for hurdle-races from 2 to 74, of race courses for horse races from 8 to 26, of sport parks for children from 2 to 18, of skating rinks from 11 to 17, of bob-sleigh tracks froms 2 to 24, of ski-jumping stages from zero to 9, of gymnastic halls from 180 to 269.

Of this progress, a large proportion was achieved by private initiative : of the total apparatus for sports in Poland (halls, stadiums, courts, playgrounds, etc.) only one-third owes its existence to the State Committee of Physical Education, not quite one-fourth to the military authorities, and nearly one-half to private organizations.

With such advance in the material equipment and in the public interest in sports, the international successes won by Polish sportsmen and sportswomen have of late been keeping pace steadily. Polish horsemen are among the winners at almost every world competition ; Polish tennis has attracted respectful attention at Wimbledon ; a Polish runner broke the world record at Los Angeles in 1932, and as a general result of the Olympic games of that year, Poland holds a high place among the nations of the world in sports, being the eighth on the final list.

## 16

From the subject of physical education we will now pass on to the closely related one of *school hygiene*.

In 1920-22 only 39 per cent. of the secondary schools, and 21 per cent. of the teachers' colleges of Poland had "school doctors" permanently attached to them ; to-day practically all the schools of this grade have such doctors, while of the three and a half million elementary schoolchildren of Poland over half a million, at any rate, are under medical control either constantly or periodically. Besides doctors, a considerable number of elementary schools in the larger towns have trained school nurses watching over the hygiene of school life. The medical personnel attached to the schools is obliged, besides actual medical attendance, to provide instruction in hygiene in the form of periodical talks in the lower, and systematic lessons in the upper forms. This propaganda of hygiene is supplemented by occasional school exhibitions illustrating the dangers of such social evils as drink or consumption. Courses in hygiene are also frequently held for school teachers. Among *school clinics* for the timely treatment of defects of health, dental ones proved to be the most urgently needed. In 1918, Cracow was the only town in Poland which could boast of a dental clinic for the pupils of its municipal schools ; ten years later, 40 per cent. of the secondary schools, and 70 per cent. of the teachers' colleges had school dentists with dental surgeries on the spot. Among the elementary school dental clinics (now fairly numerous) the institutions of this kind at Cracow are still a model for the rest of Poland. Clinics for the treatment of the children's eyes so far exist only in four of the largest cities, clinics for the cure of defects of speech in three ; excellent " policlinics " offering all kinds of medical attendance to school children are established at Lwów, Warsaw and Wilno.

Tuberculosis was a widespread scourge among the under-fed children of the early post-war years. The most effective means to combat it, especially among the school-children of the cities, was soon found to consist in the organization of " summer colonies " for sickly school-children in healthy country spots. A number of such colonies, due largely to private initiative, existed before the War, especially in Austrian Poland. After the War, the matter was largely taken in hand by the State and by provincial bodies. The number of colonies rose from 200 to over 1000 between 1922 and 1929 ; in the later years, nearly 80,000 children profited by them, besides 45,000 going out into "day colonies" for every day of their summer vacation. The colonies are partly destined for children suffering from definite symptoms of disease; these are located largely at some of Poland's mineral springs on the northern slopes of the Carpathians (such as Rabka or Rymanów). Some such colonies are permanent and connected with " sanatorium schools " ; one of the best sanatoria for children is the anti-tuberculous one at Zakopane, conducted by the University of Cracow. Among summer colonies for healthy schoolboys, those at Poremba and at Mszana near Cracow (the latter conducted by the Y.M.C.A. as a " summer camp " on the American model) deserve to be singled out. Many summer camps are organized by the Boy Scouts organizations ; the strip of Polish sea-coast is fairly dotted with them every summer, and so is the beautiful region of the rapids of the Dunajec river in the mountains of the south.

Little could be done, in the early years of the new Poland, for the health of its eager crowds of university students, both male and female. Their general poverty, the appalling lack of lodgings for them in the cities, and the after-effects of the war-time privations under which they had spent their childhood—all this resulted in the fact that tuberculosis took terrible toll among them during the first few years. Conditions have fortunately changed very much for the better since. To begin with, a comprehensive system of sickness insurance is in operation now, under which every student of a Polish university, by virtue of a moderate annual payment in addition to his academic fees, receives gratuitous medical treatment in case of need in the medical clinics of his own university. Out of the sickness insurance fund, subsidies are also granted towards the thorough repair of students' teeth, towards the provision of spectacles for those with defective eyesight, and, what is more important, prolonged sojourns in the mountain health resorts are made possible to those attacked by consumption. In the second place, the students' fees—as mentioned before—have been used for the construction of students' hostels (some of them, such as the one in Warsaw, being among the largest institutions of the kind in Europe), and these hostels have, in a great measure, put an end to the distressful housing difficulties of the first post-war years. It was out of the students' fees also, partly by means of a separate addition to them, and with the assistance of long-term loans from the Bank of National Economy, that sanatoria for consumptive students were built in various health resorts of the Tatra and Carpathian mountains under the auspices of different student relief organizations : the largest and best-equipped one, built at Zakopane under the auspices of the Association of Student Relief Societies of Poland, was happily finished in 1932. Besides sanatoria in the proper sense of the word, convalescent homes and rest homes for vacation time have arisen both by the sea-side and in the mountains, and are now peopled, every summer, by joyous groups of students, who inhabit them by monthy turns. It may be added that individual benefactors have not been lacking who, by bequeathing estates to the universities, have enabled them to establish rest and recreation homes for university professors as well : one such house, situated in a forest neighbourhood at a few hours' distance from Warsaw, and popularly known as *Mądralin* (" The Wise Men's Home " ), enjoys a certain celebrity, because important works by Polish scholars and scientist have already been written during welcome periods of retirement within its quiet walls.

## 17

The mention of *Mądralin* has brought us to the one subject which still remains to be discussed in Poland's educational system, viz., to the *research work* which is being carried on by the leaders of scholarship and science in the new Poland.

It has been explained in a former chapter, how, during the century of Poland's captivity, research and learning shared with literature and art the privilege of absorbing national energies which, in a country more fortunately situated, in large measure would have gone into various forms of active public service, political and social. Hence the surprising fact that even in the darkest periods of political oppression—such as the middle of the century, when the country is temporarily without any Polish universities, its learned societies are mostly paralyzed, and its intellectual leaders scattered in exile and struggling against poverty—organized research work never ceases to be conducted in Poland, and hundreds of volumes, chiefly illustrating historical and natural aspects of Poland itself, are continually appearing.

For these intellectual manifestations of national vitality, a material foundation is largely furnished by the generosity of noble donors. The passion of the nobility for collecting literary and art treasures as well as objects of scientific and scholarly interest—a passion stimulated in eighteenth-century Poland by the example of the French *ancien régime,* and encouraged by the last King of Poland—continued to manifest itself even in the days of the worst national disasters after the partitions. Thus, to quote one instance only, it was in the darkest moments after the calamity of 1863 that a famous collection of Greek vases[1] was ultimately organized and housed in the palace of Gołuchowo in Prussian Poland. It was largely the same landed aristocracy which munificently supported the work and publications of learned societies in Warsaw, Wilno and Poznań in the earlier decades of the century, and of the Polish Academy at Cracow in

[1] See Professor J. D. Beazley : *Greek Vases in Poland* (Oxford University Press, 1928).

its later half. And it was also from the ranks of the larger
landowners that amateur workers in various fields of research
mostly came in the earlier nineteenth century, many of them
attaining high distinction.

The actual efforts of Polish research workers in the earlier
part of the nineteenth century, under the double stimulus of the
European Romantic movement and of national memories, were
largely directed into historical channels. If the dawn of the
century was dominated, in the intellectual field, by the typical
eighteenth-century figure of Stanislas Staszic, the father of
modern Polish natural science—the 'thirties, 'forties, and 'fifties
are marked by the ascendancy of the no less typical representative of Romanticism in learning—Joachim Lelewel, who,
from his exile in Brussels, pours forth a library of studies in
history, all dominated by the Romantic sociological doctrine of
" the folk " as the chief actor on the historical stage. It is not
only Romantic thought, but the great Polish Romantic poetry of
the period, which profoundly influences research in this era,
particularly in the humanities. Poland's greatest poet, Adam
Mickiewicz, occupies the newly-created chair of Slavonic studies
in the *Collège de France* and delivers an epoch-making course of
lectures on the literatures of the Slav nations ; another poet, W.
Pol, becomes distinguished as a Professor of Geography in the
University of Cracow ; and a wonderfully prolific novelist, J. I.
Kraszewski—the Polish Walter Scott—does meritorious work in
history.

Beside the Romantic note, another dominant characteristic of
Polish learning in the earlier nineteenth century is the strength
of German influence. In spite of the constant and manifold
political relations with France, Polish intellectual culture, almost
throughout the age of captivity, bears the imprint of the German
neighbours, not unnaturally, since they at this time almost
become " the schoolmasters of the world." In the early
decades of the century, the names of some leading scholars—
such as Linde, the author of a standard dictionary of the Polish
language ; Frank, the reorganizer of medical studies in the
University of Wilno ; Groddeck, the distinguished Wilno
professor of classics, and many others—bear witness to German
origin. In the 'thirties and 'forties, a rising group of Polish
thinkers (including the great Romantic poets) is, for a time,
entirely under the spell of Hegel, (" the Christ of our times,"
as one of them called him) and his philosophy of history. In the
later half of the nineteenth century, the Universities of Cracow
and Lwów, containing the only Polish workshops of research

then available, are set within the framework of the Austro-Hungarian Monarchy and accordingly kept in close touch with the German Universities of Austria and Germany itself, at which many of their lecturers and professors received, in their youth, their professional training—some of them when exiled after the insurrection of 1863. However, new developments result in a renewed widening of the Polish intellectual horizon long before the end of the nineteenth century.

18

It was in the eighteen-sixties that the most epoch-making changes of the century took place in the development of research activities in Poland. The triumphant achievements of natural science in the west produced their repercussions in Poland ; the sobered mood of the nation after the defeat of 1863 also had its effect on learning ; and the result was that the Romantic pre-dominance of historical and literary interests ceased, and natural science once more came into its own in Polish research work, while the new note of realism made itself felt even within the sphere of the humanities. No less important was the fact that Austrian Poland, with the grant of self-government, was able to re-introduce the Polish language into its temporarily Germanized two universities, and that it received, besides, a number of higher schools of university rank, and of research organizations subsidized out of public funds (such as the Polish Academy at Cracow). Hence-forward, in this sector of Poland at least, research was no longer exclusively dependent on the generosity of private individuals, and work could be conducted under conditions somewhat like the normal ones of a free European State. A number of societies and of periodicals devoted to special branches of learning arise ; eminent professors gather groups of disciples round them and create " schools " in which chosen aims of research are pursued with consolidated effort. The activities of these Cracow " schools " extend to nearly all fields both of the humanities and of natural science, and will repeatedly have to be mentioned yet as the origins and foundations of contemporary Polish work in various domains of research. All these remarkable achieve-ments, jointly constituting a brilliant renascence of Cracow's ancient academic glories, are the combined work of a band of gifted scholars and scientists coming from all parts of the divided country. The resistance of the Austrian Government against professorial appointments, and elections to Academy member-ship, of eminent research workers from Russian and Prussian Poland is gradually overcome, and Cracow becomes a true

U

*Alma Mater* for all the best intellect of Poland.   What is equally
important, is that through this widening of the range of selection
of its teachers, Cracow, and all Polish intellectual culture with it,
becomes connected no longer with Germany alone, but with the
great centres of ideas in other western countries as well : some of
Cracow's outstanding workers in physics and chemistry at the
turn of the century come from British schools (Lord Kelvin's at
Glasgow, Sir J. J. Thomson's at Cambridge, Sir Ernest Ruther-
ford's at Manchester), the creator of the new mathematical
tradition is himself a disciple of the French ; and it is Cracow
University which sends the first " visiting professors " from
Poland, in our own days, to the universities of France, Belgium,
Italy, Britain, and the United States.

Under incomparably less favourable auspices than Cracow,
Warsaw in the later nineteenth century indefatigably endeavours
to keep the flag of Polish learning flying.   At first, some of her
distinguished scholars and scientists retain a foothold in Warsaw
University, even after the introduction of Russian as its language
of teaching ; but gradually, Russification in *personnel* as well as
in language sets in, and Polish men of learning, often of great
eminence, are crowded out into meagre administrative employment, private school teaching, or journalism, and have to be
content with such substitutes for research workshops as the
libraries of noble families, and the laboratories provided by
private generosity or social co-operation.   Of the research work
conducted under these precarious conditions in Warsaw, it is
characteristic that economic and sociological studies occupy a
prominent place in it, following the change which transforms
Russian Poland into an important industrial area.   The practical
study of medicine also stands out, because Warsaw's hospitals
give opportunity for it, and the medical practitioners of the city
make important contributions to research.   Subjects verging
on political problems are naturally difficult to cultivate under
Russian rule ; still, epoch-making work in Polish geography is
done in Warsaw ; the historical knowledge of Polish law is considerably deepened by the efforts of Warsaw scholars ; and in
the sphere of Polish history, new light is thrown—by way of
conscious reaction against the critical attitude of the Cracow
school—on the constructive achievements of the old Poland
accomplished during the very period of the partitions.   Last not
least, it should be mentioned that the lack of a Polish University in Warsaw was not without a stimulating effect on extra-
mural adult education, and much meritorious work was done in
the way of popularization of knowledge.

Prussian Poland, under the steam-roller both of German political persecution and German educational influence, naturally presents the most modest record of independent Polish intellectual effort. Its best forces are either drawn into the field of active social and economic endeavour, or if inclined for speculative thought, seek employment in the Austrian sector. Still, the learned societies of Poznań and of Toruń (the capital of Poland's old sea-side province), subsidized both by nobles and by the growing Polish *bourgeoisie* of the sector, make certain important contributions, especially to the study of the sources of early Polish history.

In addition to these brief remarks on intellectual life in the three sections of divided Poland, mention must be made of research activities among the Polish emigrants, especially in Paris. While centring round a quickly growing library and museum (which are still located at 6, Quai d'Orléans), these efforts are, in their early stages, largely marred by all-absorbing political interests and party dissensions among the emigrants. Later on, certain important labours, mainly in Polish history, are conducted largely under the influence of the " Cracow school," and that influence naturally becomes intensified when the Paris library becomes transformed into the " Paris research station " of the Polish Academy, under whose auspices it remains since. For a time, owing to the munificence of a rich Polish noble, a Polish Scientific Society leads a very productive existence in Paris, and does much not only to help Warsaw scientists to publish their work, but also to establish contacts between Polish and French science, and thus to widen Poland's intellectual outlook beyond Germany. It was in this direction also that useful work was done, until the last pre-war years, by a scholarship foundation due to the generosity of a Polish doctor in Paris. Out of a home for exiles, Paris became a source of inspiration and instruction for re-emigrants, who endeavoured to turn to practical use what they had learned in France. This evolutionary change only prefigured the important part which Paris, after the deliverance of Poland, was to play as a great centre of post-graduate studies for young Polish adepts at research work. The venerable figure of Mme Curie (Skłodowska by her Polish maiden name) vividly illustrates this aspect of Franco-Polish relations. Having risen to a dominant position in the French scientific world, she has never ceased to extend her sympathetic interest to scientific progress in her native country, and it was deservedly under her auspices and in her honoured presence that the Polish Radiological Institute, coming into existence with the help of a generous gift from her, was inaugurated in Warsaw in 1932.

## 19

Through mention of Mme Curie—a glorious " link with the past " indeed—we have entered into the field of contemporary history, and must now attempt to survey the record of research work in the new, free Poland.

As in the political and the economic domain, so likewise in that of creative intellectual effort, the deliverance of Poland, while incomparably enlarging the field of opportunity, at the same time necessarily brought with it not only very difficult new tasks—some of them diverting the energies of research workers into other fields—but also serious economic embarrassments, which were bound to hamper progress considerably. A Research Department was created in the Ministry of Education, but the funds at its disposal were always scanty, and it had ultimately to be united with the University Department of the Ministry. A new organ, however, for the promotion of research came into existence when the favourable economic conditions of the first years of the Piłsudski *régime* made it possible in 1928, to create a " National Culture Fund " of five million złoty, which has since received additional annual grants. The administration of the Fund was not subordinated to the Ministry of Education, but made independent of it, and it was entrusted to Dr. St. Michalski, who had become known long before the War as a most deserving worker in the difficult field of adult education and privately-organized research work under Russian rule in Warsaw. It is to the Fund that Poland's research workers have since 1928 chiefly been looking for subsidies, especially towards post-graduate training of young adepts of research by means of scholarships which enable them to go abroad. It is the Fund also which has made it possible to continue the publication of an annual called *Nauka Polska* (*Polish Learning*), which has now run into sixteen large volumes, and contains a great deal of first-hand information concerning the general development of research work in Poland. It contains also a good many projects outlined by Poland's leaders in research, but never realized because of the lack of means.

As explained in a former section of the present chapter, the universities, whose tradition it is to be homes of research as well as of teaching, have lately, in Poland as in other countries, become increasingly engrossed by the absorbing tasks of the mass education of students for the several learned professions. The

tendency to provide separate homes for pure research in the form
of special institutes is accordingly spreading throughout the
world as a necessity, and it has found expression in Poland, as
far as the resources of the new State allowed it.

The different institutes of this kind actually conducting
research work in Poland are being incidentally mentioned up and
down these pages. The most important among them are : an
Institute of Chemical Research, which owes its existence to the
present President of the Republic (formerly a distinguished
Professor of Chemistry himself), a State Meteorological Office,
a State Mineralogical and Geological Institute, the Radium
Institute mentioned before as created under the auspices of
Mme Curie, an Institute of Public Hygiene endowed by the
Rockefeller Foundation, a Biological Institute named after the
late eminent scientist M. Nencki, and a Hydrobiological
Research Station on the Polish sea coast.

Passing now to a more detailed review of recent Polish
research work in its aspect of personal achievement of individual
men of learning in different fields, we must begin by illustrating
one distinguishing feature of the new era which has already been
alluded to, viz., the enlargement of the domain of activities of
Polish scholars and scientists by the very fact of renewed political
existence and the needs of the new State's life. This enlargement, while increasing the social importance of the research
worker in the eyes of his fellow-citizens, often took him, temporarily or altogether, outside the limits of his proper occupation.
It was natural and inevitable that both the organization and
the actual public service of the new State claimed some of the
best forces among academic teachers and research workers. All
the three Presidents whom the Polish Republic has had so far were
Professors: the present occupant of the exalted post—Professor
Ignatius Mościcki—is well known to specialists in industrial
chemistry as an inventor with a remarkable record of achievement. There has never yet been a Cabinet in the new Poland
without one or several university professors occupying ministerial
posts in it ; professors as Prime Ministers are frequent, the most
notable figure among them being perhaps that of Professor K.
Bartel, who, by sheer personal energy and talent, has risen from
the humble employment of mechanician in the workshops of the
Engineering College at Lwów to the rank of Professor and Rector
of the institution. Professors mostly formed the advisory body
of experts who accompanied the Polish delegates to the Versailles
Peace Conference. Professors headed many foreign missions,
took part in international conferences, and drafted political,

commercial, and other agreements between Poland and other Powers. Professors acted—and still act—as Poland's diplomatic representatives in a number of foreign countries ; and it was a professor—S. Askenazy, Poland's foremost authority on nineteenth-century history—who was Poland's delegate to the League of Nations during the first few years of its existence.

In the legislature, university professors have been less prominent, because the thoroughly democratic franchise of the new Republic gave the predominance, in both chambers, to professional politicians, and the arguments and methods of party controversy kept people of higher intellect and finer moral sense out of politics in Poland as elsewhere. After the *coup d'état* of 1926, again, the cavalierly proceedings of the military group around the Dictator discouraged many academic personalities otherwise willing to co-operate in the great work of Constitutional reform, but profoundly addicted to the great nineteenth-century tradition of liberalism.

In one form, however, academic experts have uninterruptedly collaborated in the work of Polish legislation : due mention has been made, in a former chapter, of the labours of the *Commission for the Codification of Polish Law*, which was formed in the very earliest period of Poland's new existence, and composed of the foremost legal specialists in the country under the presidency of the late Professor Fierich, of Cracow. Apart from the commission's constantly increasing output of comprehensive codes of various branches of law for the new Poland, individual representatives of Polish jurisprudence have acted with distinction as law-makers. Thus, Professor F. Zoll, of Cracow, besides taking a prominent part in international work on private law and copyright law, was also the author of a most important " Valorisation Bill " which regulated the treatment of old monetary obligations after the introduction of the new Polish currency.

In connection with these labours, covering large fields of general legislation, the merits of prominent teachers of the *philosophy of law* come in for due mention. The late Professor W. L. Jaworski, of Cracow, an important figure in Austro-Polish politics before the War, being prevented by physical disability from an active share in the political life in the new Poland, spent his enforced retirement in speculation on fundamental problems of political and social law : his " Commentary on the Polish Constitution," as well as his " Project of an Agrarian Code," have furnished food for reflection to a whole generation of his pupils as well as of his adversaries. He was also the general editor of one of a number of legal encyclopædias which became necessary for the practice of law in the freshly reunited country.

Jaworski's contemporary, the late L. Petrażycki in Warsaw, had acquired world-wide celebrity, even during his work in the University of St. Petersburg before the War, by his daringly original generalizations in the vaster field of the origins and nature of law ; he continued, in the new Poland, to analyze problems of the relation of legal order to social life and of abstract intellect to practical action.

20

Not less important than the services rendered to the new State by experts in jurisprudence, were those of the specialists in *political economy* and *financial science*.

The disastrous consequences of paper-money inflation, of wasteful popular legislation, and of illusory experiments in economic policy were counteracted by sound advice from leading economic thinkers, who never neglected an opportunity to raise a voice of warning or to make constructive suggestions. Among those who resolutely adhere, in the midst of this changing world of " social planning," to the classical doctrines of economic liberalism, Professor A. Krzyżanowski, of Cracow, must be singled out as undoubtedly the foremost teacher of political economy in Poland. Besides giving to Polish economic literature standard works on the theory of money and on financial science, he showed his keen sense of vital contemporary problems by dealing with one of the most important—the problem of population and of the birth-rate—in an essay prefixed to a new Polish edition of Malthus' *Principles of Population*. In his contributions to the discussion of current economic problems, Professor Krzyżanowski constantly advocates the restriction of the expensive social activities of the State and the abstention from undue Government interference with economic development : among the numerous and important research publications of the Cracow Economic Society, whose President he is, there appeared recently a co-operative volume, giving a critical survey of state-conducted economic enterprise in Poland. Opponents of economic liberalism are not wanting, of course, and the present crisis in particular has become a prolific source of projects of state remedies against economic evils. The general tendencies of our age seem to be in favour of the advocates of " social planning," and some of their works in Poland—such as a collective volume recently published under the title *On the Economic Front*—contain serious contributions to economic thought.

Political economy borders on, and overlaps with *social studies* in their various forms. The modern science of *sociology*, while looked at askance by the older universities in the later nineteenth century, had, for local reasons of social development, appealed to active minds in Russian Poland, unfettered by academic tradition ; and it was there that E. Majewski had written a voluminous treatise on *The Study of Civilization,* and E. Abramowski had endeavoured to create a remarkable compromise between individualism and social philosophy. And outside Russian Poland, it had been the Polish province of Austria which had given to German scholarship the first author of a systematic outline of sociology in the person of the late Professor L. Gumplowicz. In the new Poland, a sociological school of importance is arising at Poznań, thanks to the efforts of Professor F. Znaniecki, who is known outside his country by his investigations into the changes in social mentality among the emigrant Polish peasantry in America. Another Polish sociologist of distinction, B. Malinowski of Cracow, passed, like Joseph Conrad in the world of letters, from the Polish to the English scene : his researches into the history and customs of Australian and Polynesian aboriginal tribes won him the chair in the London School of Economics which he now occupies. Equally remote were the objects of study of Professor J. Talko-Hryncewicz, now the senior representative of physical anthropology in Poland, who spent thirty years of his earlier life among the Buriat tribes in Transbaikalian Siberia and made a name by the investigation of their racial characteristics. His younger colleague J. Czekanowski at Lwów, who began his career by taking part in a German research expedition into Central Africa, has recently summed up his studies in the racial types represented among the population of Poland, in a large and fascinating volume, whose daring generalizations are likely to stimulate research and controversy for a long time to come. Similar interest has been excited, also in recent years, by an elaborate volume of K. Moszyński on the primitive culture of the Slav nations. Prehistoric archæology, a subject closely related to anthropology both physical and social, has lately been enriched by the results of digging in various parts of Poland, and a comprehensive *Archæology of Poland* by the Warsaw Professor, W. Antoniewicz, provisionally sums up the achievements of the movement. On the side of contemporary life, ethnology is accumulating interesting material of its own : Professors J. St.

Bystroń of Cracow and A. Fischer of Lwów are following in the footsteps of a brilliant band of Polish ethnologists of the nineteenth century, and their work on Polish proverbs and other aspects of popular culture adds much that is new to the voluminous materials collected in the last decades since the monumental works of Oscar Kolberg *Polish Folk-Songs* (1842—1857) and *The People* (1860 ff.).

### 21

From social and prehistoric studies it is an easy transition to the large field of *history* in the proper sense of the word. The important part played by the study of history in national life during the nineteenth century has been characterized in former chapters. The last few pre-war decades left Polish historical scholarship divided, in the main, into three groups or " schools." There was, first of all, the old " Cracow school," laying stress on the inward faults of the old Poland as the principal cause of political disaster ; the venerable surviving head of the school, M. Bobrzyński, after a memorable period of political activity under Austria, used the leisure of his vigorous old age to add, in 1927, a volume on nineteenth-century Polish history to the two volumes of his standard *History of Poland* of which he published a third and revised edition nearly fifty years after the first.

In opposition to the Cracow school, a " Warsaw school " had arisen towards the end of the nineteenth century, largely through the labours of T. Korzon, who, in a monumental work on the domestic history of the old Poland under her last king, had recorded the vast mass of constructive effort displayed in the very period of the partitions, and had thereby laid the foundation for a more optimistic and less condemnatory appreciation of the old Polish State.

A distinct " Lwów school " of historians, akin in its spirit of national optimism to the Warsaw group, turned its efforts first, in the works of Professor L. Kubala, towards the old Poland's heroic and successful struggles against a flood of foreign invasions in the seventeenth century ; by presenting them in fuller light, the ground was prepared for one of the masterpieces of Polish literature, viz. the great *Trilogy* of H. Sienkiewicz' novels on Poland's seventeenth-century wars. Next to Kubala, Professor O. Balzer—who died in 1933—exercised for many pre-war years an important influence from his Lwów chair by presenting the legal and institutional aspects of the old Polish State in their historical reality, and so stimulating in his hearers the sense of the vital need of political independence for national self-expression. Lastly, it was Lwów which, through the activities of

Professor S. Askenazy, became the centre of a group of younger historians, who were inspired by the example of his numerous and brilliantly-written works to examine in detail the history of military and diplomatic effort in the nineteenth century directed at the recovery of Poland's independence. It was Askenazy and his pupils who did much to keep the consciousness of the Polish cause as a great international problem, and the idea of the possibility of renewed military and political action, alive among a generation which was inclined to abandon the entire nineteenth-century tradition of struggle for freedom as Utopian. The tradition created by the Askenazy school has remained strong in the new free Poland, when the attention of historians might have been expected to turn away from the century of captivity. Among many other examples proving the vitality of the Askenazy tradition, it is enough to refer to Professor W. Tokarz' standard work on the insurrection of 1830 (published in 1930) and Professor M. Handelsman's investigations into the diplomatic history of the Polish problem during the Crimean war.

Apart from the different tendencies of the various schools, the activities of Polish historians of pre-war time had run essentially in the same directions as the general trend of European historical scholarship in that period : the publication of historical sources, and the investigation of particular problems in monographs, were the main occupations of average workers in the field. For the editing of sources, the Polish Academy at Cracow provided a convenient central institution, and a very large portion of the many series of volumes published by it was specially devoted to labours of that kind. At Lwów, on the other hand, thanks to the initiative of the late Professor L. Finkel, a large bibliography of Polish historical writings was compiled, which has recently been supplemented and is a most valuable work of reference.

The progress of the Polish cause during the World War towards complete independence naturally directed the efforts of historians into channels appropriate to the time. It was by way of searching the national conscience on the eve of the great rebirth that a distinguished group of Polish scholars co-operated to produce a joint disquisition into the *Causes of Poland's Fall* (1917). At the same time, it was appropriate, on the threshold of the peace settlement, to lend support to Polish claims by summing up. in another collective volume, *Poland's Contributions to World Civilization* (1918). After a dozen years of renewed free existence, it was no less opportune to present to the nation's eyes another co-operative picture of the historical Poland at her highest and her best, as an incentive for endeavour to enact a corresponding and similarly important part in the new European system. Such an opportunity offered itself when, in 1930, the 400th anniversary of the birth of Poland's great renascence poet Jan Kochanowski was celebrated at Cracow by a numerously-attended convention of scholars under the auspices of the Polish Academy. Out of the papers read before that gathering by the foremost specialists in various fields of history, there arose an imposing volume on *Early Polish Civilization* (1932) which presents a wide survey of sixteenth-century Poland in the splendour not only of her power and wealth, but also of her achievements in learning and literature.

It is in accordance with the general current of historical studies in contemporary Europe that in this collective work, as well as in the individual labours of historiographers in the new Poland, particular attention is devoted to intellectual culture and to the history of ideas. With regard to the period of the old Poland's political greatness, it is especially on the importance of the reformation movement in the general civilization of Poland that entirely new light has been thrown, of late years, by the works of Professor St. Kot and his pupils at Cracow, both in a periodical called the *Reformation in Poland*, and in a number of important monographs. It is among Professor Kot's many merits also to have revealed the true greatness of some Polish political thinkers of the sixteenth century (such as Andrew Frycz), to have deepened out knowledge of the history of Polish education and of Poland's intellectual relations with western seats of learning, to have presented for the first time a comprehensive view of the old Poland in contemporary western European opinion, and—last not least—to have, in a quite unique manner, popularized the nation's earlier literature among readers of to-day by his able editorship of an admirable series called *The National Library*.

As an important branch of the history of civilization, studies in the manners, customs, and daily life of the olden time must yet be separately mentioned. Poland had had a master in this field in the person of W. Łoziński, whose *Polish Life in Former Centuries* is still a standard work. He now has a successor in the sociologist, J. St. Bystroń, who has recently published an elaborate *History of Early Polish Manners*.

The *history of art* in Poland has ample materials ready to hand in the numerous relics of medieval and early modern art to be found in ancient churches, convents and palaces. The city of

Cracow, above all, is a perfect museum of art monuments, fully illustrating both the Romanesque and the Gothic period of the Middle Ages, as well as the eras of Renascence and Baroque. It was at Cracow also that modern Polish research in the history of art received its characteristic form, in which the examination of art treasures of the past is combined with care for their proper preservation. The labours of the late Professor M. Sokołowski and of Dr. St. Tomkowicz, who died in 1933, as the honoured senior of Poland's art historians, have created a " Cracow school" of art studies, which extended its influence over other academic centres in the new Poland—particularly to Wilno, which is also rich in monuments of Renascence and Baroque art. It was at Cracow also that the Director of the National Museum in the city (the most representative collection of Polish painting, old and new), Dr. F. Kopera, recently completed the first comprehensive history of painting in Poland. Corresponding work with reference to the history of music in Poland has been done both at Cracow (by Z. Jachimecki) and at Lwów, where Professor A. Chybiński is editing monuments of early Polish music. Another Polish historian of music, H. Opieński, living abroad, has extended his studies to early western European music, and popularized it actively by concerts as well as by writings.

22

Besides the history of civilization and of art, it is the *history of legal and political institutions* which has a legitimate claim on special attention in a newly reborn State. Long before the War, a manual of the constitutional history of Poland by Professor St. Kutrzeba (now General Secretary of the Polish Academy and, in 1932-33, Rector of Cracow University) had attained well-deserved popularity both within the country and abroad (having been translated into several foreign languages). In the new Poland, work in this field has been continued and extended : Professor P. Dąbkowski and his pupils are reconstructing the history of early Polish private law, and Professor Kutrzeba himself, having been engaged repeatedly in international negotiations on behalf of the new Polish State—particularly with Czechoslovakia—was obviously qualified to give a systematic presentation of the political law of the new Polish Republic, which he did in an elaborate treatise.

As a third domain of vital interest to historians in the new Poland, the comparatively recent study of *economic history* may be singled out. In this field, Professor F. Bujak at Lwów is the acknowledged master of a whole generation of research workers, and his brief outline of Poland's economic history, published in English in 1925, excellently sums up the results of modern labours in that field. More recently, a History of Polish Trade by Professor J. Rutkowski has appeared as a first comprehensive presentation of its subject. In a domain closely related to economic history, viz., the history of social classes, the studies of the late Professor J Ptaśnik in the medieval history of Polish towns deservedly hold a high place ; and as a less scholarly but very vivid account of an obscure and unfamiliar but highly important subject, the History of the Polish Peasantry by the aged Radical journalist A. Świętochowski must be mentioned.

Poland having, in consequence of her geographical position, been a frequent object of invasions and one of Europe's constant battlegrounds, there is nothing abnormal in the fact that *military history* should loom comparatively large as a branch of historical learning in Poland. A marked revival of work in that field set in a few years before the War ; it was not unconnected with the preparations for new armed effort. One of the originators of that revival—M. Kukiel, himself afterwards a Polish soldier and a general in the war of 1920—has since added many a page of brilliant writing and sound investigation to the history of Poland's armies, their leaders, and their exploits.

For the purposes of the present survey, it has been thought expedient to emphasize the achievements of historical research centring on problems of Poland ; but there is no lack of studies in foreign history undertaken without reference to Polish affairs, past or present. The admirable monographs of the late Z. Morawski on such subjects from Italian Renascence history as the *Sacco di Roma*, of the life of St. Charles Borromaeus, may be singled out as examples of such work : the author had had a predecessor in K. Chłędowski, whose entertaining volumes on the life of Italian courts and cities in the early modern era had been translated into several languages.

In a field very remote from the Italian mother-soil of European civilization, but related more nearly to the historical destinies of Poland, meritorious work has been done by J. Kucharzewski in the large volumes of his book *From the White Tsardom to the Red*, in which he traces the evolutionary connections between the old Russia of the Tsars and the Russia of the Soviets.

## 23

The *history of literature*, when it endeavours to present the development of letters in connected fashion, necessarily is a branch of general history, and there are some literary historians in whose minds interest in this " organic " aspect of the subject predominates over the fascination of individual great writers and their works. Among writers of Polish literary history, this type is represented most eminently by the venerable figure of Alexander Brückner, who, after forty years of work as Professor of Slavonic languages and literatures in the University of Berlin, does not cease to surprise his admirers, in his advanced old age, by volume after volume of new work on a large scale. The wonderfully prolific labours of Brückner's long life have thrown light over whole periods of Polish literature which were largely obscure before him—particularly the Middle Ages, the period of the Reformation, and the Baroque era. Besides a multitude of valuable monographs, he wrote the entire history of Polish literature in several different version, both in Polish and German; and in recent years he gathered up an enormous mass of accumulated knowledge of detail in a three-volume *History of Polish Civilization*. This truly monumental work, as well as Brückner's two-volume *Etymological Dictionary of the Polish Language*—the first of its kind—will no doubt for a long time occupy in Polish scholarship a position analogous to the late F. J. Furnivall's voluminous labours in the Early English field.

The unique figure of Brückner—although followed by a number of younger workers, who are elaborating suggestions of his—stands somewhat apart from the main stream of Polish literary studies.

In the intellectual centres of the country itself the great Histories of Polish literature by Professor St. Tarnowski (for many years President of the Polish Academy at Cracow) and Professor P. Chmielowski of Warsaw (later at Lwów), representing in many ways opposite points of view, divided the field between them for a generation. Tarnowski was succeeded at Cracow by I. Chrzanowski, who became the head of a great school : most of Poland's Professors of Literature in our days are pupils of his. If any common feature can be discerned as predominant in the labours of all the numerous younger scholars in the field, it is perhaps a tendency—appropriate to the new era of Poland's existence—to put less emphasis on the importance of Poland's great poetry as a national gospel in tragic times, and more on its values as high literary art, while at the same time stressing the connection with the large European movements of literary evolution. To single out only two names among many, on account of work accessible in foreign languages, it is in this new and more international spirit that the great things in Polish literature have recently been presented by Professor J. Kleiner in

German (in Walzel's *Handbuch der Literaturwissenschaft*) and by Professor. J. Krzyżanowski in English (*Polish Romantic Literature*, London : Allen & Unwin, 1931). Both were preceded in this manner of treatment by distinguished Cracow teachers who showed a truly " international mind " in their research work— Professor M. Zdziechowski, who is the author of a monumental work on religious currents in nineteenth-century European literature, and Professor St. Windakiewicz, who did more spade-work towards the ascertainment of foreign elements and in-fluences in Polish literature than anybody now alive. To-day it is gratifying to observe that the international spirit of such Polish scholars is meeting with worthy response in the shape of active interest in Polish literature manifested by foreigners, who by their monographs and translations interpret Poland's literature to other nations—such as Miss Monica M. Gardner in England, Professor G. R. Noyes in America, Dr. Paul Cazin in France, Professor G. Maver in Italy, Professor K. H. Meyer in Germany, Professor J. Horak and others (including a Pole, Professor M. Szyjkowski) at Prague, Professor Benesic in Yugo-slavia, and Professor Chernobayev in Russia.

The transition is natural from foreign studies in Polish to Polish studies in foreign literature. Different from the some-what scanty provision of pre-war time, Polish universities are now fairly well equipped with Chairs of French, German and English Literature ; nor is the traditional interest in Italian neglected by Poland's scholars. In accordance with the dominant note in post-war modern language scholarship, there is a prevailing tendency to extend the study of language and literature to the entire field of the actual life and the national mentality of foreign peoples. An excellent organ for such broad views of the foreign world is provided by the Cracow monthly *The Contem-porary Review* (*Przegląd Współczesny*), most ably edited since 1922 by Professor St. Wędkiewicz, himself one of Poland's leading specialists in Romance languages and literatures.

If books on the wider aspects of the life of foreign nations are now more common in Poland—the present writer's Polish studies of post-war Britain and America belong to that category—strictly literary studies are not neglected either : a large History of English Literature by Professor W.H. Tarnawski is in course of publication, and comparative studies of great international literary movements by Professor Z. Łempicki (*Renascence, Enlightenment, Romanticism*, 1923, in Polish) and W. Fol-kierski (*Entre le classicisme et le romantisme*, Paris 1925, Cham-pion) have supplied ample material for animated discussion.

The recent anniversaries of the deaths of Dante, of St. Francis, of Byron, of Goethe, have been duly honoured by an abundant crop of studies in Polish, the large work on Byron by Professor. A. Tretiak being particularly valuable. Besides, the work of professional university teachers is nobly accompanied by the writings of such distinguished amateurs as Count L. Piniński, a retired statesman, who is the author of valuable studies in Shakespeare, Goethe, Dante, and Marcus Aurelius.

## 24

It may seem strange that the record of recent Polish scholarship in the field of studies in the languages and literatures of Poland's Slavonic neighbours is less impressive than that in western European studies. The cause lies perhaps partly in Poland's historical relations with Russia, which result in an attitude different from that of all the other Slav nations—and partly also in a wider internationalism which looks beyond Slavonic horizons, and which was fostered in the Polish mind during the exile of Poland's *élite* to western Europe after 1831. Thus it happens that modern Polish research has so far not produced anything to parallel the epoch-making survey of Slavonic literary achievement undertaken by Poland's great poet Mickiewicz in his French lectures at Paris in the eighteen-forties. In the Poland of to-day, apart from a remarkable history of Russian literature from the pen of the inexhaustible Brückner, and important earlier studies in Russian and other Slavonic literatures by M. Zdziechowski (now followed in the Russian field by his pupil W. Lednicki), there is little being written to prove any active interest in the literatures of the other Slav nations.

The deficiency is partly made up by a noteworthy record in *linguistic research*. Poland's comparative philologists mostly study the problems of Slavonic languages with remarkable results. In this domain again, as in so many others, Cracow has become an important centre of learning in recent decades : thanks to the labours of the late Professor J. Łoś in the history of the language, of K. Nitsch in the comprehensive exploration of living Polish dialects, and of the late L. Malinowski and his successor Professor J. Rozwadowski in general linguistics, the Cracow Linguistic School has won wide international repute : it counts among its younger representatives one of the best experts in the complicated dialectal geography of Yugoslavia (Dr. M. Małecki), and it has even recently produced a brilliant English treatise on the characteristics of the Chinese language by an

American post-graduate student working at Cracow (Mr. Denzel Carr, 1932).

Warsaw possessed two great teachers of linguistics who had both for years occupied positions of authority in the learned world of Russia : J. Baudouin de Courtenay and W. Porzeziński ; both now dead, they, like the leaders of the Cracow school, had made chiefly the problems of Polish and other Slavonic languages the object of their research. Their colleague and successor, S. Szober is the author of a school text-book of Polish grammar on the lines of modern linguistic science.

Poland's age-long relations—both in the way of warfare and of trade—with the Near East make her a predestined centre of *Oriental studies* ; and in this field also research work at Cracow in particular has lately taken a predominantly linguistic turn, as in Slavonic. Cracow University can boast of possessing, in the person of Professor T. Kowalski, one of the world's leading authorities on the dialects of modern Turkish. The sister university at Lwów counts among its professors an eminent specialist in Mongolian languages—Professor Kotwicz, who spent many years in Russia. It was Lwów also which was the scene of the activities of modern Poland's most eminent Sanskrit scholar, A Gawroński, a general linguist of astounding genius, who unfortunately died young.

*Classical philology*, the common mother of all modern European studies in languages and literature, has a long and distinguished tradition in Polish scholarship. On the eve of the War, it was Professor K. Morawski at Cracow, who was the recognized head of classical studies in Poland. His monumental History of Roman Literature was concluded in the last years of his life, when he was President of the Polish Academy. Since his death, this has been paralleled by equally important works on Greek literature from the pen of his younger colleagues, S. Witkowski and T. Sinko ; elaborate monographs, like those on Plautus by Professor G. Przychocki of Warsaw, and on Epicurus and his Philosophy, by Professor A. Krokiewicz, have not been wanting ; and to a number of brilliant translations of the classics into Polish in recent times—such as the *Aristophanes* of E. Cięglewicz, the versions of the great Greek tragedies by B. Butrymowicz and by the poet Kasprowicz, the *Dialogues* of Plato by W. Witwicki and S. Lisiecki, the *Golden Ass* of Apuleius by E. Jędrkiewicz, the *Odyssey* by the poet J. Wittlin, a new complete *Plautus* by Przychocki—new additions are being made continually, in spite of the decline of classical teaching in secondary schools.

x

It must not pass unmentioned either that Poland lost, only a very few years ago, an eminent classical archæologist in the person of P. Bieńkowski, whose studies on the presentation of barbarian nations in classical sculpture enjoyed a great international reputation ; and that some of her younger specialists in the field of antique history—such as K. Zakrzewski—have shown a great aptitude for treating their subject in a thoroughly modern spirit.

Above all other classical scholars of Poland, there towers, since the death of K. Morawski, the aged figure of Professor T. Zieliński in Warsaw, who only returned to his native country after many years' work in Russia, and whose latest volumes on the classical element in the Christian religion have attracted no less world-wide attention than his older studies on the origin of Greek drama and on the relation of the modern world to antiquity.[1]

In the field of comparative religion, which Zieliński has so boldly entered in his old age, modern Poland has so far possessed only one specialist of distinction—S. Czarnowski, who had attracted attention by his early study of St. Patrick and has since remained the only Polish Celtologist.

### 25

Turning from the humanities to Polish work in *natural science* and *mathematics*, we may begin with *geography*, as being a borderland between the humanities and the sciences.

It was under the difficult conditions of nineteenth-century Russian Poland that one of the most distinguished modern geographers of the country, W. Nałkowski, conceived and developed his theory of Poland as a geographical unit. Among the men of to-day, the leader in Polish geographical research undoubtedly is Professor E. Romer, whose name and person are known in both hemispheres, and whose organizing efforts have resulted in creating a first-rate map-making workshop at Lwów. His late Cracow colleague L. Sawicki had worked with distinction in the same field ; he was also a great traveller in exotic countries (Abyssinia, Siam), and would probably, but for his premature death, have rivalled the glories of such Polish explorers as Sir James Strzelecki in early nineteenth-century Australia, or (more recently) J. Dybowski in the French colonies.

Apart from such world-wide traditions and possibilities, however, it was the obvious and immediate task of Poland's geographers to proceed to the description and mapping-out of the

[1] See, in English, his *Religion of Ancient Greece*, translated by G. R. Noyes (Oxford University Press, 1926).

newly reconstructed State. A number of good maps of Poland in her various aspects have come from Professor Romer's Institute, and a Military Geographical Institute in Warsaw is also busily producing new Ordnance Survey maps of the whole territory of the Republic. A literary corollary to this work is being created by the excellent studies of Polish landscape from the pen of Professor J. Smoleński at Cracow.

Besides the geographers, it is no less evidently incumbent on Poland's mineralogists, geologists, botanists and zoologists to register and describe the natural wealth of Poland. A State Mineralogical and Geological Institute in Warsaw, superintended by Professor J. Morozewicz, is investigating Poland's mineral resources ; the Cracow botanist, W. Szafer, is producing a comprehensive work on the flora of Poland ; and among zoologists, Professor M. Siedlecki of Cracow has accomplished particularly meritorious work towards the proper scientific appreciation of the fauna of the sea along Poland's newly regained coast ; he is Poland's representative on the International Council for Sea Research.

Mention has before been made of the efforts of some Polish scientists to turn certain mountain territories on the southern border, and portions of a large forest in the north-east, into reservations which will serve as natural parks and keep many interesting species of plants and animals intact and safe from extermination. The combination of efficiency and enthusiasm displayed by Professor W. Goetel, of Cracow, in this matter, has earned him well-deserved recognition, and Poland figured prominently at an international Congress for the Protection of Nature held in Paris in 1925.

The attention necessarily paid to tasks connected with Poland's renewed political existence does not, however, interfere with the pursuit of research work of a general nature, especially where a tradition of it is firmly established. The pre-war labours of Professor H. Hoyer and his school at Cracow in the field of comparative anatomy of animals are successfully continued ; those of Professor Kreutz in crystallography have become extended and attract much attention among foreign specialists. Of the great achievements of Polish scientists— such as the late Professor E. Godlewski—in plant physiology, mention has been made before in connection with agriculture. In several fields of applied zoology and botany the Agricultural Schools of Poland can boast of eminent experts—such as the late Professor E. Załęski at Cracow, who was an authority of international repute in the domain of seed culture.

*Mathematics*, like classical philology, can look back on a very old and glorious tradition. The Cracow mathematical school, made famous through the work of Professor S. Zaremba before the War, has continued to develop since, and Professor Rosenblatt is well known on foreign lecture platforms and at international congresses as a representative of it. A distinct school of mathematics has since the War grown up in Warsaw under the guidance of Professor W. Sierpiński ; its special field is mathematical logic, and its importance was recognized by the election of its head to the Presidency of the International Mathematical Association.

In *physics* and *chemistry* it was Cracow again which before the War possessed a perfect galaxy of distinguished research workers. Besides the late K. Olszewski, whose method for the liquefaction of air made him known all over the world, Cracow in the persons of two successive occupants of the Chair of Experimental Physics, Professors A. W. Witkowski and M. Smoluchowski, possessed research workers of high rank, and she still possesses in Professor W. Natanson not only her foremost original thinker in the domain of natural philosophy, but also a writer on scientific subjects whose excellence of style has made him a classic of Polish prose. In physics and physical chemistry, as in mathematics, Warsaw since the War, can claim equal importance with Cracow : two of its Professors, St. Pieńkowski (whose special field is optics) and W. Swiętosławski (who devised a new standard of thermodynamic measurement)— both of them the chiefs of excellently organized laboratories— are well known outside Poland. In astronomy, the prestige of the Cracow chair—whose pre-war occupant, the late M. P. Rudzki, was the author of an important work on geophysics—is well upheld by Professor T. Banachiewicz, whose school has become known by the discovery of two new comets. In chemistry, Cracow now chiefly holds its own through the work of Professor K. Dziewoński and his pupils, which has important bearings on the technology of chemical industries, especially of the rising dye industry of Poland.

With the labours of the Dziewoński School at Cracow, we have reached the border of the vast domain of *applied sciences* and its services to industry. Technical research in Poland is conducted in the laboratories of two large Universities of the Technical Sciences—Warsaw and Lwów—and of the School of Mining Engineers at Cracow ; and the *élite* of technical research workers has been organized in a special academy under the Presidency of Professor M. T. Huber, himself a distinguished expert in technical mechanics. Constant stimulation is being given to technical research by the possession of the industrial area of Silesia, as well as by the development of new industries in other parts of Poland ; and it is perhaps a fit expression of the very active movement in this field as one of the chief characteristics of the new Poland that an eminent specialist in industrial chemistry, Professor Ignatius Mościcki, has risen to the Presidency of the Republic. The large extent which technical studies soon reached in the State, led to the production of a plentiful crop of fundamental text-books, of which Czopowski's *Mechanics*, W. Broniewski's *Metallography*, Z. Straszewicz's *Theory of Motion*, H. Mierzejewski's *Theory of Measurement*, and B. Dobrowolski's monograph on *Ice* are outstanding examples. Into the manifold work on particular problems of the technical sciences—work often subsidized by the industrialists in their own interests—this is not the place to enter : it constitutes—or constituted until the present crisis—an important portion of the total volume of intellectual work in Poland, and although debarred by its nature from spectacular popularity, it meant a worthy continuation, under new and more hopeful conditions, of the distinguished work done by Polish engineers in foreign service, especially in Russia, during the nineteenth century. Practical results of such work in the form of inventions are not uncommon, and show a marked increase ; the agenda of the Patent Office of the Republic has developed by leaps and bounds during the few years of its existence, and more would no doubt have been heard of Polish inventions abroad if many of them had not remained unexploited through lack of capital. But in some cases even now, the eminent abilities of Poles for constructive technical work win recognition abroad. The Chair of Aerodynamics in the University of Ann Arbor (Michigan) is held by a Pole, Professor Pawłowski, who is one of the few authorities in this field throughout the world.

Poland herself, it may be added, possesses a well-organized Institute of Aerodynamics in Warsaw, conducted by Professor C. Witoszyński and provided with a fine building in 1927. The notable victory of the Polish airman, Lieutenant Żwirko, in the Central Europe Challenge Flight of 1932 was a triumph not only for the victorious airman's own personal courage, skill and endurance, but also of Polish technical achievement, since the machine used on the occasion had been built by the students of the Engineering College in Warsaw. This success was unfortunately followed within a very few days by the death of the victorious airman and of the constructor of his machine,

Engineer Wigura, through an accident in Silesia, where they were caught in a storm in their way to Prague.

## 26

*Medicine* in Poland had had, like other branches of learning, its most important centre at Cracow. The Cracow Medical Schools were famous even in the early centuries of the University's existence : the glory of some of Cracow's medical teachers in those ages has recently been revived by the French historical writings of Dr. Bugiel, a Polish doctor resident in Paris. From among the distinguished research workers who occupied Chairs in the Cracow Faculty of Medicine immediately before the War Cracow lost in the early years of the new Poland one of the most eminent : Professor N. Cybulski, a physiologist who had chiefly become known through his invention of an instrument for the measurement and registration of the movements of the heart; the distinguished anatomist K. Kostanecki—now President of the Polish Academy —is happily still in the ranks of Cracow's active university teachers. The occupant of the Chair of Chemistry in the Medical Faculty of Cracow, Professor L. Marchlewski, had before the War attracted much notice abroad by the discovery of the chemical identity of chlorophyll in plants with the pigment of the human blood ; he has since conducted no less important research work on vitamins. It was at Cracow also that Professor E. Godlewski, jun., established an international reputation for himself by his studies in the theory of heredity, summed up in an elaborate German work. A great bacteriological album by the Cracow Professor, J. Nowak (who was to become Prime Minister of the new Poland) was also published in Germany. At the same time, publishing activities on a large scale in Polish, to provide Poland's medical students with manuals of the different subjects of their studies, were undertaken by the Polish Academy ; Cybulski's *Physiology*, and Bochenek and Ciechanowski's *Anatomy*, both published before the War, have since been followed by an excellent manual of *Gynæcology* from the hand of the late Professor A. Rosner, and by a voluminous *General Pathology*, begun by the late Professor K. Klecki. The *Histology* of Professor W. Szymanowicz of Lwów, besides its Polish issues, has run into six editions in German, and has also been translated into English and Italian ; The *Roentgenological Dentistry* of Professor W. Cieszyński (Lwów) was published in German, and an elaborate Polish *Neurology* by Professor W. Dzierżyński was the fruit of many years' work in Russia. The standard handbook of *Forensic Medicine* by Professor L.

Wachholz, the master of all Polish specialists in the field, has run into several new editions since the creation of three new Medical Faculties in the free Poland.

Warsaw before the War had no Polish Medical Faculty of its own ; but hard-working doctors in private practice and in hospital did what they could to maintain the honourable tradition of medical research in that part of the country. To quote but one example, it was in the Russian sector of Poland that Dr. Sokołowski deposited the labours of a lifetime on the subject of tuberculosis in a voluminous work.

When Warsaw, Poznań and Wilno received their Polish Universities after the War, the theoretical chairs had indeed to be filled mostly with lecturers called in from Cracow ; but the clinical chairs could largely be manned with eminent local doctors, with the addition of a few who came back to their native country rom university posts in Russia. It was not to Russia only, but to some western countries that Poland had given distinguished medical research workers ; the Chair of Anatomy at Geneva was occupied for many years by a Pole, Professor Z. Laskowski ; French medical science possessed in Dr. J. Babiński a leading authority on nervous diseases, and it has in Dr. Kopaczewski a prominent specialist in an important field of recent medical research, viz., the colloid chemistry of the blood.

Some of these Polish occupants of medical chairs abroad came back to Poland : Professor Jurasz, one of the creators of modern laryngology, exchanged his chair at Heidelberg for one at Lwów and afterwards at Poznań ; Professor J. Szymański, the present chief of the Eye Clinic at Wilno (for a time Chairman of the Upper House of Parliament) won his reputation as an oculist in pre-war days at Santiago de Chile.

The rebirth of the Polish State created special tasks for medicine, as it did for other sciences. Polish medicine, as mentioned in a former chapter, had to fight its own battle on behalf of the new Poland, not only by serving the Army in its wars, but above all, by defending Poland—and all civilized Europe together with her—from an invasion of epidemics which had accompanied the invading Red Army in 1920. This defence, with some assistance from the League of Nations, was largely accomplished by the organizing talent and unstinted effort of Professor E. Godlewski of Cracow (mentioned above as a research worker of merit). His work as General Commissioner for the fight against epidemics in 1920 and 1921 was continued, in peace-time, by his prominent participation in the development of the Public Health Service of Poland. It is mainly to his energies and devotion that the community is indebted for two excellently conducted large sanatoria for children, one for tuberculous ones at Zakopane, and one for trachomatic ones near Cracow, both of them reflecting high credit on the University of Cracow, under whose permanent protection they are placed.

If Professor Godlewski, and many other leaders of medical study in Poland besides him, had to devote a large amount of energy to the social aspects of medicine in the new State, they did not become so absorbed in them as to lose sight entirely of their several domains of research work. On the contrary, many a valuable chapter has been added since the War to Poland's record of medical research. To quote a few instances, we may begin with the name of Dr. Casimir Funk, who has become known all over the world as the creator of the theory of vitamins (now so universally popular), and who is a Pole by birth. Among Poles occupying medical chairs in Poland's Universities, we may single out Professor K. Lewkowicz of Cracow, who has become well-known abroad as the inventor of a new surgical treatment of meningitis ; the late Professor K. Rzętkowski in Warsaw, who was widely known for his investigations of residuous nitrogen in the blood and its importance for various diseases ; the late Professor J. Hornowski, in Warsaw, who was the author of a new classification of tumours ; Dr. Hirschfeld and his wife in Warsaw, who have investigated the connections between race and the qualities of the blood and obtained results of importance for anthropology and for forensic medicine ; and the late Professor Klecki at Cracow, who also specialized in investigations of the blood, which threw important light on some physiological problems. Dr. M. Rose of Cracow (now at Wilno) did valuable work concerning the structure of the human brain, which won for him even a post in the Institute of Brain Research in Berlin. Professor Karaffa-Korbutt at Wilno (formerly at St. Petersburg), a distinguished specialist in hygiene, is the author of a unique, comprehensive study of the hygiene of human work. The investigations of Professor R. Weigl at Lwów on the subject of spotted fever deserve particular mention ; being concerned with a scourge which threatened to devastate the whole population of Poland after the Bolshevik War, and which never is quite absent from the Eastern regions, Professor Weigl's researches are of the utmost social importance. They are conducted under difficulties and dangers which make them truly heroic, and the Polish Academy has recently rewarded them with a well-deserved prize.

We will not attempt to penetrate further into the recesses of special research in medicine, which must necessarily remain *terra incognita* to the layman. It must, however, still be added summarily that one great movement in contemporary medicine, viz., the reaction against extreme specialism and the return to the "constitutional" treatment of disease with due regard to the whole personality of the patient, had had its important repercussions in Poland ; it is represented in the theoretical field of anatomy by Professor J. Loth and his school in Warsaw, and it was brilliantly applied in practice by the late Cracow gynæcologist, A. Rosner, who achieved excellent results in the treatment of women's diseases by envisaging in every case, in a truly modern spirit, the entire sexual organization of the sufferer.

To return, in conclusion, to those social aspects of medicine which necessarily claimed such attention in the early years of the new State, it may surely be interpreted as a tribute to Poland's achievements in that field that a Polish public health expert—Dr. Rajchman of Warsaw—occupies a distinguished post on the permanent staff of the League of Nations and has rendered it much useful service on special missions to such distant countries as China and others.

### 27

*Philosophy* claims its traditional place apart and may be fitly considered at the end of our survey.

Polish philosphical thought, as has been mentioned several times before, was in the early nineteenth century powerfully stimulated by the tragic enigma of the nation's disasters and sufferings, and at the same time profoundly influenced by Hegel's philosophy of history, then in the heyday of its European vogue. Shaped by these two factors, there arose a national system of thought which in the hands of Poland's great romantic poets acquired the dignity of a gospel of patriotism ; it has passed into history under the name of "Messianism" from the part of a "Messiah among nations" which it assigns to Poland as suffering for the sins of them all. Among a group of distinguished writers of philosophical prose, who developed more or less "Messianic" conceptions in their works, the figure of August Cieszkowski towers above the rest, both by moral nobility and intellectual power ; his great work *Our Father*, of which the second part only appeared long after his death, well deserves international attention even to-day in the abridged English version in which it appeared recently.[1] Nor must another less

[1] A. Cieszkowski, *The Desire of all Nations*, being an English edition (abridged) of *Our Father*, prepared by W. J. Rose, London, Student Christian Movement Press, 1919.

unambiguous figure pass unmentioned here—that of J. M. Hoene-Wroński, whose voluminous and abstruse writings (mostly in French), dealing with nearly all domains of human thought, are in our days being republished and extolled by a sect of enthusiastic admirers recruited from many countries and united by a belief in Hoene-Wroński as the greatest and most universal of all modern thinkers.[1] Critics have not been wanting who have gone quite as far in the opposite direction and made Wroński appear as little better than a pompous charlatan : he figured in that aspect in his own days in Balzac's novel *La recherche de l'absolu*, and it is in the twilight between the two extreme views that his enigmatic figure still stands in the eyes of unbiassed observers to-day.

It was Wroński who invented the term " Messianism " for his philosophy ; it is, however, not in his personal acceptance of the word, but in the entirely different meaning given to it by the Romantic thinkers and especially the great poets of the nineteenth century that " Polish Messianism " has taken its place in Poland's spiritual history. The noble illusions of the Romantics' philosophy of history have long been superseded, in Poland as well as elsewhere, by the several successive systems of thought which have risen into ascendancy since and been dethroned in their turn. One strange figure among the living, however, must be mentioned as a staunch upholder of the lasting vitality and universal applicability of Polish Romantic philosophy. It is Professor W. Lutosławski who, many years ago, made a name in England by epoch-making studies in Plato. He has not ceased to proclaim, for the last thirty years, the essential truth of Polish Messianic doctrine as interpreted and developed by him, together with another favourite belief of his—of which his Indian studies are the source—viz., the belief in reincarnation. His post-war English books *The World of Souls* (London : 1924, Allen and Unwin) ; *Pre-existence and Reincarnation* (ib. 1928), and *The Knowledge of Reality* (Cambridge University Press, 1930) have reawakened international interest in what is certainly a unique and brilliantly gifted personality.

To pass from this continuator of the Romantic tradition to representatives or more or less contemporary currents in philosophical thought, and to use names which have international currency as symbols, we may say that, while Bergson and William James divided the allegiance of Poland's philosophical youth between them before the War, it is under the names of the

---

[1] See, in particular, F. Warrain : *L'Armature Métaphysique établie d'après la Loi de Création de Hoene-Wroński*, 1925.

late Cardinal Mercier and of Bertrand Russell that we can classify some of the best philosophical efforts in the Poland of to-day. The revaluation of medieval philosophy by the late Cardinal Mercier and his school is receiving important new confirmations from the research work of Father C. Michalski, Professor and recently Rector of the University of Cracow. The lead, on the other hand, given to the development of mathematical logic by the *Principia Mathematica* of pre-war fame has been followed up by Poland's numerous and distinguished mathematical logicians of recent days, whose patriarch, Professor J. Śleszyński at Cracow, died not long ago. It is on the borderland between mathematics, natural philosophy and metaphysical speculation that a former member of this school, Professor L. Chwistek, moves in his interesting work *The Pluralism of Reality*; and it is to the philosophy of Mr. Whitehead that Dr. J. Metallman has devoted an elaborate special study.

Only a few instances of work along the predominant lines of latter-day philosophy could be given here ; it is not possible either to register all the attempts which have been made, under the pressure of practical academic necessities in the new Poland, to garner the harvest of the past in comprehensive work for the use of students. While an admirable but unfortunately unfinished *History of Greek Philosophy* by the late Father S. Pawlicki of Cracow is still unforgotten, it is a brilliant survey of the entire history of philosophy, in two volumes, by Professor W. Tatarkiewicz of Warsaw, which now holds the field as the standard text-book of its subject. Of particular sections of systematic philosophy, *Logic* has received comprehensive treatment in a memorable work by the late W. Biegański (a medical practitioner by profession), *Æsthetics* is the subject of an encyclopædic work by Professor M. Sobeski of Poznań, and a large treatise on *Ethics* became the *magnum opus* of Professor W. Rubczyński of Cracow. It is in accordance with the general temper of our own age that problems of *conduct* have particular prominence in Polish philosophical work to-day ; and in connection with this, certain important achievements in the field of *educational theory* deserve to be mentioned. The modern application of experimental psychology to problems of education had its pioneer in pre-war Poland in the person of J. W. Dawid of Warsaw ; and it was a research worker of Polish nationality, Mademoiselle Joteyko, who (working at Brussels) contributed materially to recent progress in intelligence measurement and educational statistics. The new Polish Republic, at work on the building-up of its own educational system, is eagerly utilizing all foreign experience in the field. The Montessori method, the Dalton Plan, *Gestaltpsychologie*, the doctrines of Claparède, of Dewey, of Kirkpatrick, are all household words among Polish educators to-day ; elaborate works on leading educational tendencies abroad have come from the pens of Dr. H. Rowid and Dr. M. Ziemnowicz at Cracow ; the founder of the first academic laboratory of experimental psychology in Poland, Professor W. Heinrich at Cracow, has lately devoted his energies to the organization and development of a large Educational Institute in the same University, and another institute of the same kind is working at Warsaw. These institutes, together with several periodicals devoted to educational problems, also communicate current foreign educational experience to Polish teachers of all grades. Altogether, there is if anything, perhaps rather a danger of too much readiness to " try out " all new foreign methods on Polish ground, however inapplicable they may be under Polish conditions. But then, as has been stated at the beginning of the present chapter, Poland has begun her renewed free existence in the midst of a world full of educational ferment and teeming with educational experiments.

## 28

Something remains to be said of the forms of organization and the system of international relations in which Polish research work moves and has its being.

Mention has repeatedly been made before in these pages of the Polish Academy at Cracow, as the most authoritative organization for pure research in Poland. Since the War, the Academy, in spite of financial calamities, has never interrupted its large publishing activities (represented by many hundreds of volumes by this time)[1]. This constant continuation of the Academy's work in the difficult post-war times was rendered possible by the fact that generous donors have again made their appearance. Foremost among them, the former Austrian Archduke Charles Stephen Hapsburg—an old friend of the Poles, and now a Polish citizen—must be mentioned as having made the Academy a royal present of part of his estates and forests.

The Academy consists of three sections, devoted to philology and art history, history and philosophy, and mathematics and natural science respectively. A fourth section, devoted to

---

[1] For an account, in English, of the Academy's history, organization, and its various series of research publications see *The Polish Academy of Sciences and Letters*, 1872–1930, published at Cracow in 1930 by the Academy itself, with illustrations.

medical research, has recently been added, replacing a separate Academy of Medicine which existed for a time, and a similar movement towards fusion is afoot with regard to the Academy of Technical Sciences, which still exists. The work of the Polish Academy ranges over the whole of Poland, through the co-operation of the eminent scholars and scientists, who are its elected members, and the collaboration of others who belong to its thirty special " Commissions " for different branches of research. Contact with foreign research work is established through the election of foreign members, and through interchange of publications with other learned research societies all over the world ; and organized research work abroad—particularly in the field of history—is conducted through the agency of two Polish research stations, one in Paris and one in Rome, which are superintended by the Academy.

The reunion and deliverance of Poland undoubtedly gave scope for unhampered expansion of the Academy's activities, especially in certain directions indicated by the needs of the new State. Even before the War, the Academy had undertaken the production of a co-operative work on a large scale— a *Polish Encyclopædia* in systematic arrangement, giving elaborate and authoritative information on all aspects of Poland—historical, literary, economic, social and scientific. A number of volumes of the Encyclopædia had appeared when the War broke out ; some of these have been republished, and others added, in the new era of freedom. The Encyclopædia is to receive a companion in an equally important work of reference —a *Polish Dictionary of National Biography*, which the Academy is at present preparing.

The fact that Cracow, the seat of the Academy, is not the political capital of the new Poland, has given rise to a tendency to place Warsaw institutions on a level with the Cracow Academy in name and dignity. Warsaw has a " Learned Society " of more than a hundred years' standing and of very distinguished traditions ; she has, besides, in the " Mianowski Foundation," an institution for the publication of research work which was created entirely by private initiative under the greatest difficulties, over fifty years ago, and has since published some of the most monumental works of modern Polish scholarship. Besides these Warsaw organizations, there are large and active societies of a similar kind, with a fine record of published work, at Lwów, Poznań, and Wilno, besides minor organizations of merit in such smaller provincial cities as Płock, Toruń, and Przemyśl. Even, however, if the Warsaw Learned Society should in the near future be raised to the rank of an academy (which seems not unlikely), or if some other associations mentioned should receive the same title (which is a more remote contingency), it is highly probable that well-established historical authority will assert itself, and the Polish Academy at Cracow retain a central and supreme position, like the *Académie Française*, among a group of institutions of the same name.

It was the Polish Academy at Cracow which, long before the War, was largely instrumental in promoting wider international contacts for Polish research work, beyond the established relations with German, Austrian, and Russian academic centres. Such wider connections could naturally be much more freely developed under the conditions of regained independence after the War ; but at the same time the links existing before had for the most part been so thoroughly broken by the War itself that large labours towards reconstructing the entire comity of the world's research workers have had to be undertaken. These labours, owing to political antagonisms, have not yet attained complete results ; Poland has had an active part in them. She has a permanent seat in the " International Research Council," created in 1919 at Brussels with the aim of co-ordinating world-wide effort in natural science ; and Polish representatives play a conspicuous part in the activities of the twelve associations devoted to particular subjects, and working under the auspices of the Council : Professor Świętosławski (in chemistry) and Professor Banachiewicz (in astronomy) have undertaken work of international importance on behalf of different of these sub-sections of the Council.

An analogous organ for the no less difficult task of co-ordinating the research work of all civilized nations in the field of the humanities was re-created in 1919 in the shape of the " International Academic Union," likewise residing at Brussels. Here again, Polish representatives have made their mark ; Professor Sternbach of Cracow has renewed his eminent participation in the pre-war international scheme of re-editing the Fathers of the Church, and Professor Michalski has given the initiative for a co-operative collected edition of the works of the chief medieval philosophers.

To the Council and the Union, which are bodies of delegates of the chief learned societies of different countries, there was added, under the auspices of the League of Nations, an organization of wider scope and with an elaborate permanent apparatus of its own—the " Committee of Intellectual Co-operation " in Paris. The University section of that Committee was presided over by two Polish scholars in succession—Professor O. Halecki of Warsaw and Professor W. Folkierski of Cracow.

### 29

An important part of the labours of the Committee of Intellectual Co-operation consists in editorial work on a proposed international bibliography of published research work. Poland's distinct status in the bibliography is, of course, assured, and will contrast favourably with the pre-war situation, when the work of Polish scholars often figured, in international bibliographies, among the work of Germans or Russians. Similarly, at international congresses of research workers in particular fields, there was hardly ever any opportunity, before the War, of asserting the independent part played by Polish research. Since the War, Poland has not only had her separate representation at all such congresses, but that representation has often figured prominently. To quote one instance only : of over one hundred papers read before the World Congress of Geographers at Cairo in 1925, no fewer than twenty-two were by Polish authors. What is more, a number of congresses of great international importance, such as a world congress of chemists, one of botanists, and one of agricultural experts, have already since the War, been held in Warsaw, and the international congress of historians to be held there in 1933 bids fair to become a worthy addition to the series.

Apart from the general organizations of research workers, such as the Polish Academy and other societies mentioned above, Poland now possesses an abundant crop of national associations devoted to special branches of learning ; and almost every such society possesses a periodical as its organ. Some wider fields such as history, philosophy, or the study of Polish literature, are covered by several periodicals each, usually originating in different academic centres. All articles in learned periodicals (and indeed most of the serious Polish contributions to research in book form, as well as the Transactions of learned societies) appear accompanied by summaries (or, as in the case of the Polish Academy, separate *Bulletins*) in one of the principal world languages (French, German or English), so as to make the results of Polish research work accessible to foreign specialists. Some of the perodicals, such as the *Eos* at Lwów (devoted to the classics), or the *Fundamenta Mathematicæ*, or the recent *Archivum Neophilologicum* at Cracow, appear in foreign languages entirely, and have successfully attracted foreign collaboration. Such collaboration also often assumes the form of visits of eminent foreign lecturers to Poland's Universities ; French

Professors have of late been particularly frequent guests in Poland, and the Mathematical School, as well as the School of Political Science in the University of Cracow, have in recent years even had courses of lectures by French visiting Professors for one term in every academic year. Lectures by Polish university teachers in Paris have, for the last ten years, not been uncommon either ; with the neighbouring Republic of Czechoslovakia, and its chief University, Prague, an almost constant exchange of visits of lecturers is now in progress ; and permanent Polish lecturerships have been established in the School of Slavonic Studies of London University, in the Universities of Rome and Brussels.

Of all foreign nations, France has so far shown the greatest interest in maintaining and developing relations with Poland in the field of academic teaching and of research work : not only does she maintain an *Institut Français* for such purposes in Warsaw, but she grants a considerable number of scholarships to Polish University students every year for studies in French seats of learning, and she provides Polish libraries with French learned publications at reduced prices.

Next to France, America must be mentioned as having done much to promote the exchange of ideas between research workers. The Carnegie Endowment has been generously supplying to Poland's libraries, as to those of other European countries, its numerous and valuable publications free of cost. The Rockefeller Foundation has its page of honour in the annals of medical science in Poland, having not only provided books, periodicals, and materials gratuitously to Poland's medical schools in the early post-war years, but also founded a model School of Nursing at Cracow and an Institute of Public Hygiene in Warsaw, and, above all, having helped, by the annual grant of a number of scholarships, to give opportunities for special training abroad to many of Poland's younger research workers in medicine, and, more recently, also in social studies. While the activities of the two great American institutions embrace Poland only as one of the many countries to which they extend their work, a special instrument for the exchange of students and teachers between the United States and Poland has of late years been created in the shape of the Kościuszko Foundation in New York, financed by Americans of Polish origin, subsidized by some generous American friends of Poland, presided over by President H. N. McCracken of Vassar College, and administered with untiring devotion by a Polish-American scholar, Professor Stephen P. Mizwa. Benefiting by assistance from the Foundation, a number of Polish students have by this time spent years in American Universities and usefully supplemented their studies in such subjects as English literature, financial science, banking, engineering, mining, social psychology, and educational method ; a number of American students, on the other hand, have been enabled, by residence in Polish Universities, to become familiar with the language, literature, history and contemporary problems of Poland. The sojourn of Americans in Poland under the auspices of the Foundation has even materialized in such successful literary work as Professor E. P. Kelly's three historical novels centring round old Polish cities (Cracow, Wilno, and Halicz) ; and more such work—in the shape of translations of works on Polish literature into English by American students—is anticipated. It is to such endeavours that we must look for those results in the way of mutual understanding, respect and sympathy, which the exchange and co-ordination of intellectual effort between nations is bound to produce in the long run for the common benefit of humanity.

## CHAPTER IX

# LITERATURE AND ART

## I

EVEN during the century of Poland's eclipse, when the Poles were indulgently smiled at as political Utopians or even condemned as an international nuisance, they never ceased to be held in high regard as a nation producing great poets and artists. It was, in fact, the glamour of high achievement in the sphere of the creative imagination which contributed greatly to the widespread sympathies for the Polish cause in nineteenth-century Europe. And, what seems more to the purpose now, an entirely unique part in modern history was played by literature and art in Poland as constituting, for many years, the mainspring of national vitality in an age of captivity. We have to go back to the inspired books of the prophets of Israel to illustrate that extraordinary phenomenon by an adequate comparison from the annals of humanity's literary experience.

That unique function of literature and art—repeatedly mentioned before in these pages—was entirely the outcome of the peculiar conditions in which the early nineteenth century placed the Polish nation. During the preceding centuries, Poland, with regard to the development of literature and the other arts, and of their *rôle* in national life, had more or less followed the course of other European communities. Quite as Polish architecture, whose historical pageant we behold in the churches and palaces of Cracow, Warsaw, and Wilno, had passed through the normal periods of Romanesque, Gothic, Renascence, Baroque and Rococo, so in literature, a glorious outburst of creative energies in poetry and prose under the double stimulus of Humanism and the Reformation in the sixteenth century had, in the seventeenth, been duly followed by the passionate exuberance and amazing oddities of Baroque writing (largely to be rediscovered, in its peculiar excellence, only in our own days), and these again had been replaced, in the eighteenth, by the chastened harmonies and the dry light of the era of rationalism.

Eminent and original as had been the creative record of some of the literary masters of these earlier epochs—such as especially the poet *J. Kochanowski* and the preacher *P. Skarga* in the sixteenth century ; close as was the union, in the eighteenth, between its best literature and noble efforts at social and moral reform, in the activities of such men as *I. Krasicki* the satirist and *S. Staszic* the political thinker : yet the time when a powerful international current of literary ideas was to be transformed into something completely distinct, supremely important and transcendently beautiful in its Polish expression, only came with the advent of Romanticism in the first quarter of the nineteenth century. It was under the combined influence of the new Romantic enthusiasm for national elements in art, and of the mournful speculation of exiles on the deeper meaning of the nation's disasters, that the works of Poland's three greatest poets, *A. Mickiewicz, J. Słowacki* and *Z. Krasiński* were created and became not only the perennial masterpieces of Polish literature, but also the canonical books of a national gospel. Not only did they enshrine the tortured people's inmost aspirations in forms of language which in themselves constituted an indestructible political palladium against all attempts at suppressing nationality by foreign education and speech ; but, by upholding belief in a divine aim to be attained through Poland's sufferings for the common good of all humanity, they inspired the flower of the nation with that readiness for disinterested sacrifice and that capacity for heroic effort which were again and again to surprise the very foes of Poland down to our own days. Not for nothing has the word for " prophet " —*wieszcz*—like the Latin *vates*, ever since become the chosen appellation in Poland of those three greatest poets, and of them only.

2

The great poet-prophets of the Romantic era did not stand alone in their wonderful historical function : besides a number of poetic satellites—some of them brilliant—they are accompanied by the genius of *Chopin*, whose immortal music, instinct with Polish folk-song and dance-tune and changing them into " something rich and strange," bears noble witness not only to the unbreakable strength of national tradition, but also to a high sense of moral dignity born out of the midst of helpless degradation and suffering. The same moral elevation is imparted to heartrending scenes of ruin and disaster from the desperate national rising of 1863 by the hand of *A. Grottger*,

the great elegiac poet among Poland's masters of the brush and
pencil, comparable to Goya in his portrayal of the horrors and
pathos of partisan warfare.

But other times were coming, and it seemed, in the decades
after 1863, as if literature and art were going to yield pride of
place in national estimation to economic and social activities.
Yet so strong is the established sense of the importance of
literature, that even the new social and moral doctrines, arising
out of industrial progress and scientific discovery, find their
most authoritative expression in Poland in the widely read
novels and popular *Weekly Chronicles* of *B. Prus* and in the
lofty, intellectual poetry of *A. Asnyk*. And in the very middle
of the period of realism and of addiction to the positive tasks
of the present, the stupendous genius of *H. Sienkiewicz* suddenly
takes flight into the Romantic past and in the great *Trilogy*
of historical novels on Poland's seventeenth-century wars
(*With Fire and Sword, The Flood, The Little Knight*) stirs the
hearts of his countrymen by images of heroism victorious against
overwhelming odds, and of political prestige founded on the
sense of a civilizing mission in eastern Europe. Following up
this great national success with the world-wide one of *Quo Vadis ?*
(which won him the Nobel Prize), Sienkiewicz became, in his
later years, quite as much of a recognized spokesman of the
nation as Mickiewicz had been half a century before. And as
the Romantic poets appear side by side with Chopin, so Sienkiewicz' genius and national leadership are paralleled in the
field of another art by his contemporary, Poland's greatest
painter *J. Matejko*, who, by his huge canvases of memorable
scenes from Polish history, likewise lifted the national imagination out of the baseness of present servitude to the heights of
ancient splendour, and thereby once more inspired the nation
with life-giving dignity and self-confidence.

To these names of great artists who were all great spiritual
leaders of the nation, one other must be added which illustrates
the continued working of Polish literature and art as a mainspring of national energy, even within the memory of living
generations. The Cracow painter and poet, *St. Wyspiański*—
who died at the age of thirty-eight in 1907—in his powerful verse-
plays once more shook the national consciousness out of the
torpor of acquiescence in a debased existence, and while thundering against the " tyranny " of the Romantic poets' word,
himself conjured into the words of his poetry a compelling
vision of coming rebirth into freedom through mortal struggle,
and an unshaken faith in the ultimate triumph of spiritual

forces over the brute reign of material power. Secure for ever now in his historical position of the last one among enslaved Poland's poet-kings, he did not live to see the day when an inspired musician was to rule a redelivered Poland as Prime Minister ; but it is safe to say that he would not have found the spectacle either strange or unworthy.

### 3

In spite of the symbolism of *Paderewski's* tenure of highest office in the new Polish State, it might well have seemed assured that from the day of political resurrection the glories of literature and art as transcendent national powers were necessarily gone for ever. In fact, it might have been interpreted as another and more pathetically potent symbolism of events that in the very beginnings of Poland's renewed existence the greatest lights of pre-war Polish literature quickly went out one after another. The great heart of *Sienkiewicz* broke in the midst of his nation's war-time miseries, before liberty was regained at their cost. The second Nobel Prize winner whom Poland produced, *W. S. Reymont*, having completed before the War his *magnum opus*, the four-volume prose epic *The Peasants*, added only some less significant work to his record after the War, and died before a decade of Poland's new freedom was out. Equal to him in importance, and much more popular among the younger generation, *S. Żeromski*, had voiced in his pre-war novels, with piercing lyrical intensity, all the pain and pathos of Poland's captive existence : the same tragic pessimism pervaded his pictures of futile if self-sacrificing modern attempts at social improvement and redress (as in his first masterly novel, *Homeless People*) and of the desperate armed struggles for national independence in the earlier nineteenth century—as in his *magnum opus*, the three-volume novel *Ashes*, presenting the pageant of Poland's share in the Napoleonic wars. With all the pessimism inherent in his personal outlook, Żeromski yet had, even before the War, given comfort to the national consciousness by depicting (on the ground of his own recollections) the fruitlessness of all attempts of foreign educators to uproot Polish tradition in the souls of youth (*Labours of Sisyphus*), nay, the ultimate, instinctive recovery of individual victims of the system from seemingly complete Russification (*The Charm of Life*). Having become, with all the bitterness of his tragic stories, the idol of Poland's youth, Żeromski lived on during the first few difficult years of the new Poland, and again oscillated, in his post-war work, between exultation in the glory of regained liberty—especially of regained access to the sea (voiced in his cycle of historical sketches, *The Wind from the Sea*)—and equally passionate expression of the inevitable disillusionment which attends the realization of cherished ideals (in his famous novel of early post-war Poland entitled *Before Spring Comes*). Being indeed much more intimately in touch with the mentality of post-war Poland than his more classic contemporary Reymont, Żeromski also died all too soon—in 1924, within a few days of the other great master. Last of all, *J. Kasprowicz*, the most powerful of modern Poland's lyric poets, having increased his rich gift to Polish letters by two of his most inspired volumes of song during the War and since, was likewise taken away out of the midst of a generation of younger poets who almost all looked up to him as their leader and master.

The reason why the genius of Kasprowicz, in particular, seemed a lode-star to the young poets of the new post-war era, was that he had risen, in his mature poetry, above preoccupation with the earthly joys and sorrows, whether of personality or nationality, into the realm of absolute values and eternal mysteries. In some of his noblest pre-war poems he had struggled, like the greatest poet-thinkers of all ages, with the problem of Evil and the problem of God ; in what is perhaps his crowning achievement—the lyric cycle *The Book of the Poor*, published in full War time, he had—not unlike Wordsworth —found refuge from the horror of world convulsions in the healing contact with Nature in her everyday mood on the familiar mountain-side ; and through the enchanting melody of his last songs (*My World*, 1926), the calm of acquiescence in a divine world-order was breathed from the heart of a poet actually in the grip of lingering mortal disease. Such philosophic universality of poetical inspiration had been given only to few modern lyrists of Poland. Two leaders of an " emancipation of personality " proclaimed by a Cracow group of writers at the turn of the century, survived indeed into the new days in the persons of *K. Tetmajer* and *St. Przybyszewski*, but the creative strength of both had been exhausted long before the death of the later and the living death of the former. The only poet of the older generation who lives on in undiminished productive power, *Leopold Staff*, had certainly also been a model, to his younger followers, of inspiration by personal emotion, and of deep and large humanity ; but the exquisite poetic workmanship which makes him the recognized master of lyrical form in the Polish literature of to-day, does not go together with the mighty sweep of intellectual fervour which had marked Kasprowicz ; and Staff himself, in fact, treads in the footsteps of Kasprowicz' passionate metaphysical meditations in his recent fine volume of religious musings in verse entitled *The Eye of the Needle*.

### 4

Such were those whose recent memory or surviving creative power summoned *the young poets of the new Poland* to gather round the standard of a great poetical tradition. Some of them, following the call, sought for inspiration in the revival of one component factor of the great Romantic fabric of a hundred years ago—viz., of its folklore element. *E. Zegadłowicz* became the head of a poetic school centring—bodily and literally—round the *Beskid* hills in the south-west of Poland, with their varied charms of idyllic scenery and their rich store of popular legend and custom. In deliberate opposition to the mechanized civilization of the cities, these poets extol the wisdom which has its source in country nature and country life. They look for their material to the stories told by pedlars and village artisans, and for form to the songs of the people. But a refinement originating in literary culture transforms these popular crudities into somewhat hybrid poetical products, which occasionally trespass into affectation.

Another group of poets, the *expressionists of Poznań* in former Prussian Poland, also professed to be harking back to old Romantic slogans, but were really influenced by contemporary German literary currents, through the mediation of the veteran *Przybyszewski*, who in his stormy youth abroad had been closely associated with German and Scandinavian " moderns." The existence of the Poznań group was not of long duration ; but one rather isolated member of it, *St. Bąkowski*, continued to produce poetry or religious inspiration, which, in the quiet intensity of its thought and feeling, certainly makes us think of a modern German master of the religious lyric— Rainer Maria Rilke.

If German influence, in spite of political severance, was marked here, it was Italian influence of pre-war date which dominated the somewhat belated but clamorous doings of Poland's "futurists," who followed in the wake of Marinetti's revolt against established verse form, and even against the grammar, spelling and vocabulary of tradition. It was at the very seat of old traditions in Poland—in the historical city of Cracow—that the young futurist group noisily displayed its radical programme for a few short post-war years. Their radicalism, in some

cases, extended into the social and political field under the
influence of such poetic revolutionaries of Soviet Russia as the
late S. Mayakovsky. The group even received its own theory
of poetry at the hands of one of its most active members,
*T. Peiper*. Futurism has survived only in the chastened and
subdued form of *vers libre* and of a new boldness of metaphor
and expression in the writings of some poets not otherwise
connected with it, such as *J. A. Gałuszka* of Cracow.

A central place—not only geographically, by virtue of its
location in the capital, but also morally, by the greater permanence of its achievement—is held in contemporary Polish
poetry by a Warsaw group of poets which consolidated in the
later years of the World War, and afterwards became identified
with a periodical called *Scamander*. The outstanding talent
among this group is *J. Tuwim*. While socially a revolutionary
in many of his utterances, and sometimes even emulating the
formal extravagances of Mayakovsky—he has at the same time,
shown a deep sense of the value of his historical inheritance as
a Polish poet, and has recently manifested this in a volume
dedicated, by its very title, to the sweetness of sixteenth-century
Polish poetical speech (*Rzecz czarnoleska*). And while re-
echoing the pulse of modern urban and industrial civilization in
some of the *tours de force* of his poetry, Tuwim has also proved
capable of ecstatic absorption in the beauty of Nature and of
rapturous meditation on the mysteries of the Divine. If anybody, it is he who may be singled out as a leading figure among
the Polish poets of our generation. Of his companions in the
Warsaw centre, *B. Leśmian*, who set the pace for them all by a
volume of exquisite lyrics in 1920, has become silent too soon ;
the noble inspiration of *J. Lechoń* is too fitful and too scanty
in volume to secure for him the highest rank ; *A. Słonimski*,
certainly a most gifted lyrist, is carried by his temperament into
the domain of journalism, which he cultivates with rare distinction indeed, but at the expense of the concentration required
for high poetry ; *K. Wierzyński*, at his best, so far, in a volume
entitled *Olympian Laurels*, which celebrates the glories of modern
sport, has not yet gone beyond a somewhat narrow range of
enthusiasm over the physical beauty and richness of life ; and
*J. Iwaszkiewicz* dangerously borders on *préciosité* in his devotion
to elaborate and complex forms of versification ; too much
attachment to the *beau geste* of style also spoils his novels.

To these names, recent years have added a number of others,
not a few of them coupled with works of great promise. Of
writing lyrical verse in Poland, in fact, there seems to be no

end, even in these hard and difficult days of economic and political realities. It would not serve any useful purpose to select even a few of those newer names for mention in the present survey ; but a word must yet be added on the *poetesses* of modern Poland. In *M. Konopnicka*, the era of captivity had produced a melodious and warm-hearted singer only inferior to the very greatest among men poets ; and some other women, mostly, alas, cut off in their prime, like *K. Zawistowska, B. Ostrowska, M. Grossek-Korycka*, had constituted a worthy sequel. In our own days, *Miss J. K. Iłłakowicz*, wide in range, deeply human in feeling, almost classically clear and simple in expression, and enchanting in the straightforwardness of her melody, stands easily supreme among women poets, and equals the best among the men. The gift of melodious sweetness is possessed also by the more subtle, delicate, and strictly feminine talent of *M. Pawlikowska*, whose charming poetical filigree work nowhere approaches the " grand manner," successfully attempted by Miss Iłłakowicz in some of her utterances on important events in national life, or on the perennial beauties of forest and field.

## 5

In the domain of *prose fiction*, as in that of poetry, the memory of great writers recently dead hung like a cloud over the efforts of the younger generation ; and here again, literature, under the new conditions of regained political freedom, found its traditional occupation gone—the occupation, that is, of comforting and upholding the spirit of an enslaved people. The energies of some of the best and most active personalities, which, in the nineteenth century, had often of necessity flowed into channels of literary expression, now found an outlet in direct social action. In spite of the changed situation, however, the number of writers in the new Poland is not at all smaller than before, and fiction is represented in their output quite as abundantly as lyrical poetry. But a resolute sense of direction and definite aim is lacking even in writers who live on into the new period with a respectable record of pre-war production to their credit. Sometimes, their powers even seem temporarily paralysed by the great change.

The most significant example of this kind is that of *W. Berent*, one of the outstanding masters of Polish prose fiction in our century. Having made a name before the War by some short novels full of penetrating insight into current changes of social mentality, he found detachment enough in himself, in full War

time, to produce a most lifelike vision of medieval civilization
in his most elaborate and fascinating work, *Living Stones*.
But in the new Poland, he lapsed into a long silence ; this was
broken only after more than ten years by the beginnings of a
new large-scale production—half novel, half historical study—
entitled *The Sword and the Spirit*, and presenting, in a highly
original light, the effects on Poland's intellectual life of the
new contacts with old western European culture which were
produced by the turmoil of the Napoleonic Wars and the knight-
errantry of exiled Polish soldiers.

More aged representatives of the pre-war literary tradition
are not, indeed, silenced by the unfamiliarity of the new conditions, but are not stirred by them, either, to move beyond their
accustomed lines. The veteran conspirator and long-term
Siberian exile *W. Sieroszewski* continues to draw upon recollections of life among the Far Eastern races for vivid exotic stories ;
he does not suceed in an ambitious attempt at historical fiction.
Another veteran writer with a well-established literary physiognomy of his own, *J. Weyssenhoff* (who died in 1932) likewise
never ceased to move in the invariable *milieu* of his stories—
the life of the landed aristocracy and gentry, mainly in Poland's
eastern border provinces, of whose landscape he has given
incomparable descriptions (*The Sable and the Girl*). Constitutionally a conservative, Weyssenhoff was under no delusion
as to the seeds of decay inherent in all the old-world charm of
palace and manor. A more idealized picture of this dying
world and of its importance for the Polish tradition on the
eastern border is drawn in the numerous novels of the venerable
*Mary Rodziewicz*, which combine attachment to old chivalrous
ideals with a seasoned art of story-telling. In providing a whole
generation with novels always interesting yet never deviating
from high moral standards, she has worthily followed in the
footsteps of the greatest Polish woman novelist of the period
of realism, *Mme. E. Orzeszko*, whose favourite sphere had also
been the life of the Polish country gentry on the eastern border.

Among younger writers, some owe the very awakening of
their talent to the upheavals of War time, but afterwards follow,
with little variation, this or that well-worn path. An eminent
instance is supplied by Poland's foremost woman novelist of
the new period, *Mme. Kossak-Szczucka*. Having lived through
the horrors of rural Bolshevism on the Russian border in 1917–
19, she related her experiences with great literary power in
a book of memoirs called *Blaze* (*Pooga*), which set the fashion
for a series of similar autobiographical works, some of them

equal to hers in talent. After this first success, she became
a novelist, and in the best of her latter-day works, has deliberately
resumed the great Sienkiewicz tradition, even in her choice of
subjects for historical novels—one from Poland's seventeenth-
century wars, and one from the remote Middle Ages ; occasionally rising to the height of Sienkiewicz in historical intuition,
she remains his inferior in force of invention. But she has
recently opened up an unworked mine of literary themes in the
shape of the historical traditions of *Silesia*, the province in
which she has made her new home. She has thus joined the
ranks of the " regionalists," who try to add life and colour
to their productions by drawing on the peculiarities, customs,
and traditions of particular provinces. In Polish literature, a
great regionalist had arisen in pre-war days in *W. Orkan* (pre-
maturely dead since) who had made the dire poverty of mountain
villages in the south-west his chosen subject. Since the War,
the most notable fact in this domain has been the appearance
of Polish Silesia among the provinces with a literary tradition
of their own : in *G. Morcinek*, the author of pathetic stories
from the hard existence of coal-miners, Silesia has her own
laureate now.

Another writer for whose career, as for that of Mme. Szczucka's,
War-time experiences meant the starting-point, is *F. Goetel*,
now the President of the Polish P.E.N. Club. He turned his
Russian captivity in Turkestan to good account in a number
of vivid stories placed in that strange old land. But after
these, neither his experiments in a new form of fiction (*From
Day to Day*), nor his literary exploitation of further travels
(Egypt, Iceland, India) seem as yet to give evidence of settled
artistic purpose.

Goetel's reputation, although international by this time,
was preceded and far surpassed by the quick and cosmopolitan
fame of *F. Ossendowski's* sensational accounts of wanderings
and adventures in Mongolia and elsewhere. Their world-
wide success is not likely to be of long duration. Neither is
the purely domestic popularity of some striking " War books "
in the manner of the German Remarque, written with precocious
talent by the two young writers, *J. Kossowski* and *T. Kudliński*,
but not followed up by greater achievement. A novelist of
longer experience and more assured literary position, *A. Strug*,
who had begun his career by a story illustrating the revolutionary ferment in Russian Poland about 1905, has since the
War tried his hand on subjects from the immediate war-time
and post-war experience of his nation (including captivity and

exile in Russia), but has not risen above somewhat crude melodrama in his manner.

A phenomenon calling for deeper reflection is constituted by the career of *J. Kaden-Bandrowski*, whose early works were likewise rooted in war experience. His war novels (containing thinly disguised portraits of historical figures) were surpassed in range and power by a trilogy of social stories giving a panorama of conditions in the coal-mining district of former Russian Poland : the cycle may be described as a Polish counterpart of Zola's *Germinal*, the analogy extending even to such less pleasing features as unstinting realism in the presentation of sordid details, and unmitigated pessimism of the author's outlook both upon social relations and individual character. A strange contrast to *Black Wings* (such is the suggestive title of the colliery series) is formed by a group of Bandrowski's books which embody reminiscences of his childhood and youth. Beginning with *The City of my Mother*, they have won the hearts of a large number of readers by their delicacy of touch and tenderness of sentiment, which sometimes even fade into an allusiveness almost too subtle for the average public. In this manner of his—diametrically opposed to that of *Black Wings*—Bandrowski approaches his predecessor *T. Rittner*, a writer of great charm, who died while still young, leaving behind a few stories and plays of the same allusive, reflective and sensitive nature, in Polish and German. As for Bandrowski himself, he has lately, like many gifted younger writers, become of necessity absorbed in journalism, and his more recent books also bear the journalistic stamp.

Side by side with Bandrowski, it is fit to mention *Z. Nałkowska*, whose rank among Polish lady novelists is founded partly on pre-war achievements ; but she has succeeded in retaining popularity among the contemporary generation. Her novels, even when drawing on post-war life for their material, breathe a pre-war air of refined psychological analysis together with a certain relativist scepticism. Only in some of her quite recent work—a volume of novels from prison life and a play on a man's return from prison (which was produced with success in England) do we see her productive inspiration animated by a deeper faith in ideas of social reform. With her undiminished feminine sensitiveness to world-wide currents in literary life she remains a model representative of catholicity of taste and cosmopolitan breadth of culture in the Polish literature of to-day. That element of literary culture is only present in the form of technical skill in the glibly-told and well-constructed novels of *W. Perzyński* (recently dead), who both as novelist and playwright was for decades the typical exponent of the average life and average mentality of Warsaw ; his work will probably appear more interesting to sociologists than to literary historians in the future.

We are transferred to an entirely different atmosphere in the books of one of the most prominent among the youngest group of novelists, *J. Wiktor*. He began his career by stories of animals. In this domain he had had a great predecessor in *A. Dygasiński*, whose prose epic of wild animal life in the Polish countryside, entitled *The Feast of Life* (1902), is now recognized as a landmark in modern Polish literature. Wiktor wrote unpretentious stories of domestic animals—particularly dogs—with charming insight and in a spirit of almost Franciscan sympathy. The same sympathy was manifested with equal intensity on a higher level, when the author next passed to literary pictures of the life of the poor in the cities. His own experience embracing the " lower depths " of social life both of the Polish towns and of the centres of Polish emigrants in search of work in France, he reproduces what he has seen with a noble humanity which does him honour, and with a simple faithfulness to fact which is far from the deliberate squalor of the late " naturalist school " and thereby all the more deeply moving in its appeal. Wiktor's early masterpiece *The Rainbow above the Heart* won him a well-deserved literary prize.

Side by side with him, a woman writer has of late years quickly risen into eminence among the group of younger lady novelists. Her name is *M. Dąbrowska*. Having made a mark by sketches of farm servants and delightful pictures of animal life in the farmyard from the perspective of a childhood spent in a country house, she has since embarked on a more ambitious undertaking—the life history of a married woman—which has revealed her as possessed of masterly psychological penetration and a life-giving realistic touch in the treatment of the most common details. (*Nights and Days*.)

If any defect may be noticed in the unfolding biographical epic of Dąbrowska's, it is the scarcity of humorous relief. A gift for *humour* had been one of the outstanding features of the two great masters of realism in the Polish novel : *Sienkiewicz* (in whose great historical trilogy it had inspired the figure of Zagłoba, the Polish Falstaff) and *Prus* (whose novels and short stories of Warsaw life in the second half of the nineteenth century abound with humorous traits). A humorist *par excellence* arose among the later pre-war generation in the person of *K. Makuszyński*, but his recent works suffer from monotonous repetition and an overdose of sentiment. He has, however, struck a new and very happy vein in writing excellent humorous books for children—a category of literature in which Poland was none too rich before him.

Post-war Poland has eminently witty satirists in verse and prose ; the humorous essay is being cultivated with conspicuous success by *Z. Nowakowski* (until recently a distinguished actor and theatrical manager). Nowakowski has also made a mark by a capital novel of schoolboy life, *The Cape of Good Hope* (which is about to appear in English). But larger Polish works of fiction entirely pervaded by humorous inspiration are still comparatively scarce ; an exception like *P. Choynowski's* rollicking story *Youth, Love, Adventure*, remains isolated even among the works of its own author. And we can hardly classify as works of humour the remarkable productions of one of Poland's most gifted men in the present day, the portrait-painter and writer *St. I. Witkiewicz*, whose two amazing novels, as well as his more numerous and no less astonishing plays, stuffed with an abundance of Rabelaisian crudities and obscenities, also fairly burst with an overwhelming exuberance of the most surprising ideas.

### 6

Passing from fiction to the *drama*, we enter a field of singular aridity, not in Poland only, but throughout contemporary Europe. A general reason for this fact may be sought in the decay of the contemporary theatre through the withering competition of the film. In Poland, there is the additional cause that dramatic production in Polish literature had never had much of a continuous record : the classical comedies of *A. Fredro* in the earlier decades of the nineteenth century, the romantic tragedies of *J. Słowacki* towards the middle of it, the visionary poetic plays of *S. Wyspiański* at its end—all these had been somewhat isolated outbursts of great dramatic genius against a background of comparative insignificance.

If the literary tradition of modern Polish drama is fitful and broken, there is, side by side with it, a strong and sustained tradition of *popular dramatic art*, centring round the holidays of the Christian year and the old rites and ceremonies at weddings. This tradition of folk plays, retaining occasionally features even of pre-Christian belief and practice, has recently received more attention than ever before. Dramatic innovators and reformers in Poland have gone to it for refreshing inspiration.

Thus, *L. Schiller*, a most able stage-manager, built up, out of elements of traditional Christmas plays, carols, and folk-songs, a most charming dramatic *Pastoral*, in which the adoration of the Divine Child by the shepherds is clothed in the garb of Polish village life and custom. Again, a spectacle composed entirely of folk-rites and ceremonies, *A Wedding among Kurpian Peasants*, organized by a village priest, *Father Skierkowski*, has of late years been successfully performed by peasant actors in all parts of Poland and become a great stimulus to local production of a similar kind. A special *Department of Folk Theatres* in the Polish *Ministry of Education*, under the able superintendence of *J. Cierniak*, is constantly promoting the activities of village dramatic associations and their playwrights on lines of genuinely popular tradition.

This strong admixture of folk-lore to Poland's theatrical tradition—corresponding to the new social importance of the peasantry in the reborn State—will perhaps, in the future, modify the character and style of Poland's entire dramatic literature. Some such effect was already perceivable, at the beginning of the present century, in the poetic plays of *Wyspianski*, whose great drama *The Wedding*, for instance, was modelled in structure on the comic dialogues in the old Christmas folk-plays. And another great poet, *Kasprowicz*, had used the grotesque figure of the ribald *Marculf* from the old chap-books for powerful symbolism in a drama modelled in its form on the ancient morality plays.

Apart from such single instances, however, dramatists both new and old still seem content to follow the modern literary models which they find dominant at home and abroad.

Among dramatic writers of pre-war fame, *K. H. Rostworowski* is one of the most prominent. He had begun by verse plays which were influenced by the style of Wyspiański, although they dealt mostly with subjects outside the Polish tradition (*Judas Iscariot, The Emperor Caligula*). The rebirth of Poland and the victory over Bolshevism inspired him for a number of further poetic plays filled even to obscurity with symbolic imagery. A third phase came when he turned from symbolical abstractions to social realities and, in a trilogy of plays, developed, with great melodramatic force, a theme in which Balzacian motives of criminal greed work as a hereditary curse in the fashion of the " fatality plays " of German Romantics.

A younger dramatic poet of somewhat similar type, *L. H. Morstin*, who also took Wyspiański's poetic dramas for his first models, has not shown much capacity to move beyond lyrism and reflexion into the realm of the strictly dramatic, even in his plays of contemporary life. Neither has the distinguished lyrical singer *E. Żegadłowicz* in his poetic tragedies from Polish peasant life.

Among younger prose dramatists, *J. Szaniawski* has won the greatest measure of recognition by his talent. Like his eminent Russian contemporary Yevreinov, he is chiefly concerned in his plays with the great problem of the relation of art to life, of illusion and make-believe to reality and action. That is why we usually move in his plays on the border-line between commonplace everyday existence and fantastic worlds of the imagination, and we have to make the effort of understanding allegorically much of what we see on the stage. In spite of the doubtful and hybrid character of these plays, there is something refreshing in the way they lift us, momentarily and bodily, out of workaday life into wonderland, and their successes prove that they meet a real spiritual need of the people of to-day.

Apart from the somewhat isolated phenomenon of Szaniawski there is not much among the average dramatic production of Poland's writers to-day which would seem to deserve singling out for values of depth or permanence. There is no lack of competent historical plays for patriotic pageants (such as *King Stephen Bathory*, by *K. Brończyk*), nor of witty drawing-room comedies. In the latter *genre* writers of Jewish blood excel by their racial gift for pointed dialogue. One of them, *Alfred Savoir* (originally *A. Poznański*, of Łódź) has even won international laurels as a writer of brilliant comedies in French. Among those writing in Polish, *B. Winawer* is perhaps most remarkable by his combination of piercing satirical wit with an almost idolatrous worship of modern natural science. One of his amusing yet thoughtful little plays, *The Book of Job*, was even found worth the labour of translation into English by no less a man than Joseph Conrad.

### 7

In connection with dramatic literature, it will perhaps be appropriate to add here a few words on the *theatre* in Poland.

The theatre, which had begun to flourish in eighteenth-century Warsaw under the enlightened protection of the last king of Poland, was one of those institutions which most manifestly demonstrated the vitality of the national spirit throughout the period of Poland's captivity. The first great actor-manager and popular dramatist of modern Poland, *W. Bogusławski*, crossed and re-crossed continually, with his Thespian cart, the fresh partition frontiers in the very first years after the old Poland's fall, as if deliberately protesting against the dismemberment of the country. And many is the glorious chapter which Polish actors and managers have since added to the record, often under circumstances of political repression and material distress. For the present purpose, it may be sufficient to single out, as an instance, the queenly figure of *Helen Modrzejewska* (*Modjeska*), who, after a speedy rise into fame on the Polish stage, succeeded in later years in captivating English-speaking audiences on both sides of the Atlantic, and in winning a popularity among them equal to Paderewski's. And like Paderewski's, her heart remained unwaveringly attached to her country throughout a career of world-wide renown : and it was in Polish earth, at Cracow, that this heart finally found its last resting-place.

At the dawn of our century, it was the stage of the municipal theatre at *Cracow* which, under the memorable management of *T. Pawlikowski*, became the place of production of modern Poland's highest achievements in dramatic literature—including the verse plays of Wyspiański, who, as a painter, himself collaborated in scenic design and decoration. It was Cracow also which attracted the best of rising talent among young actors. But the actors, when they had risen into eminence on the Cracow stage, often proceeded to Warsaw where larger audiences and better material conditions awaited them. It was perhaps due to the Russian's innate strong liking for theatrical art, and perhaps also to a desire to divert national energies towards side-issues, that the authorities of the Tsar's Government treated the theatre in Warsaw more leniently than other Polish institutions : some Warsaw repertory theatres (including the Grand Opera) were actually subsidized by the State and maintained, in spite of the rigours of political censorship, a very high level indeed both of literary repertory and of artistic performance.

Thus Warsaw, when she became the capital of a reunited Poland and thereby also naturally the heart of the country's theatrical life, had a very good foundation in her own theatrical tradition to go upon.

The *Polish Theatre* of Warsaw, founded in 1913 by *A. Szyfman*, had under his management become one of the best theatres in Poland. Besides introducing certain technical innovations, then as yet unknown elsewhere (such as the revolving stage) it attracted a perfect galaxy of the very best actors—some of whom have themselves become well-known producers and stage-managers since—as well as modern Poland's two best scene-painters—*W. Drabik* and *K. Frycz*. The *Little Theatre* and the *Comedy Theatre* also came under Szyfman's management, and all the three playhouses conducted by him became known as models of careful and thoroughly modern stage production, distinguished by the constant endeavour to fuse decoration and performance into one harmonious æsthetic whole. This was, in fact, the ideal of one of the best theatres in pre-war Europe—the " Art Theatre " of Stanislavsky in Moscow. Polish actors, driven by the War into the interior of Russia, there became acquainted with the great achievements of modern Russian theatrical art, and this contact bore manifold fruit afterwards. Even in Russia, the eminent tragic actress *S. Wysocka* founded, at Kiev, a Polish dramatic *Studio* or experimental theatre modelled on the several famous institutions of this kind in Moscow. But greater things were to come. It was under the influence of his Russian memories that *J. Osterwa*, in the grey dawn of the new Poland, in 1919, formed out of noble enthusiasts a company of players called *Reduta*, which became something like a religious brotherhood devoted to the propaganda of high art. Thorough analysis and joint discussion of works to be performed became the foundation of stage production, an earnest and lofty zeal united the whole group, and thus *Reduta* became the synonym not only of a very high level of accomplishment, but of a liberal education for actors and a perfect spirit of co-operation. After several years of work in Warsaw, and a year of dispersal, the revived *Reduta* toured the provinces, especially the eastern border, and did wonders, not only in stirring the stagnant waters of intellectual life in country towns, but also in awakening admiration for the literary achievements of Polish genius among people brought up under predominant Russian or German influence. Scattered since upon many stages in Poland, the *Reduta* actors have become a pervading and ennobling leaven in Polish theatrical life. Their leader, Osterwa himself, assumed the management of the Cracow theatre in 1932 and will, it is hoped, bring back something of its pre-war glories.

Next to Osterwa, it is perhaps *L. Schiller* who will have left the deepest trace behind in the post-war development of the Polish theatre. Schiller has been mentioned above as the creator of the Christmas play, *Pastoral*, out of traditional folklore stuff. The height of his activities was reached in 1924–26 when he conducted the Bogusławski Theatre in Warsaw. Adding a fine ear for music and a gift for composing to his talents as an actor and producer, Schiller succeeded in giving rhythmical beauty to mass movements and choral speeches on the stage, and in producing, with good effect, dramatic works supposed to be utterly untheatrical in their structure. In this, it must be admitted that a somewhat unscrupulous boldness in the manipulation of dramatic texts stood him in good stead ; and the assistance of two decorators of very " advanced " type—the *Pronaszko* brothers—enhanced the impression of striking originality which his productions give.

A third prominent figure, no less well known than Osterwa and Schiller, is *R. Ordyński*, a disciple of the German Reinhardt, whose stage version of the Early English moral play of *Everyman* he transferred to the Polish stage at Cracow. Having made a name both in Europe and America, Ordyński (like so many other men of the theatre) has recently devoted his energies to the screen ; he was the creator of one of the first films produced in Poland—a film based on the great national epic *Pan Tadeusz*, by Mickiewicz—and has since collaborated in the production of other Polish films both dramatic and comic, which are becoming more and more numerous, and technically more and more perfect. The emphatically spectacular tendency which Ordyński acquired in the school of Reinhardt, is also to some extent characteristic of the work of *T. Trzciński*, likewise a disciple of Reinhardt's. Trzciński's outstanding achievement during his eight years' tenure of Cracow theatre was perhaps his open-air production of a sixteenth-century Polish classical play— *The Dismissal of the Greek Envoys* by Kochanowski—in the magnificent Renascence courtyard of the old Royal Castle.

The efforts of the eminent stage-managers here mentioned, and of some others, would not have been crowned by their great successes without the collaboration of a body of distinguished *actors*. The names of such surviving representatives of the " Old Guard " of pre-war stage talent as *L. Solski*, the aged king of the tragic stage, and *M. Frenkiel*, supreme in comedy, are household words in Poland ; and so are the names of ladies like *Mme. Solska* and *Mme. Siemaszko*, who worthily upheld the standard set by the great Modjeska. Among younger men, *K. Junosza-Stępowski* (excellent as King Magnus in Shaw's *Apple Cart*) and *S. Jaracz* (unforgettable as *The Captain of Koepenick* in a remarkable Germantragi-comedy), might perhaps be singled out, together with *Mlle. Malicka* (recently great as Queen Elizabeth of Valois in Schiller's *Don Carlos*) and *Mme. Zaklicka* (the best Polish *St. Joan* in Shaw's drama). But this is an arbitrary choice, based on the personal preferences of a playgoer, and a number of other names undoubtedly are equal to those here selected.

Even the present cursory survey of the new Poland's theatrical life would be incomplete without a mention of the *revue* stage. The music-hall stages of Warsaw, such as the *Qui Pro Quo* and some others, have become the arena for brilliant displays of political and social satire by Poland's younger poets ; and in the persons of *Mlle. Ordon*, the foremost *diseuse* in the Poland of to-day, and of numbers of other gifted singers, reciters and dancers, they possess a capital of artistic talent of very high order. They are always extremely popular ; no wonder that recently a remedy against the present theatrical crisis should have been sought in fusion of one of the august literary theatres —the *Polish Theatre*—with the leading *revue* theatre of Warsaw.

### 8

It was in accordance with the national mission which Polish literature had to fulfil in the era of captivity that *literary criticism* also very largely concerned itself with the making of programmes of collective life and insisted on the need for close attention to the social tasks of the hour. In the light of Poland's nineteenth-century history it is not to be wondered at that one of the most eminent literary critics of the last pre-war years, *W. Feldman*, was an active fellow-worker of a group preparing a new armed struggle for independence, and another critic—a theorist of great influence on the young writers of his day—*St. Brzozowski*, endeavoured, with the utmost fervour of a rich if somewhat confused intellect, to weave literature into the texture of a scheme of life and of society centring round glorified labour (*The Legend of the Young Poland*, 1909).

The recovery of political independence deprived literature of its high position in national life, but at the same time set it free from the cramping obligation of perpetually doing duty as a national institution. No wonder that theoretical thought on the essential tasks of literature now fairly runs riot among extreme conceptions as removed as can be from pre-war notions on the function of literature. One young critic (*J. N. Miller*) in his eagerness to open up for Polish literature the wider fields of " universal " ideals went the length of decrying the recognized masterpieces of Poland's Romantic poetry as " provincial " ; another—the brilliant *St. I. Witkiewicz*— in his plea for " pure form " as the supreme value of art, proclaims the critical principle of utter indifference to the problems and ideas which are the subject-matter of the works considered by the critic. Contrary to him, a third outstanding critic, *K. Irzykowski,* brought up in the school of German philosophy, does indeed always pay attention first and foremost to the spiritual contents of any given work of art, but takes a detached and purely intellectual view of them ; hence the abstract air of his critical appreciations, abounding in *isms* and forcing personalities and works into their categories.

It needs a very strong sense of reality to tread a path of moderation in this atmosphere of very natural excitement over thoroughly changed conditions of literary life. Such a path was followed for a time by *T. Żeleński*—better known by his pen name of " *Boy* "—who is perhaps, the best critical writer in the Poland of to-day. His intellectual horizon had been widened, even before the War, beyond the limits of traditional Polish conceptions of the functions of literature, through his indefatigable work on translating the masterpieces of French literature into Polish. His translations—filling more than a hundred volumes already!—are a great service to the nation's literary culture and, by their qualities of style, an ornament of modern Polish letters. As a critic, he has taken the theatre for his special province, and stands easily supreme in that field : his theatrical criticisms, collected in an ever-growing array of volumes, form a vivid record of the recent history of the Polish stage. Unfortunately, an inveterate *penchant* for the pursuit of sensation in the recesses of great men's biographies, and a newly developed zeal for the propaganda of such social causes as birth control, are diverting the energies of this brilliant writer into channels alien to his highest gifts.

### 9

If thus we see literary criticism in post-war Poland torn between tendencies diametrically opposed to each other, a spectacle of conflicts and often of contradictions, this is but the necessary reflex of the state of things which prevails in the larger area of *literature* itself. In literature, as in literary criticism, the consciousness became predominant that in this new era of regained political freedom the days of literature as a mainstay of national life and a sacred national institution were irrevocably past. At the same time it was realized that literature could play an honourable and important part within the aggregate life of the community also under the new conditions if only it did no longer make national preoccupations the excuse for indifference to problems agitating the literary life of humanity at large, whether they were problems of theme and idea, or

problems of form and style. In this sense, the responsibilities
of literature in a free country could be conceived as not only by
no means smaller or less weighty, but greater even than in the
age of captivity. The literature of re-delivered Poland must,
by its products, supply part of the moral justification for the
reconstruction of the Polish State as a worthy and useful
member of the comity of civilized nations. In their endeavours
to live up to the level of these new tasks, the young writers of
Poland inevitably fell into extremes, either of vagueness of idea
in their internationalism, or of inanity of formalism in their
care for expression.

Most of these writers are still young : their first writings
of any distinction go back no farther than War time or (in most
cases) the first post-war years. Some further progress towards
maturity both of idea and of form may, accordingly, still be
expected from many even of those who have reached fame or
popularity. If such progress has so far not been greatly
promoted by deliberate acquisition of wide and deep literary
culture ; if, on the contrary, Poland's young writers of to-day
seem to possess more than the common contempt of post-war
youth for historical experience and tradition, and more than
the ordinary assurance and self-confidence of the young of all
times, this surely is sufficiently accounted for by the peculiar
position of a literary generation who are separated from the
historical past by a gulf of political and social change, and,
to assert themselves and achieve anything of value, had to
struggle against the overwhelming superiority and almost
religious authority of Poland's great literature of the age of
captivity.

That literature has, so far, not been equalled in the new free
Poland by anything of equal distinction or permanence. The
last undeniably great writers of a truly heroic age of Polish
letters—Sienkiewicz and Reymont, Zeromski and Kasprowicz—
died out quickly in the very first years of the new era which was
opened up by the thunders of 1914. Harvests of genius, like
harvests of grain, are incalculable. We may be entering on a
prolonged period of literary dearth in Poland after a century
of magnificent fruitfulness. But we may also be on the eve of
another golden age of abundance, which will emerge from the
ferment and uncertainty of these our days. One thing, at any
rate, is certain : that literature, even if it may not, in a re-
delivered country, claim the dignity of a national *palladium*,
as in the time of captivity, yet can become, and should become,
an important component of the fabric of Poland's reconstructed

national civilization, and a valuable asset in her contribution
to the spiritual stock of the humanity of to-morrow.

### 10

Before passing on from literature to the other arts, it seems
appropriate to insert here a short account of the Polish *periodical
press*—a domain of activity which, in modern societies, absorbs
much of the best literary talent, and often provides authors
with a living when they cannot make one by their books.

The Press in its modern form was one of those institutions
which owed their development in the eighteenth century to the
cultural influence of the enlightened last king of Poland on the
Warsaw of his day. Besides an official gazette (called *Monitor*
then as it is called again in the new Poland) a number of moral
weeklies on the model of Addison's and Steele's English ones
began to be published, and the debates of Poland's " Long
Parliament " on constitutional reform (1788–92) were accompanied by the utterances of Poland's first political newspaper,
the *Domestic and Foreign News*, conducted by the poet *J. U.
Niemcewicz* and voicing the wishes of the patriotic reformers.

In the nineteenth century, the Press shared the vicissitudes
of fortune to which a captive and divided nation was subject.
A brief efflorescence not only of political daily papers but of
high-class literary periodicals in the University cities of Warsaw
and Wilno during the first post-Napoleonic era was soon followed
by the period of repression which set in as a consequence of the
disaster of 1831. The best writers of Poland being driven into
exile, the greatest among them did not disdain, in the atmosphere
of ferment prevailing throughout Europe on the eve of 1848,
to use the instrument of the Press for the popularization of their
ideas. Poland's supreme poet and national leader, *A. Mickiewicz*, for a brief and remarkable period of his later career,
became the editor of a French periodical called *La Tribune des
peuples*, and his articles written for it were no less conspicuous
for the advanced radicalism of his social and political programme
than for his eloquent advocacy of such liberal ideas as that of
the freedom of the Press.

In Poland itself, both before and especially after the unfortunate second insurrection of 1863, Warsaw became a great Press
centre : the great historical novelist, *J. I. Kraszewski* (Poland's
Walter Scott) not only became prominent in daily journalism,
but was for many years the editor of a monthly periodical of
high literary level entitled *Ateneum*.

The times after 1863, as has been recounted in detail elsewhere in this book, were favourable to absorption in day-to-day tasks of social improvement within the narrow limits of what was possible under foreign rule. Reaction against romantic and hopeless armed struggles for independence, and with it, reaction against the nation's romantic attachment to certain traditional ideals, became a dominant current in national thought. It was under the threefold watchword of modern democracy, scientific free thought, and a sense of political realities (especially with regard to Russian Poland's position within the Russian Empire) that the most fiery and temperamental Polish journalist of the later nineteenth century, *A. Swięto-chowski*, conducted for many years a vehement campaign against the idols of tradition in his periodical called *Truth* (*Prawda*). In a much more moderate and balanced way, with far greater sense of the values of historical tradition, with a saving sense of humour as refreshing as it is rare in Polish journalism, and with deep and tender human pity for the wronged and oppressed, the great novelist, *B. Prus*, acted for several decades as preceptor to the nation on the vital problems of the hour in his memorable *Weekly Chronicles*. Both in his writing and that of other brilliant Warsaw journalists of his time, the conditions imposed by Russian censorship favoured the development of a studiously subdued style, full of reticences and skilful circumlocutions—perhaps not altogether harmful as a curb on the flamboyant and rhetorical Polish temperament, and certainly useful as a means of educating the public, who had to exercise their acumen by reading between the lines.

An entirely different situation, favourable to unrestrained discussion and to hustings oratory in print, was created for the Press in the Austrian sector of the country by the grant of provincial self-government to Galicia in 1867. Long before that date, in the revolutionary days of 1848, a daily paper named *Czas* ("The Times") had been founded at Cracow, where it has not ceased to appear since. During the half-century of Galician home rule, being served by a succession of eminent writers, it steadily represented a conservative programme of political realism combined with firm adherence to Poland's Catholic tradition and to the established predominance of the land-owning class in the social and political life of Galicia. The Conservatism of the country gentry was blended in the columns of *Czas* with a philosophical conception of politics based on sound historical scholarship and expounded mainly by Professors of Cracow University, who were (and largely still are) contributors to the paper. *Czas* had a concomitant of more serious bulk in the monthly *Polish Review* (*Przeglad Polski*), which, together with the *Bibljoteka Warszawska* of Warsaw, represented a highly cultured and dignified style of periodical writing.

As time went on, the educated middle class of the cities came to hold in Galicia a position of equal importance to that of the country gentry. Standing for a more democratic and liberal programme, it created a highly popular organ of its own, called *Reform* (*Reforma*, later *Nowa Reforma*), which was for a time served by the able pen of the philosophical poet *A. Asnyk*.

*Lwów*, the other great city of Austrian Poland and the official centre of its political life, had its counterpart to the Conservative *Czas* in the *Gazette* (*Gazeta Lwowska*) brilliantly edited for years by the distinguished novelist *A. Krechowiecki* ; and it also had a paper representative of urban middle-class Liberalism, like the *Reform* of Cracow, in the shape of the *Courier* (*Kurjer Lwowski*), no less ably conducted by the ardent democrat and progressive educational worker, *B. Wysłouch*.

As the end of the century approached, a new political force gathered strength, which soon began to appeal to the educated middle class of the cities more strongly than the mild Liberalism of *Reform* at Cracow. This force was *Nationalism* in its modern form, not content with day-to-day social work within the three sections of the divided country, but intent on preparing the way for national reunion and independence. In the Austrian section, it was Lwów which, in its exposed position in the midst of the rising tide of Ukrainian Nationalism, became a stronghold of the Polish nationalist movement. As an organ of this movement, the daily *Słowo Polskie* (*The Polish Word*), under the editorship of *Z. Wasilewski* (who was also a distinguished literary critic) rose into eminence. The movement also created for itself a high-class monthly called *The Pan-Polish Review* (*Przegląd Wszechpolski*) which, by its very title indicates its ambition to appeal to Poles of all the three sections of the divided country and, in fact, maintains close contact with the nationalist movement in Russian Poland, then growing in importance through the leadership of *R. Dmowski*.

In contrast to Nationalism with its unifying tendencies, we observe towards the end of the century the growth of *class parties*, emphasizing the existing social antagonisms and advocating more or less radical schemes of social reform. A fiery-tempered Catholic priest, *Father S. Stojałowski*, became the founder of a *Peasant Farmers' Party* largely through the agency of a widespread paper called *The Garland and the Bee* (*Wienieci*)

*Pszczłóka*) which gave scope to his brilliant gift for popular journalism. At the same time, the rising power of *Socialism* received an organ at Cracow in the still existing daily paper *Naprzód* (*Forward*), and soon afterwards one for Russian Poland called *Robotnik* (*The Working-man*). This was at first secretly published and circulated by no less a person than *Joseph Piłsudski*, then the leader and organizer of the Polish Socialist Party. In course of time, the paper emerged into open daylight, and it still remains the outstanding organ of Polish Socialism.

It may have been noticed by the reader that the above account of the pre-war Polish Press is confined to the Austrian and the Russian sector. As a matter of fact, the *Prussian province of Poland*, although superior in general literacy to the two others, was too absorbed in the day-to-day economic struggle against Prussian colonization to produce a Press of high refinement or interest. Its outstanding papers, such as the *Poznań Courier* (*Kurjer Poznański*), seem singularly jejune in comparison with Polish papers of the other sectors even to-day. On the other hand, it must be emphasized that some of the papers of this province, owing to the high level of education among the country people, reached figures of circulation then unknown elsewhere in Poland—such as the *Gazeta Grudziądzka*, of which 100,000 copies used to be printed. It is in the Prussian sector also that the entire modern Polish national movement in a large province long exposed to systematic Germanization— viz., Prussian Silesia—was practically created by a popular newspaper under the title of *The Catholic* (*Katolik*).

## II

Passing over the highly interesting but temporary developments in Polish journalism in War time—such as the growth of a number of Polish dailies, weeklies, and monthlies in the interior of Russia between 1915 and 1917—we now come to the history of the *Press in the new Poland*.

Owing to the close connection between the Press and political fluctuations, it took a number of years to replace the Press laws of the three partitioning powers by a unified Polish *Press Code*. And when that Code was at last promulgated in the form of a Presidential decree in 1927, it turned out to contain rigorous provisions directed by Piłsudski's Government against the political parties opposed to it, and it aroused much protest for undue interference with the freedom of the Press. Parliament refused to ratify it, but did not replace it by a new law.

In the meantime, the growth of the Polish Press had also been profoundly affected by the changing economic fortunes of the new Poland. Paper-money inflation produced a mushroom growth of periodicals, as it produced a mushroom growth of business undertakings. The tide fell again, and it rose once more with the settled currency conditions of 1925, only to ebb away a second time during the present crisis. The net balance, however, was one of increase : at the end of ten years the new Poland numbered twice as many periodicals as in 1918, that is to say, over 2200, of which total four-fifths were in Polish. The distribution of the circulation of these as between country and town, and as between the different provinces of Poland, is very unequal ; and the entire volume of the circulation can only be estimated very approximately. It was placed roughly, in 1928, at $1\frac{1}{2}$ million copies of periodicals daily, which would constitute an average of one copy to every twenty persons of the total population. The average for Warsaw, however, is one in seven, and it is similar in other urban centres. The gap between country and town in the circulation of newspapers is equalled in width by the gap between Poland's west and east in the number of newspapers published.

Thus, in 1928, the western border province of Poznań had 272 Polish periodicals and 40 German ones, while in the eastern border province of Volhynia no local daily paper was published at all.

Of the total number of periodicals published in Poland only somewhat over one-third are devoted to political and social affairs ; but of these, taking them together, twenty times as many copies are published as of all the rest. Of daily newspapers in Polish alone there were, in 1928, over a hundred, and their total *tirage* was estimated at slightly over a million copies. Of all the periodicals, one-third appeared in Warsaw alone ; of the daily newspapers, about one-fifth.

Warsaw papers are naturally widely read in the provinces ; on the whole, however, the three pre-war sections of Poland remain influenced, in the matter of newspaper reading, by their respective old centres. It is significant that the one daily paper in Poland which has succeeded in making itself read from one end of the Republic to the other, is not a Warsaw paper, but a Cracow one—the *Illustrated Daily Courier* (*Ilustrowany Kurjer Codzienny*). It owes this success to the organizing capacity of its editor, *M. Dąbrowski*, who skilfully imitated such popular features of the modern American Press as : a quick and abundant news service, sensational headlines, a profusion of illustrations, copious Sunday supplements, simple comic cartoons, and a persistent appeal not only to the craving for excitement, but also to some of the rooted prejudices of the man in the street. Even the large " Press Palace " housing the *Courier* at Cracow is built and organized on the model of American offices. Round the *Courier* are grouped a number of weekly and fortnightly pictorial and comic papers. The *Courier*, while professedly independent, in the main supports the Piłsudski Government.

Of other centres than Cracow, the cities of Warsaw and Poznań have widely read *Couriers* of their own, whose popularity, however, does not reach beyond the province of each. They are both nationalist papers, the Warsaw one more mild, the Poznań one more fervent in tone. It is, in fact, the Nationalist Party which counts, among all political groups, the largest number of Press organs of its own. Its leading newspaper, the *Warsaw Gazette* (*Gazeta Warszawska*) also can boast of being the oldest paper now appearing in Poland, as it has been published without interruption since 1774.

As against the more or less Nationalist Press, which is largely read by the *intelligentsia* of the towns, the present Government counts among the papers supporting its cause two large Warsaw papers of respectable tradition—the *Morning Courier* (*Kurjer Poranny*) and the *Polish Courier* (*Kurjer Polski*) ; it also subsidizes a large paper of its own called *The Polish Gazette* (*Gazeta Polska*). A measure of support is given to the Government by the old-established Conservative *Czas* at Cracow, which continues to maintain a high standard of intellectual culture and journalistic good manners, and by a Wilno paper called *Słowo* (*The Word*) which represents the somewhat distinct interests of eastern Poland's land-owning gentry, and counts one of Poland's most brilliant younger journalists, *St. Mackiewicz*, among its contributors.

Among the organs of the outstanding parties other than the nationalists and the Government *bloc*, the leading Socialist paper, *Robotnik* (*The Working Man*), must here be mentioned again as holding its old position. The Peasant Farmers' Party, led by the former Prime Minister Witos, commands a popular organ called *Piast*. The Christian Democrats (a party akin to the nationalists, but distinct from them) have developed their old organ, *The Voice of the People* (*Głos Narodu*) at Cracow, into one of the popular political newspapers in that part of the country. The Radical Peasant groups and the small fractions approaching Communism have only a scanty and fitful Press representation.

Some particulars may here be added on the Press of Poland's national and racial *minorities*. A few of their organs only, such as the Zionist papers, *The New Journal* (*Nowy Dziennik*) at Cracow, *Our Review* (*Nasz Przegląd*) in Warsaw, and *The Hour* (*Chwila*) at Lwów, are published in Polish. Others appear in other languages, constituting altogether about one-fifth of the total number of periodicals published in Poland. Foremost among them in number of organs and in circulation stands the *Jewish Press*, published in *Yiddish* and printed in Hebrew letters. Of its 130 newspapers nearly one-half appear in Warsaw ; the most popular one among them is *Moment*. Periodicals in *Hebrew* are only nine in number, and mostly devoted to religious affairs.

Second in importance, there is the *German Press* in Poland. Subsidized from Germany it counted, in 1928, no fewer than 118 periodicals, of which 55 were political newspapers ; the *Deutsche Rundschau* (*German Review*) of Bydgoszcz and the *Kattowitzer Zeitung* in Silesia are the most popular among them, while the *Deutsche Wissenschaftliche Zeitschrift für Polen* represents German research work done in Poland.

Third in the scale, there stands the *Ukrainian Press* with 72 periodicals. Its only daily, *The Cause* (*Diło*), published at Lwów, has a long tradition of many decades behind it ; it is now the official organ of the Ukrainian Nationalist Party. The list includes also a *Literary and Scientific Review* (*Literaturno-Naukowyj Wistnyk*), likewise published at Lwów, and likewise of old standing.

Among the Press of other minorities (White Ruthenians, Lithuanians, Czechs, Russians) we may single out the Warsaw Russian paper *For Freedom* (*Za Svobodu*) which is one of the outstanding European organs of Russian emigrant opinion.

### 12

We now pass from more or less political papers to the *non-political periodicals* (mostly weeklies and monthlies) ; here, we are confronted by a picture of intense progress and development, which only the crisis in recent years has affected adversely. In 1928, there were two Polish periodicals devoted to bibliography and three statistical ones ; 70 represented various aspects of religion, 40 medicine, 30 education, 15 the law, 20 engineering, 50 economic affairs, 50 agriculture, 11 military science, 15 the interests of women and 6 philosophy and mathematics, to say nothing of the specialist organs devoted to particular branches of research and industry, or to the affairs of various professional associations. The number of historical, literary, and political reviews of serious importance was considerable, but several of them have since ended their existence owing to economic difficulties. Prominent among them were : *The Warsaw Review* (*Przegląd Warszawski*) and a more recent monthly called *The Path* (*Droga*) in Warsaw, and *The Contemporary Review* (*Przegląd Współczesny*) at Cracow. The latter, edited by Professor St. Wędkiewicz of Cracow University, is particularly distinguished for breadth of outlook on world affairs : its special numbers devoted to Italy, to Switzerland, and to Belgium, presented comprehensive surveys of the life of those countries by eminent authorities. *The Universal Review* (*Przegląd Powszechny*), published by the Jesuit fathers at Cracow, also holds a high and well-established position among Poland's monthly reviews. As for weeklies, the *Tygodnik Ilustrowany* of Warsaw is the time-honoured favourite picture weekly of the Polish home, while the *Literary News* (*Wiadomości literackie*) has of late years rapidly risen into wide popularity as the organ of the younger writers and of the most brilliant literary criticism in Poland. Under the management of its editors, there appears also a French review of Polish literary life (with occasional articles in English and German) under the title *La Pologne littéraire*. The economic aspects of Polish life are presented to the foreign reader by a French *Bulletin*, and by a periodical in English, called *The Polish Economist*.

A few data must be added concerning the *Polish Press published abroad*. As mentioned in a former chapter, there are nearly seven million Poles living outside Poland, about two-thirds of the number being inhabitants of the United States. Accordingly, of the 200 Polish papers published abroad, 120 appear in America, Chicago alone producing ten of them, with a joint circulation of half a million copies. The one million Poles in Germany have 15 Polish periodicals, and the more recent, and now almost equally numerous, Polish emigrants in France, the same number ; the needs of the Poles in Czechoslovakia (nearly 150,000) are served by 10 periodicals ; Polish colonies in other countries both around Poland and far away have their isolated Press organs : there is even a Polish weekly at Harbin in Manchuria.

In 1928, Poland had 32 *press agencies*, of which the three outstanding ones, with the State-subsidized *P.A.T.* (Polish Telegraph Agency) at their head, supplied foreign news, and the *A.W.* (" Agencja Wschodnia," Eastern Agency) specialized in economic information.

The journalists of Poland are organized in a number of *professional syndicates*, which again are united in a Central Association. This, in its turn, belongs to the *Fédération Internationale des Journalistes*, and Poland is represented by some of her ablest newspaper men at its periodical congresses, such as the recent one in London in 1932, at which Dr. A. Beaupré of the Cracow *Czas* figured not inconspicuously.

For over ten years now, Poland has also had a *Higher School of Journalism* in Warsaw, among whose lecturers both leading journalists and distinguished experts in the social sciences figure prominently.

13

Polish *painting*, like Polish literature, had, in the nineteenth century, served as an instrument of national self-expression and self-assertion when the normal political organs of national life were absent. Mention has been made before of the king of modern Poland's painters, *J. Matejko*, whose huge canvases from Polish history—similar in their technique to the manner of Rubens at his grandest—have never ceased to draw crowds of pilgrims from all parts of Poland to the halls of the National Museum at Cracow, and to awaken in them certainly as much patriotic as æsthetic emotion. Matejko's powerful personality dominated for many years the Cracow Academy of Arts, in which he was a teacher ; it even left a strong imprint on the genius of his greatest pupil *St. Wyspiański*, who won no less high a place among Poland's painters than he holds among her poets.

It was under the influence of Matejko also that Polish art criticism in the late nineteenth century became accustomed to rate paintings according to their appeal to national feelings rather than the qualities of their workmanship, and it was towards the end of the century that the excellent art critic and gifted writer *St. Witkiewicz* (himself an eminent landscape painter) was obliged resoundingly to reassert (in a memorable book entitled *Art and Art Criticism in Our Country*, 1891) such common-place truths as the dependence of the artistic value of a picture on execution rather than on the choice of theme.

In the meantime, gifted painters (who are being rediscovered to-day) had passed without due notice and influence. A great era of Polish painting had been inaugurated by the enlightened protection which the last king of Poland extended to the arts ;

such representatives of that efflorescence as *Norblin* or *A. Orłowski* (who lived at St. Petersburg after the partitions) are only now being appreciated duly, the one for the exquisite perfection of his views of eighteenth-century Warsaw, the other for the racy vividness of his scenes and figures from old-world country life. Similarly, *P. Michałowski*, who was absorbed in social and political interests and only in his leisure hours dashed off sketchy little pictures, mostly of horses and battles, is now only being recognized as perhaps the greatest genius in earlier nineteenth-century Polish painting.

In the period of Matejko himself, only *H. Siemiradzki*, a Polish Alma Tadema on a grander scale, was admitted to approach the great master by the monumental character of his large canvases (such as the famous " Torches of Nero " in the National Museum at Cracow) ; but the national imagination did not warm to his classic themes and statuesque attitudes. It was certainly more attracted by the numberless scenes of horsemanship and battle in which *J. Kossak* (the founder of a dynasty of popular painters of that name) expressed his cult of old Polish ideals of chivalry ; and it needed all the literary eloquence of St. Witkiewicz—author of excellent books both on Matejko and on Kossak—to demonstrate that Kossak, with the small size of his pictures (mostly in water-colour) and drawings, and his non-monumental style, was also a painter of great and unique genius. It was Witkiewicz again who drew attention to the advanced Parisian methods admirably exemplified in the little-known landscapes of *M. Gierymski* ; or to the wonderful realism of *J. Chełmoński's* pictures of country nature and country life, such as his famous " Four-Horse Team," galloping at the visitor out of a large picture in the National Museum at Cracow.

As the nineteenth century drew to its close, and the domination of Matejko began to wane, studies abroad—mostly in Munich and Paris—began to tell on the technique of current Polish painting, and new great foreign models asserted their influence. A Polish Boecklin made his appearance in the person of *J. Malczewski*, whose long and glorious career was only terminated in the days of the new Poland. His strange pictures, in which figures of every-day Polish life and weird allegorical shapes jostle each other, are as admirable for their purely pictorial qualities as they are enigmatic in their adumbrations of phases of the national tragedy or of problems of the artist's relation to the world. He found a follower in his disciple *V. Hofman*. While less severe and intellectually exacting in the character of his compositions, more lyrical and full of human pity and tenderness, Hofman yet remains generally akin to Malczewski in his allegorical style and the peculiar colouring of his pictures ; he is now himself one of the senior masters of the Cracow School.

Most of the new styles and technical modes which release each other in western European painting during the last fifty or sixty years, are tried by turns, with ever-youthful vigour of personality, and applied to the painting and drawing of Polish landscapes in the numberless water-colours, designs and etchings of *L. Wyczółkowski*, who now, in his green and unceasingly active old age, enjoys a well-deserved full measure of appreciation throughout the country. The cities and villages, mountains and fields, forests and rivers and skies of all parts of Poland— no modern Polish painter's work presents them more fully and more characteristically than his. In the technique of water-colour painting he had a rival only in his late colleague *J. Fałat*, an equally prolific and masterly painter of Polish landscape in all its variety of place and season ; while as a painter of diminutive but exquisitely coloured oil landscapes (chiefly of Italian scenes) *J. Stanisławski* won a unique place, still attested by the roomful of his little masterpieces in the National Museum at Cracow.

14

The few outstanding examples selected above from the record of Polish painting during the last few decades are sufficient to illustrate the fact that the dawn of the twentieth century saw pictorial art in Poland vividly in touch with the dominant contemporary currents of western Europe, and at the same time represented by powerful, productive personalities. *Organization* —a secondary if important concern—was hampered by the political conditions of a divided Poland ; but Societies of Friends of the Fine Arts, holding periodical exhibitions, were flourishing both at Cracow under Austria and in Warsaw under Russia.

In the reunited Poland after the World War, an administrative organ for the protection of Art by the State was formed, and a certain measure of government assistance in the form of scholarships, subsidies, prizes, and purchases for state collections was shown, as far as Poland's financial difficulties allowed. Local societies organized periodical exhibitions no longer at Warsaw and Cracow only, but at Poznań, Lwów, Łódź, and Zakopane as well—and the exhibitions in the galleries of picture dealers (particularly the firm of Cz. Garliński) reached once more the level of distinction for which they were known—especially in Warsaw—before the War. The organization of the artists themselves in the name of common interests, ideals and programmes, was no longer restrained by the partition frontiers. In this particular matter, however, it was soon apparent, as it was in so many other domains, that regained freedom and unrestrained possibilities for co-ordinated and systematic effort had come to Poland at a time of unparalleled world-wide ferment. It is not to be wondered at, then, that the tracing of anything like clear lines of development, whether in the different categories of painting or in the work of leading personalities, is perhaps even more difficult here than in the realm of letters.

One of the most powerful and memorable currents which spread from France all over Europe in the later nineteenth century, modifying the crudity of naïve realism by emphasis on the personal note—the current of *impressionism*, in a word— had a powerful organ in pre-war Poland in a numerous association of painters called " *Art* " and centring at Cracow. The organization survives in the new Poland, and now mostly unites painters and sculptors of the older generation, adhering to more or less traditional standards of technique. Some of them are among the pillars of the Cracow Academy of Art, where they teach, and most of them hold the established position of classics of Polish painting. Such are : *Professor T. Axentowicz*, the ever-graceful and poetic painter of heads of women ; *Olga Boznańska* (living in Paris), one of Poland's outstanding women artists, a portrait painter of high psychological refinement, with a *pointilliste* manner ; *St. Filipkiewicz*, the favourite landscape painter of the unsophisticated lovers of country nature ; *W. Jarocki*, equally popular by his gaily-coloured scenes of eastern Carpathian peasant life ; *St. Lentz* (dead too early), a classic portrait painter of the best old type ; *A. Markowicz*, who has specialized in *genre* scenes from the Jewish *ghetto*, in a manner reminiscent of the old Dutch masters ; *S. Noakowski*, who came back to Poland to die after many years in Russia, and who remains unrivalled as a painter of old architecture ; *F. Pautsch*, who revels in splashes of strong colour with a passion like Frank Brangwyn's ; *F. Ruszczyc*, who discovered the beauty of the old city of Wilno and became the leader of its artistic life ; *K. Sichulski*, once a daring experimenter in line and colour, and renowned also as a caricaturist ; *W. Weiss*, a model of traditional correctness not devoid of vigour in colour

and design ; and many others of no less importance, whose
names cannot all be given here, but whose works the foreign
reader of these pages may occasionally come across at international picture exhibitions, because this group of painters
mainly represents Poland abroad.

### 15

These " academicians," as they may in a wider sense collec-
tively be called, became, according to an immemorial law of
historical development, the butt of attack for groups of younger
painters in the early years of the new Poland. Under the
slogans of expressionism, and then especially of "*formism,*"
this youthful reaction against what seemed too purely " repre-
sensational " and accordingly servile in traditional art, began to
run riot, not without influences from German expressionists,
Russian constructivists, and the fading futurism of pre-war
Italy. This noisy and muddled movement, however, did not
produce much evidence of real talent and barely stirred, for a
short time, the surface of artistic life at *Poznań* and at *Cracow*,
where it had its centres.

Another and a stronger counter-current to academic impressionism came from *Wilno* in the shape of a new *classicism*,
fostered perhaps largely by the dominant idealism of the pre-war
Art School of St. Petersburg, where the Wilno painters mostly
had been educated. *L. Ślendziński* stands at the head of the
Wilno group, which includes several personalities of note.
Following the great Italian models of the Renascence period,
the Wilno painters aspire above all to clear-cut design and
noble simplicity of composition ; their pictures (largely portraits) accordingly produce a somewhat sculptural effect, and
even in their technique sometimes border on the bas-relief.
Wilno, thanks to this brilliant and active group, has regained
recently some of that glory as a centre of Art which it possessed
in the early nineteenth century, and for which the beauty of its
landscape surroundings and its exquisite Baroque architecture
make an ideal setting.

Poland's capital, *Warsaw*, also became the seat of a strong
young anti-impressionist group united under the name of *Rhythm*,
since 1922. More heterogeneous in composition than the
Wilno School, it included in its ranks some prominent representatives of very advanced tendencies, such as *E. Zak*, who became
well known in France before his premature death. Other
distinguished " rhythmists " are *Z. Stryjeńska*, the ablest young
woman painter in Poland to-day, whose decorative panels

(such as " The Seasons,") as well as her compositions on the subjects of Polish national dances and popular customs, are marked by an almost musical eloquence of sweeping design, by irresistible fire of temperament and by a sense of humour rare among modern painters, and certainly unique among women. The " Rhythm " group also includes *W. Skoczylas*, the supreme master of the woodcut in modern Polish art. Both Skoczylas, in his treatment of the wiry mountain peasant figures which are his favourite subject, and *T. Pruszkowski* in his oil portraits, show distinct leanings towards the sculptural neoclassicism now dominant at Wilno, but without Wilno's neglect of the element of colour. Another resemblance to the Wilno movement was constituted by the fact that the pupils of T. Pruszkowski's class organized in 1928 into a guild called *The Brotherhood of St. Luke* which, like the Wilno School professes classical ideals of design, but takes the Dutch painters of the seventeenth century for its chosen (and, indeed, somewhat too exclusive) model.

In our wanderings between the extremes of traditionalism and revolt we now return to that old art centre, *Cracow*. After the futile and passing tumult of expressionism, Cracow has recently begun again to play a part more appropriate to its fine tradition by uniting, under the name of *The Unicorn*, a group of young painters intent above all on discipline and expert knowledge of their art, and professing enmity to all accepted shams and easy commonplaces. In the case of some of them, such as *L. Misky* in landscape painting and *St. Żurawski* in the portrait, this is almost equivalent to a recurrent wave of the old impressionism ; others, like *R. Orszulski* or *T. Seweryn*, are resolutely crude in their endeavour to be sincere.

*Poznań*, like Cracow, once the haunt of noisy expressionists, now houses a more moderate group called *Plastic Art*, which advocates a careful study of problems of form, and is willing to nourish the Polish creative imagination with the experience of the West. *W. Lam*, who has left phases of cubism and neo-classicism behind him, and *L. Dolzycki*, who is distinguished by a strong personal sense of colour, are the leading figures of this group.

Both the new Cracow and the new Poznań organization, through the medium of the many Polish painters always resident in Paris, are subject to the strong influence of the latest French fashions in painting—not invariably to their advantage. They are far, however, from the extremism of the *ultra-modernists* united recently in a group called *Praesens*. In the intellectual abstractions of their art, geometrical design really takes the place of painting in the traditional sense of the word.

With this mention of an extreme not unconnected with similar phenomena in the western European painting of our time, this rapid survey must end, although there is no end to the formation of new groups of young artists, and, as a matter of fact, new and promising organizations have made their appearance at Warsaw, Cracow, and even in the industrial city of Łódź within the last three or four years.

### 16

In addition to the above cursory survey of latter-day Polish painting, a few observations may be offered on such *education* in the arts of painting and sculpture as is provided to the citizens of the new Poland.

In this connection, foremost mention is due to the *Cracow Academy of Arts*, repeatedly named before as constituting, since Matejko's days, the chief stronghold of traditional education in painting. It had been founded in the early nineteenth century as an Art Faculty in the old University of Cracow, and only in 1879, after temporary degradation to the level of a section in a secondary school, it attained independence as a separate institution, receiving at the same time the building which it still occupies ; in 1900, it was granted academic rank, which it retains in the new Poland. If Matejko was the greatest master who ever taught in it, his successor in the headmastership, the eminent landscape painter, *J. Fałat*, was the great reorganizer and modernizer of the School ; it was to his efforts that a number of outstanding Polish painters owed the chairs they occupied in it. In the new Poland, some more chairs of painting and sculpture were added, and the teaching of architecture, of history of art, and of some branches of applied art and technical accomplishments, were placed on a broader basis. Unfortunately, at the same time, the fairly large number of scholarships available to students in pre-war days, shrank to insignificant dimensions, owing to Poland's financial troubles. The actual facilities for study abroad were considerably diminished, although educational assistance was organized by the creation of a branch office of the Academy in Paris, with a Polish painter permanently resident there (J. Pankiewicz) for its head. Somewhat later, a rest home for the Academy's professors and students was founded in the Polish mountains at Zakopane ; it serves the additional purpose of providing the proper material and surroundings for landscape and open-air painting.

The Academy, with an average attendance of 200 students, remains the educational centre which produces most Polish painters of note.

If the education of young painters in the history of their art through prolonged visits to the great foreign art collections is rendered less easy to-day by the economic difficulties of post-war time, this is all the more to be deplored, as another instrument of the æsthetic education both of artists and of their public is insufficiently developed in Poland : the country does not, for manifold historical reasons, possess those old and large *museums and galleries* which are the pride of happier nations. The Renascence was indeed, in Poland as elsewhere, a period in which kings and nobles passionately collected masterpieces of art and and ornate valuables : but large quantities of those objects were lost and dispersed, or deliberately sold or pawned, during the distressful period of costly wars and ruinous foreign invasions which afflicted Poland in the seventeenth century. In the eighteenth, the enlightened and art-loving last king of Poland laid the foundations for great national art collections ; but his efforts were thwarted by the tragedy of the country, and a certain portion only of what he so judiciously collected has quite recently been recovered from the Bolsheviks. In the nineteenth century, fear of the rapacity of the partitioning governments discouraged collectors from creating museums on Polish soil : the art treasures of the Czatoryski family were, for many decades, kept in Paris, and a Polish historical museum was founded in 1869 at Rapperswyl near Zurich in Switzerland, where it remained until the days of the new Poland. It was only in self-governing Austrian Poland during the second half of the nineteenth century that the establishment of a national museum in the country itself could securely be thought of. Such a National Museum arose at Cracow in 1883 through the initiative of an enlightened mayor of the city (Dr. J. Dietl) and the munificence of the great painter H. Siemiradzki, who presented to the Museum his own huge picture " The Torches of Nero," and whose example was soon followed by other artists. This remained, until our own time, the principal and most important art collection of Poland ; enriched in course of time by the private collections of F. Jasieński (including valuable specimens of Japanese art) and E. Barącz (Oriental rugs and other objects of applied art), the Museum to-day suffers acutely from the want of an adequate home, and leads a cramped existence in the historical city which is its natural and proper setting.

Besides the National Museum, Cracow in the later nineteenth century came to house a number of other collections of private origin and lesser extent, but valuable and full of interest. Foremost among them stands *the museum of the Czartoryski* family, including, besides many historical objects and a rich collection of old books and MSS., also a small but choice collection of pictures by old masters (with a Leonardo among them). Another art collection of importance is growing up in the *Royal Castle* on Wawel Hill at Cracow, whose rooms, as they are being restored, are filling with valuable old furniture and objects of art presented by generous donors : a number of exquisite pictures by old masters has been contributed by Count L. Piniński, one of Poland's foremost connoisseurs and collectors.

*Lwów*, with a Municipal Gallery and the rich collections of the Lubomirski and Dzieduszycki families, as well as two Ukrainian museums, suffered much through the War, but is regaining a worthy place. *Poznań* is transforming a museum left behind by the Germans (with some valuable nineteenth-century German pictures in it) into a representative gallery of modern art, in which Polish painters and sculptors of the last decades figure prominently. *Warsaw*, which possessed only a small gallery of modern pictures in pre-war time, is now in possession of the huge new building to house the central National Museum of Poland, which is in the making. A certain number of pictures by old masters, which formed a gallery connected with the Warsaw School of Fine Arts, has entered into this new Museum as its groundwork ; a considerable number of Polish pictures, illustrating the whole history of painting from the Middle Ages onward, has recently been added to it, and important additions to the stock of foreign pictures have also been made. The Rapperswyl collections from Switzerland (mentioned above) have also been incorporated in the Museum, which bids fair to grow rapidly.

The smaller towns of Poland are lately showing a noble ambition to develop local collections of their own. Some of these are based on diocesan museums, others evolve from the collections of noble families or local learned societies ; in some cases—as at Bydgoszcz (Bromberg) and Toruń (Thorn)—Poland has inherited such local collections from her German rulers in the nineteenth century, and is maintaining and enlarging them with all due care. A new provincial museum is rapidly growing up at Katowice in the industrial district of Silesia ; so is a new municipal gallery in the factory town of Łódź. Thus, even in centres of economic preoccupation, the education of the people n art and history is being intelligently attended to.

17

For *sculpture*, the Slavonic races have generally shown but little aptitude or inclination, in remarkable contrast to their high achievements in painting. A Slavonic sculptor of towering genius, like the great Yugoslav Ivo Mestrovic in our days, is a comparatively rare phenomenon.

Poland had produced very few gifted sculptors to match her distinguished painters of the nineteenth century.

At Cracow, *Professor K. Laszczka* represented before the War, and continues to represent now, a typically academic style of sculpture, calm in its careful elaboration and certainly noble in the irreproachable beauty of its classical forms. A more agitated and romantic, but also largely traditional and declamatory style was represented by the late *W. Szymanowski*, the creator of the Warsaw monument to Chopin, with a wind-swept Polish tree over Chopin's listening head. Among sculptors who may be said to have reached maturity now, *E. Wittig* is a prominent figure. He has passed through several phases. His recumbent figure of "Eve," the outcome of entranced absorption in sheer beauty of outline, has found an honourable permanent place in the Trocadéro Gardens in Paris. More recently, his monument to Poland's fallen airmen in Warsaw has given full evidence of the grandeur and concentrated power of conception of which he is capable. But the most passionately daring genius in the field of sculpture in Poland to-day undoubtedly is *K. Dunikowski*. He may have owed a large share of his original inspiration to the bold and rapturous attitudes of Baroque statuary in some of Poland's seventeenth-century churches; and the masterpiece of his own early years, an "Annunciation" altar-piece in the new Jesuit Church at Cracow, has Baroque characteristics. But he has since reached greater depths of reflection and a boldness of more sublime simplicity in his studies of "Maternity" which created much sensation; he has shown himself a perfect master of individual expression in the numerous "heads" which are to look down upon the visitor from the *cassettes* of the ceiling of one of the restored rooms in the old Royal Castle at Cracow; and in his huge models of statues of Saints for the front of a projected new cathedral at Katowice in Silesia, he has shown true monumental *calibre*. He definitely holds the supreme place among Polish sculptors to-day.

Among those who are so far conspicuous rather for promise than for achievement, mention is due to the much-discussed talent of *St. Szukalski*, suffering hitherto from an admixture of irritating mannerism borrowed from various ancient styles (such as the Assyrian and the Chinese) and dangerously bordering on the grotesque by weird combinations of the human form with those of fantastic animals. We may further mention *Mme. M. Szczytt-Lednicka*, a worthy disciple of the eminent Frenchman Antoine Bourdelle, and *A. Zamoyski*, outrageous but always interesting in his ultra-modern, deliberate simplifications.

From sculpture it is an easy transition to *architecture*. Like sculpture, and even to a higher degree, the art of building is indebted for impulses and monumental tasks to the great political change of our days, and especially to the reassumption by Warsaw of the functions of a capital city.

The two opposite poles between which Polish architecture oscillated on the eve of the War, were national tradition and the imitation of great historical styles. The national tradition was typically represented by the old houses of the Polish country gentry—mostly low, oblong structures, not rising beyond a wide ground floor, and marked by a porch on two columns in the middle of the front side. Of course, this type of home did not lend itself to adaptation for the purposes of public buildings ; but it has been largely adopted as the model of family houses in the new suburbs of Polish cities, such as Żoliborz in Warsaw ; and—in a more original way—it has also been used for new railway stations in the country, which with their white walls, two graceful little front columns, and pretty gardens, produce a very pleasing effect indeed, vastly different from that of the raw-looking and grim red-brick structures of pre-war time.

The imitation of historical styles of monumental architecture in the construction of public buildings mostly went, in the immediate pre-war era, in the direction of Renaissance or Empire classicism, with imposing rows of large columns along the front. Buildings of this traditional type have risen in the new Poland in considerable numbers, the model being sometimes not unpleasingly varied by a rounded outline by way of adaptation to the site. In Warsaw, the new homes of several government departments (such as the new Education Office) represent large-scale examples of this style, and it must be admitted that they mostly harmonize well with the palaces of the Empire era in which the city is particularly rich. Cracow, which had developed, in the Renascence period, a kind of " Tudor Gothic " of its own (imitated in nineteenth-century red-brick structures like the new University College of 1884) absorbs the large

colonnades of modern buildings in the strictly classical style
less easily ; several of them, however, have been introduced
into the physiognomy of the city since the War.

Side by side with time-honoured monumental classicism,
a new large-scale style of building has made its appearance in
post-war architecture, and more and more specimens of it are
springing up at conspicuous points in Poland's old cities. The
characteristic features of this modern style—perhaps best
summed up in the German slogan *die neue Sachlichkeit*—are
by this time quite familiar to the traveller in contemporary
Europe. They consist mainly in smooth frontages, flat roofs,
and square ironwork balconies like the balustrades of pier
walks or steamer decks. The obvious origin of this new departure in style was the desire for undisguised and even ornamental
use of such new elements as ferro-concrete, large glass surfaces,
or wire netting ; also a liking for the solid contours of tall
square blocks, as in the case of the American sky-scrapers ;
sometimes—as in the use of corner windows—a wish to be
strikingly original at any price ; but generally a reaction in
favour of stark simplicity after the profusion of largely mere-
tricious ornament in which nineteenth-century architectural
eclecticism had fairly revelled.

In Poland, the new style—for it is becoming nothing less
than that—is already represented by such landmarks as the
large new building of the Bank of National Economy, in the
very centre of Warsaw (at the crossing of the two main thorough-
fares of the city), designed by *Professor R. Świerczyński* and
finished in 1931. At Cracow, significantly enough, one of the
first buildings of the kind was the home of the Y.M.C.A., designed
by *Professor W. Krzyżanowski* on the American model. More
recently, an even larger building, to house the offices of an
insurance company, has been designed by *Professor Szyszko-
Bohusz*, and, in spite of loud protests and violent controversy,
has boldly taken its place in the ancient market-place of the
city, among historic houses mostly several hundred years old,
opposite the graceful Renascence structure of Drapers' Hall,
and at a stone's throw from the venerable fourteenth-century
Gothic pile of St. Mary's. Few things indeed could illustrate
so visibly the remarkable fact of historical Poland's resumed
life in a new and utterly different epoch.

## 18

This striking juxtaposition of the very old and the very new
in such historical cities as Cracow reminds us of the fact that,

besides urgent and important tasks in the way of building, the new Poland had to face a duty which it owed to its past, viz., that of *preserving the monuments* of nearly a thousand years of history in the shape of some magnificent old architecture.

The War had done much to ruin such historical monuments in all parts of Poland, and accordingly it was an early concern of the temporary Government in 1918, even before the new Polish State was definitely formed, to organize official protection over the relics of old architecture by a special decree. Unfortunately, financial difficulties made it impossible subsequently to create more than seven offices for the preservation of architectural monuments in the whole Republic, and the experts in charge of them are doing what they can, with the scanty means at their disposal, to promote and subsidize local effort directed at the maintenance of Poland's ancient architectural glories. Considerable materials towards a complete inventory of architectural and art relics have been prepared, and the registration of all such objects was made compulsory by a new decree in 1928.

Romanesque and Gothic *churches* of the Middle Ages, often of great beauty, are to be found in out-of-the-way corners of the country; many of them had grievously suffered through artillery fire during the War. In 1928, it could proudly be stated by the official organs that all such damage had in the main, wherever still possible, been repaired; in many cases this involved the accurate re-building of entire steeples, walls, pillars or vaultings. Local piety, sometimes expressed by heavy sacrifices in money, helped to renew or reconstruct the interior decoration of the churches. The greatest example of the co-operation of government assistance and private effort in this domain consists in the outward and inward restoration —now almost completed—of St. Mary's at Cracow, Poland's most magnificent Gothic church. Besides larger churches of brick and stone, many small village churches built of wood, and five or six hundred years old, preserve features of their old character and beauty of outline. They have sometimes to be preserved from the undiscriminating zeal of ambitious parish priests, who naturally wish to replace them by stone ones. These wooden churches have lately become an object not only of particular care, but also of assiduous and sometimes surprisingly fruitful study. In some cases, in the eastern provinces, Roman Catholic churches had been transformed under Russian rule into Greek Orthodox ones, and features of Byzantine architecture engrafted on them; a number of such churches have now regained their pristine purity of style. Often, the restoration of the interior of churches has led to important discoveries in the history of religious art : thus, at Toruń in Pomerania, valuable frescoes of the fourteenth century were laid bare in the Church of St. John, and fifteenth-century Byzantine fresco paintings of exceptional interest were found in the Castle Chapel of Lublin. A special workshop for the restoration of old pictures has been created in Warsaw, and among the achievements in this field the careful restoration of the famous picture of the " Black Virgin " at Częstochowa (now proved to be early Sienese work under Byzantine influence) stands to the new Poland's credit. Sometimes even chemical research has to be called in to aid the preserver of ancient monuments : thus, chemical experts helped in protecting the coffins of the kings of Poland in the crypts of the Cathedral at Cracow against a process of decomposition described as " tin lepra."

Passing now from ecclesiastical to *secular architecture*, we can only summarily mention the restoration of numerous old aristocratic palaces in *Warsaw*, now occupied by central government institutions. The eighteenth-century palace of Minister Brühl in " Saxon Square " (now housing Poland's Foreign Office) is a particularly fine specimen of the kind. But foremost among such works of restoration there must be mentioned the restoration of the Royal Palace in Warsaw, now almost complete again in the ancient splendour of its halls, and used by the President of the Republic.

Before the kings of Poland transferred their capital to Warsaw at the end of the sixteenth century, they had used the Royal Castle on Wawel Hill at *Cracow*, which in its extant shape is a masterpiece of Renascence architecture. The restoration of Wawel Castle was taken in hand under Austria, a few years before the War, but real progress was only made with it in the new Poland, and now the enchanting beauty of the arcaded courtyard, as well as the spacious magnificence of dozens of rooms and of the ample staircase, can once more be admired by the visitor.

Of a number of old palaces in various parts of Poland—some of them still belonging to noble families, others turned to public uses—this is not the place to speak in detail ; most of them were restored in the first ten years of the new Poland's existence. Besides these palaces of the modern era, Poland is by no means poor in *ruins* of medieval castles, and the more important ones of these also are being secured against further decay, such as, e.g., the remnants of the early medieval castle overlooking the city of Wilno.

Besides government initiative in these matters, the intelligent interest taken by some city communities in their old architecture deserves recognition. In this respect, Cracow, with its old and very active Society of Antiquaries, is an example to the whole of Poland ; among the numerous and valuable publications undertaken by this Society, there figures also the English edition of L. Lepszy's book on the history and monuments of the city (" Cracow," translated by R. Dyboski, London: T. Fisher Unwin, 1912). It is due to the influence of such organizations on municipal administration, that the ancient beauty of cities like Cracow is being safeguarded against, or even freed from the hideous excrescences of modern commercialism and advertisement. Wilno, a city ranking in beauty next to Cracow, has recently followed her lead in these matters with laudable zeal and enlightened judgment. It is to be confidently expected that the growing volume of such efforts will effectively protect the glories of Poland's historical monuments from disappearing under the cheap and colourless coating of a standardized civilization.

## 19

The account given above of the preservation of Poland's historical relics would not be complete without brief mention of the *recovery of art treasures and valuable objects of historical interest* which had been carried out of Poland by her invaders and despoilers since the partitions.

Libraries, archives, picture collections, the artistic furniture of royal palaces, much of all this had gone into the interior of Russia long ago in the eighteenth century ; more had followed after the rising of 1831, and some very precious items had been evacuated during the World War, when the Imperial Armies were abandoning Russian Poland to the Germans.

The conditions under which the Riga Peace Treaty between Poland and the Bolsheviks was concluded in 1921, made it possible to include in it fairly sweeping provisions for the restoration of all such valuable property taken by Russia from Poland between 1772 and 1915. But the task of carrying these provisions into effect was indeed staggering : in the chaotic state of Soviet Russia, it seemed next to impossible to locate anything whatever, and in many important cases documentary evidence for Poland's claims was not easy to produce. An army of the best experts of Poland in all the relative spheres of scholarship was mobilized to assist the " Delegation for Revindication " acting in Moscow. Against it were arrayed, in due time, some of the most eminent historical scholars and art experts of Russia, as far as they had survived the first years of the Bolshevik revolution and emerged from the Soviet prisons into which they had been put as " bourgeois " and " counter-revolutionaries."

The labours of revindication dragged on for half a dozen weary years, and Poland could at best hope to recover a portion only of the priceless treasures of which she was robbed in the course of a century and a half of depredations. Considering the great difficulties of the work, however, it is astonishing and gratifying to see how much has actually been recovered, and it would be unjust not to make honourable mention of the names of those who first achieved definite results in the difficult early stages, viz., the skilful diplomat Minister *Olszewski*, his secretary the eminent art expert *M. Morelowski* (now professor in the University of Wilno), and the library specialist *E. Kuntze* (now chief librarian to the University of Cracow).

Among the items of first-rate importance and value recovered in the very first years of work, pride of place is due to the 120 priceless large arrases or wall-hangings of sixteenth-century Flemish design and manufacture, representing Old Testament Scenes, which once adorned the state rooms of the Royal Castle at Cracow and have now returned to them. In the second place, we may mention the furniture of the Royal Castle in Warsaw, and the even more valuable, highly artistic furniture of the last king of Poland's charming Rococo summer palace called *Łazienki* (" The Bath House ") in Warsaw. Of the same art-loving monarch's large picture collection, twenty-one pictures painted in eighteenth-century Warsaw by the Venetian, Antonio Belotto-Canaleto, and 120,000 etchings of the period have been restored to their Polish home. Other capital items now easily accessible to the visitor in Warsaw are Thorwaldsen's noble equestrian statue of the Napoleonic Polish hero Prince Joseph Poniatowski, and Matejko's huge historical picture of the battle of Grunwald (fought by Poles and Lithuanians in 1410 against the Knights of the Teutonic Order). Passing over the extremely valuable art collections of a number of prominent Polish noble families of the borderlands, we may yet mention a collection of 100,000 etchings belonging to the University of Warsaw, and some 7,000 bells taken out of eastern Poland's churches in 1915, during the retreat of the Russians.

Such were the results, obtained amid endless friction, and with prolonged interruptions, during the first few years. In 1927, after another serious political complication, and a pause of two years, a " General Agreement " was concluded which was to cover all the outstanding claims of Poland and to put an end to the whole process. Among the objects enumerated in this agreement and *de facto* recovered since, there are the following important items of historical interest : the coronation sword of the kings of Poland ; the sixteenth-century state banner of the kingdom ; a number of trophies brought home by King John Sobieski after his rescue of Vienna from the Turk ; a considerable number of pictures by such masters as Watteau, Rembrandt, and others (collected by the last king of Poland) ; a large collection of coins belonging to Warsaw University (nearly 12,000), etc. More important were the definite gains in the matter of *libraries and archives*. Of Poland's best and largest library of the eighteenth century, the Załuski Library (mentioned before in this book), which had served as the groundwork for the St. Petersburg Public Library, a considerable portion of the more valuable early books, as well as 1,100 MSS. have been recovered and now form part of the new National Library of Poland in Warsaw. And the historical material in the way of charters and other documents regained for Polish archives, has provided the students of sources for Poland's political, legal, social, and economic development with objects of research for many years ahead.

Considering the way in which history is either disregarded or twisted to party uses in Soviet Russia, the revindications of Poland in the way of historical material constitute important salvage work for the great western European tradition of historical scholarship, while her revindications of works of art have restored part at least of that abundance of beauty in all forms which was a marked characteristic both of the Renascence Poland of the Jagellon Kings and of eighteenth-century Poland under the unfortunate but highly cultured Stanislas Augustus.

## 20

The discussion of the art treasures recovered from Russia has carried us from the domain of architecture into the cognate one of *decorative arts*, and it seems appropriate now to say something of the evolution of these arts in the new Poland.

Here, as in the sphere of oil painting, the great name of *Matejko* stands for a landmark. By executing, with the help of his pupils, the huge labour of decorating the entire interior of St. Mary's Church at Cracow with fresco paintings and ornaments, he set an example which inspired many younger men. Foremost among them, there stands *J. Mehoffer*, now himself a professor in the same Academy at Cracow where he was Matejko's disciple. Mehoffer's international fame securely rests on the imposing array of stained-glass windows painted by him for the Roman Catholic Cathedral of Fribourg in Switzerland ; at home, he is also known as an etcher, an illustrator, a painter of theatrical decorations, of posters, and of frescoes : some of his finest fresco work adorns the great hall of the Cracow Chamber of Commerce. His fellow-student in Matejko's class, *S. Wyspiański*, has been mentioned before both as a great dramatic poet and as a painter ; some of his grandest pictorial work consists of cartoons of stained-glass windows for Cracow Cathedral—showing ancient kings and princes of Poland in the awful majesty of death—and of fresco wall decorations and stained-glass windows in the Franciscan Church at Cracow, the latter (St. Francis of Assisi, St. Salomea, and God Father separating light from darkness) being among the most powerful Polish work of the kind. Crowding an almost incredible amount of inspired work into the precarious few years of his mature life, Wyspiański did not disdain the tasks of furniture designer, of book decorator, of scene painter for his own dramas, and in all these fields of decorative art his work bears the stamp of great genius.

Another pioneer—mentioned before as an epoch-making art critic—appeared at the same time in the person of *St. Witkiewicz*, He discovered for Polish public opinion the beauty of the architectural outline, the carved ornamental patterns, and the home-made furniture of the cottages of the mountain peasantry at Zakopane, and he used his brilliant gifts as a writer to advocate the idea that the " *style of Zakopane* " be made a national style for the whole of Poland. The style proved too florid for general use, and what is more important, being a style peculiar to wood architecture, it resisted all attempts at adaptation to brick and stone architecture. The movement broke down after a few years of popularity ; but the Zakopane style remains a great force in the moulding of characteristic Polish artistic furniture, and its influence is manifest in such masterpieces of recent Polish woodcarving as the interior of a chapel of the Virgin, designed by *J. Szczepkowski* and exhibited at the International Exhibition of Decorative Arts in Paris, 1925.

A more lasting impress than by the noble personal initiative of Witkiewicz was left by a society formed in 1901 at Cracow under the name of *Polish Applied Art*, whose organizer, *J. Warchałowski* still remains the most active propagandist of decorative art in Poland. It was he and his fellow-workers who, like Morris and his compeers in England, awakened in modern Polish society not only a strong sense of the need for beauty in man's everyday surroundings, not only a proper appreciation of decorative art as Art, but a new enthusiasm for the inspiring quality of the art of peasant folk, as manifested in the shape of objects of daily use quite as vividly as in folk-song or folk-music. Now the charm of ornament peculiar to hand-woven rugs (*Kilims*) as used by the peasantry in many parts of Poland, became apparent to the eyes of the educated public. " Kilim " workshops, began to spring up, and form at present one of the most flourishing branches of artistic handicraft in the country, Polish kilims being by this time widely known and very much in demand among foreign amateurs.

In 1912 the new " Applied Art " movement had sufficiently progressed to organize an impressive exhibition of Polish domestic architecture and interior decoration at Cracow. Shortly afterwards, the " Cracow Workshops " and the " Industrial Museum " at Cracow became active centres of propaganda, training, experiment, and high-quality production in the field. With the reunion and deliverance of Poland, the whole of the wide domain of highly diversified peasant art in all the different provinces of the country was really opened up for loving observation, and a popular movement called (in western European fashion) " *regionalism* " made not only local history, local nature study and local folk-lore, but also the study and glorification of local folk-art its aim. At the same time, the central Government took applied art under its protection and organized a number of new *Arts and Crafts Schools* in the principal cities, added Departments of Decorative Art to existing Art Schools, and enlarged such old-established institutions as the Artistic Woodcarving School at Zakopane. *Workshops* connected with all such schools are stimulating artistic production among their pupils, and a model *co-operative*, founded a few years ago by the professors and students of the College of Arts in Warsaw under the name of *Ład* (" Order "), has done much to raise the level of all recent endeavour in the field, and to place it on the broader footing. Its organization was due to the highly encouraging successes achieved by Polish work at the Decorative Arts Exhibition in Paris in 1925.

Among prominent personalities active in various branches of decorative art, we may single out : *K. Młodzianowski* (dead a few years ago after meritorious work as a soldier and administrator in the new Polish State), the first director of the pre-war

Cracow Workshops ; *E. Trojanowski,* who years ago first
transplanted the movement from Cracow to Warsaw ; *J.
Czajkowski,* now director of the Warsaw College of Arts, the
most prominent recent leader of the whole movement, distinguished both as a painter and an interior decorator ; *K.
Maszkowski,* now the head of the Arts and Crafts School at
Poznań, an excellent practical organizer of production ; *W.
Jastrzębowski,* a master in the planning of interiors ; *K. Tichy,*
a pioneer in the field of artistic pottery ; *K. Frycz* and *W. Drabik,* mentioned before as the most gifted theatrical scene painters
in the country ; *K. Stryjeński* (recently dead, alas, in the
prime of manhood), the highly gifted reorganizer of Polish
woodcarving ; *B. Treter,* the creator of the finest modern
" kilims," *J Bukowski,* Poland's foremost book decorator ;
*B. Lenart,* the leading promoter of artistic bookbinding ;
*L. Gardowski* and *A. Półtawski,* distinguished for innovations
in beautiful printing ; *Mlle. Z. Kogutówna,* an eminent artist
in the production of the kind of tapestry called by the Malayan
name of " batik " ; *Mme. Łazarska,* popular as the creator of an
artistic type of folk-lore doll named after Mme. Paderewski.

To this list of names of eminent artists and teachers, a few
details may be added concerning the general organization of
*education* in the decorative arts in the new Polish Republic.
One of its principal instruments is the *Cracow School of Decorative
Arts and Artistic Industries,* an institution of pre-war origin,
on which many similar schools in other cities of Poland have
modelled their structure. The Cracow School consists of a
general and special section. The general section provides the
pupil with the rudiments of nature study, of composition and
ornament, of the technical organization of different decorative
art workshops, adding some elements of geometry, perspective,
art history, anatomy, the chemistry and physics of materials,
as well as book-keeping and civics. The special section is
divided into half a dozen departments devoted to such branches
of applied art as interior decoration, decorative painting,
etching and woodcutting, textile work, pottery and ornamental
sculpture in wood, stone and metal. The school has sent out a
number of designers and artistic directors into Poland's industrial establishments ; it is also constantly furnishing to those
establishments artistic patterns and designs of its own production, which have already won hundreds of prizes at competitions
and exhibitions. Its influence as well as the influence of the
two other schools of the same type (at Poznań and Lwów)
may be said to be more and more permeating large spheres of

Polish industry. Warsaw, in its *School of Fine Arts*, possesses a unique institution, which combines academic instruction in painting and sculpture with the teaching of the decorative arts on the same academic level, and so provides for the constant and fruitful penetration of the domain of applied art by influences from the more abstract regions of artistic creation.

Surveying the whole field of recent Polish effort in the way of carrying art and beauty into the daily life and daily surroundings of the people, we may say without exaggeration that the noble band of "Applied Art" workers has rescued decorative art in Poland from subjection to the commonplace standards of international industrialism, and secured for it a distinctive note of its own, harmonized with national tradition and inspired by the creations of the folk.

### 21

Polish *music*, like literature and painting, while not by any means poor in remarkable productions during the early modern centuries, yet reached the very highest pitch of achievement in the period of captivity and exile, when art had to serve as a vehicle of national self-expression, and when banishment lent the glamour of homesick longing to everything pertaining to Poland. Better known throughout the world than Poland's great Romantic poets, their contemporary and fellow-exile *F. Chopin*, speaking to all nations in the great world-language of music, breathed into his compositions not only all an exile's idealizing worship of Poland's historical greatness, not only all the temperament of the nation, chivalrous and poetic and fiery and dreamy, but also a wealth of melody inspired by the dance tunes and songs of Poland's country folk. It is this connection of so many of Chopin's masterpieces with Polish folk-music which gives his work the hall-mark of something profoundly and primevally Polish, in spite of the composer's emigrant French ancestry.

Unlike the poet Mickiewicz and the painter Matejko, whose suns are surrounded with constellations of lesser lights, Chopin stands comparatively alone. The only great name besides his in mid-nineteenth-century Polish music—a name little known outside Poland—is that of *St. Moniuszko*, whose *Halka* (*Helen*) remains the supreme and most typical of Polish operas, while other works of his—such as *The Haunted Country-house* (*Straszny Dwór*)—also hold a permanent and honourable place in the repertory of the national operatic stage. Other Polish composers of Moniuszko's era and of the following decades—

such as *W. Żeleński* and *Z. Noskowski*—are rather epigones than satellites of the great genius of Chopin.

It is only with the appearance of Poland's greatest song composer, *M. Kartowicz*—unfortunately killed in early manhood by an avalanche in the Tatra mountains a few years before the War—that a breath of new and high creative inspiration once more pervades the domain of Polish music. He became the head and leader of a group of young composers, some of whom survive as the outstanding representatives of Polish music to-day. This new development, soon interrupted by the World War, did not gain in strength and depth by the recovery of Poland's independence. About post-war Polish music, as about post-war Polish literature, there is a feeling as if art had a less vital and august message among a free nation than among a captive one. Political obstacles had prevented the consolidation of a strong tradition of national style in music in the nineteenth century, and such a style did not consolidate now, when all such obstacles were removed.

The musical world of Poland in the early post-war years was divided into two main groups, which differ also in age. The older composers all more or less represent the ideals of the great *Romantic movement* in nineteenth-century European music. To these belongs *I. J. Paderewski* not only by his unique renderings of Chopin, but by his own opera *Manru* and his other well-known lesser compositions. Others of this group are the eminent song-composers *St. Niewiadomski* and *F. Szopski* ; the symphonist *F. Nowowiejski*; the late distinguished pianist, *H. Melcer* ; the musical historian *H. Opieński* ; and the eminent representative of Polish music in America, *Z. Stojowski*. Some of the group, like the gifted *J. Wertheim,* went back even beyond Romantic music, to the age of classicism for their models of style.

Opposed to these traditionalists, there stands (as in painting), a younger group of *musical modernists*, much less homogeneous in its composition, because comprising strong and highly differentiated personalities. It can only be said by way of broad generalization that the moderate wing of the modernist group, not altogether remote from traditional standards, is led by *L. Różycki*, while an advanced wing, marked by complicated technique and intellectualism, is headed by the commanding figure of *K. Szymanowski*, now perhaps best known to fame of all living Polish composers.

Różycki marks his connection with the Romantic tradition by drawing on Polish folk-lore both for the subject-matter and the musical garb of his highly successful ballet *Twardowski* (a legendary magician, Poland's Dr. Faustus), while his operas —such as *Beatrice Cenci*—are characterized by boldness and strength of dramatic effect, also a typically Romantic feature.

Opera remains the almost exclusive domain of Różycki's creative activities ; others of the moderate progressive group also cultivate the symphony ; prominent among them are *W. Maliszewski*, an instrumental composer of great subtlety of invention and high perfection of form ; *L. M. Rogowski*, remarkable for the exoticism of his Oriental and archaic themes ; *A. Wieniawski*, a cultured follower of the French impressionists ; and *E. Morawski*, a disciple of such masters of programme music as Berlioz and Liszt.

*K. Szymanowski*, the leader of the Left in Poland's music of to-day, now aged fifty, has a rich and interesting personal evolution behind him. Influences of R. Strauss, of Scriabin, of the French impressionists cross each other in the early growth of his genius and threaten to overpower his independent personality, quite as the extreme polyphonic complexity of some of his compositions almost buries the creative idea under an overelaboration of mere technical invention. A return to greater simplicity becomes necessary and is happily accomplished in the sphere of song composition, and with helpful inspiration from the folk-melodies of the Polish mountain peasantry, to which Szymanowski has recently done eloquent creative homage in his *Mazurkas*. With all this refreshing change of form and structure, however, his music still remains true to its constant and dominant tendency towards intellectual abstraction and metaphysical brooding, which in such a masterpiece of his as the *Third Symphony* penetrates us with a haunting fear of the vast mysteries of the universe. Even in his historical opera, *King Roger*, it is an essentially abstract idea, that of struggle between living spirit and inert material form, that is conveyed in musical terms.

The great phenomenon of Szymanowski is flanked by other representatives of the intellectual abstraction of " pure " music, such as *C. Marek*, to whom, however, as to Szymanowski himself, a Romantic admixture of folk-lore melody is not foreign. Neither is it absent in the extremely modernist compositions of *A. Tansman*, better known abroad than in Poland. Composers of the youngest generation, like *A. Maklakiewicz* and *P. Perkowski* in Poland, *K. Rathaus* in Berlin and *T. Jarecki* in America, inevitably are largely under the spell of Szymanowski's fascinating polyphonic style. It is safe to predict that the present era of Polish music will in history be known by his name.

## 22

To the above survey of the creative work of composers in the new Poland, a few particulars may now be added concerning the *organized cultivation of music and singing* in the Poland of to-day.

*Choral singing*, that simplest and in some ways most important social expression of musical culture, was most popular in the former Prussian provinces of Poland (Poznania and Silesia), where organized Polish choral song was opposed to German : it is well known what great part choral singing played in modern German education and national life.  Next to the west, it was the south-east—the eastern part of Austrian Galicia—where choral singing flourished most :  here it was the old-established, fine tradition of choral song among the Ukrainian peasantry which acted as a stimulant.  In the new united Poland, efforts were made to promote the noble practice of choral song throughout the whole country, and a state-wide *Association of Polish Choral Societies*, with a *Musical Review* for its organ, was founded. It originated in the former Prussian province of Poznań, where also the first congress of Poland's Choral Societies was held in 1924.  A year before, a Warsaw Choral Society with an old tradition behind it, called *Harfa* (" The Harp ") had won a first prize at an international choral singing contest in Amsterdam, and the Cracow Society called *Echo*, had been awarded honourable mention.  Cracow also possesses, in the University Students' Choral Society, one of the best and oldest organizations of its kind in Poland, and it has at present, in the person of *B. Wallek Walewski* (also well known as a composer), one of the ablest conductors of choral song in Poland, equal to such older conductors as the late *J. Gall* at Lwów (well known also as a song composer) and *P. Maszyński* in Warsaw.  The composition of choral songs is an important item among the creative work of Poland's greatest musical masters, e.g., *K. Szymanowski*, whose *Stabat Mater* for mixed choir and orchestra is one of his most famous works.  A series of prize competitions organized in the new Poland, has revealed some valuable young talents in this particular field of composition.

*Opera* had four regular stages devoted exclusively to it in Poland (Warsaw, Lwów, Poznań and Katowice), besides an Amateur Operatic Society at Cracow, and less sustained efforts at Wilno.  The present crisis has hit opera (in Poland as elsewhere) harder than other branches of dramatic art, as being particularly expensive—and Poland's opera houses are closing their gates one after another. Looking back upon their activities in the days of relative prosperity, we must single out the *Opera of Warsaw* as a first-rate operatic stage : its excellence was due not only to munificent subsidies from the Government and the Municipality, but also to its long-continued and admirable management by the eminent conductor and composer, *E. Mlynarski*. Apart from the new operas of Polish composers (mentioned above), the Warsaw stage attracted attention by a brilliant production of Wagner's *Parsifal* in its entirety. Among the names of eminent Polish opera singers, those of *Adam Didur*, *Ada Sari* and *Jan Kiepura* may be mentioned as being well known abroad, both on the European and the American stage, as well as through the more popular media of the gramophone, the radio and the operatic film.

Side by side with such well-known stars of Polish song, it is fit to mention some of the foremost of Poland's *instrumental performers* of the present day. The supreme glories of *Paderewski* as an interpreter of Chopin are rivalled though not reached, by *Z. Drzewiecki*, *I. Friedmann*, the aged *A. Michałowski*, *E. Petri*, *A. Rubinstein*, *J. Śliwiński*, *J. Turczyński*, and a number of other Polish pianists of great distinction, including *W. Landowska*, who has specialized in performing on that archaic instrument the clavecin. As a violinist, *B. Huberman* has made a well-established international reputation ; and *P. Kochański* is known on both sides of the Atlantic.

What the Warsaw Opera House meant for opera in Poland (until the present crisis), the *Warsaw Philharmonic Society* meant, and happily still means, for symphonic music ; its fine concert hall and excellent orchestra, together with a brilliant succession of capable conductors, have made it a first-rate centre of musical culture. The glories of the *Cracow* and *Lwów Musical Societies*, very high in the nineteenth century, have comparatively faded, owing to the centralization of post-war Polish art in Warsaw and to the impoverishment of the intelligent public, as well as to the recent competition of cheaper forms of musical entertainment. Still, it must be mentioned that a special *Oratorium Society* at Cracow is indefatigably doing its best to offer worthy renderings of great musical works of the past.

If secular music has suffered from the stress and distraction of the times, *religious music*, stimulated by a marked revival of Catholicism throughout contemporary Europe, is in a comparatively flourishing condition in Poland. *The High Masses at*

*Poznań Cathedral* (now made accessible to listeners all over Poland by radio) enjoy a particular and well-deserved reputation for excellent music and song. And the *Cecilian Choir* at Cracow has done much to popularize the best church music of past ages. The renascence of *Gregorian Chant*, inaugurated in the Catholic Church at the beginning of our century, has worthy exponents in Poland in the *Missionary Fathers*. There are also several periodicals devoted to church music in particular.

What is being done for *musical education* in the new Poland, has partly been recorded in the foregoing chapter on " Education and Research." Here it may be briefly noted that progress has been particularly marked in former Russian Poland, where all education had been so sadly repressed under Russian rule : of the twenty-nine Schools of Music now extant in that sector of the country, twenty were founded since the War. In the Austrian province, well-organized music schools of higher grade had existed in all the principal towns since the 'eighties of the last century, and the number of their pupils has considerably increased since the War, especially at Lwów. The new Polish Government has created two state-supported Musical Academies or " Conservatoria," as they are called in Continental Europe, viz., in the cities of Warsaw and Poznań (Cracow and Lwów had had theirs before the War), and the attempt has recently been made—not very successfully so far—to raise the Warsaw Academy to university rank. A successful and important organizing achievement of the Polish State consists in the introduction of competent inspection of all music teaching in Polish schools, which has been very helpful in raising the general standard of musical education. The same end is served by periodical public performances of instrumental music classes, both of government and private schools. All in all, Poland now has over seventy schools of music of various grades, including a few schools specially devoted to singing and some for the training of organists. There are nine musical periodicals, the most important among them being the monthly *Muzyka* (" Music ") which has been appearing in Warsaw since 1924, under the able editorship of *M. Gliński*. Research in the history and theory of music, conducted by the professors of the subject in Polish universities (*A. Chybiński*, *Z. Jachimecki*, and *L. Kamieński*), has produced not only a fairly large crop of text-books for students, and monographs of important composers, but also some very important editorial work, which has given new publicity to the works of forgotten Polish composers of earlier centuries. Editorial efforts have also been devoted to the music of the country people, to which the works of Chopin and other great Polish composers owe so much, and it is especially the music of the Tatra mountaineers (among whom the bagpipe, as in Scotland, is a popular instrument) which has lately been illustrated by carefully prepared and well-produced collections. They will certainly not fail to give renewed strength to the perennial and invigorating influence of folk-music on the creative activity of composers.

## CHAPTER X

# POLAND'S POSITION IN THE WORLD OF TO-DAY AND TO-MORROW

I

IT might be considered as one of the ironies of history that the deliverance of Poland, striven for with so much suffering and sacrifice during a century and a half of captivity, should at last have been attained in an era in which hard facts are apparently compelling the world to realize that the " self-determination of nations " is not a panacea, and that, by the rearrangement of central and eastern Europe on a basis of nationality, at least as much has been lost economically as may have been gained politically.

To this argument—which is undeniably strong in these days of raging crisis and universal tariff war—a Pole will oppose the comforting consideration that a Poland composed of purely and strictly Polish territories—if it had at all been possible to carve them out unerringly—would indeed have been amorphous and unfit to live, while the Polish State as it exists to-day, built up on other foundations besides national ones, combines in its larger bulk a number of requirements for an existence economically sound as well as politically independent.

But it was this very creation of a " greater Poland " which not only entangled the new Republic in inevitable conflicts with almost all her neighbours, but also called forth remonstrances from among the western European authors of her restoration. In a well-known collective publication, organized under the auspices of the *Encyclopædia Britannica* and entitled *These Eventful Years* (1924), the eminent journalist Mr. J. L. Garvin, summarizing the historical results of the World War, expressed a common British opinion when he described it as a mistake that Poland was re-established in somewhat like her wide eighteenth-century frontiers, which once already had been the cause of international complications and of disaster to the country itself.

Such opinions—not perhaps much less prevalent in western

Europe and America in 1933 than they were ten years ago—make it seem appropriate to begin a conclusive account of Poland's place in the world to-day with a discussion of *territorial problems* ; and these can best be grouped according to the former partitioning powers, at whose expense Poland had been built up again.

In these matters, the question foremost in the minds of the average European and American, because most acutely controversial to-day, is that of Poland's relation to her western neighbour, *Germany*.

Germany has not become reconciled to the loss of several large provinces into which, since she took them from Poland, she had put a great amount of organizing effort and also of capital. Her territorial revindications—continually trumpeted into the ears of western Europe and America—concern not so much the agricultural province of Poznania (which, indeed, is as purely and indisputably Polish as any part of Poland can be), but in the first place the south-eastern portion of industrial *Silesia*, and the strip of land on the western bank of the lower Vistula, constituting Poland's access to the sea and called " *the Polish Corridor.*" With regard to *Polish Silesia*, Poland's case undeniably rests on somewhat remote history, as the whole of Silesia had been lost to Poland since the middle of the fourteenth century (although annexed by Prussia only in the eighteenth). But the very fact that the Polish tradition, in language and religion, after such long severance, should have been strong enough right through the modern era to give Poland, in 1921, a majority of the popular vote in those districts which were accordingly awarded to her, surely speaks for itself. And it must not be forgotten that a large and compact body of Polish country population (constituting a considerable portion of the one million Poles who now live under Germany) has remained outside Poland, in Prussian Lower Silesia. Taking the matter on other than national grounds, we are confronted by the fact that Poland possesses, in her portion of Silesia, the only large coal reservoir in a thirty-million State—the only substantial foundation for industrial progress and economic balance—while Germany, in possession of rich and excellent coalfields in her western regions, is by no means menaced in her economic existence by the cession of the Silesian mines. These mines remain largely in the private possession of German capitalists, and in the crisis which has affected the world's coal trade for years now, they would perhaps even be an embarrassing item if included in Germany's national household.

That is, perhaps, the reason why, in spite of much local friction, the Upper Silesian issue as a whole has not lately been quite the first point in the list of Germany's anti-Polish territorial grievances.

2

That place has been held for years by the question of the *"Polish Corridor."*[1] It is safe to say that many newspaper readers in the world of to-day have only that one single notion definitely and permanently associated with Poland in their heads : that it is the country which has a quarrel with Germany over a " Polish Corridor " through German territory.  German propaganda does not shun endless repetition in this matter, and repetition must not, accordingly, be shunned here in summing up the Polish case.  It must, then, once again be emphatically stated that East Prussia, now separated by the " Corridor " from the body of Germany, had been a German island in the midst of non-German populations ever since the Teutonic Knights began to colonize it in the early thirteenth century ;  and that territorial connection with Germany was only established by cutting Poland off from the sea in the period of the partitions.  Secondly, that Poland's historical sea-side province (of which the miscalled " Corridor " is only a portion) had not only been part and parcel of the Polish State until the partitions, but had, after them, remained predominantly Polish in the character of its population, not only to the extent of sending Polish deputies into the German Parliament, but of being marked, in authentic German official maps and statistics of pre-war time, as one of the centres of the " Polish danger " to the German Empire.  The " Corridor " is well over 80 per cent. Polish in its population now, as has repeatedly been verified by British and other foreign observers on the spot.  The Kassubians, who form the fishing population on the coast, speak a Polish dialect, and have often in the past manifested their attachment to the Polish national tradition, with which they are also connected by their Roman Catholic religion.

It is difficult even for Germans to deny these patent facts concerning the history of the " Corridor " territory and its population.  The argument, however, which is usually brought forward in support of the German case for frontier revision,

[1] This wrong and misleading appellation of the Polish province of Pomerania has unfortunately, owing to the efforts of German propaganda, become so common in English that it has been decided—under protest—to use it in inverted commas, in this book.

has reference not so much to the " Corridor " itself as to East Prussia. It is alleged that the isolation of East Prussia effected by the Peace Treaty is unnatural, unique in the modern world, and ruinous to the province so separated from the body of Germany.

As against this, it must be emphasized that similar " corridors " are not unknown elsewhere ; and the Canadian " corridor " to Vancouver—to mention only the instance most familiar to British and American readers—has never been an obstacle to the development of Alaska as part of the United States, or a cause of enmity between the two nations.

With regard to East Prussia, it is a well-established fact that German transit across the " Corridor," as safeguarded by international conventions, and often checked both by official authorities and private foreign observers, is facilitated in every way, and Poland has never declined to discuss further extensions of these facilities.

But, it is pleaded, East Prussia has suffered gravely in her economic life through her detachment, and a movement of emigration from that province into the interior of Germany has actually set in. The German budget is burdened with large expenditure on " relief to the East " (*Osthilfe*), which, as a matter of fact, is largely used for the political end of promoting and strengthening Germanism along the Polish border.

The complaints regarding the economic situation of East Prussia are not altogether unfounded, but are certainly exaggerated. The conditions, described as effects of the isolation of the province, are part of the general economic situation of Germany, which is due to a great many factors other than the territorial settlement. They are also part of the economic relations of commercial diffidence or open " tariff war " now unfortunately so general between European States. If Germany made up her mind to ratify the commercial treaty at last concluded in 1931, and long ago ratified by Poland, this would bring economic relief to East Prussia by providing her with a Polish Hinterland. It is, however, East Prussia herself which stands in the way of such ratification, the agrarian class-interest of her large landowners—a thoroughly reactionary and fanatically nationalist group—being allowed to carry undue weight in the councils of Germany's rulers.

Without discussing more fully such purely domestic German problems, it must plainly be stated that, in the last resort, the issue lies between greater or less economic inconvenience for one German province on the one hand, and the existence or non-

existence of the entire thirty-million Polish State on the other.
Poland can point to her historical experience in the partition
period, which shows that the annexation of her sea-side lands
by Prussia at the second partition in 1793 meant the cutting of
the jugular artery of her political organism.

This historical lesson, having been embodied (at the suggestion
of Colonel House) in President Wilson's Fourteen Points, was
taken into consideration by the framers of the Versailles Peace
Treaty. A compromise was created, by which a minimum of
direct access to the sea was given to Poland. The situation
which has developed since, has made this irreducible minimum
of access even more vital to Poland than ever before. Placed
between a Communist Russia with whom normal trade is
impossible, and a Germany who will not buy what Poland has
to offer—whether agricultural produce or coal—Poland has been
compelled to re-orient the direction of her entire foreign trade
in the sense that the main current of that trade no longer
runs between west and east, but from south to north. Britain
has become an important purchaser of Poland's agricultural
produce, the Scandinavian countries of her coal, and more
distant oversea lands buy in increasing quantities what cannot be
sold to Poland's continental neighbours. Poland once more, as
in the sixteenth century, must be a Baltic Power, or not be at all.

It is one of the constant German complaints before the League
of Nations and elsewhere that Poland, having by the Peace
Treaty obtained a measure of control over the port of *Danzig*,
a few years later began, with the assistance of French capital,
to build up close to Danzig on her own sea-coast the port of
*Gdynia* as a rapidly growing menace to Danzig's prosperity.
Now the compelling reason for the building of Gdynia consisted
not only in Danzig's persistent disloyalty to Poland, in her
constant evasion of treaty obligations, her organized encouragement of smuggling on a huge scale, and her general active
enmity to Polish interests—but also in the fact that the deadlock
in economic relations with Germany made the forcible development of Poland's sea-borne trade a vital necessity. And the
results of the fantastically quick evolution of Gdynia have been
truly surprising. It soon became fully apparent that there were
sufficient possibilities in Poland's trade to secure prosperity
both for Danzig and Gdynia, and perhaps even a third port
would become necessary in course of time. Danzig remained
infinitely more alive and prosperous than she was before the
War, when Hamburg overshadowed her entirely ; Gdynia
began to spread out year by year, like any modern American

city; and Tczew (further up the river) may soon come to act as a " port of distribution " for the two. The process accomplished before our eyes within a few short years could now be reversed only at the cost of complete economic ruin, and consequently of political destruction, to the entire fabric of the new Polish State. It is an axiom of Polish public opinion—regardless of party—that unimpeded access to the Baltic is a fundamental condition of Poland's continued existence.

### 3

Polish opinion is no less solidly united on the point that no discussion aiming at revision of the existing arrangements (a revision so clamorously demanded by Germany) can be entered into by Poland. Suggested alternatives to the " Corridor " will therefore only be briefly mentioned here in order to show how utterly unacceptable they are for Poland.

The absorption of the " Corridor " together with Danzig and East Prussia into the body of a reunited Germany could, it is said, be compensated to Poland by the right to use all north-eastern German harbours from Stettin to Königsberg. But everybody who has a knowledge of present-day international conditions, must realize that any guarantees which could be given for the inviolability of such commercial " rights of way " are worthless in a Europe deprived of a strong international executive. The same objection lies, *a fortiori*, to the idea (which would certainly not be relished either by Germany or by Poland) of erecting Danzig together with the " Corridor," and possibly with East Prussia, into a neutral political unit under international administration. The " Free City " of Danzig alone has caused more than enough trouble to the League of Nations in the last twelve years; a larger territory under international control in that part of the world would prove much more unmanageable, and would only be a source of constant quarrels and anxieties.

There remains a third proposal, which has tentatively been broached and is understood to be favoured by some British statesmen. Its main idea is that in return for the territory of the " Corridor," and for access to the sea by way of Danzig, Poland should receive access to the sea further east, by way of *Memel*, through territory which is now Lithuanian. Now Memel certainly commands as her natural Hinterland not only the whole of present-day Lithuania (over 50,000 square kilometres), but an equal amount of Polish territory, viz., the basin of the river Niemen, covering a large part of north-eastern

Poland. But in the present territorial constitution of the larger, united Poland, such an arrangement would imply a violent, unnatural and entirely impracticable twist of the country's whole system of communications by 45 degrees, a twist all the more difficult and wasteful as exactly those territories for which a direct route to the sea is most vital, viz., the Silesian coal mines, would then be farthest away from Poland's sea outlet, being right at the opposite end of a diagonal line. Besides, the Memel plan would involve a thorough change in Poland's relations with *Lithuania*—the re-establishment, in fact, of the historical union between the two countries. Now Lithuania, while vociferously reclaiming her old capital, Wilno, and its district at the hands of Poland, shrinks from the very thought of a renewal of the union, because she fears that, in such a union, her national distinctness would be endangered through weight of numbers and through Polish cultural influence.

Apart, however, from the question of Lithuania's attitude there is yet another, and major, aspect of the problem to be considered, which is imperfectly visualized by western observers. The fact that Balkan antagonisms had arrayed Germany and Russia against each other in the World War, obscured the memory of a very old and very real *community of interests between Germany and Russia* in the domain of eastern European affairs. That community, cemented in the eighteenth century by the partitions of Poland, has since the World War, been fully revived. While using Soviet Russia (her ally since the Rapallo Treaty of 1922) as a convenient basis for large armaments impracticable at home under the Peace Treaty, Germany at the same time pursues, more strenuously than ever, the aim of turning the whole of the vast Russian lands into a colonial territory for German enterprise of all kinds. That pursuit is naturally intensified by the loss of Germany's pre-war oversea colonial possessions. Poland once again, as in the eighteenth century, is an obstacle in the way of such aspirations ; and if Germany so strongly resents the existence of the " Polish Corridor," it is certainly not only because the " Corridor " cuts off East Prussia from Germany, but because it is a barrier between Germany and Russia. What Germany wants to effect by the removal of the " Polish Corridor," is the creation of a new and much broader " Corridor " over the head of Poland, uniting Germany with Russia. The small Baltic States, particularly Lithuania, would then serve but as a continuation of a German " Corridor " so conceived. It is plain, then, that it is not against the " Polish Corridor " as it exists now but against *a* " Polish Corridor "—in fact, against any and every " Polish Corridor " to the Baltic—that the efforts of Germany are and will be directed.

It is, on the other hand, equally plain to anybody possessed of a modicum of historical knowledge and political imagination, what danger to the whole European system an effective contiguity of Russia and Germany and a close combination of the Imperialist forces of both countries would imply. If this danger is to be avoided, the maintenance not only of Poland as a whole, but of her outstretched territorial arm towards the sea, appears a dictate of truly wise and far-sighted European policy.[1]

## 4

The discussion of Germany's new-old Russian alliance has already carried us from the orbit of Polish-German into that of *Polish-Russian relations*. Although less strained at present than those with Germany, Poland's relations with her eastern neighbour are no less difficult and no less fraught with dangers.

When Poland had saved herself and Europe from a deluge of Bolshevism by the victory of Warsaw in 1920, she was soon in a position to dictate her own peace terms, and might there and then have extended her frontiers to those of 1772, before the first partition. This, however, would have been incompatible with a continuation of her function of Europe's safeguard against Bolshevism, because the vast eastern territories in question had already become permeated with Bolshevist propaganda, and the Polish landowning gentry, which represented western European civilization in those regions, had largely fallen a prey to pillage and massacre. The solution ultimately found consisted simply in dividing the borderlands and their population—which is, in its bulk, neither Polish nor Russian but White Ruthenian in the north and Ukrainian in the south —between Poland and Russia, so that Poland only regained the eastern frontier which had been left to her after the second

---

[1] The above remarks were written several months before Adolf Hitler became Chancellor of Germany. His drastic anti-Communist policy has since led to the cancellation of the Rapallo alliance. A new factor has also been introduced into Russo-German relations by Mussolini's recent project of a Four-Power Pact including Germany while excluding Russia.

On the other hand, non-aggression pacts have been concluded with Soviet Russia recently both by Poland, and by France.

The question of Germany's relations with Russia, however, is one of permanent interests reaching beyond the shifting combinations of a feverish period of international uncertainty.

Whatever the future of these relations may be, the vital necessity for access to the sea and the unique practicability of the present territorial arrangement under the given conditions remain unshaken principles of Polish political thought.

partition of 1793, and before the third and final one of 1795. This, while saving Poland from the inclusion of dangerous elements within her borders, produced a new difficulty of a different kind. The Bolsheviks, by creating national White Ruthenian and Ukrainian Republics on the Polish border within the Soviet Union, skilfully pandered to national ambitions ; and as a matter of fact, White Ruthenian and especially Ukrainian nationalism within Soviet Russia, while at first rigidly kept within bounds by Moscow centralism, have in course of time outgrown this control, and are active forces. It is only as long as life in Soviet Russia means a hell of distress and oppression, that Poland is in no serious danger from irredentist movements among her own White Ruthenians and Ukrainians. But it is also as long only as this state of things lasts, that Poland has the opportunity to win the firm and permanent adherence of those border populations of hers. Why it has been very difficult, so far, for all successive Polish Governments to frame a definite line of policy in these matters, especially with regard to the vast Ukrainian problem, has been explained elsewhere in this book ; but neither the difficulty of the task, nor the fact that conditions of life in Soviet Russia are still very far from improvement, does render the task itself less urgent or less important. A truly constructive and far sighted Ukrainian policy remains a capital *desideratum* of Polish policy.

No less important than a definite policy in the borderlands is a resolute and consistent policy of Poland in the *Baltic* region. If Poland is to be safe, the Baltic must become neither a German nor a Russian, nor a Russo-German lake. To keep it free from exclusive control by one of these great Powers or by both, is obviously the common interest of all the Baltic States. It is on the basis of that common interest that friendly relations have developed between the new Poland and her ancient rival in the Baltic, Sweden, in spite of Sweden's traditional German sympathies. But friends on the other side of the Baltic, whether in the shape of Sweden or Finland (with whom Poland is on terms of perfect amity) would be of comparatively little avail, if support of a more definite kind were not sought nearer home. Poland's continued safe existence depends quite as much as do, let us say, British trade interests in the Baltic, on the maintenance of the smaller south Baltic states. With one of them only, viz., Estonia, is Poland living in a political harmony untroubled by any differences. With another —Latvia—there has occasionally been serious friction, on account of Poland's interest in the fate of Poles under Latvian rule, especially in the border province of Lettgallia ; and Latvia, in her precarious position, is always on the brink of being drawn into either the Russian or the German sphere of interests. Worse still, Poland's relations with her nearest Baltic neighbour, Lithuania, remain unregulated unto this day, on account of the old quarrel over the Wilno region ; and the fact of present-day Lithuania's economic dependence on Germany certainly does not strengthen Poland's hold on the Baltic shore. The Lithuanian problem, next to the Ukrainian one, undoubtedly remains an outstanding *crux* for Polish statesmanship.

Poland's interests in the sphere of the other sea to which she once had immediate access, viz., the *Black Sea*, are indirectly promoted to-day (as they occasionally were in former centuries) by her close alliance with Rumania. To Rumania, on the other hand, the support of her big Polish neighbour is a mainstay in her relations with Russia.

Recently, Poland, by concluding her non-aggression pact with Russia in 1932 regardless of the state of negotiations between Rumania and Russia to the same effect, has perhaps shown a due sense of proportion : a measure of security and stability in her relations with Russia must mean more to her than all the alliances and friendships with minor neighbouring nations. It cannot be denied, however, that the failure of Poland to organize joint action with the smaller Baltic States on the occasion of a former similar pact with Russia a few years ago, and now the separate action of Rumania in this important matter, are both proofs of the power of Soviet diplomacy : Poland is being consistently prevented from becoming the rallying centre of all the European outposts against Bolshevism in eastern Europe.

5

If, regardless of the shifting policies of her smaller neighbours, Poland continues to think of herself as still " the bulwark of Europe " against Bolshevism—as she was for centuries the bulwark of Christianity against Islam—it is certainly in no Quixotic vein that the idea is entertained either by Polish public opinion or by Poland's rulers. Fifteen years of unbroken Bolshevik rule over Russia have convinced everybody who has a sense of reality, that neither is there a revolutionary overthrow of the system from within to be expected, nor can armed intervention, even in the form of an international crusade, be thought of with any prospect of success. As Russia's next-door neighbour, the Poles are necessarily better aware than western Europeans or Americans, of the vast mass of unspeakable human suffering by which every day in Russia's life and every step in the policy of her rulers are still marked ; and they are certainly much less liable to delusions concerning the solidity of Soviet Russia's economic or cultural achievements, or as to the immediate advantages to be derived from trade with her to-day. At the same time, however, by virtue of being neighbours, they also realize more fully the ultimate possibilities inherent in economic relations ; and the undeniable importance of those relations for Poland in particular induces them to exercise the utmost political patience even in the face of continuous subterranean Communist propaganda and Soviet espionage throughout Poland. Under endless provocation, Poland has succeeded, as stated elsewhere in this volume, in maintaining unbroken diplomatic relations with Soviet Russia since 1921— that is to say, for a longer period than most other States who entertain such relations at all. And it must be admitted that this attitude has not been entirely fruitless. Some branches of Poland's heavy industry—especially the iron-foundries— owe their uninterrupted existence through the years of the present crisis largely to Soviet orders connected with the Five Years' Plan ; others—such as the textile factories of Łódź— must reckon with Soviet Russia as their largest export market in any future situation. It is true that Soviet dumping has done ruinous harm to Poland's timber trade ; but neither does Poland stand alone in suffering from " the menace of Red Trade," as described by Mr. Knickerbocker in his sensational book, nor (it must be added) is Soviet Russia unique in the world of to-day for practising dumping on a large scale. The difference is not one of principle, but rather of methods, the slavery of forced labour being freely used in Russia to cheapen production. Whatever the *pros* and *cons* of the present situation may be, it is, at any rate, sufficiently evident that Poland stands to gain from trade relations with Russia in the future, not only through the sale of her own products, but through transit at a time when commerce between Russia and western Europe will once more have assumed important dimensions. Over and above this, Poland has good reason to expect relief for her population difficulties from relations with Russia in the future : not only will she be able to send to Russia her own surplus of trained specialists of all kinds—badly needed in a country whose pre-war educated class has been largely destroyed, and whose own new education is still in the experimental stage—but the possibilities of commercial development as well as of settlement on the land in various parts of the vast domains of Russia (especially in Siberia with its immense potential wealth) may present the prospect of an outlet, through emigration, to congested and distressed masses of Poland's rapidly growing population, whether landless peasants in the western provinces, or proletarian Jews in the country towns of the eastern border. It may seem fanciful to speak of such prospects now, when they are obviously very distant at best ; but it must be remembered that since the United States have closed their doors to emigration, and France has absorbed as much emigrant Polish labour as she seems able to support, the problem is likely to become calamitous very soon for a country whose population will, within the next decade, have equalled that of France, while her area is only three-fourths of that of the French Republic. Poland is not—and is not at present likely to be soon—in possession of any colonial territories ; the possibilities of South America (now a great reservoir of Polish emigrants) have, by bitter experience, been proved to be limited ; and Russia, however strange the idea may seem, is the only imaginable outlet in the immediate future.

When all these things are duly considered, they necessarily dictate an attitude widely different from that of 1920. It is not a conquest of Bolshevik Russia for European civilization that can be in question now, nor even the creation of a *cordon* cutting it off entirely from all intercourse with civilized Europe, but the peaceful penetration, by European cultural influences, of a country now in the grips of a fanatical and furiously propagandist doctrine. Deeply and instinctively as all Polish minds, whatever their education or party creed, abhor the extremism of Bolshevist doctrine, both in its theoretical and practical aspects, Poland is obviously destined and (in the persons of her more far-sighted citizens) quite willing to play a part of some importance in the great task of re-converting Russia to our common civilization.

Again, it may seem highly fanciful to think of countering world-wide and intense Bolshevik propaganda by the exercise of European cultural influence on Russia. Yet the plain fact is that determined efforts to bring such influences to bear are actually being made both in the field of economic and of spiritual relations. And whether the approach be commercial or religious, the unique position of Poland as a basis of operations cannot be overlooked.

As regards *commerce*, the historical fact has been mentioned elsewhere in this book that the economic (and shortly after it, the political) importance of Poland, as well as that of the Venetian Republic, began to decay when, on the one hand, the gates of the East were barred for centuries by the Turkish conquest of Constantinople, and, on the other hand, the discovery of America shifted the world's centre of economic interest to the shores of the Atlantic. With the possibilities of the Russia of to-morrow before us, we may, at this moment of history, be on the eve of a great revival of economic life in eastern Europe ; and history may solve the present disputes about the relative importance of agriculture and industry for Poland's future in the unexpected sense that it will be neither of these two but commerce which will become the dominant feature of a future Poland. The country may once again become, as it was in the Middle Ages, an important junction in the network of Europe's and of the world's great trade routes.

Passing from commerce to the remote subject of *religion*, we observe that the Vatican, in its age-old wisdom, has already realized the historical opportunity which Soviet Russia's war against religion offers for an attempt at Catholic reunion. A *Pro-Russia* missionary campaign has been started in Poland's eastern provinces, which has aroused misgivings among the Poles and called forth some loud protests. The objections of Polish opinion are : firstly, that the formality of allegiance to Rome, with the maintenance of separate ritual, will not be enough to bridge over the immemorial gulf between Latin and Byzantine civilization, and real conversion of the entire, huge Greek Orthodox world to Latin Christianity can at best be only a very distant goal ; secondly, that it was short-sighted of Rome resolutely to dispense with the collaboration of Poland's Catholic forces in the task on the ground that Poland was " politically interested."

Whatever the further course of this important process may be, it must be fairly clear to everybody possessed of the elementary facts of history and geography that Poland, quite as she may in the near future once more become a great trade centre, may also be destined to serve as a clearing-house for the different great historical forms of the Christian religion now attempting to come closer to each other again and to reconstruct Christendom as a civilizing world force.

6

Turning away at last from the Russian Sphinx and her vast riddles, we will, after the west, the north, and the east, direct our attention to the south, and after Germany and Russia, examine from the point of view of Polish interests that which has taken the place of the third partitioning Empire—*the Austro-Hungarian Monarchy*. For of all the three, this one only has been entirely broken up by the World War. Its territories, apart from a diminutive Austria and a mutilated Hungary (which both constitute European problems in themselves) are now divided between three "*Succession States*," all of them political units well known in history, one of which has been entirely reconstructed, and the two others considerably enlarged, out of the lands of the late Monarchy.

*Czechoslovakia*, *Yugoslavia* and *Rumania* have, under the auspices of their common protectress France, combined into a "*Little Entente*" whose political object is the preservation of the *status quo* created by the Peace Treaties in their section of Europe.

Poland, as mentioned before, is in close alliance with Rumania. Her relations with Yugoslavia, always untroubled by any causes for disagreement, have of late become particularly friendly. As regards Czechoslovakia, it took some time to live down the territorial disputes of the early years, which had even found expression in a local war ; and the treatment of the strong Polish minority in the Czechoslovak section of Silesia gave ground for complaint until recently. Of late, however, the relations between the two States have presented a picture of steady progress towards better understanding, and a renewal of friction is practically out of the question.

It may seem surprising why a sense of the obvious community of interests between the two newly risen States of Poland and Czechoslovakia should not sooner have got the upper hand over their temporary differences. The reason lies in a certain constitutional disparity between Polish and Czech ways of thinking. The Poles, for centuries the defenders of Europe against the Islam, necessarily acquired characteristics of impulsive readiness for heroic effort and disinterested sacrifice, but also of aversion to plodding labour and patient realism ; the romantic, militant country gentleman, who made up the *élite* of the nation, also formed its notions of human perfection. The modern Czechs, on the other hand, are a thoroughly democratic race : they have the sterling qualities of industry, endurance and thrift proper to a nation of small farmers and artisans, but are apt to be lacking in the airs and graces dear to a people traditionally led by country gentlemen. The Czechs, again, have since the Middle Ages been emphatic rationalists in religious matters, while the Poles have a mystic and sentimental attachment to their Catholicism. The Czechs, finally, in the nineteenth century, became believers in Pan-Slavism under the auspices of Russia as a safeguard against the German danger, while the Poles, oppressed by Russia, never could muster up much enthusiasm for the Pan-Slav ideal.

Many of these things, however, are changing. In the first place, modern Poland is undergoing a very thorough process of democratisation, and losing the distinctive, aristocratic tinge of her mentality. Secondly, pre-war Pan-Slavism has gone down into limbo together with the old Russia, and notions of the part to be played in the world by the Slavonic races can now be more easily harmonized, when Slavdom is principally represented on the European stage by peoples having an emphatically western civilization in common, as the Poles and the Czechs have it.

Even in the satisfactory state, however, which relations with Czechoslovakia as well as with the other two partners of the Little Entente have happily reached of late years, Poland finds it impossible to join this regional group of European States. The reasons for Poland's aloofness are manifold. To begin with, her vital interests are centring more and more in the Baltic region, while those of the Little Entente belong rather to the sphere of the Adriatic, and of the Danubian river-basin. In the second place, the maintenance of the *status quo*—which is the avowed aim of the Little Entente—implies diplomatic repression of all the unceasing and passionate demands of curtailed and encircled *Hungary* for a revision of the frontiers in her favour. Now Poland is bound to Hungary by a thousand strong ties of historical association and temperamental sympathy. Constituting for centuries an outpost of Europe against the Islam, very much like Poland, the Hungarians acquired the same soldierly characteristic as the Poles : dashing horsemen and foolhardy fighters like them, they also coupled chivalry with nonchalance, and romanticism of disposition with refinement of manners, in the fashion set by the country gentry, which in Hungary as in Poland, was the *élite* and model of the nation. This found expression even in a marked resemblance between the picturesque national costumes of the noblemen in both countries, and in the long domination of Latin eloquence in Hungarian and in Polish public life. That public life itself was characterized in both countries by an early development of parliamentary institutions, when these were still unknown to their neighbours ; both Poland and Hungary were "gentry democracies" in their political structure, and always cherished their tradition of representative government.

Besides these resemblances, there were direct historical connections of the most memorable sort : one of Hungary's greatest kings, Lewis of Anjou (d. 1382), had also occupied the throne of Poland ; his daughter Jadwiga, as Queen of Poland, had created the great Polish-Lithuanian Monarchy by her self-sacrificing marriage ; and the greatest king who ever ruled that Monarchy, Stephen Batory (d. 1587), had also come from Hungary, being a Transylvanian Prince. In the nineteenth century, when both nations were struggling against foreign rule, a Polish General, J. Bem, had commanded the Hungarian insurrection against Austria in 1849 ; and in the twentieth, Hungary alone among Poland's neighbours stood by her side at the moment of her supreme danger in 1920 with an offer of men, and effective assistance in munitions.

## 7

The ample historical grounds which exist for Polish-Hungarian sympathies are bound to affect Poland's Little Entente policy. But deeper issues than mere sympathies are involved. The relations between the Little Entente and Hungary have become one of the unfortunately numerous causes of post-war tension between *Italy* and *France*. Italy, whose Adriatic ambitions clash with the interests of Yugoslavia, has lately given open support to Hungarian aspirations. Now, if there is anything against which Poland must always make a resolute stand, it is a demand for revision of the existing frontiers, because this could be extended at once to Poland's frontiers as well. But in the case of differences between France and Italy, Poland is fundamentally in a painful dilemma, although the French alliance is a corner-stone of her international policy. Italy has historical claims on Polish sympathy no less strong than those of France. Renascence Poland, through the Italian marriage of one of her kings, was more deeply permeated with influences of Italian art, scholarship, literature and general civilization than with the influence of almost any other country in her history. Modern Italy had sent noble sons of hers (Francesco Nullo and others) to die for Poland in the insurrection of 1863, and Poles had fought in the ranks of Garibaldi. And the Italian Parliament was the first in the allied countries to raise its voice on behalf of a free Poland in the World War (1916).

Apart from the Polish nation's traditional and very deep Italian sympathies, however, there is an aspect of the Hungarian issue which suggests to the Polish observer a solution different from the present policy of the Little Entente. As an eventual result of the maintenance of the *status quo* with regard to the position of Hungary there always looms one highly threatening possibility. Neither Austria nor Hungary in their present reduced shape have much economic vitality in them, and their existence is being artificially kept up by loans from the League of Nations or (as lately in the case of Austria) from France. In Austria, strong political forces are in favour of the *Anschluss* or incorporation into Germany, the preparations for which in the form of administrative and other assimilation are continually proceeding. France and the Little Entente cling to the conviction that the *Anschluss* can be prevented ; Polish observers taking a more distant and detached view—such as the experienced veteran politician R. Dmowski—think that in the long run it cannot. Dangerous as the prospect of such an aggrandizement of Germany must seem to some of the neighbours immediately concerned (such as Czechoslovakia), a really great danger to the whole European system as reconstructed by the Peace Treaties would only arise if Hungary were to follow Austria's example and seek relief from what she feels to be an intolerable situation in union with Germany and Austria. In that case, the pre-war group of the Central Powers would have almost entirely become a reality again, and renewed expansionist pressure in the direction of the Balkans and the Near East would only be a normal sign of life on its part. In that sense, the little Hungary of to-day has the key of the central and eastern European situation in her hands.

If the *Anschluss* of Austria to Germany, in the view of some, cannot ultimately be prevented, the inclusion of Hungary in the German-Austrian aggregate perhaps might be forestalled by the creation of a *bloc* composed of the Powers of the Little Entente and Hungary together. The plan of a Danubian Federation on a larger scale, including Austria, was recently broached by France ; it failed, perhaps because of the difficulties arising of its largeness. Within the smaller framework of the Powers of the Little Entente *plus* Hungary, great difficulties in the shape of violent antagonisms and resentments would certainly also have to be overcome. But the common aim of saving the general scheme of present-day Central Europe would justify every effort, and the plan might have the advantage of reconciling Italian and French interests in that region.

Poland, while probably not seeking inclusion in such a Danubian group, might view its rise favourably as a guarantee of international security, provided, of course, that the new *bloc* would not constitute another bar to Polish commerce on the southern side, like those already constituted by the attitude of Russia and Germany along her western and her eastern frontier. On the contrary, it would be in the best interest of all concerned if such a *bloc* did constitute the southern, and Poland, together with the smaller Baltic States, the northern wing of a larger group interposed between Germany and Russia. Such a larger group would not only be an effective bar on the danger to the European system which would arise out of a re-establishment of contiguity between Germany and Russia ; it would also have the immense advantage of presenting a larger section of Europe to the rest of the world in harmonized and settled condition. " The Balkanization of Eastern Europe "—that taunt of Mr. Lloyd George's so bitterly resented in all the new states east of Berlin—would then lose the last shred of justification which it may yet possess in the eyes of the British or American spectator of Continental European affairs. For to these spectators in particular—detached and impartial as the best among them are—the picture hitherto presented has inevitably appeared bewildering and unintelligible, and with its simmering hostilities, averse to all compromise, has necessarily produced the impression of impermanence and waste to their eyes, whatever the constructive achievements within the individual new States.

8

The above suggestions are the results of a dispassionate student's musings, not the proposals of a politician inspired from official quarters. The author is well aware that they do not imply a *maximum* of advantages for his own country, and, indeed, might call for sacrifices on the part of all nations concerned. But the wearisome history of fruitless diplomatic conferences during a dozen post-war years, and, last not least, the spectacle of the imperfections and the weakness of the League of Nations, has made it clear to many thoughtful observers that regional arrangements should precede continental and world-wide ones. A settlement, in something like the form outlined above, of all the still existing antagonisms among the States occupying the space between Germany and Russia, would be an important stage on the road towards the consolidation, and perhaps, ultimately even the confederation, of Europe. It would certainly make it possible to end, within some larger groups of countries, the present fierce tariff war of everybody against everybody,

which makes it impossible, even literally, to call the present
state of Europe one of peace. It would also create a necessary
preliminary towards a sincere and effective international
discussion of *disarmament*.

In this matter of disarmament, now the subject of the debates
of a great but, so far, ineffective international gathering, Poland
is not merely the blind partisan of the views of her powerful
ally France. She has her own bitter historical experiences to
guide her—experiences unique among those of the Powers
represented at the conference. In the partition period, as
early as 1717, she actually agreed voluntarily to partial disarmament, only to be ultimately dismembered soon afterwards,
in spite of heroic efforts. In the light of such data from her
own history, Poland is bound to consider the creation of an
atmosphere of *security* an indispensable preliminary condition
of disarmament. If the citizens of countries armed much more
fully and expensively than she, choose, in view of this, to call
her an "adventurous militarist State," she can only regret
their imperfect understanding of her situation, and continue
imperturbably to collaborate in all efforts to secure lasting
peace with the same good will which she showed in the
days of the Geneva Protocol, and which she has recently
manifested again by her League proposals concerning "moral
disarmament."

If the world is to be enabled to proceed whole-heartedly with
its work on those tasks of our common civilization which all
claim co-ordinated international effort, a certain measure of
political and economic stability is an indispensable requirement.
And, however wide the framework of organization may be by
which such stability is to be ensured, history has shown with
sufficient clearness that it is not through the suppression of the
factor of nationality, but through the recognition of its constructive value that the end can be achieved. The ghost of a
buried Poland constituted one of the elements of restlessness
in nineteenth-century Europe ; the body of Poland risen from
her grave must be allowed the rudimentary conditions of
safe existence in order that she may take the part which
her past and her present alike show her to be qualified for
in the huge collective labours lying before twentieth-century
humanity.

9

From the grave international problems, in whose coils the
new Poland necessarily is entangled, we may now pass to the

outstanding *domestic issues*, with which the reconstructed State has had to struggle, and no doubt will yet have to struggle for some time to come.

These issues, mostly discussed in some detail in the foregoing chapters, may conveniently be summarized under four headings : national consolidation, political structure, social evolution, and cultural effort.

The reunion of Polish lands into an independent and comparatively large State naturally did not involve the automatic re-establishment of *national unity*, undermined as this had become by a century of division. *Russian rule*, while calling forth heroic and self-sacrificing patriotism by its oppressive character, had at the same time accustomed Poles to the easy-going and wasteful Russian ways in economic matters ; while conducive, by its bureaucratic absolutism, to private initiative in organization and even largely to action by conspiracy, it had thoroughly extinguished in the minds of Russia's Polish subjects the respect for law, and had implanted in them the idea that bribery and corruption were necessary concomitants of all organized public life.

Under *Prussia*, where the struggle, in the era of German colonization, was conducted chiefly by economic means, disciplined organization on the German model, together with industry and pedantic efficiency, became a habit of the Poles ; but intellectual and æsthetic culture of the higher kind were largely left to starve in the midst of plenty, since the achievement of material success absorbed all the best energies.

In systematic higher education, *Austrian Poland* came to surpass both other sections, since, with self-government, the province received a network of Polish schools of all grades. Having a parliamentary and administrative public life of its own, the Austrian sector became also the only real training-ground for the political organization of the new Polish State. The minds of Austrian Poles became as imbued with a sense of legality as those of Russian Poles were devoid of it ; but Austro-Polish legality occasionally degenerated into mere bureaucratic formalism, fatal to initiative and action, especially in economic matters—the more so, as half a century of home rule by country gentlemen was not sufficient to raise the country from the depths of impoverishment into which the previous half century of predatory Austrian administration had plunged it.

It was, then, with *three distinct mentalities*—each of them marked by certain excellences and certain defects, that the Poles entered into their new reunited existence. Those three mentalities still largely prevail in the three former sectors, and clashes between them are not infrequent at the centre of affairs. The older generation cannot be expected to change its mental habits ; and it is only in the minds of the young, growing up in a united, free Poland under a uniform system of education, that the old sectional differences are becoming obliterated. The process is comparatively rapid, and even now the dividing lines among Poland's young citizens are no longer those of regional origin, but rather those of party.

The *Polish party system* cannot, unfortunately, be said to have developed normally, so as to fit itself to the exigencies of the new political existence. The ultra-democratic constitution of the Republic in the first years favoured the fissiparous and factious tendencies proper to the political life of inexperienced communities. Then again, Piłsudski's dictatorial *coup d'état* of 1926 broke up the existing party system entirely, smashing larger and smaller party organizations indiscriminately. As a result of it all, there is indeed, in present-day Poland, a clear-cut division into two political camps, the Government *bloc* and the Opposition, but neither of the two is homogeneous enough to produce a constructive political programme. Among the supporters of the Government, former Socialist revolution-aries of 1905 rub shoulders with Conservative landed magnates, and militant believers in legislation by decree and in economic planning by the State are confronted by intellectual Radicals, who remain attached to the doctrines of nineteenth-century liberalism and to parliamentary methods.

The Opposition presents a picture of even greater contrasts, being merely a common name for all old parties which did not consent to absorption in the *bloc*. In a strange alliance, then, we find here the Socialists who would not resign their party creed in favour of the dictatorship of a *quondam* comrade, and their old adversaries the Nationalists, to whom Piłsudski and Socialism together had traditionally been " the enemy." In equally strange juxtaposition we see the battered remnants of the once powerful Peasant Farmers' Party, led by the skilful parliamentary tactician Witos (three times Prime Minister of Poland in his day), and the Agrarian Radicals, representative of landless rural labour under the guidance of intellectual fanatics.

It is utterly unsafe to predict at the moment when this is being written, what kind of government and what kind of programme may ultimately emerge, in case the present virtual dictatorship should once more give place to parliamentary rule in substance as well as in form. It only remains to be hoped that individual personalities may appear on the scene which will frame definite policies adapted to a time of great changes in all the essential conditions of political life. The task is certainly rendered particularly difficult both by Poland's international insecurity and by her economic ruin through the crisis.

### 10

So far, we have surveyed the difficulties of the consolidation of Poland as far as the predominant nation is concerned. It remains to be remembered, however, that the Polish State includes an unusually numerous and variegated admixture of national and racial *minorities*.

The enormous difficulties, both domestic and international, created for the new Poland by these minorities, have been passed in review in a former chapter of this book. Looking back upon the problem for a last time here, we may briefly repeat that the *German minority* chiefly remains unmanageable because of the strong support it receives from its mother-country across the frontier. The growth of Poland's international *prestige* as well as the progress of Polish culture in Poland's western provinces are sure to bring relief here, if great international conflicts do not supervene.

The case seems worse with regard to the *Ukrainian minority*. As stated before, Poland has not proved capable so far of evolving a constructive and consistent Ukrainian policy, and the fault of this lies as much with the violent tactics of the irreconcilable Ukrainian Nationalists (very like the Hindu Nationalists in their attitude) as in the frequent and dramatic changes of government on the Polish side, and ultimately in the incapacity of a military dictatorship to combine liberalism with firmness. If a comprehensive Ukrainian programme is not devised and resolutely carried out soon, the calamity of an irredentist movement in favour of a larger Ukraine across the Soviet border may overtake Poland in a possibly none too distant future.

A comprehensive and constructive programme providing for future contingencies, is, alas, entirely out of the question with regard to the *Jewish problem*, which is all the more difficult for not being confined to one particular territory, and which must be dealt with anew in every new phase. As I have tried to make clear elsewhere, the Jewish problem in Poland is essentially a problem of numbers : the numerical proportion of Jews (the highest, percentually, in Europe) and their local congestion under conditions of *ghetto* separatism makes the one and only normal solution, viz., assimilation, impracticable and even abhorrent to Jews and Poles alike. " Numbers " in the Jewish sacred books is next-door neighbour to " Exodus," and it seems hard to avoid the conclusion that the Jewish problem in Poland will in the long run only solve itself in the normal way of assimilation (as predicted by some of the most judicious and dispassionate men on both sides), if an outlet for emigration is opened up, of which large numbers of Polish Jews will find it to their economic advantage voluntarily to avail themselves. America has ceased to be such an outlet ; Palestine, the land of noblest Jewish dreams—be it said with regret—cannot possibly develop into one ; and the present writer is again driven back on his seemingly fantastic conclusion that only Russia can provide such an outlet in the future. The medieval movement of the Jews from the west to the east of Europe may, in due time, be continued farther in the same direction, and again, in new domains, prove a useful stimulant to economic development.

## II

In the matter of *constitutional structure*, as in that of national consolidation, certain weighty problems necessarily remain imperfectly solved by Poland after fourteen years of her new existence. As emphasized on several former occasions, she entered into possession of her new freedom in an era of unparalleled world-wide ferment affecting all the fundamentals of social life. That ferment extended also to the great question of democratic government. Parliamentary democracy, in the course of the nineteenth century, had been developing towards extreme forms through wider and wider extension of the franchise ; and with the progress of this development, the limitations of parliamentary rule had begun to become apparent. Increased popular control almost inevitably meant a decrease of expert efficiency in administration: it was in France under the thoroughly democratic *régime* of the Third Republic that the winged phrase *le culte de l'incompétence* was coined by a famous critic.

Apart from recent European (and American) developments, Poland had her own historical lessons to go upon : her own parliamentary system, fully developed since the beginning of the sixteenth century, had at an early date manifested certain typical weaknesses ; what was in theory a " gentry democracy," became in practice the anarchical competition of a few noble houses for supremacy, with the mob of the minor gentry for its instrument. In view of this distortion of constitutional freedom, some of the noblest and wisest of the old Poland's statesmen and political thinkers had advocated the strengthening of central authority as vested in the crown. Nothing definite, however—not even hereditary monarchy in the place of the ruinous election of kings—was achieved till the eighteenth century, when the efforts of a generation of enlightened patriots culminated in the glorious Constitution of the Third of May, 1791. This, at one sweep, did away with all the pseudodemocratic abuses of the old Polish Commonwealth by giving a full measure of power to the executive, and at the same time provided for a broadening of the basis of democracy by granting the rudiments of political rights to burghers and peasants. Unfortunately Poland, soon after this supreme achievement in political regeneration, fell a prey to her rapacious neighbours.

It is, alas, a fact sufficiently attested by historical examples that nations, as a rule, do not profit by the lessons of their own past or that of others. The new Poland did verbal homage to the great Act of the Third of May in the preamble to her own preliminary Constitution, but the definite Constitution of the new Republic, as voted in 1921, was modelled on the doctrinaire extremes of the French Constitution of the Third Republic, and the animosity of parties hostile to the dominant personality of Piłsudski added a surplus of features of weakness to its provisions concerning the central executive authorities. With the imperfect preparation of large masses of the people for the responsibilities of freedom, the results were not long in coming. Costly administrative inefficiency, even corruption, and the constant interference of party politics with urgently-needed measures of administrative organization and legislative initiative, constituted blots upon the record of the nation's early struggles against its enormous difficulties.

Marshal Piłsudki's *coup d'état* of 1926 was to remedy these crying evils. The remedy was in keeping with a widespread mood among modern European democracies : the longing for dictators is well-nigh universal among the disillusioned peoples, and the example set by *Fascismo* in Italy was no doubt a particularly strong stimulant.

As set forth in detail in another part of this volume, the Piłsudki *régime* succeeded, in its first years, in introducing administrative order into large domains of Polish life, which needed it urgently. It accomplished some long overdue tasks of legislation ; it raised Poland's *prestige* abroad considerably ; it preserved peace without and within ; it obtained a large American loan, and it has managed, in these days of crisis, to maintain

DD

the Polish currency unshaken and to keep Poland among the very few States in the world which have not, so far, imposed any restraint on the freedom of exchange.

These are successes which will undoubtedly stand to the Government's historical credit. But it has not carried out, so far, that programme of constitutional reform which was one of the principal objects of its assumption of power. It has not done so, although it now possesses an overwhelming and disciplined majority in Parliament, and although that majority itself has actually produced the draft of a new constitution. Legislation by decrees, high-handed administrative measures, some ill-considered projects of laws (such as the University Reform Bill of 1932) and drastic party patronage in State appointments, have made the Piłsudski Government less popular even with many of its adherents, and it is open to doubt, as these words are being written, whether this Government will crown its historical achievements by a new Constitution for Poland. With the general helplessness of the States of to-day in the face of the economic crisis and of international complications, with the fascination which Bolshevist " planning " and the constructive record of Fascismo exercise over the minds of Europe's democracies at present, it seems more difficult than ever to find that *via media* between liberty and authority which is the ultimate secret of successful government under modern conditions. That *via media* cannot possibly be the same for all communities, but must be found by each nation for itself. The new Poland is, so far, still at a loss for its own formula, and profoundly divided on the subject. It does not stand alone in that respect ; but its difficulties are seriously aggravated by the fact that other European States, with a longer unbroken tradition to look back upon, at least are in possession of a firm and well-tried substructure of *local government*, while in Poland this important component of state organization is still in the making. The fashionable movement of " regionalism," mentioned elsewhere in this book, is helpful in many ways as stirring up life in the provinces into creative activity in education, research, art and social welfare ; but it has of late shown a tendency unduly to invade administrative theory and practice in Poland, and that would certainly be fraught with dangers for the solidity of a political fabric freshly constructed and still far from having completely coalesced into an indivisible whole.

Altogether, as we see, the second decade of Poland's new existence is still rife with constitutional problems of the first order, which will severely tax the brains of her political theorists as well as of her practical statesmen. Let us hope that decade will carry the country, in some of the essentials at any rate, towards solutions of at least relative durability.

12

During the century of its captivity, Poland lived through the great *social changes* in the modern world which made that world thoroughly democratic. In Poland, the most important stage in this social evolution of the nineteenth century was the successive abolition of serfdom in the three sections of the divided country. It has been related elsewhere in this volume, how peasant emancipation was followed up by the growth of a strong peasant owner class through gradual purchase of land ; how that class, under Prussia and under Austria, became a political power ; and how, with the educational opportunities afforded by Austrian Poland, it began to infuse its younger blood into the educated class of the towns.

With all the rapid growth of a peasant-born *intelligentsia* in the Austrian sector, Poland still remained, on the eve of the War, a nation represented mainly by the country gentry as its *élite*. All the leaders of the nation in modern times, whether in war or peace, in political or economic action, in learning or in art, had almost without exception come from the class of the country gentlemen. The predominance of this class in the formation of the national *élite*, and the relative absence of an old-established Polish middle class in the towns, gave to social life of Poland, even in the strongly democratic days of the later nineteenth and early twentieth century, a specifically aristocratic character, produced (as in England) by the ambition of the masses to imitate in manners, and even in views, the privileged class which furnished the *élite*.

While it was still under the same social auspices that the new free Poland began her existence, while Piłsudski, Dmowski, and Paderewski, in whose hands her earliest fortunes lay, all still came from the landed gentry class, certain historical events could not fail to produce a rapidly modifying effect. To the restoration of Poland's independence, the most active contribution had been made by the sometime revolutionaries of 1905, whose younger years had largely been spent in radical Socialist propaganda among the industrial proletariat of Russian Poland. One of the first Prime Ministers of the new Republic was W. Witos, a peasant farmer by birth, who had risen into a commanding position in Austro-Polish parliamentary politics. The higher administrative offices of the new Polish Government were largely filled with trained officials from Austrian Poland, many of whom represented the new peasant *intelligentsia* of that sector. The constitution of the new Poland, formed on thoroughly democratic lines, gave the old landed nobility and gentry no possibility of parliamentary representation as a social group ; and one of the first legislative measures was Land Reform (described in a previous chapter), whose admitted aim it was to strengthen the peasant farmer element of the country by forcibly quickening the break-up of the possessions of the old landed classes.

What was begun by Land Reform, is now being even more rapidly finished by the economic crisis which hits agriculture—and especially larger estates—most severely. Thousands of those estates are continually being sold at auction, and there can be no more doubt at the present moment that the nobility and gentry will very soon have melted away, as a class, from the surface of Poland's social life.

In view of the inevitableness of the process it would be futile to indulge in any criticism of it. The country house, with all the glamour of its traditional associations, is vanishing from the Polish scene, as it has been vanishing from England for some time past. For the ultimate good of the nation—it must confidently be hoped—the prophetic words of the poet Wyspiański are coming true : " The peasant is a power, and there's an end ! "

However, as we are witnessing now not the end, but only the beginning of peasant power, the immediate consequences of what is happening before our eyes deserve a moment's consideration ; for they will have to be faced resolutely by the men and women of our time.

To begin with, the peasantry, impoverished to the extreme by the world-wide fall of prices for agricultural produce, are for the present unable to profit much either by Land Reform or even by the sales at auction of the larger estates. In fact, they are momentarily losing a great deal, because the small peasant farmer can on longer eke out his income by working, in his spare time, as a hired labourer on the neighbouring manor, as he used to do. And the prolific growth of peasant families and consequent subdivision of land counteract the work of Land Reform, which was to change the face of the Polish countryside into a net-work of middle-sized and prosperous peasant farms. Even if the depression should soon pass, it will assuredly take a long time before a tolerable degree of saturation of the peasant masses with land is reached, subdivision of peasant property effectively stopped, a satisfactory outlet for the surplus village population provided, and co-operative organization sufficiently developed to place rural prosperity on a solid footing. It is a long, long way, in a word, from present-day Poland to Denmark, whose condition, under the given circumstances, must appear as the only possible goal for the social development of the Polish country-side.

13

The transition from the Poland of the old country gentry to a Poland of competent and contented peasant farmers is not only sure to be marked by a long phase of economic difficulties—it will also be characterized by a serious crisis in Poland's *intellectual culture*.

It has been stated in a former chapter that the singular charm which even an enslaved and miserable Poland possessed in the eyes of the world, was largely constituted by admirable achievements in art, and an intellectual refinement manifest in works of learning and research. These glories of nineteenth-century Poland could only shine in that atmosphere of individualism, which was the very life-breath of an essentially aristocratic social system. As far as its effect in the domain of intellect and of art was concerned, the individualism of Poland's country gentry corresponded to that classical middle-class liberalism in England which inspired some of the greatest achievements of the Victorian age.

In both countries, that nineteenth-century individualism is now replaced by the more recent collective spirit, which, in its extreme form, is manifest in modern American civilization. Under the circumstances dictated by historical development, it is an unavoidable necessity for Polish educational effort and organization to concern itself largely with quantity for the present, to the detriment of quality. Until the time when a satisfactory general level of popular education will have been secured, a mass of pupils must somewhat summarily be attended to in Poland's educational institutions. Again, as in economic matters, there is good reason to hope for the best in the end ; a national civilization resting on the firm basis of a prosperous peasant element will no doubt evolve creative achievement of a high and distinct type all its own. In the meantime, however, a prolonged formative period may intervene, during which Poland will possibly not astonish the world by such individual works of genius as came from her in the nineteenth century. Probably even, the Polish national character will not, during that period, be distinguished by such clear-cut and at the same time engaging features as the predominance of the chivalrous country gentleman type still gave it in the not very distant past.

There is yet another weighty reason why Polish education, in a transition period which is now in progress, must resign itself to certain standardizing tendencies. It has repeatedly been emphasized in the foregoing pages what profound intellectual differences, for certain very definite historical reasons, still separate in Poland not only the country and the town from each other, but the large former Russian section from the two others, and particularly the east from the west of the country. An enormous educational labour in the way of " levelling-up " has to be accomplished, and no wonder that this sometimes appears as " levelling-down " to the minority whose level was especially high before. If a new *élite* is to blossom forth—as, God willing, it shall—from a mass permeated by more or less uniform new culture, the base on which it is to flourish must not itself be strikingly uneven.

The golden harvest from the level ground so prepared and fertilized may be long in coming : it is a difficult lesson to learn for the quick and impatient Polish temper, but it is a lesson which, after fourteen years of trial and error, must consistently be applied throughout all domains of the new Poland's life—the lesson, we mean, conveyed in Tennyson's majestic words :

" Slow and sure comes up the golden year."

## 14

It may indeed seem the very reverse of a " golden year " that is dawning upon Poland and upon humanity as these concluding sections of the book are being written in the early days of January, 1933. The gloom of world prospects around may, in fact, have affected even the present final summary of Poland's general situation. It is quite deliberately, at any rate, that the author has preferred not to avoid in his presentation any of the moments of doubt and danger in which that situation abounds. The insecurity of Poland's frontiers—especially of her vital access to the sea—the lack of strong support for her among her neighbours, the imperfect inner consolidation of the new State, the unsolved constitutional problem, the economic difficulties attendant upon the great social transformation of Poland, the detrimental effect it is bound to have, for a time, on the creative forces of the spirit,—all these are facts disquieting enough when

considered over and above the political uncertainty and economic collapse which prevail throughout the world at large
in these days.

But a sense of dark realities need not, even now, inspire
extreme and wholesale pessimism, which is the most sterile and
paralysing view that can be taken of human affairs. In the
case of Poland, confidence in the future is not only an abstract
act of faith. It certainly has in it something of the attitude of a
believer in dogma : Polish patriotism has not only always been
closely associated with the Poles' national conception of their
old religion, but has also itself had the fervour and firmness of a
religious creed. *Credo quia impossibile*—that glorious paradox of
early Christianity often comes to our minds when we meet with
manifestations of unshakable belief in Poland's future at the
darkest moments of her nineteenth-century captivity and
oppression.

But there is something more to go upon than the faith which
moved the mountains heaped upon the grave of Poland. There
is an element perhaps even more valuable under the circumstances of to-day : it is *historical experience*. Economists, bewildered by the vastness of the present world crisis, often specu-
late on the question whether there has been any crisis in history
comparable to it in depth and extent. A Pole need not go deep
into the history of his nation to be convinced that it has survived
predicaments more catastrophic than the present one. He
remembers that Poland was, apparently hopelessly, split up into
petty principalities during nearly the whole of the twelfth and the
thirteenth centuries, to become reunited and grow into the
large Polish-Lithuanian Monarchy ; that, in the seventeenth,
she was over-run, ravaged, and torn to pieces by a multitude of
foreign invasions from all sides—to re-arise as the Power which
saved Vienna and Europe from the Turk in 1683 ; that in the
nineteenth, not only political existence was cancelled, not only
was the land being forcibly wrenched, piece by piece, from its
Polish owners, but the most strenuous efforts were made both by
Russia and Germany to extinguish Polish tradition and Polish
speech among the young—and yet, in the very same century,
Poland roused the whole civilized world to admiration by the
very greatest achievements of Polish genius in literature and art.

In the light of such ineffaceable historical evidence, neither
the rebuilding of a strong Polish State from the wreckage of the
most thoroughly devastated one among the theatres of the World
War can seem inexplicable ; nor can the " miracle on the
Vistula," as Poles are accustomed piously to call their victory

of 1920, properly appear a miracle at all. That a nation freshly risen from its grave, amidst appalling ruin, to face an existence of starvation, put a million men into the field and drove back the whole huge force of Soviet Russia from the gates of Central Europe, is neither more nor less surprising than Sobieski's victory at Vienna after the ruinous welter of Poland's seventeenth-century wars.

There can be only one general explanation to account for it all —the proved fact of an indomitable *national vitality*. And if that explanation may be said to explain little, because it is in itself a term of mystery, why, so are all the scientific formulæ for the inmost facts of life. Whatever its intellectual value, it certainly is sufficient to provide the Pole, at any rate, not with a creed merely, but with a certainty. Quite as Poland's heroes and martyrs, and her exiles and prophets, throughout the nineteenth century, never ceased to believe and hope that a Polish State would rise again, however wildly improbable this seemed at the time—so the Polish citizen of to-day, with the record of his nation's history before him, instinctively knows and never for a moment doubts, that whatever forms may evolve out of the present world-wide ferment, Poland will be a living and active organism among them.

# BIBLIOGRAPHY

Two lists of books in English relating to Poland have recently been published, one in England and one in America, viz. :

National Book Council, London, Book List No. 136 : *Poland*. Compiled by the Polish Bibliographical Institute, Warsaw. June, 1932.

Eleanor E. Ledbetter : *Polish Literature in English Translation*. A Bibliography, with a list of books about Poland and the Poles. Published under the auspices of the Polish National Alliance by the H. W. Wilson Company, New York, 1932.

Numerous articles on various aspects of Poland, historical and contemporary, are to be found in the *Slavonic (and East European) Review*, published for the School of Slavonic and East European Studies (University of London) by Eyre & Spottiswoode, London (10 vols., 1922 ff.), and in the monthly *Poland*, originally published by the American-Polish Chamber of Commerce in New York, and now continued as *Poland America* by the " Poland America Company," 60 South St., Ware, Mass., U.S.A. See particularly *Poland*, vol. IX, No. 11 (November 1928)—an " Anniversary Number " issued to commemorate the tenth anniversary of the independence of Poland.

The bibliography given below is a selection of recent works of general interest, dealing with Poland and Polish problems, and published in English. Books which are out of date or out of print, have not been included in the list.

## I. The Old Poland.

## II. Poland under Foreign Rule.

Fuller information on the past history of Poland, as well as a bibliography of books in English or particular subjects from Polish history, may be found in the present writer's *Outlines of Polish History* (a course of lectures, delivered at King's College, University of London), 2nd ed., London : Allen & Unwin, 1931.

For the relations between Poland and Russia in their historical development, see F. Nowak, *Medieval Slavdom and the Rise of Russia* (Berkshire Studies in European History), New York: Henry Holt, 1930.

On the historical relations between Poland and the United States, see M. Haiman, *Poland and the American Revolutionary War*, Chicago, Ill., 1932 (published by the Polish Roman Catholic Union of America). W. J. Thomas and F. Znaniecki, *The Polish Peasant in Europe and America*, 2nd ed., New York: A. Knopf, 1927 (a sociological study based on original letters and family documents).

III.  *The World War and the Rebirth of the Polish State.*

IV.  *Ten Years of the New Poland.*

The fullest up-to-date account, in English, of the rise and development of the new Poland is given in Robert Machray's *Poland, 1914-1931*, London : Allen & Unwin, 1931 (with bibliography).  See also the elaborate monograph by H. H. Fisher and Sidney Brooks : *America and the New Poland*, New York, Macmillan, 1928.

V.  *Geographical Aspects and Administrative Structure.*

For detailed encyclopædic information on all domains of life in the new Poland, see *The Polish Handbook*, a guide to the country and resources of the Republic of Poland, edited by F. Bauer Czarnomski, London: Eyre & Spottiswoode, 1925 ; and on a larger scale : *Poland of To-day*, edited by K. Bader (text in Polish, French, English and German, 1155 illustrations, fol.) Vienna, published by *Wiener Allgemeine Zeitung*, 1927.

For statistical figures, illustrating all aspects of the new Poland's life, see the *Concise Statistical Year-book of Poland* (published by the Central Statistical Office of the Republic), Warsaw.

Among shorter comprehensive accounts of Poland, published in English in recent years, the following may be singled out : A. E. Tennant, *Studies in Polish Life and History*, London: Allen & Unwin, 1924.  C. Smogorzewski, *Poland of To-day*, Paris: F.I.D.A.C., 1926. Karski St., *Poland, Past and Present*, Warsaw: 1927.  Orłowski, M., *Poland and its Curiosities*, Warsaw, published by the Ministry of Communications, 1927.  Pawłowski, J. I., *Poland and her People*, Detroit, Mich., 1929. G. Humphrey, *Poland the Unexplored*, Indianapolis, Ind. : Bobbs-Merrill, 1931.

A brief guide-book to Poland for tourists, with illustrations and a map, has recently been published by the *Orbis* Travel Office in Warsaw under the title *See Poland Next* (110 pp., 1933). For Cracow in particular, see Gąsiorowski and Jarosławiecka, *Cracow*, translated by M. H. Dziewicki, Cracow and Paris, Gebethner, 1924.

## VI.  *Minority Problems.*

R. Dyboski, *Poland and the Problem of National Minorities,* London, " Journal of the British Institute of International Affairs," September, 1923. Stephens, J. S., *Danger Zones of Europe* (Mertens Lectures on War and Peace, No. 3), Hogarth Press, London, 1929 (pp. 53-74 : *Minorities in Poland*).

## VII.  *Economic Life.*

History : Bujak F., *The Economic Development of Poland,* London : Allen & Unwin, 1925.

The current economic problems of Poland are discussed in English in the *Polish Economist,* a monthly review of trade, industry and economics in Poland (published by the Ministry of Commerce and Industry), Warsaw, 1925 ff.

The different stages of the financial and economic development of the new Poland may be studied in English in the official reports of Poland's British financial adviser, Sir Hilton Young (1924), of the American Financial Mission headed by Professor E. W. Kemmerer (1926), of Mr. Charles S. Dewey, for three years financial adviser to the Bank of Poland (1929-1931), and of the Commercial Secretary of the British Embassy in Warsaw, Mr. R. E. Kimens, (H. M. Stationery Office, 1925, 1931). An up-to-date summary has recently been given be E. Kwiatkowski (sometime Minister of Commerce and Industry of Poland): *The Economic Progress of Poland* (reprinted from " The Polish Economist " ), Warsaw, 1932.

On Poland's Social Policy, see F. Sokal, *Social Insurance in Poland,* Geneva, 1925.

## VIII.  *Education and Research.*

*Education in Poland,* 1918-1928 (published by the Ministry of Education), Warsaw, 1929. *Educational Year-book of the International Institute of Teachers' College, Columbia University,* 1926, edited by J. L. Kandel, New York: Macmillan, 1927 (pp. 321-350, *Poland,* by R. Dyboski and K. Zbierski). *The New Era* (a Quarterly, published at 11, Tavistock Square, London, W.C.1), No. 41 (January 1930) ; special number, devoted to education in Poland.

## IX.  *Literature and Art.*

Literary History : R. Dyboski, *Periods of Polish Literary History* (Ilchester Foundation Lectures), London: Oxford University Press, 1923. *Idem, Modern Polish Literature* (lectures

at King's College, University of London), *ibidem*, 1924.
J. Krzyżanowski, *Polish Romantic Literature*, London: Allen &
Unwin, 1930. See also the books on eminent Polish authors by
Miss Monica M. Gardner : *Adam Mickiewicz, the National Poet of
Poland*, London: Dent. 1911. *The Anonymous Poet of Poland,
Sigmund Krasiński*, London: Cambridge University Press, 1920.
*The Patriot Novelist of Poland, Henryk Sienkiewicz*, London: J.
M. Dent, 1926.

Translations of short stories and poems from the Polish, as well
as critical articles on modern Polish writers, appear in nearly
every number of the *Slavonic Review* (London) and of *Poland*
(New York). A representative collection of modern Polish
short stories in English translations is included in the " World's
Classics " series: Benecke, E. C. M., and Busch, M.; *Selected
Polish Tales*, London : Oxford University Press, 1929.

Among modern English translations of outstanding larger
works by some of the Polish authors mentioned in this book, the
following are particularly worth notice : Fredro, A., *Ladies and
Hussars*, a comedy in three acts, translated by F. and G. R.
Noyes, New York, S. French, 1925. Goetel F., *From Day to
Day*, a novel translated by W. Cooper, introduction by John
Galsworthy, London : Matthew and Marrot (New York: Viking
Press), 1931. Kochanowski J., *Poems*, translated by G. R.
Noyes and others, University of California Press, Berkeley, Cal.,
U.S.A. (London : Cambridge University Press), 1929. Konopnicka
M., *The Brownie Scouts*, translated by K. Żuk-Skarszewska,
illustrated by M. Bukowska, Warsaw, M. Arct 1929 (one of
Poland's classics for children). Kossak-Szczucka Z., *The Blaze :
Reminiscences of Volhynia*, 1917-1919. London: Allen & Unwin
1927. Krasiński, Z., *The Undivine Comedy*, translated by H. E.
Kennedy and Z. Umińska, preface by G. K. Chesterton,
London: Harrap. 1924. *Idem, Iridion*, translated by F. and
G. R. Noyes, London : Oxford University Press, 1929. Mickie-
wicz, A., *Konrad Wallenrod and other Writings*, translated by
G. R. Noyes and others: University of California Press,
Berkeley, U.S.A. (London : Cambridge University Press), 1925.
*Idem, Pan Tadeusz, or the Last Foray in Lithuania*, translated
by G. R. Noyes, London: Dent ("Everyman's Library"), 1929.
Nałkowska, Z. R., *Kobiety (Women)*, translated by M. H. Dzie-
wicki, New York: Putnam, 1920. Ossendowski, F. A., *Beasts,
Men, and Gods*, London : J. M. Dent (New York: Dutton), 1922.
Reymont, W., *The Peasants*, translated by M. H. Dziewicki, 4
vols., New York: A. Knopf, 1924-25 (in one vol., 1927). *Idem,
The Promised Land*, translated by M. H. Dziewicki, 2 vols., New

York: A. Knopf, 1927. Sienkiewicz, H., *With Fire and Sword* (1890) ; *The Deluge* (2 vols., 1891) ; *Pan Michael* (1910) ; *Quo Vadis?* (1896 and later); *Knights of the Cross* (2 vols., 1930); all translated by J. Curtin, and published by Little, Brown & Co., Boston, U.S.A. *Idem, In Desert and Wilderness* (a story of African adventure for children), translated by M. Drezmal, illustrated by R. Schuyler, Boston: Little, Brown & Co., 1923. *Idem, Tales*, edited by Monica M. Gardner, London: J. M. Dent (Everyman's Library), 1931 (with bibliography of other English translations from Sienkiewicz). Słowacki, J., *Anhelli*, translated by D. Prall Radin and G. R. Noyes, London: Allen & Unwin, 1930. *Mazeppa*, translated by C. D. and C. F. Wells, Alumni Press, Ann Arbor, Michigan, U.S.A., 1929. Weyssenhoff, J., *The Sable and the Girl*, translated by K. Żuk-Skarszewska, London: Allen & Unwin, 1929. Winawer, B., *The Book of Job*, a Satirical Comedy, translated by Joseph Conrad, London: J. M. Dent, 1931. Żeromski, S., *Ashes*, translated by H. Stankiewicz-Zand (2 vols.), New York: A. Knopf (London: Allen & Unwin), 1928.

X. *Poland's Position in the World of To-day and To-morrow.*

Joseph Conrad, *Poland Revisited* (1915) ; *A Note on the Polish Problem* (1916), *The Crime of Partition*, (1919), all included in *Notes on Life and Letters* (Uniform Edition, London, J. M. Dent, 1924) ; see also his *Prince Roman* (in *Tales of Hearsay*) and his *Personal Record : some Reminiscences* (1923, with *Author's Note* and *Familiar Preface* in the Uniform Edition). These writings of the great English novelist, who was a Pole by birth, although remote by their very date from the problems of to-day, throw most significant light on Polish national tradition and mentality. A noble interpretation of the Polish national character was given in War time by Miss Monica M. Gardner in her book, *Poland : a Study in National Idealism*, London: Burns, Oates & Washbourne, 1915. Of the domestic and foreign problems which beset Poland in the first years of their new existence, a clear and succinct account was given by Professor Charles Sarolea in his *Letters on Polish Affairs*, Edinburgh: Oliver & Boyd, 1922.

Among books which have a more immediate bearing on the problems of Poland in more recent years, and particularly on those discussed in the final chapter of this book, the following must be especially mentioned :

A. Skrzyński (Foreign Minister of Poland in 1923 and Prime Minister in 1925, d. 1931), *Poland and Peace*, London: Allen & Unwin, 1923. " Augur," *Eagles, Black and White: the Fight for the Sea*, 2nd ed., London and New York: Appleton, 1929. C. Smogorzewski, *Poland, Germany, and the Corridor*, London: Williams & Norgate, 1930 (a documented reply to Sir Robert Donald's *The Polish Corridor and its Consequences*, London: Butterworth, 1929). E. W. L. Newman, *Britain and the Baltic*, London: Methuen, 1930. J. Weinstein, *Upper Silesia, a Country of Contrasts*, Paris: Gebethner & Wolff, 1931. A. Plutynski, *The German Paradox: a study of German political and economic life, with special consideration of the problem of East Prussia*, London, Wishart & Co., 1933.

## ADDENDA

Pp. 23–4 : on the partitions of Poland, see :
Lord Eversley, *The Partitions of Poland*, London, T. Fisher Unwin, 1915 ;—Robert Howard, Lord, *The Second Partition of Poland* (Harvard Historical Studies, vol. XXIII), Cambridge, Mass., 1916 ;—R. H. Lord, *The Third Partition of Poland* (in *The Slavonic Review*, London, vol. III, No. 9, March, 1925).

Pp. 21, 35, 423, 424 : on King John Sobieski, see :
J. B. Morton, *Sobieski, King of Poland* (with plates, including portraits, and maps), pp. xvii, 286, Eyre and Spottiswoode, London, 1932 (European Biographies).

# INDEX

431

Printed in Great Britain at the KEMP HALL PRESS, LTD. in the City of Oxford